RONNIE SCOTT'S
JAZZ FARRAGO

**dedicated to Ronnie Scott and Pete King,
the co-founders of Ronnie Scott's Club**

Published by Hampstead Press
16 Heathville Road,
N19 3AJ,
London,
United Kingdom

ISBN 978-0-9557628-0-2

Illustrations and photographs are reproduced courtesy of the following copyright holders, credited accordingly. The publishers have made every effort to trace copyright holders and any omissions will be corrected in future editions.
Tom Ballenger, Jody Boulting, John Byrne, Richard Cole, Codge, Mel Calman, Diz Disley, Gene Deitch, Al Fairweather, Wally 'Trog' Fawkes, Dana Fradon, Mike Hatchard, Hazeldine, Mark Herman, Al Hirschfeld, Chick Jacob, Joy Johnson, Stephen Nemethy, Johny Parker, Jack Pennington, Hedley Picton, David Redfern, Marta Rusin, Mr. Tidy, Ken Sims, David Sinclair, Bill Stott, Monty Sunshine, Antony Wysard

A special thanks to Michael Pointon, Ron Rubin and Matthew Wright whose collective beady eyes mercifully fell on the many literals and this editor is deeply grateful.

Layout and design by Marta Rusin

Printed and bound by Drukarnia GS, Krakow, Poland

RONNIE SCOTT'S JAZZ FARRAGO

A motley assortment of characters, happenings
and history on the modern British jazz scene

edited and with contributions
by JIM GODBOLT

foreword
by GEORGE MELLY

HAMPSTEAD
PRESS

CONTENTS

CONTENTS

Photos from Ronnie Scott's on Contents pages:
Marta Rusin, private collection, 2005

FOREWORD by GEORGE MELLY

George by Wally 'Trog' Fawkes

It has been a strange turn of events that has linked my name with Jim Godbolt's and Ronnie Scott's Club, but I had a previous connection with Jim, one that started in 1950.

From that date, I spent twelve years on the road singing with Mick Mulligan's Magnolia Jazz Band (we went in for fancy names in those days). After we had murdered a few early gigs as semi-pros, Mick invited Jim Godbolt for his opinion. For Mick and the rest of us Jim was a formidable figure in that he had managed George Webb's Dixielanders, arguably the first Revivalist trail-blazers in this country. After Jim had heard us, he conferred for some twenty minutes with Mick. Then Godbolt left and Mick rejoined us to give us the verdict. It was typical, 'He says we should give up.'

Well, we didn't, and in time improved and began to attract a growing body of fans, yet it was somehow unlikely that Jim soon became and remained our agent until Mick disbanded in 1963. It was a 'gentleman's agreement'. There was no signed contract.

BRIEF ENCOUNTER
Yet it was just as unlikely, if not more so, that Jim, for so many years the most unbending revivalist, should brave the Scott Club to suggest to Pete King, Ronnie's business partner and the Club's co-founder that the Club has a house magazine. King, Ronnie's best friend, his ex-sax player and manager of the Holy Grail in Frith Street, agreed, but who did Jim suggest as the editor? Himself!

Pete's reaction was predictably, one of shock/horror. The arch 'mouldy fygge' (the boppers' contemptuous nickname for the revivalist) proposing to edit a house magazine in this high church of bebop — blasphemy!
Pete told Jim to get lost. There was, it was true, much against him, not least his musical tastes, nor had Jim's tongue held back in denigrating the modernists. However, in his favour, he had edited with some flair a few jazz magazines, and by 1979 was perhaps less rigid in his views than thirty years before. The first issue, August-September 1979, had only eight pages in red print, but this was increased in size as the years went by to twenty four pages and two bumper issues of forty pages celebrating the Club's 40th and 45th anniversaries. Jim also produced a special issue — a tribute to Ronnie following his death in December 1996.

A TRAUMATIC MOMENT
It may amuse readers here of whatever musical taste (for the bitter wars are over) to describe an early visit that Godbolt and I made, spies and denigrators as we were, to the 'Club Eleven', one of the early rebel camps of bop before Pete and Ronnie opened their own premises. This took place around 1949, (see Wally's cartoon on page 3.)

We were satisfactorily appalled. The music (music?!) was as dreadful to our ears as we'd hoped, and especially the drums — 'bomb-dropping' we called it, but then the liberties with chords and bar-lines, the endless solos, the incomprehensible titles and scat-singing, the 'cool' ambience — it was all, for us, a nightmare.

It was not just a different world, but a different cosmos. The modern musicians tended to dress sharp too. The girls, mostly well-groomed, lacked the art student scruffiness of our supporters. The East End was in complete contrast to the predominantly suburban, if enthusiastic, ambience we were used to. We left, Jim and I, looking forward to a thoroughly enjoyable and destructive review of what we'd seen and heard in the nearest pub.

ACCEPTANCE OF CHANGE
So how and why did we become more tolerant? Right from the off there was the late Welsh pianist, the elfish Dill Jones, who could play in both idioms, and did his best to act as a kind of United Nations advocate of peace between the factions. There was Jim's period as an agent, which inevitably required a wider spectrum, but perhaps, most influentially, was the lifting, in 1956, of the ban on visiting musicians, after endless 'will you, won't you' prevarication from our Communist-led Musicians' Union and their American opposite number, James Petrillo. Louis Armstrong and his All Stars appeared at the Empress Hall and then toured the country and later, jazz of all periods from New Orleans to 52nd Street crossed the Atlantic, while Norman Granz's 'Jazz at the Phil' packages, while of a deliberately 'rabble-rousing' nature, incorporated great musicians, many of them 'mainstream'.

Ronnie and Pete too, even before they moved a quarter of a mile up the road to Frith Street, hired Zoot Sims, and since then signed up an amazing regiment of great Americans, both individually and collectively, and even a few of the earlier schools before mainstream. John Chilton's Feetwarmers, for example, and after his well-earned retirement after 30 years at Ronnie's, Digby Fairweather since, have collectively played there every Christmas with me fronting them. 'And George Melly — God help us!' said Ronnie, announcing our forthcoming appearances every November. How John and I established these long-lived appearances is another tale, as unlikely perhaps as Godbolt's *JARS* editorship, but not especially relevant here.

So there it all was: opposition from all schools against the MU's blind intransigence helped establish a truce. Exposure to great musicians blowing their gospel in promiscuous circumstances, social contact on the road, everything led us all to realise that those we, and they, had despised were human beings. By the time Jim Godbolt made his apparently preposterous offer, it was not, after the initial shock, surprising but right that RS and PK should eventually have accepted it.

A UNIQUE HISTORY
Now this book is an anthology, selected by Jim, to show that *JARS* is not a simple plug for whoever is appearing next, or even the printing of the menu (Ronnie used to say that pygmies came all the way from Africa to dip their arrows in the chef's soup). To show its scope, I can do nothing better than quote its range from Jim, in his letter asking me if I would write this preface. It contains: 'a compilation of features, poems (by

the admirable Ron Rubin), drawings by the acerbic Wally Fawkes, other cartoons, photographs, bill posters, invitation tickets etc.'

All true, and no point in my elaborating on this, as you hold the book in your hand (I quite envy you finishing or abandoning this foreword and diving in). I would however bring to your attention the marvellous pre-posthumous obituary; a proof, if needed, that drummers are not all 'bomb-heads', but in Tony Crombie's case for example, sensitive, observant and very lovable members of the human race. The same list of qualities applies, despite his sometimes gruff manner, his heart-felt cry of 'Do us an effing favour' (as Jim Godbolt would write it) of Pete King.

And then there was Ronnie, that highly-strung, witty, non-judgmental (except musically) and tolerant of most things boss. He was a true romantic, and it gave him much pain. He haunts this book as I suspect he still beneficently does the club he founded. 'Missed by all,' they used to write in obituary adverts in the provincial papers. In Ronnie's case it's completely true.

FRIENDLY TIT-FOR-TAT
Finally, a tiny bone to pick with Jim Godbolt. His pen portrait of me, here printed and not all together alleviated by a few favourable comments in conclusion. It is hideously accurate, but I can't really complain. In my first book, *Owning Up*, a memoir of the Revivalist Jazz World of the Fifties, I describe Jim as he observed the much-hated public school boys and their noisy girlfriends (Hooray Henrys and Henriettas as he called them) as 'having eyes as cold and watchful as those of a pike in the reeds'.

The pike and the Hoorays — Jim, Mick and I, have become good friends and, despite reservations as to their unfortunate educational background, so have several others. This book, Jim, to return finally to your vigorous and long-lived service at the wheel of *JARS*, is an enjoyable and unsycophantic picture of a world that has enclosed and formed us all. Congratulations, my 'council school chum' (your phrase) from your old public school raver.

December 2006

Above, tradders, Jim Godbolt clutching a Bix Beiderbecke album and Melly a Bessie Smith compilation, reeling in horror at the sound of bebop, 1950.
Pictured right, Melly and Godbolt at the launch of Godbolt's *A History of Jazz in Britain 1919-1950*, published by Quartet, at Kettner's Restaurant in 1984. It was an occasion attended by musicians and critics representing all the styles.
George Melly wrote the above foreword in 2006. Sadly, George died in July 2007, his passing receiving an extraordinarily large coverage in the national and provincial press and on TV and radio, such was the impact he made with his colourful lifestyle.

Illustration: Wally 'Trog' Fawkes; Photo: Jody Boulting

INTRODUCTION by JIM GODBOLT

Jim Godbolt, the editor of *JARS*.
Photo by trumpeter Ken Sims
at George Melly's funeral , 13 July 2007

My introduction into the world of jazz, in 1940, was collecting 78rpm records, some purchased from record stores, others rescued from piles of bric-a-brac in junk shops. Jazz being associated with nameless depravity, I eagerly entered this saturnalia by attending weekly meetings of the 161 Rhythm Club meeting at the Station Hotel, Sidcup. Another member was Wally Fawkes, later to become a noted jazz clarinettist and one of the country's leading cartoonists. There were approximately twelve of us seated at a refectory table playing records on a turntable plugged into the electric light bulb. I suppose that becoming the club's secretary was my first 'job' in the business, albeit that this was merely paying the landlord five shillings for hire of the room and placing our weekly advertisement, giving names of our recitalists and their subjects to the *Melody Maker* to run in their club column.

This club column was a standard feature in the *MM*, as the paper was affectionately described by aficionados. The *MM* sponsored the first club of its kind, the Number 1 Rhythm Club, in 1933, and thereafter all other clubs were numbered consecutively, our number in swinging Sidcup was 161.

GEORGE WEBB'S DIXIELANDERS

Service in the Royal Navy from 1941 to 1946 saw me out of the country, but on demobilisation I was passionately caught up in revivalist fervour, becoming manager of George Webb's Dixielanders, playing every Monday at the Red Barn, Barnehurst, Kent. The Dixielanders were fervent purists who modelled their style on the music of the New Orleans pioneers: Louis Armstrong, King Oliver and Jelly Roll Morton. Their slogan was 'jazz and only jazz'. They were semi-professional, comprised of factory workers, an electrical shop proprietor, a draughtsman and a librarian. The band's patent sincerity and enthusiasm for the 'old' jazz brought them a following, a fair amount of publicity in the *Melody Maker* and severe criticism from professional musicians for their poor technique and intonation.

I organised monthly concerts in London's West End under the name of the Hot Club of London featuring the band and the few musicians playing in that style. It was before the so called trad boom where literally hundreds of young musicians in this country were playing traditional jazz.

HUMPH

In April 1947, a young man, ex-captain in the Brigade of Guards but studying at the Camberwell School of Art, Humphrey Lyttelton, joined the band, which considerably enhanced their reputation. Lyttelton left in November 1947 taking with him clarinettist Wally Fawkes, then establishing himself as a cartoonist in the *Daily Mail*, and trombonist Harry Brown. It was the end of the Dixielanders.

At the time I thought this was to be the end of my association with the music business and I became a nomadic farm labourer working from agricultural camps organised by the Ministry of Agriculture and Fisheries and then as a clerk in a sign writing firm, still with no contact with music. The Lyttelton band had a weekly residency, first with the Leicester Square Jazz Club, 37 Leicester Square and then at the London Jazz Club holding its meetings at Mac's Rehearsal Rooms, opposite the Windmill Theatre, Great Windmill Street, near Piccadilly. I attended both clubs as a member but contributed a weekly broad-sheet called *The Puffo* under the name of 'Odbot'.

WORKING FOR WILCOX

The London Jazz Club was run by Bert Wilcox, who owned an electrical and record shop in St John's Wood, north London, and I worked there packing records. Wilcox, who had his sights on being an impresario, moved to an office in Earlham Street, off Cambridge Circus, but had started a magazine called *Jazz Illustrated* whilst in St John's Wood. The production of this, initially standing at the edge of a table, was largely by me and once in Earlham Street, I became its editor. Wilcox had started a band agency representing the Johnny Dankworth Seven, Kenny Graham's Afro-Cubists and, on an extended visit to England, Graeme Bell's Australian Jazz Band. *Jazz Illustrated* folded and by accident I found myself handling the date sheets of the bands Wilcox represented. Wilcox engaged in disastrous ventures that saw the end of his agency and in 1951 I set out on my own as an agent, earning a living in this capacity for the next twelve years, principally booking Mick Mulligan and his band featuring George Melly and other traditional style bands. When 'mainstream' became a fashion, I represented the bands of Fairweather-Brown, Bruce Turner's Jump Band and Wally Fawkes's Troglodytes. Overall, my associations were decidedly traditional.

DIFFERENT WORLDS

When my own agency folded I worked for the Bron Organisation booking Colosseum, Bonzo Dog Doo-Dah Band and Juicy Lucy, all far removed from the bands I had previously represented It was a totally different milieu. I wasn't at ease in this new situation and the volume of the bands I booked was hard on my ears.

In 1973 I left Bron's to become a writer and failed miserably. To earn a living, I became a meter reader with the London Electricity Board for four feet-plodding years. At the end of this foot-punishing experience calling on two hundred addresses a day

The first cover of *JARS*, August, 1979

and battling with a variety of dogs,* I persuaded Roger Horton running the 100 Club in Oxford Street, to have a house magazine.

SHOW ME A BANJO !

Horton's policy was almost wholly traditional, thus furthering my associations with that side of the jazz fence. In the summer of 1979 I was possessed by what may have seemed a mad idea of approaching Ronnie Scott's Club and suggesting that they too have a house magazine. I say 'mad' as the Scott's Club policy was utterly different from Horton's whose plangent cry was 'Show me a banjo and you show me a profit!' I hardly knew Ronnie Scott and only vaguely knew his partner Pete King, whom I had approached for advertising in a magazine called *Jazz Circle News* and had occasionally met when I was with the Bron office. Horton had no objection to me approaching Scott's as both clubs drew almost entirely different audiences.

George Melly recalls in his foreword the look of absolute amazement that manager Pete King gave me when I proposed that he should have a house magazine and I would like to be its editor. He saw me as inveterate tradder who, with my banjo-addled ears, was the last person to edit the house magazine of a club internationally famed for its modern policy.

In August 1979 I produced the first issue of *Jazz at Ronnie Scott's* which became known as *JARS*. It comprised a mere eight pages printed in vivid

red and, frankly, it wasn't production of the highest order, but it improved sufficiently for me to produce 159 issues over the next twenty six years, each twenty-four pages, until the club changed hands.

ABOUT THIS BOOK

This book is a selection of features, photographs and cartoons and reflects the extraordinary history of Ronnie Scott's Club, but I have included articles relating to the history of modern jazz generally.

Regarding the overall concept of the book, I have omitted the then 'current news' and the record and book reviews, concentrating mainly on comment, profiles and interviews. These are largely reproduced as initially published. I have retained the originall tense of most of the features and certain references to time, as it would be near impossible to alter all the copy, realising that the magazine is no longer published and many of the characters featured no longer alive.

This volume is a jazz farrago — a motley assortment of characters, happenings and history on the modern British jazz scene. The aim of the book is to serve as a reminder of what an achievement it was for Scott and King to run a jazz club on a seven nights a week basis and sticking to their jazz policy. The reader will note that many of the features have no direct connection with the Club's activities, but from the start neither Ronnie nor Pete insisted on a publication that was purely a house magazine in its content.

I wrote most of the articles and the pseudonymous gossip column under different headings and using such nom-de-plumes as Paul Pry, Talcott Malagrowther, Clark 'Clarky' Tewksbury, Slawkenbergius and Lance Fairfax. I have also attempted to reduce the number of times my name appears, but there are some occasions where the personal pronoun makes a signature inevitable. Regarding the 'Interviews' with Ronnie, these are mostly fictitious, but those with the likes of Sir John Dankworth, Ruby Braff, Charlie Watts, Spike Milligan and George Melly were for real and therefore require a signature.

PRODUCTION PERILS

It was naive of me to think that it was a simple matter of transferring material from one format to another. Not so: the big problem was what to select from a hundred and fifty-nine issues to make a balanced whole and fit into the mere two hundred pages.

As for the jokes and anecdotes, repetition over a quarter century for a transient readership was permissible, but not between hard covers. After all, Ronnie Scott was not averse to repeating his jokes and some of the tales, incidents and anecdotes, often in a different context, I have retained. A lot of rearrangement was necessary, and then there was the urgent matter of eliminating errors, mostly misprints of proper names in the original issues and subsequent typing.

Another setback was that several issues of *JARS* on the net that could have been adapted were accidently wiped out when the new website was implemented. As a result most of the copy had to be arduously retyped, frequently introducing more errors.

In the production of this volume I have to gratefully thank Marta Rusin for skilfully making the transfer from one format to another possible, but not without heated disputes!

Illustration: Jack Pennington

The above somewhat unflattering illustration of myself by Jack Pennington was a regular feature illustrating my editorial comment. At a launch of the republication of Ronnie Scott's book *Some of My Best Friends Are Blues* at Ray's Jazz Shop in Foyle's, Charing Cross Road, London, a total stranger approached me with the words, 'Hello, Jim'. I was curious as to how he recognised me and the shattering reply was that he had seen the Pennington cartoon...

* detail in *All This And Many A Dog* by the author, Northway Publications

RONNIE SCOTT'S: FROM GERRARD TO FRITH STREET AND ITS GENESIS

On 23 October 1959, the following advert appeared in the Classified section of the *Melody Maker*:

Ronnie Scott's Club, 39 Gerrard Street, W1. Fri. 7.30pm. Tubby Hayes Quartet; Eddie Thompson Trio and the first appearance of Jack Parnell in a jazz club since the relief of Mafeking. Membership 10/- until January 1961. Admission 1/6d (members).

The following week, the *Melody Maker*, dated Saturday 30 October 1959, on sale on Friday 29th, the actual date of the Club's opening, ran the following announcement:

The genesis of this historic event starts with the general popular music pattern in Britain in the late forties when traditional jazz was on the upsurge, and many young white men elected to play the 'old' music of the black New Orleans pioneers, Louis Armstrong, King Oliver and Jelly Roll Morton in the bands of George Webb's Dixielanders, John Haim's Jelly Roll Kings and the Crane River Jazz Band among many others.

Other young musicians of the time were influenced by the highly successful big US bands of Benny Goodman, Artie Shaw, Harry James, Gene Krupa, Tommy Dorsey and Jimmy Dorsey. It was also a time when foreign musicians were not allowed to play in this country, the British Musicians' Union imposing their will in this regard on the Ministry of Labour, the body that actually issued the work permits.

GERALDO'S NAVY

In this situation, the new jazz called bebop, or rebop, played by the likes of Charlie Parker and Dizzy Gillespie in America, was unknown over here until some of the musicians who actually visited America on transatlantic liners brought back these revolutionary new recordings. These musicians did not travel as passengers but as players in bands which were described as 'Geraldo's Navy'. Geraldo was a very successful bandleader in Britain who was the booker for the music on the liners Caronia, Mauritania and the Queen Mary.

These recordings were played at the Bloomsbury flat of drummer, collector and record producer Carlo Krahmer, planting the seeds of interest among British musicians, most of whom had played in jazz sessions, principally at Feldman's Swing Club at 100 Oxford Street. Among these young musicians who played in Geraldo's Navy, principally to spend a few hours listening to the bebop bands on 52nd Street, barely a walk away from the New York docks, was Ronnie Scott, and visiting these clubs implanted in the nineteen-year-old the idea of one day having his own jazz club.

RONNIE'S EARLY CAREER

This had to wait for quite a few years as he earned his living playing with a variety of big bands, including those of Ambrose, Ted Heath and Vic Lewis, before forming his own nine-piece in 1953. During this time he and fellow spirits gathered to form the Club Eleven. This proved to be the seedbed of bop in Britain, and many of his colleagues appearing weekly in a grubby basement in Great Windmill Street, opposite the Windmill Theatre near Piccadilly, were to be in Ronnie's various bands, one of which was his famed nine-piece, conceived over innumerable cups of tea in a café run by George Siptak, a Czech émigré, who quickly cottoned on to his patrons' occupation and renamed his café the Harmony Inn.

This was in Archer Street, a small thoroughfare near Piccadilly, connecting Wardour and Rupert Streets, that was the unofficial open-air labour exchange and social club for dance/jazz musicians. The street remains, but is a ghost of its former identity.

In January 1953 the band commenced two years of intensive touring, principal figures in the establishment of modern jazz in Britain's dance, drill and concert halls. The nine-piece was succeeded in 1955 by Ronnie Scott's Big Band which, although an artistic success, was a commercial failure.

RONNIE IN THE STATES

In February 1957, Ronnie took his sextet to the USA, as part of the newly instituted exchange system for bands agreed between the American Federation of Musicians and the British Musicians' Union, a fraudulent stratagem which at least had the merit of breaking down the artistic barrier that prevented American musicians from playing in the UK. (Subsequently, these visitors have proved to be the lifeblood of the Club right up until the present day.)

The visit to the USA was not a happy one. The sextet, playing just one number, was part of an all-black rock'n'roll package. Ronnie quipped, 'They needed a British bebop band like they need a synagogue in Damascus.'

THE JAZZ COURIERS

In 1957 Ronnie teamed up with the brilliant young tenor saxophonist

Tubby Hayes, calling themselves the Jazz Couriers. When they folded in 1959, it was time for Ronnie, with Pete King, who had played tenor with and managed the nine-piece and Big Band, to open a club at 39 Gerrard Street, but in those days the MU ban still barred solo Americans; only British musicians were able to play. It was not until 1965, when this stupid ban on soloists was lifted, that the Club engaged a string of great American jazzmen, including Zoot Sims, Sonny Rollins, Stan Getz, Ben Webster, Sonny Stitt, Coleman Hawkins and many, many others, who fashioned the shape of post-war jazz.

In 1965, they borrowed £35,000, a very large sum at that time, from agent/impresario Harold Davison and the Club moved to its present abode in 47 Frith Street. Opening on 27th November, the *Melody Maker* reported that the night was a tremendous success but the Club had a novel ventilation: 'There was no front door'. Wires hung from the ceiling and there was only one toilet, but it was the start of an era that transformed Ronnie's from operating in a grubby basement to achieving a nightclub ambience in a prime West End site.

THE ROLL CALL
The prestigious names appearing at Frith Street included the big orchestras of Stan Kenton, Count Basie, Woody Herman, Harry James and Buddy Rich, and individual artists, often with British rhythm sections, included Dexter Gordon, Ben Webster, Chet Baker, Wayne Shorter, Ruby Braff, Benny Carter, Elvin Jones, Illinois Jacquet, Roland Kirk, Charles Mingus, Thelonious Monk, Archie Shepp and many more.

There were singers such as Sarah Vaughan, Ella Fitzgerald, Anita O'Day and Betty Carter. The stream of great American musicians and singers continued to establish Ronnie Scott's Club as a brand name. A feature of the Club's presentation was the wise-cracking persona of Ronnie Scott, entertaining audiences with his famed jokes as well, of course, as leading his own group.

With this succession of American stars the best of British jazz was also presented as a salient part of the Club's policy.

RIGHT ON THE NIGHT
Whilst there was no doubt that the move to the more up-market premises at 47 Frith Street, eventually enlarged, was an improvement on Gerrard Street, there were many musicians and fans who preferred the 'Old Place' (as 39 Gerrard Street became known, continuing after the Club opened at Frith Street), probably because it was more in line with the ancient jazz club tradition of a smoky basement — and, of course, the old typically viewing the past through rose-tinted glasses. Whatever, such memories were encapsulated in this valedictory poem in homage to the Old Place by Ron Rubin that appeared in *JARS* 120, September–October 1999.   J.G.

I REMEMBER, I REMEMBER
I remember, I remember
That joint in Gerrard Street,
The poky, smoky basement club
Where you and I would meet;
There wasn't room to swing a cat
But how those cats could swing!
In London's hip new jazz room,
Thanks to Messrs Scott and King.

I remember, I remember
A grubby cubby hole –
'The Office' it was fondly called,
There Pete was in control;
Whilst up onstage stood Ronnie,
Content to do his bit,
Emceeing, playing, joshing,
With his legendary wit.

I remember those all-nighters,
And the gifted guys who blew –
It was wall-to-wall musicians
(And perhaps some punters too...)
Some played, some listened, some got stoned,
And when the night was done,
They'd stagger up those steps again
To face the morning sun.

A cynic said that distance
Lends enchantment to the view,
But giants graced that stage! – the list
Reads like a Jazz Who's Who.
The club moved on to Frith Street,
And greater things, we know,
But I remember Gerrard Street
Those forty years ago.
RON RUBIN

The chaotic state of 47 Frith Street prior to its opening in December 1965 with a somewhat worried-looking Ronnie in sheepskin coat, flanked by Soho character Bobby Schwartz, with two workmen, one of whom appears to resent the photographer, the other leaning on his shovel, probably reassuring Ronnie that everything would be 'all right on the night, guv'. In the event the premises turned out to be famous world-wide and Ronnie Scott's became a brand name.
So much so, letters addressed 'Ronnie Scott's, London', reached their destination and the affectionate term for the Club became simply 'Ronnie's', a Mecca for jazz enthusiasts around the world.

UK BOP: THE PIONEERS
by ALUN MORGAN

In January 1947 drummer Laurie Morgan came back from a visit to New York bringing with him some 78rpm records of Charlie Parker, probably the first to be seen or heard in Britain. At that time Sunday afternoons were usually set aside for a select group of jazz musicians to meet at 76 Bedford Court Mansions, the large apartment owned by drummer–bandleader Carlo Krahmer. Laurie's new discs were played over and over again as such musicians as Tony Crombie, Pete Chilver, Lennie Bush and Denis Rose tried to come to grips with this new music. Ronnie Scott, a regular at Carlo's, said later after hearing Parker's *Red Cross* (with guitarist Tiny Grimes): 'I was totally stunned. I'd not heard jazz like this before. After that experience I could only "hear" Parker when I was playing. He made me realise what musical direction I had to take from then on.'

EARLY BEBOP RELEASES
In April 1947 EMI issued *Our Delight* coupled with *Good Dues Blues* by the Dizzy Gillespie Orchestra on the Parlophone label, sandwiched in between releases by Zep Meissner's Dixieland Band and Slim Gaillard's *Yep Roc Heresi*. A few months later Parlophone put

An LP sleeve cover illustrating, inaccurately, the fascia board of the Club Eleven at Mac's Rehearsal Rooms, Great Windmill Street, Soho. The man in the neck-tie inviting punters in, is manager, Harry Morris.

out *One Bass Hit* and the frantic *Things To Come* by Gillespie's big band, then, right at the end of the year, *Shaw Nuff* and *Loverman*, the first British release to feature Gillespie and Charlie Parker. By now word of mouth and more unofficial importing of Dial and Savoy recordings were spreading the bebop message. Younger musicians such as Johnny (as he was then) Dankworth, trumpeter Leon Calvert, pianist/vibraphonist Tommy Pollard, pianist and trumpeter Denis Rose and of course Ronnie Scott were actually playing bebop, or 'rebop' as it was often called.

Years later Dankworth told writer Tony Hall: 'At that time only a few of us realised that the new music was a complete alteration harmonically of everything that had preceded it; that this was an entirely new conception of harmony and not just a new stylisation or way of phrasing. That's where some British musicians fell down. For instance the leading saxophonists of that time. They tried hard to assimilate Parker into their playing, but fell into the trap of merely incorporating what you could call 'bebop phrases', almost clichés.' This is borne out by a track from a rare Columbia 78 made at a *Melody Maker* Jazz Rally held in the EMI studios on 29 June 1947, when alto saxist Harry Hayes played Bird's *Thriving From A Riff*. Hayes, a superb player in the Benny Carter style, lacks the natural ability to play bebop as exemplified by guitarist Dave Goldberg, who also solos on this track. At thirty-seven Hayes was then almost twice as old as Dankworth, Scott and the rest of the Young Turks from those Sunday afternoons at Carlo's place.

DENIS ROSE
The musician who first grasped the essentials of bebop in Britain was certainly Denis Rose. It was Denis who schooled Tommy Pollard, Tony Crombie, Scott, Dankworth

etc. and they, in turn, helped such talented youngsters as Vic Feldman and trumpeter Terry Brown. By the end of 1948 there was a powerful nucleus of British beboppers, but many lacked regular employment (several established bandleaders had a strong anti-bop attitude) and all were looking for somewhere to play. In December 1948 a new club opened at Mac's Rehearsal Rooms in Great Windmill Street named Club Eleven, home to Ronnie Scott's Sextet and the Johnny Dankworth Quartet. Bebop in Britain now had its own headquarters.

But what these aspiring boppers lacked was close and continuous contact with leading exponents of the new music from across the Atlantic. It was one thing to work aboard the Queen Mary in order to spend a few hectic hours in the 52nd Street jazz clubs, but another to have American jazz stars booked to play dates in Britain. A dispute between the American Federation of Musicians and our Musicians' Union had prevented a free interchange of players since 1934 and was not to be relaxed until 1956. When a Jazz Fair was staged in Paris during May 1949, men such as Dankworth, Scott etc. flew to the French capital to hear the Charlie Parker Quintet (with Kenny Dorham, Al Haig, Tommy Potter and Max Roach) and the Miles Davis–Tadd Dameron group (with James Moody and Kenny Clarke), players denied an appearance in Britain.

THE SEMINAL CLUB ELEVEN
In July 1949, the stupidity of the union disagreement was highlighted when Benny Goodman and his pianist Buddy Greco were allowed to play at the London Palladium for two weeks. The MU advised the Ministry of Labour that these men were 'variety artists' and the issue of work permits was in line with the union's policy. Greco, a fine bebop player before he found greater fame and fortune as a singer,

was welcome at Club Eleven after his Palladium duties were over for the night.

In 1950 Spike Robinson from Wisconsin came to Britain as a musician in a US Navy band. In those days he played alto and although he was virtually unknown to the British fraternity, his powerful Parker-like solos soon alerted us to his importance and he was frequently to be seen and heard in the gloom of Club Eleven. Carlo Krahmer recorded him on three separate dates for the Esquire label before he returned to the USA. Spike played an important part in the growth of British bebop and it was satisfying to have this most amiable and talented of men actually resident in the country for a time.

MODERN JAZZ
ESTABLISHED IN THE UK

In less than three years those first British bebop pioneers who had gathered in Krahmer's flat had assimilated the new music to the point where they were teaching and acting as inspirations to others. Trumpeter Jimmy Deuchar came out of the RAF in May 1950 and went into the important septet formed by Johnny Dankworth. The following year a sixteen-year-old from Raynes Park named Tubby Hayes joined Kenny Baker's band. Drummer Tony Kinsey and pianist Ronnie Ball came down to London from the Midlands and the burgeoning

A jiving couple of the fifties displaying a disciplined coordination of movement. Note all the high-heeled shoes are white, obviously a fashion, and the boy – a sharp dresser, probably a customer of Cecil Gee's Outfitters, Shaftesbury Avenue. Sartorial elegance not to be found in traditional jazz clubs.

British 'modern jazz' scene went from strength to strength.

Self-deprecation was a quality sometimes displayed by British jazzmen during the growth of bebop in Britain, but nowadays, thanks to those important style-setters, our local men are at least the equal of

jazzmen anywhere in the world. As the late Spike Milligan wrote in his 'Coda' to Ronnie Scott and Mike Hennessy's book *Some of My Best Friends are Blues* (1979): 'Whenever I see [Ronnie's] group billed as the house band, more often than not he outshines the US stars.'

RONNIE'S JOKES

Although the Club Eleven could get pretty smoky and sweaty, it had so much more atmosphere than some of the dance gigs we had to play. I remember we did a date once at a place right out in the sticks where it was so quiet they had to shoot an old man to start a cemetery.
If more than three people stood together they thought it was a riot.
The night life there finished in the afternoon.
I asked a cab driver where all the action was and he took me to this place where they were fishing illegally.
It was so dull up there – they had one set of traffic lights in the whole town. They changed once a week. People used to come out and watch. It was the kind of town where you plugged in your electric tooth brush and the street lights dimmed.
We got so bored having nothing to do that we used to sit in the band bus and mix LSD with chopped liver and take trips to Israel. Actually it was a combination of dubious substances that was to put the Club Eleven out of business in the spring of 1950.

Ronnie and Pete by Trog

RONNIE & PETE
two East-Enders who made their mark 'up West'

I hardly knew Ronnie before I started his house mag in 1979 and I am not much wiser about him all these years later.

I attempted a pen-portrait of him in the September/ October 1983 issue of *JARS* which, with startling originality, I called 'The Essential Scott', but I owned up that my monograph was hardly an in-depth picture. Even had I known him from the Club Eleven days I doubt if the sum total of my knowledge of RS would be much greater. He plays his real self close to the chest.

Those who read *JARS* from the off will know that I managed to come up with several 'Interview' features based on 'conversations' with him, but that was a stark case of building bricks with the merest wisps of straw, and about sixteen months ago I gave up battering my head against that Scott wall of non-communication. I mean to say – how far can you get with someone who, when asked what he considered to be the highlight of his career, replied 'I had saxophone lessons from Jack Lewis and he's Vera Lynn's father-in-law!?'

Nor could I refer to his files. Files! There's a joke! He has not kept a single press cutting or photograph of himself, nor does he possess one record he's made. Not that he is unsentimental about the past. He speaks wistfully about the East End of his childhood and adolescence — warmly recalls the spirit and community feeling in that multilingual area. He is even forthcoming about his early days in the business, particularly with Johnny Claes Band, he loves the bands of Artie Shaw, Benny Goodman and Glenn Miller — but he's not one for hanging on to memorabilia. Probably because he is on the indolent side and keeping a scrapbook involves some effort, however minimal. In current terminology he is rather 'laid-back' — relaxed to the point of torpor I would say. Indeed, he doesn't exert himself — except when playing tenor — a fact, it has to be said, often tough on those around him, but perhaps that's his survival secret.

OFFICE TELLY

He has a telly in his office; he gazes at it — whatever the programme — and although the box is but a yard away from where he normally sits, a remote control panel saves him the excruciating effort of getting up to press the buttons. If one is lucky the remote control is operated to turn down the volume a little should I ask him a question but he rarely turns the box off — not at all if there is a comedy show on.

We are in accord, even converse freely, about the subject of humour on TV. We are agreed that 'Soap' is the funniest series on the TV screen. The names of Jessica, Burt, Chester, Jody, Billy, Mary, Corinne, Benson (succeeded by Saunders), Detective Donahue, and all the other superb characters that pop in and out of this remarkable series frequently come up in our chat. Other shows that we admire are the British 'Porridge', 'Fawlty Towers', 'Rising Damp' and 'Hi-De-Hi' and agree that these shows hold up a mirror to the human condition as much as Greek drama or Shakespeare, heretical as that may sound to many. He becomes almost dewy-eyed about Laurel and Hardy. He raves about the comic writers —Perelman, Thurber and Henry Root. He displays animation in his castigation of critics; with almost all musicians, these do not rate highly in his estimation. In this regard he is very forthcoming.

LAID BACK

For someone so laid back and of quite humble origins he has an unmistakable and rather forbidding presence which I find difficult to describe, but make no mistake, that presence is there alright. 'A born leader' is how Pete King described him and Pete has known him long enough not to carry any vestige of hero-worship in his estimation. I can confirm that Ronnie's peremptory manner echoes Pete's words. He's not a man you trifle with.

His 'soft' side is exemplified by his visits to sick musicians in hospital — something many would shrink from. I can think of the late Dill Jones and Pat Smythe whom he went out of his way to see.

A SHARP EYE

There are, of course, certain aspects of his character about which I am very well aware. He has a sharp eye for grammatical or punctuation errors and misprints and jumps on those he sees in *JARS* with tigerish speed. The laid-back image disappears in a flash. He is apt to make comments like. 'You know Jim, you should have asked about... I could have told you that'. Considering the hundreds of questions I have asked him about himself and his contemporaries in the five years of *JARS* existence and all I got was a shake of the head, those little thrusts are hard to take.

I've recently made a few broadcasts and, naturally, mentioned Ronnie, his records and the club as often as

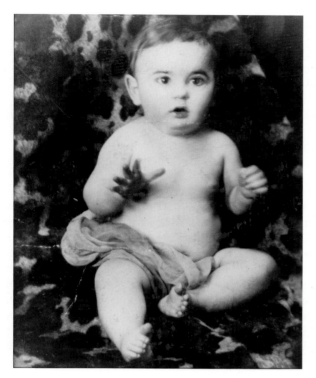

Little did chubby Ronald Schatt, born 28 January 1927, at 23 Tenter Street, E 1, realise as he sat, modestly betassled, that one day he would have his name in lights and be awarded the OBE. The protuberance peeping from his swaddling clothes is his big toe. His Royal Highness, Prince Edward, in line for the throne, was a visitor to the Stepney Green hospital and likely set eyes on this cherub.

PORTRAIT OF PETE

Should I ever become famous — and considering the biblical allotment of three score years and ten I'm cutting it a bit fine to achieve this — and was becoming overblown with the plaudits the famous ingest — I would hie myself to Pete King to have the wind taken out of my sails.

It wouldn't be a subtle put-down the like of which you would get from a bland Ronnie, nor the gently delivered but lethal thrust characteristic of practised lifemen like Wally Fawkes, Humphrey Lyttelton or George Melly. No: it would be a bull-like charge at one's ego, this deflating of the inflated accompanied by a flow of choice expletives and a ferocious glare.

I'm a few years older than Pete, but he frequently manages to make me feel like a naughty little boy. Indeed, a blunt character, often discomfortingly so, but at least you know where you stand with him. But this demeanour is the surface image – there's a lot more to P. King than I have indicated. He has many, many other qualities, qualities that have kept the institution that is Ronnie Scott's Club going for an unbelievable twenty-five years — unbelievable because very, very few jazz clubs in the whole wide world keep going for anywhere near this amount of time and Ronnie will be the first to agree that it has been Pete's determination and persistence that has made their Jubilee possible.

JOB AND HOBBY

The Club is Pete's job and hobby. I was in his office recently when someone asked him — 'Where are you going for your holidays?' '47 Frith Street,' came the laconic reply and that just about sums up the dedication he has to the Club.

He arrives at his office at about 2 p.m, and his first job is to deal with the banking. He grimly recalls the occasions when there has not been a lot to bank. He and Ronnie have had a few financial crises over the years but have always managed to pull through. The rest of the afternoon is spent on general administration, including often tricky negotiations with American artists. These can develop into lengthy hassles bedevilled by a fluctuating and often adverse exchange rates, not to mention cancellations, postponements, alterations in personnels and the

I could, but my queries as to personnel, dates etc have met only with that shake of the cranium — that's if he's feeling energetic — energetic for him that is. Often it's the glazed eye approach that signifies I look elsewhere for that information. And retaliation gets you nowhere. Reading his funny *Some of My Best Friends Are Blues* (co-authored with Mike Hennessey) I thought I had discovered (apart from an obvious misprint) an error in fact. I checked: not so, but I admitted to Ronnie that I thought I had been near a retaliatory triumph.He said: 'You know, I've only been wrong once, and that's when I thought I was wrong and found out that I wasn't.' His features were graven as he spoke, but there was a twinkle in his eye. It is not only on the bandstand that he's a joker.

▶▶

RONNIE'S JOKES

I was born in a room over a Jewish pub in the East End of London called the Kosher Horses. Ours was a very poor family and my father was always out of work. He was a shepherd. But my parents used to go around the house all day singing the blues. Used to drive me crazy. Then one day I heard Mantovani and I said to myself, 'That's my music- these are my people.'
Actually I am not a Jew. Just Jewish. And Jewish people have very strong bonds of affection for one another. But my uncle Ruben and his wife were constantly at each other's throats. I remember my aunt saying to Ruben after a particularly violent argument, 'What would you do if you came home from work one day and found me in bed with another man?' And my uncle said, 'I'd kick his guide dog.'

occasional fly character who books his relatives (or lady friends) into the hotel and charges the Club! During the evening he has to deal with the many problems of running a night club, including the odd fractious member, staff rosters, musicians keeping to schedules — and free-loaders, especially the famous who think their standing entitles them to sail past the cash desk without payment.

He locks up his office about 3.30 a.m. and drives home to Elstree. He gets to bed at about 4.30, but often the phone rings in the forenoon and he's back at the desk at 2 p.m. a gruelling, punishing routine, but he says, philosophically, 'It's a pit I've dug for myself and I've got to lie in it- but I'm lucky to be doing something I really enjoy–despite the aggro.'

DOWN ON THE FARM

Born in Bow in 1929 he was evacuated to a farm in Budleigh Salterton, Devon, during the war. He worked on the farm and at his host's insistence studied at Budleigh Salterton Agricultural College, but for family reasons returned to London and became a coach builder's apprentice, until the music bug got him and he's been in the business ever since.

Seeing him in that small windowless and airless office, usually packed with instruments and amplification equipment, and considering the long hours he spends in this barely lit space, it is a little difficult to imagine that but for a quirk of fate he would have become a farmer exposed to the elements out on the broad acres of Devon.

A former musician (on tenor and clarinet) he started playing at the age of sixteen in Jack Oliver's Big Band at Stoke Newington Town Hall and was later in a variety of bands — including Oscar Rabin's, Leslie 'Jiver' Hutchinson's, Jack Parnell's

A great double act: Pete King and Ronnie Scott
Photo: David Redfern

and Ronnie's nine-piece and big band.

Pete had been interested in motor-racing since a teenager, but music and then running the club had to take priority over this interest. It was not until April 1970 that Pete (and Ronnie) were to join other musicians who raced on the track — trumpeter Johnny Claes, tenor saxophonist Buddy Featherstonhaugh, drummer Les Leston, trombonist Chris Barber, and more recently, Nick Mason of Pink Floyd.

In 1970 Martin Hone opened a club in Birmingham named the Opposite Lock–so-called as it was opposite a canal and had mechanical connotations. It was Martin who made available his Porsche 904 for Pete to compete. John Webb, of Brands Hatch, Kent introduced 'Celebrity' races in Ford Saloons and Ronnie Scott and Pete were invited to participate. Both went to Brands every week to complete their training, Ronnie going on to win the Radio Luxembourg Trophy. Both became part of a camaraderie they are very proud to belong to. Pete, with the aid of Shell Oil, Ford and Pirelli, competed for the Ford Escort Championship from 1973–76 — winning some and losing some. In 1977 with John Webb and David McPherson he represented Britain in European touring Car Championship. These were three to four endurance tests and took them all over Europe to compete. Their first victory in this International Championship came in Austria in 1978. They also added victories in Jarana, Spain, Zandvoort, Holland, Zolder, Belgium and finished second-in-class overall in 1979.

'WHAT A NICE FACE'

Pete's built like an ox; barrel-chested, powerful forearms and a square jaw that juts alarmingly when roused. These physical and facial characteristics have come in useful when dealing with the occasional rough customer. Fortunately, these have been few and far between in the Club's long history but there have been occasions when — to quote Pete — 'I've had to steam in'. I wouldn't relish him 'steaming in' on me, but I make no bones about my admiration and liking for Pete King, a fundamentally kind and generous man, even though, I have to admit, I am never entirely at ease with him.

Only once I have seen him put down. I took a lady friend to hear Houston Person and Etta Jones — no contribution to the coffers here — and I expected Pete's usual good-natured banter on the matter, but he was quite nonplussed when I introduced him and she said, 'What a nice face you have,' which completely took the wind out of his sails. I enjoyed that moment. Ronnie and Pete — sounds like a pre-war music hall double act, but in essence, a double act is what they were. Two utterly different characters, yet totally complementary and both destined for the unique roles they were to fill in the history of jazz in Britain.

To have kept a jazz club going for nigh on fifty years is a tremendous achievement.
Despite Ronnie's death in 1997 Pete has kept his name in the forefront.   J.G.

JAZZ AT THE PHIL
a historic event, a natural disaster the catalyst

On Sunday, March 8th, 1953, there was a significant jazz happening in London. Norman Granz's 'Jazz At The Philharmonic' played two concerts at the Gaumont State Theatre, Kilburn. The ostensible reason was to raise money for the National Flood and Tempest Distress Fund, launched by the Lord Mayor of London, following the flooding of some 150,999 acres of East Anglia in January that year, a disaster that accounted for the loss of 370 human lives, and thousands of head of livestock, and considerable damage to property.

It was a grim irony in the history of jazz in Britain that a calamity of such magnitude should be the catalyst for allowing American musicians to appear here with official blessing.

Prior to this, American musicians had been forbidden to play in Britain. The British Musicians' Union had imposed their wishes on the Ministry of Labour, claiming the US jazz musicians appearing here would be taking employment from British musicians. The argument was nonsense, but it stuck, and since 1934 only a handful of Americans, working as 'variety' artistes, had been granted the essential permits.

THE M.U. IN A CORNER

Norman Granz's offer for his JATP to appear in London without charge and the entire proceeds to be donated to the Fund put the MU in a corner. They could not be seen to be standing in the way of such philanthropy. The concert was organised by promoter Harold Fielding in association with the *Melody Maker*, who gave it their all. The box office was inundated with enquiries, much to the astonishment of the theatre's manager, Mr. G. Conway, who had told Fielding, 'You must be mad.'

8,239 fans of all stylistic preferences, (paying 7/6d, 10/- and 15/- for tickets) attended the two concerts. Mr. Conway said, 'I take back what I said. In twenty six years of show business I've never seen anything like it.'

That particular JATP package comprised Charlie Shavers (trumpet), Lester Young, Flip Phillips (tenor saxophones), Willie Smith (alto saxophone), Barney Kessel (guitar), Oscar Peterson (piano), Ray Brown (bass), Gene Krupa, J.C. heard (drums) and Ella Fitzgerald, supported by British bands – Harry Hayes and his Band, Eddie Thompson Trio, Norman Burns Quintet with Tito Burns, and a contingent from the newly-formed Ronnie Scott band that had driven down specially from Manchester to play the concert.

OSCAR PETERSON

Melody Maker staffman Tony Brown wrote a full page review headed 'ONE DAY THE IMPOSSIBLE HAPPENED', and offered the opinion that only one British musician (un-named) on the bill was 'fit to take place in the JATP unit.'

Many musicians in the audience were quoted, including Vic Lewis, who wasn't that impressed. 'I think there was nothing the best of our musicians couldn't have done.' But Lewis, like most others, was highly impressed with Oscar Peterson. As was Steve Race: 'Since my particular interest is the piano, perhaps one of the British lads' brigade will tell me which British pianist is a superior jazzman to Oscar Peterson. Jazz aside, perhaps one of them will write and tell me who has a superior technique, a finer touch, or a more advanced harmonic sense. For good measure they might like to add the name of the British dance-band pianist who is fit to dust the piano lid with him. I'll print the names of all nominations, and let the nominees decide. Let's hear from you, gentlemen!'

Race didn't receive one nomination, or any other kind of communication in response. The whole show had made the point of American superiority, that no British musician would be on the breadline if the masters were allowed to play here.

'BELLS, MAN!'

But the critics rightly praised the efforts of the British musicians, Tony Brown describing Ronnie Scott as 'brilliant'. Of course, it was a hard task for them all in those daunting circumstances. Terry Brown, playing in the Harry Hayes band (which included Benny Green) recalls: 'Let's face it. Everyone was there to hear the Americans. We had to kick off the first house. I remember we walked off to the patter of our tiny feet.'

Terry is exaggerating a little, but there is no question as to who the packed house had come to see.

Ronnie Scott recalls Lester Young's comment after the Scott set.' 'Bells, man!' he said. At least I think, and dearly hope, that's what he said. It was a moment to cherish and I thought Lester played superbly despite comments to the contrary.' ('Bells', by the way, was Lester's much quoted term of approval.)

These fifty years later, it is still a matter for wonderment that a natural disaster should have been the reason for American jazzmen to play in Britain with official sanction, but the embargo remained until 1956 when, after insistent campaigning by the jazz fraternity, an 'exchange' system was agreed between the British Musicians' Union and the American Federation of Musicians and, at last, British aficionados were allowed to see and hear their heroes in the flesh — and British bands played in America — but that's another story.

A photograph of Ronnie Scott with Lester Young was in Pete King's office, but some wretch stole it. It would have been a pleasure to reproduce here a shot of that historic meeting. J.G.

Right: A graphic poster advertising the event.

JARS 150: NOT OUT!
by JIM GODBOLT

This article was published in the 150th issue of *JARS* which as well as being an anniversary issue for the magazine, also celebrated the Ronnie Scott's Club 45th year. The Trog cartoon below, but with 100 on the 'scoreboard', was drawn to celebrate the 100th edition of *JARS*, July–August 1996. Pete King is the umpire to the left and Ronnie to the right, and although Ronnie is no longer with us I thought we should include the original in its entirety with an updated score.

Pete King, in his column*, finds it difficult to believe that it is an amazing forty-five years since he and Ronnie Scott commenced business at Gerrard Street. I, too, can scarcely believe that this is the 150th edition of *JARS*, having covered events at Ronnie's for a quarter of a century. Understandably, this issue will include congratulations on the Club's birthday and *JARS* reaching 150. No apologies for these, the longevity of both Club and its house magazine is a record and certainly nothing to be modest about.

Sometime in June 1979 I suggested to Pete King that the Club should have a house magazine. Pete agreed, but when I proposed I be the editor, the essence of his reply was would I kindly be on my way and be quick about it. Actually, as those who know Pete will confirm, this wouldn't be his mode of speech, and the reason for giving me the turn-down was that I came from the traditional side of the jazz fence having, in the late forties, managed George Webb's Dixielanders, the seminal New Orleans-style band in Britain, and later represented trad bands including Mick Mulligan's with George Melly. To Pete, I was a traddie. But I didn't 'eff-off' and the first issue, dated August–September 1979, comprised a mere eight pages printed in shocking red. So here I am, twenty-five years later, taking pride and pleasure in editing and publishing the magazine that represents what has been described as 'the greatest jazz club in the world'.

NOT PURELY A HOUSE MAG

Naturally, its pages primarily reflect the Club's activities, but from the start neither Ronnie nor Pete insisted on a publication that was purely a house mag in content, allowing me to include many features that had no direct connection with Ronnie's, but which, I like to think, have been worthy contributions to jazz literature — some of which I have reprinted in this anniversary issue, such as Ron Rubin's poetry and Trog's cartoons

The production of *JARS* has always been a team effort and I have been lucky in having so many erudite contributors: Terry Brown, Campbell Burnap, Roy Davenport, Brian Davis, Derek Everett, Digby Fairweather, Barry Fox, Charles Fox, Mike Garrick, Mike Gavin, Wally Houser, Alun Morgan, Chrissie Murray, Paul Pace, Chris Parker, Jimmy Parsons, Jack Pennington, Alain Presencer, Ron Rubin, researcher Bob Glass and online editor John Richardson. Thanks, also, to David Redfern and David Sinclair for their splendid photographs, and for cartoons by Barney Bates, Wally Fawkes, Jack Pennington, Hedley Picton, Bill Stott and Monty Sunshine, their graphic talents gracing our pages. On the production side, I have

---

* Pete's column was a regular *JARS* feature

received invaluable help from Mike Gavin, Cindy Hacker, Janet Law, Chrissie Murray, Paul Pace, Chris Parker, Anne Piombini and Jim Rothwell.

REFERENCE VOLUMES

Like all hacks, I lean heavily on the standard reference books and am particularly grateful for the works of John Chilton. His *Who's Who of Jazz and Who's Who of British Jazz* are constantly at my side, knowing that the information I seek is as correct as you'll find anywhere in jazz journalism.

I have made many good friends and, alas, a few enemies as well. One adversary, Steve Voce, writing in *Jazz Journal*, referring to my sight problems, generously described me as 'the Ray Charles of jazz journalism'.

I have reproduced in *JARS* many of the potty things that have been written about jazz, often supplied by the eagle-eyed Ron Rubin. One comment I recall was made by John Gill, 'contemporary' composer Graham Collier's partner, who solemnly declared that under no circumstances would Collier ever descend to playing Dixieland, which was an enormous relief to me, but the nagging doubt persists that he may change his mind.

HOWLERS

Of course, *JARS* has contributed its share of howlers and typos that escape one's notice before going to the printer. One concerned Ellington trombonist Laurence Brown. I wrote that he gave up playing at the age of sixty-five. This appeared as 'gave up laying' which, at his age, may have well been the case, but was not what I'd written. An absolute horror was a caption under a photograph of a Ronnie Scott sideman, alto saxophonist Dougie Robinson. This appeared as 'Druggie' Robinson and Dougie was never an addict. Another clanger, on the front page, was a picture of a white female singer captioned as the black American tenor saxophonist Ben Webster. Mercifully, I spotted this before publication, but I get the horrors merely thinking about it. How the boys would have loved that one! Especially the pedantic pest who religiously keeps me informed of our errors, but then in this game we are all pots ascribing a particular blackness to kettles. Of course, the other fellow's niggles are petty but we point out errors purely in the interests of a higher truth…

For instance, reader Adrian Hill (who expertly set up my internet connection), viewing the Ken Burns jazz series on BBC2 in 2001, spotted that the train ostensibly bearing Louis Armstrong from New Orleans to Chicago in 1923 was in fact a British LNER B2, a fact confirmed by film historian John Huntley, leading us to wonder whether Mr Burns was as hazy about US locomotive history as he appeared to be about jazz. Humphrey Lyttelton, on his 'Best of Jazz' programme, obviously read our comments and referred to us as 'nit-picking anoraks', as though he himself had never been guilty of such in the course of his thirty years at the microphone.

TEMPERAMENTAL TECHNOLOGY

Inevitably, the mechanics of preparing our copy have changed. When I started it was a manual typewriter, then a sophisticated electric model, then to an Amstrad, the pages going to typesetters, often with the most gruesome results. You would never believe how drastically those chaps could change meanings or render one's profundities into unintelligible gobbledegook. Now we work with the computer and printer in my front room, technology that is absolutely miraculous when handled properly and totally disastrous in the hands of someone, like me, rooted in the age of the quill and pewter pot of ink. I would have been defeated by this monster had it not been for Mesdames Hacker, Law, Murray and Rusin and Messrs Gavin, Hill, Pace and Rothwell. My thanks to you all!

THE PERILS OF HUMOUR

We have tried to maintain a level of humour. After all, Ronnie Scott was a very funny man and we would wish to follow his example, but I have no illusions about the pitfalls of attempting to be funny. Responses to humour are highly subjective. In short, it doesn't make everyone laugh. In music hall-terms, when a joke dies a death the comic dies with it. In one issue, I wrote, in respect of the ageing process, that I had been humming *November Song*. Ronnie Scott, quick to pounce on errors, said, 'You mean *September* Song', don't you?' I replied that, in this context, I thought *November Song* would make a good joke. *Really?*' was Ronnie's rejoinder. Moral: Don't try your funnies on comics. It was a lesson I should have learned interviewing Spike Milligan.

INTERVIEWING THE FAMOUS

As well as Spike, I have interviewed several famous people for *JARS*: Kenneth Clarke, then Chancellor of the Exchequer (our conversation took place in the vast Treasury Room);

David Steel, then leader of the Lib Dems; the Rolling Stones' Charlie Watts; the outrageous George Melly; the eminent John Dankworth; and the cantankerous cornetist Ruby Braff. I was accused of ingratiating myself with the renowned and my answer was that people are more interested in the opinions of the famous than in those of the man-in-the-street. My job is to make *JARS* as readable as I possibly can.

'YOUR CHEQUE IS IN THE POST'

JARS is independently produced by me and my income depends almost entirely on advertising revenue. I wish to earnestly thank those advertisers who have supported the paper and without whom there would be no *JARS*, but the financial aspect of this nexus is, to put it mildly, fiscally unfriendly — meaning that advertisers' accountants never rush for their chequebooks.

That great comic Groucho Marx once remarked, 'Don't lend people money. It gives them amnesia,' to which he could have added, 'Don't send them an invoice either, as the mere sight of it will cripple their writing arm.'

How true! This is no reflection on my advertisers, God bless them all, but on their accounts departments where it is written in stone that immediate payment of invoices will result in instant dismissal. The excuses I have been given are legion: your cheque is in the post; we don't appear to have received your invoice; the accountant is in Tenerife; the computer is down; and one that I particularly like, by virtue of its originality, 'You can't speak to the accounts lady as she is on fire drill.' But it is all part of the game and I consider myself lucky to have the job.

THE INEVITABILITY OF CHANGE

Over the years, there have been enormous changes in the music itself and, sadly, many of the pioneers have passed away. But the essential pulse is perpetuated by newcomers whose developments, it has to be said, are not entirely accepted by the old guard musicians and fans. The greybeards, grunting over their beer, mutter that things have changed for the worse and deplore the word jazz being wantonly, as they see it, attached to music far removed from once generally accepted forms.

The inevitability of change, like it or not. The old guard emphatically do not. The upstarts are upsetting their treasured conceptions and categorisations; the ancients arguing that chalk is chalk, cheese is cheese, and, if mislabelled, the buyer will find the former inedible and the latter useless on a blackboard. But no art can remain static and considering the entire history of jazz and how much it has developed since the first genuine jazz band recording by the Original Dixieland Jazz Band from New Orleans in 1917, eighty-seven years ago, jazz has become an infinitely more variegated music.

Ronnie and Pete have recognised the winds of change, and the magazine that represents the institution that is Ronnie Scott's Club, and its ethos, has to reflect these changes, but never should the musicians who established jazz as a potent force be forgotten or dismissed as old hat. We have profiled many of those great names whose enormous creativity led the way for the scene as we know it today, and we will continue to do so. Without the past, there is no present.

Slawkenbergius

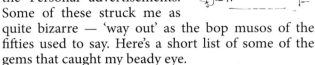

I recently chanced across a copy of the *Melody Maker*. Oh dear, oh dear! Is this the paper that supported the jazz movement for over fifty years? It doesn't seem possible. However, I was intrigued by the 'Personal' advertisements. Some of these struck me as quite bizarre — 'way out' as the bop musos of the fifties used to say. Here's a short list of some of the gems that caught my beady eye.

Young man, tall, 20s, seeks older woman, 30-35, for spiritual relationship…
Wealthy lady, 30, tall, slim, seeks dynamic guy into Police and Madness…
Guy, Leamington Spa, loves folk and rock. Into Dana Gillespie and Kate Bush…
Long haired guy into Cliff Richard, fantasy and whole foods…
Coloured guy, seeks freakish chick. Must be into rock and roll and other things. Own London flat…

Dammit, I thought, be a devil and use *JARS* to help me find my soul mate. Here goes:
Guy, not born yesterday, or the day before, Caucasian, own Highgate flat, six feet, hairy head wise, cut short back and sides, greying, bit of an old smoothie

round the chest, lower hirsute adornments original colour and curliness (centre piece not guaranteed), vegetarian, non-smoker, alcoholic heavily into Miff Mole, Horsecollar Draper and Ponzi Crunz, seeks friendship and other things with sympathetic chick, 18, or thereabouts, measurements 32,24,32 or thereabouts, who must be into Miff, Horsecollar and Ponzi. Send photograph of any of this holy trinity as proof of sincerity. Advertiser proud possessor of Salon Model Lyceum Wind-up Machine, 1927 vintage, with Astra Sound Box and extra supply of extra-loud Songster needles for midnight freakouts. Please, no mizzogs.

I'll let you know how I get on.

HANDSOME FEATURES A-CLOUDED

Now, after that untypical bit of sweetness and light, I revert to type so not as to disappoint my following when I refer to a telephone call that clouded my handsome (see Hedley Picton's drawing above) features. The call was from a querulous bandleader who enquired did we know that the country's greatest jazz trumpeter was in his band for a week at the Club? Not being clairvoyant, and rusty with the crystal ball, no, we didn't. It was up to him to let us know his personnel. We haven't the time to ring round and breathlessly enquire of Jack, or whatever his name may be, who he's booked. Consider yourself ticked-off, Jack — or whatever the name may be.

THE CHUCKLE SLOT

There are some nights when the happiness juice just doesn't seem to work. I say to myself — Slawky, old boy — what can I do to lift the blues? If it's a Sunday I always have the answer. I tune into the Chuckle Slot, billed in the *Radio Times* as *Sounds of Jazz*, Radio 2, 11p.m. to 1a.m., and dig those ace chucklers, Peter Clayton and Tony Russell. In this riot of 'ho-ho-ho' and 'ha ha ha', I'm cheered up no end. By golly, they do like a chuckle. It was a bitter disappointment to me when producer Keith Stewart turned me down as a guest chortler. It's not that I want the money — just the honour. But, living in hope, I keep practising my brand of guffaw. Now… some loon is likely to deliberately twist this, as indeed one loon already has, to have it that I'm after a presenter's job. Not so: I couldn't even pretend to be the least interested in some of the stuff they are compelled to play in the interests of a spurious broadmindedness. I'm not blaming producer or presenters for this state of affairs. It's the planners, for giving the programme only two measly hours a week. The chucklers have no choice but to appear 'broadminded', or upset the various factions, and what with the creeping paralysis of 'fusion', there are more people than ever to satisfy. No, I just wanted to show that I like a good ho-ho. Come on! Give a chap a break!! Fair dues for other chucklers, I say!

'We've still got five minutes. Play some more of that Rebop again!'
Illustration courtesy of *New Musical Express*

PERSONAL VIEW

MELODY MAKER

It has taken me twelve months or so to learn that the weekly paper *Melody Maker* has folded after 75 years in existence, its longevity surely one for *The Guinness Book of Records*? Since it became pop saturated, I had long given up reading a publication that, for some 30 years, was a weekly pleasure.

The dear old *MM*, as we affectionately called it, was an extraordinary journal. It was fundamentally a trade paper promoting the output of song publishers and musical instrument manufacturers, but from its birth, in January 1926, until the mid-Seventies, when it went over completely to pop, there was a hard core on its staff dedicated to jazz.

Indeed, it was the first publication in Europe to run jazz news and record reviews and, in many respects, giving more coverage to the music than any American counterpart. It became the weekly bible for both musicians and aficionados. Its succession of editors, commencing with Edgar Jackson, allowing the jazz 'hot-heads' space whilst still continuing to 'serve the profession' in its wider aspects. It was truly broad-based stylistically and, in its later days, covering dance music, swing, traditional and bebop jazz, and for many of us, its contents were the groundwork of our jazz education.

I have a special affection for the *MM*: in June 1941, the first article I ever had published was in that paper. In a previous issue an RD Ramsey proclaimed that jazz was dead and, full of youthful outrage, I charged in with a denial of the premise. The article was headed 'Jazz Jeremiahs', whom I slated for burying the music, simply because the current developments were not to their liking. I received the handsome sum of two guineas for this slashing attack.

Naively, I thought this was immediately going to launch me into a glittering career of journalism, but HM Government and the Admiralty had other ideas about my immediate future. Recently re-reading my piece, I blushed at the repetition and syntax, but, at least, I got it right that jazz had not expired. In fact, the twin upsurge of revivalism and bebop was just round the corner, and gave the music a wider audience, this leading to a situation from the late forties where British musicians could actually earn a living playing jazz.

QUAINT PHRASEOLOGY

I recently looked up some old copies of the *MM* and was tickled by the quaint phrases they used in the thirties and forties: clarinets were 'gobsticks', trombones were 'sliphorns', the bass was the 'dog house', pianists were '88ers', guitarists were 'frettists', drummers were 'vellum-sloshers' or 'skin-bashers', male singers were 'crooners' and the females were 'chirpettes' or 'canaries'.

The *MM* was fond of the heading 'Bombshell Hits The Profession' – this often leading to the riveting news that violinist Sidney Simone, leading a 'sweet' band at a West End restaurant, had ceased connections with that venue, and would be 'pursuing his extensive freelance connections in town', which meant that Mr Simone would

Masthead of the very first *Melody Maker*, January, 1926

be seen in Archer Street, the open-air social club and unofficial labour exchange for musicians, near Piccadilly, looking for another berth.

These Archer Street gatherings, now long gone, breached some ancient by-law and, every so often, musicians were charged with 'loitering' and fined at Great Marlborough Street magistrates' court, a stupidity against which the *MM* fiercely railed. Balmy days…

THE EDITORS

The editors, starting with Jackson, were Percy Mathison Brooks, Ray Sonin, Pat Brand, Jack Hutton, Ray Coleman and Richard Williams, its contributors including Spike Hughes, Leonard Feather, Ralph Venables, Rex Harris, Sinclair Traill, Bill Elliot, Max Jones, Bob Houston, Bob Dawbarn, Laurie Henshaw, Brian Case, Chris Welch, Steve Lake among others. Alas, these names don't mean much in a scene that has vastly changed, but they all made their contribution to spreading the gospel.

Archer Street, is a small thoroughfare in London's Soho connecting Great Windmill Street in the west and Rupert Street in the east. In the '20s–'60s it was thronged, particularly on Mondays, with dance band musicians seeking work. This 'labour exchange' and social club was known by its denizens simply as 'The Street'. On the right hand side facing east was the Harmony Inn where the first Ronnie Scott band was conceived. With the collapse of the dance band industry in the '60s 'The Street' has become virtually a ghost alley. J.G.

17

GREEMAR HARRIOTTSON (Greemar, *who?*)

We are printing this transcript of Charles Wolf's preamble to a recent unique broadcast on 'Jazz in Britain' on Radio 3 because of that broadcast's musical and historical significance.

In my view it was an event ranking with King Oliver's entry into the Gennett Studios, Indiana, in 1922, the electric partnership at the Okeh Studios between Louis Armstrong and Earl Hines, the innovatory saxophone of Lester young with Count Basie in the mid-thirties, the orchestral colourations of Duke Ellington over four decades, the revolutionary liaison between Monk, Bird and Dizzy at Minton's in the mid-forties, and the assaults on Western tonality by Ornette Coleman and Don Cherry in the sixties. Regrettably, the transcription was signed 'Anon'.

The percussionist in jazz has been traditionally concerned with 'time', using a kit comprised of a bass drum, snare drum, tom-toms and several cymbals, occasionally expanding to include orchestral percussion, like the tubular bells Sonny Greer used to play with Duke Ellington in the 20s and 30s.

Greemar Harriottson is a musician who, with considerable experience in all fields of jazz behind him, has now developed to the point where he has chosen to focus purely on sonority, or sound for its own sake, and I think it should be added that his present work is deeply influenced by his strong religious and philosophical beliefs.

INDIAN BULLOCK BELLS

Tonight we shall be hearing a performance of his new work 'S.U.D.S' or 'Suds', in which Harriottson plays on a wide variety of percussion instruments from Apache Indian Bullock bells to pre-Celtic meditation pots which, according to the rich folklore surrounding them, have traditionally more functions than merely musical! There is also a rare group of Alaskan pentatonic icicles, specially imported and, indeed, played tonight in a thermally insulated fridgidaire.

Although Greemar is improvising, he will be doing so against the background of a prerecorded tape (which he himself has made) of the spontaneous sound originating from a custom-built washing machine constructed to his own specifications, and going through its 25-minute heating, washing, rinsing and spinning cycle; the intensity

Cartoon: Monty Sunshine

and periods of calm in the improvisation responding to the machine's various meditative and climactic peaks.

MEDITATION SOCKS

So, although Harriottson's performance is improvised, it is at the same time tightly controlled and carefully timed by the machine's computerised programme – which in its turn is determined by the number, weight and texture of the soiled meditation socks which are being kindly lent for the broadcast by a group of young monks from the new order to which Greemar belongs – (and who, on occasion, act as his 'roadies') – the Ultimate Nostril Deterrents.

Indeed, the Deterrents themselves remain in the studio throughout, thereby adding several further dimensions to the mood of the performance by adopting their basic religious postures of positive or expectant waiting, which after all, serve to underline the essential nature of this kind of piece.

So, with the sound of the Celtic meditation pots reacting to the spontaneous and random kicks of the barefoot monks (and thereby tilting a trifle precariously) we begin 'Suds – A New Aural Experience' and, I might add, for those of us here in the studio, a distinctly (sniff) olfactory one too.

JARS is more than happy to lend its support to such genuinely creative music-making, especially as the astounding imagination employed in this broadcast involved the importation of Alaskan pentatonic icicles, which can't have been easy, even in the sort of summer we've had.

Notwithstanding this help from nature, Greemar Harriottson and the Ultimate Nostril Deterrents are to be warmly congratulated for this vital surge in the forever ongoing process of jazz creativity and our thanks to Charles Wolf (who knows his Miff Mole, Horsecollar Draper, Jimmy Cannon and Adrian Rollini as much as the forward-looking giants of our day) for persuading 'Jazz in Britain' producer Derek Drescher that this was to be one of the richest and stimulating musical experiences of the eighties.

OBSCURA LABEL

Readers will be delighted to know that Greemar and the UNDs will be recording 'Suds' on the Obscura label in the near future and with special thanks to the British Musicians Union for their kind permission to allow the UNDs (who are Transylvanian) to record in this country. Normally the MU frown on foreign monks (even those from behind Iron Curtain) doing British monks out of gigs, but thanks to MU officer and jazz enthusiast Brian Bane pleading their special qualities the go-ahead was given.

It's comforting to know that the new regime don't think in the same illogical and restrictive manner as their predecessors who obdurately denied the opportunity for American jazz musicians to play in this country from 1933 to 1952 on the grounds that such visits would deprive British musicians of work. The album will be produced by Ewan Harker, which follows, and the sleeve notes will be by Sal Hilmer which is a surprise since all the participants are white.

COMPLEX SONORITIES

Judging by the broadcast I can't pretend that this 'new aural experience' is for those whose jazz appreciation is cast in conventional mould. Indeed, even for those determinedly up-to-date buffs who keep tabs on the weekly changes in jazz fashion it will require some intense, not to say agonising, concentration unravelling the complex sonorities which would defy even Richard Williams's prosy examinations of like exercises, although it may well not be beyond the circumlocutions of the *Melody Maker's* Brian Case.

ICICLE IMPORTATION

I fervently hope that jazzers of all dominations will earnestly apply their ears and summon an iron will to grasp the import of this new experience and not be put off by the album's cost — a rather steep £20. I'm told by Ewan Harker that the price would have been higher had it not been for the prevailing weather conditions making the icicle importation less expensive. He also points out that Apache bullock bells and Ms. Hilmer's services are not cheap. We hope readers will not thinks all this is a load of old bullocks..

J.G.

WHISPERS, MURMURS & ASIDES

FREE AND GAY

Listening to those 'free-form' exercises is one thing, and indeed, I heard all of Graham Collier's Hoarded Dreams on Radio 3 last October and reported that it was a very long hour and twenty minutes, but it was a difficult kettle of fish actually watching this work being performed on the box. (Channel 4). It was an unlovely spectacle: skilled musicians, some with the most worthy jazz credentials, writhing and twisting, their features contorted as they honked, squealed and squawked. It had me thinking: what a good thing Art Themen was in the sax section. At least there was a doctor in the house in the case of ruptures, broken blood vessels, self-induced hysteria and cardiac arrest, all of which seemed on the cards as the guys freaked out. I was particularly worried about one of the trumpet players, a Finn, I believe. He got himself into a dreadful tizz.

This performance was advertised in *TV Times* as the Arts Council's *Jazz* (my italics) Commission at the 1983 Bracknell Jazz Festival. Two distinguished pundits, Brian Priestley and Charles Fox, made obeisant noises, the latter making comparisons with Duke Ellington, thus piling sacrilege upon travesty. Tut, *tut*, Charles...

There was another commentator, one John Gill, who made a big thing of being Collier's lover and made critical judgement about his man's music. At the end of the show this couple kissed each other.

Illustration: Hedley Picton

GREEMAR AND THE COBRA

Club member Alain Presencer (alias Greemar Harriottson), Tibetologist, and Player of Tibetan Singing Bowls (Saydisc SDL 326), was in Tashigong, south east Tibet, (illegally, as he had no visa) and sought refuge in a disused Buddhist shrine, called a stupa, this shelter by kind permission of its usual occupants, some Tibetan bandits. Settling down to

Illustration: Monty Sunshine

sleep he looked up to see a large white cobra intently staring at him. The beast looked at Alain for four hours, the object of his chilling scrutiny hardly daring to breathe, much less move or close his eyes. Later he discovered the cobra was non-poisonous, but even if he was in two minds about this, Alain wasn't prepared to put the matter to test. The things some of our members get up to!

BAT BITING

Allowing that many jazzmen's behaviour hasn't been exemplary, their misdemeanours, however, pale into insignificance compared with the excesses, off and on the stage, of many posturing rock and roll yobs. Granted I am prejudiced against them and their music (so called) but even I, with some personal experience of these people (for my sins) gaped at an item in *The Standard* about a certain Ozzy Osbourne undergoing treatment for rabies on account of having bitten off the head of a bat.

Illustration: Hedley Picton

Whether this topping of *vesperilio* is part of his 'act' or one of his pastimes, I wouldn't know — both, probably — but he bit off more than he could chew, didn't he? Serves him right! I have no particular brief for bats (except, now I come to think about it, they lend a certain eerie dimension to nights in the country which I like) but they don't do us humans any harm, and I don't see why frenetic young beasts should go about biting their heads off. Yes! Serves Ozzie right!

PAUL PRY

INTERVIEW...
of sorts...

A certain jazz journalist hoping to scratch a shilling or two from a scene littered with the bones of similar masochists phoned the office of Mr. Ronald Scott, tenor saxophonist, raconteur, club owner and latterly, author. A young lady answered the telephone. The hack enquired: 'Can I speak to the master, please?'

'Which one?'

'How many have you got then?'

'At least half a dozen.'

'Can I have the one called Ronnie Scott?'

'Do you know him?'

'Only about eighty years?'

'Oh, that's all right then.' (Pause) 'But he isn't in.'

'When will he be back?'

'I dunno. He's gone out to eat.'

'Doesn't he eat at the Club?'

'What! You gotta be joking!'

Her hand obviously went over the mouthpiece, but her comments clearly heard.

'Here, Shar! Guy here thinks Ronnie eats at the Club!'

Shrieks of girlish laughter permeate the pretty little hand over the mouthpiece.

'Cor, you've got a right one there, Trace.' Some days later the hack actually entered Mr Scott's sanctum. He had the hangdog demeanour of a door-to-door brush salesman after an unproductive day in Stockton.

It transpired that it wasn't to be the easiest interview he had conducted with a creative artiste.

'Ah, come in, Mr...er...'

'Godbolt, Jim Godbolt'

'Of course, please sit down Mr Goldberg.'

'Where?'

'Bloody hell! Someone's nicked the chair. Must have been a customer. Makes a difference, y'know, playing to an audience! Can't wait to get out there and show him! However, what can I do for you...er...'

'Godbolt. Jim Godbolt. I want to interview you for *Jazz Circle News*.'

'Ah, yes, that irregular monthly.

Certainly. Go ahead. But I hope the paper can publish the article soon, or else it'll be an obituary. I've just had a horrendous week with a neurotic genius and don't feel too good. Many of my idols proved to have feet of clay, but this one had his head packed with the stuff!'

'Sorry about that.'

'Indeed, it's tough at the top. Now, I must warn you. Anything I say doesn't constitute a contract. And let's keep it straight. Lots of people are beginning to think I'm a joke artist instead of a saxophone player.'

'It is quite an understandable misapprehension. I've just been reading on one of your handouts that your premises can be hired out for indoor riots, underwater tennis and barmitzvahs.'

'Ah, I was having a little joke about underwater tennis, but I don't need to hire the place out for riots and we do a very nice barmitzvah. For *you*, I can do a very special price! You could tell your friends, Mr. Goldstein. You are...er....?'

'No, but some of my best friends are...'

I'm pleased to hear it. We're all brothers under the skin, aye? I don't care what colour or race they are myself, as long as they pay at the door that is.'

'It also says in that handout that some of your patrons are gangsters.'

'Only very nice gangsters who help old ladies across the road. Excuse me, the phone's ringing. My partner Pete King normally attends to calls, but he's on holiday. In Miami. Got his yacht there. He's named it Ron. A nice touch, don't you think?'

'Hello! Yes, this is Ronnie Scott's. The band any good? I should hope so! I'm paying them enough! What's this? The cover? Only the bolt hole I use when my gags fail. Terrible lot last night. As much chance of raising a laugh as a joint in a nunnery. Oh, that cover. A mere five pounds, sir. It's a gift. No. Sir, no Trad here. Often thought about it, though. A touch of the old 'Muskrat Ramble' would make a change from

interminable choruses of 'Green Dolphin Street'. Clothes? Yes, sir, they should be worn, especially by your wife in this part of Soho. Oh, I see what you mean. As informal as you like, sir. Not at all. Hope to see you tonight. Now, where were we — er — what did you say your name was?'

'Doesn't matter. It's said by many that the ordinary jazz fan can't afford to attend your Club.'

'God may know what constitutes the ordinary jazz fan and I suspect he's as hazy about him as I am, but students and Musicians' Union members, for instance, are admitted for £2.00 or £2.50. For this pittance they get five hours of first class jazz and there's no obligation whatsoever to buy food or drink. Of course we object when they bring their own sandwiches. In what other London night club would you find such a facility?'

'I wouldn't know. I can't afford night clubs'.

'You want to get yourself a steady job Mr. Godlett. Try the LEB. It's the day of the proletariat y'know. To be quite frank most of my clientele are well heeled yobs. The quality can't afford to go 'up west' any more. We get the occasional Hooray, but that's all. Pity, because I'd like a bit of class about the place. Only joking. You like a laugh and a joke Mr. — er — Goddolt?'

'Depends on the jokes.'

'The old ones are the best, I know!'

'I must say there are a few of them in your book. Ghosted by Mike Hennessey, wasn't it?'

'Ghost, indeed! The book was finished years ago and he haunts me still — for his money. Well, I must be off, got to think up a few snappy gags — a few hot licks, I mean — before I go on. And get something to eat. I can recommend a nice little Greek place down the road.'

The interviewer reeled out of the premises. Once home, he immediately rang the personnel department of the LEB, murmuring, 'This must be an easier way of making a living'. J.G.

A Day in The Life... of the Editor

ESMERALDA'S JAZZY JULIE?

In the *JARS* office, an enormous complex with a wide range of multi-coloured telephones for me to bark out orders to a myriad of dedicated minions, we have a name for the quintessential PR lady — 'Esmeralda' — whose knowledge of the jazz scene is, at best, slight, and who has my name as Goldblatt.

My mind no longer boggles — too old in my tooth and too long in my lobes — but it does make one wonder just how these Esmeraldas get — and hold — their jobs. A recent example being a lady at Decca Records, who sent us — the house magazine of Europe's most famous jazz club — a Julie Andrews CD for us to review. Yes, the thoroughly wholesome Julie, who captivated your parents in the sixties with *The Sound of Music*.

Now! Do we ever get jazz CDs from Decca?

You, the assuredly perceptive readers of this column, will have got the answer in one!

DIFFUSED OR DEFUSED?

In my beef about misuse of the word 'jazz', the word 'diffused' was printed as 'defused' — which, in that context, is probably just as appropriate, but saxophonist Iain Ballamy takes me to task for resisting change.

Graciously, I accept the inevitability of change. If jazz had stayed at the level of the Original Dixieland Jazz Band — the first jazz band on disc — it would have died an early death, but I am suspicious of the word 'progress' as necessarily indicative. Without doubt, the atom bomb is an enormous advance on the bow and arrow as a killing weapon, but if it bodes well for humankind and the earth's atmosphere, that is quite another matter. Similarly, some of the directions which jazz has taken are equally questionable and I object to people changing the linguistic goalposts about jazz and of the improvement misconceptions that can arise from this misuse, especially on the few jazz programmes on the air.

For instance, a series on BBC Radio 3's Jazz File on rare 78s, by cartoonist Robert Crumb, of world pop music from the twenties and thirties had, in no respect whatsoever, anything to do with jazz. In this regard, I have no compunction in complaining about the word jazz being 'diffused', or 'defused', over the air or elsewhere. I rest my case, m'lud.   J.G.

WHISPERS, MURMURS & ASIDES

NOISE POLLUTION

Pianist Ron Rubin's letter about noise pollution in a recent *Daily Mail* expressed sentiments with which I am in utter accord. For business reasons I had to enter one of those pop emporiums in London's West End. Here, strident pop is played at such horrendous, mind-blowing and frightening volume it had me scurrying in undignified haste to the relative peace and quiet of litter strewn Oxford Street. A security man, spotting my hasty exit, grabbed me as though I was making off with a nicked Boy George album. During my brief stay in this horror house of dire noise I managed to detect two lines of an opus that was blaring from the speakers:

'Biby, whoi carn oi be wiv yew.' 'Biby, whoi carn I'ava a liddle screw wiv yew?'

Not wishing to clutter my mind with totally useless information and having an overwhelming urge to beat it hot-foot out of this approximation of hell on earth, I didn't bother to ascertain the name of the pustular delinquent delivering these eloquent lines. While this yob's desire to — ahem — cohabit with his 'biby' was quite understandable, the lyric, or that which I heard of it, was hardly in the Cole Porter class and rather lacking in what my generation quaintly called 'romance'.

SEX DISCRIMINATION

Recently I came across a guy into feminism — there's a lot of this about — who had seen The Guest Stars, given in *JARS* as an 'All-Girl Band' and said they, The Guest Stars, would not like the reference to their gender. 'You might as well have said they were performing dogs', this feminist added.

Really! What is this all about for chrissake? What is one to say: 'Persons of the opposite gender to the person who is writing the piece? Since the playing and appreciation (and writing about) jazz is largely a male activity and the sociologists and anthropologists can have a go at working out why if they wish — it seems only reasonable that any departure from the norm is mentioned, and such intelligence will arouse healthy curiosity. As Dr Johnson said, 'Sir, a woman preaching, is like a dog walking on its hind legs. It is not done well, but you are surprised to find that it is done at all'.

Of course, Johnson was a right old MCP, but he had a point, and happily, there are increasing number of female (dare I say!) jazz players and — dare I say — what a fine band The Guest Stars are.

CLARK 'CLARKY' TEWKSBURY

CLUB ELEVEN
as remembered by BRIAN DAVIS

In the late forties a group of ten musicians and one non-musician formed the Club Eleven. Until then the new jazz called bebop or rebop had been played sporadically in various London clubs, but the Club Eleven was the first regular gathering of like-inclined musicians who fervently wished to adopt the music of Dizzy Gillespie and Charlie Parker. This at the time when traditional jazz inspired by the New Orleans pioneers was in the ascendancy. At first the Club Eleven musicians were playing for themselves, with no idea of the commercial success that such startlingly nonconformist music would bring them.

However, the news spread around and before long they were actually charging admission and these sessions were the genesis of bebop bands taking the road and bringing their music to dance and concert halls throughout the country. In issue No 4 of *JARS* Brian Davis, discographer, writer and acknowledged historian of British bebop, recalled those early, heady days.

I first heard of the Club Eleven via that late and most underrated British drummer Benny (Dave) Goodman, then a resident of Southend where a group of us eager youngsters were struggling to master instruments. Benny was well ahead of the rest of us and was just beginning to get into London jazz scene. This was early 1949. I was in the RAF stationed at High Wycombe, and would rush home every weekend for the feverish activity of the Southend avant-garde and Benny was enthralling us with tales of happenings in a fantastic London basement. 'It's all the gear there, man! It's all happening there, man!'

Dear old Benny was a character and probably more impressionable than the rest of us. Anything new, real or imagined, Benny was on to it. I can see him now, one warm spring evening sitting with us in our local café hangout, his thick Birdseye overcoat down to his knees (very much the fashion of the time), hunched over a bowl of tomato soup. 'Yeah! Everybody is drinking tomato soup, man!'

Whether or not tomato soup was the fashion of the 'with-it' is questionable, but there was no mistaking that his enthusiasm for The Club Eleven was real and so we decided on a midweek visit; the 'Civvies' up from Southend, myself hitching a lift from High Wycombe.

BEBOP SEEDBED

We met at the Club's entrance, which was a narrow doorway at 41 Great Windmill Street, opposite the Windmill Theatre 'which never closed'. Immediately to the left of the entrance was a steep bare wooden stairway painted a dull red around its well, descending to a basement level. An upturned box served as a cash desk and behind this stood manager Harry Morris who collected the 3/6d admission fee in between other duties. Harry was the non-playing, eleventh man, the other ten being musicians, and apart from being cashier, he was organiser and compere. It's his voice on a historic Esquire 78 of a Club Eleven concert in April, 1949, welcoming you to the 'club' between the opening bars of 'Wee Dot'.

Actually, this was recorded at King's George's Hall, Gt. Russell Street, off Tottenham Court Road, where the Hot Club of London (secretary Jim Godbolt) pioneered traditional jazz concerts in London two years before.

The stairs led to a bare room, and I do mean bare! The floor; the walls; naked electric lights enhancing the starkness of the décor. Immediately to the right of the entrance was a small stand with an upright (just about!) piano. There were a few hard chairs in front of the stand with, if I recall correctly, space for dancing either side of the room.

However, there was a touch of luxury — two or three, off-grey, moth-eaten Victorian sofas alongside the stand and down the side wall. These sofas could tell a few tales of the famous who had sat on them, and of the shapely posteriors of the girls who used to frequent the club, all looking cool and attractive and performing an unhurried type of jive

Club Eleven session, circa 1949. Left to right: Pete Pitterson, Johnny Rogers, Nat Gonella, Tommy Pollard, unknown singer, Ronnie Scott. Armstrong disciple, Gonella, unsuccessfully, essaying bebop. Note Pitterson's expression

with dirndl skirts a-swirling; so much more sophisticated than the frantic antics of the trad club and dance hall jitterbuggers…

THE EARLY BOPPERS

As for the 'famous', well, actually, I sat on 'No.1 sofa' myself absolutely mesmerised by, and less than two feet away from, the exotic cross rhythms of Ginger Johnson's bongos against the straight jazz cymbal dinning of drummer Tony Crombie. Similarly in the same spot I watched a very young Victor Feldman totally absorbed by the driving swing of drummer Laurie Morgan, undoubtedly the first British drummer to wholly grasp and be able to interpret the rhythms and accents of bop drumming.

Certainly for us, newly exposed to a few American bop records, Laurie was the closest thing to Max Roach; and incredibly creating such enormous swing sometimes with nothing more than a snare, hi-hat and bass drum! With Laurie were bassist Joe Muddel, pianist Bernie Fenton and alto saxophonist Johnny Dankworth to complete the quartet. Sometimes trumpeter Leon Calvert would join Johnny; other times Leon would be alone as Johnny was doubtless doing a gig elsewhere. The quartet's repertoire was mainly up — very up-tempo Birdlike things, but interspersed with some Dankworth original 'heads'. The group would tackle a ballad, which is more than the larger alternative group would do.

This was a septet fired by Tony Crombie, bassist Lennie Bush and the exceptional pianist Tommy Pollard, often wearing a sort of baseball cap. Tommy took to bebop from the onset, favouring a percussive style with a rather sparse melodic line. Ginger Johnson spiced the rhythm section, whilst the front line was basically Ronnie Scott (not, at this time really a bebop player, more a — well — Ronnie can tell it much better than I!), Johnny Rogers was on alto, a very physical player who strung together choruses of rather jerky Parkerish phrases and, finally on trumpet, if he felt like playing, 'the teacher' Denis Rose.

DENIS ROSE

Frequently though, Denis was missing

Left to right: Pete Chilver, Denis Rose, Tony Crombie, Jack Fallon, Ralph Sharon, Ronnie Scott, and Sid Gross. Gross was a pioneer promoter of jazz concerts in London

or if there just not playing, in which event Hank Shaw, bursting with enthusiasm, (as of today) would be the trumpet man, digging everything, unable to keep still, and always in a curious blue jersey with three wide yellow stripes unaccountably stitched on the left sleeve. Then at times when Johnny Rogers was elsewhere, another long since forgotten alto man would be blowing up a storm; a Parker devotee, but with more flow than Johnny and a fiery exciting sound. This was Alan Doninger. Whatever happened to Alan?

Going back to Denis Rose, he was a bit older than the others and didn't view things with the same youthful fanaticism. I recall on one occasion when I was listening in my usual state of euphoria (which always overcame me from the first few notes of the septet's relentless music) he was seated on sofa 'No.2', leafing through an illustrated magazine, apparently disinterested in the whole proceedings.

This appalled me, as to be almost sacrilegious, such was my uncritical acceptance of what, in hindsight, was pretty raw stuff. Nevertheless, Denis's attitude early on was at variance with most of the others who all seemed to concentrate intently on what the other fellow was putting down and obviously playing for themselves and giving scant attention to the audience (equally serious about the proceedings), packing the place every time I was there. Once I asked Hank

Shaw from my, as always, front seat who an unknown (to me) tenor man was: 'Schh, man', replied Hank, eyes tightly closed, 'I'm listening — isn't he great?' came the afterthought. I never did find out who that tenor man was.

LIVING THE MUSIC

This indeed was the special aura of the Club Eleven — both participants and listeners alike lived the music. Its 'exclusiveness' fired the imagination of the young and impressionable and assuredly one was never the same after catching the heady atmosphere of that basement, not only in one's jazz outlook and appreciation but in one's everyday behaviour, which must have been insufferable to those on the 'outside', which was almost everybody!

I don't recall many of the Club's special 'characters' because I was too absorbed to notice extra-musical activities, but I do remember a rather pathetic figure called Solly, the sweeper-up, who, I believe officiated at the Windmill Theatre. I had the impression that he lived in one or the other as he was constantly around. He obviously loved the music, but was a little disconcerting with his bizarre, although harmless, behaviour.

Back to the music, though. 'Sitters-in' had to be 'acceptable' to this fast company. I saw pianists Ralph Sharon and Eddie Thompson and one memorable night heard some of the most Bud Powell-like piano by Buddy Greco, then appearing with Benny

▶▶

Left to right: Ronnie Scott, Johnny Dankworth (now, Sir John), Denis Rose, Tommy Pollard, Lennie Bush, Tony Crombie.

Goodman and five British musicians as a Goodman Sextet under the guise of a variety act at the London Palladium. Other names come to mind like Harry Klein, on alto only then, and the first homegrown bop baritone saxophonist Derek Neville, stalwart of the No1 Rhythm Club jam sessions, and an early convert to the new jazz.

BIRDSONG

Another vivid memory is the sight of a thin, cropped-haired young alto player with an ancient looking silver instrument whose playing turned everyone around. Everything is relative, but even today I still think back on that stranger's playing as being the closest to Parker I've ever heard. I caught Ronnie Scott in a non-playing moment to enquire who he was: 'He's Spike Robinson' and an unsolicited follow up comment from the normally taciturn Scott, 'He's an American merchant seaman, really fantastic, isn't he?'

At least Spike is preserved on record. Recently four titles under Ronnie's name, with this extraordinary player were released on an Esquire LP: there remain four titles under Tommy Pollard's name and four quartet titles under Spike's own name available since the original 78s. The Club Eleven concert at King George's Hall went down in recorded history on three 10" and two 12"78s, plus a few unissued tracks.

Thirty years later this is a somewhat tentative and gauche set to listen to, but redolent of the tremendous air of excitement always to be found in that dingy, sweaty and smoke-filled basement where British bop spawned, and legendary figures either began their careers to become household names or at least top artistes in jazz circles. The less fortunate have remained in undeserved obscurity for decades since.

BRUSH WITH THE LAW

The Club Eleven moved to Carnaby Street in 1950 and made the headlines after the police raid in search of drugs. Several musicians were arrested and spent the night in cells and then appeared at Marlborough Street magistrates' court, before a Mr. Daniel Hopkin, charged with offences under the Raw Opium Regulations and the Dangerous Drugs Act. In his book *Some of My Best Friends Are Blues* Ronnie Scott described the court case as 'pure Beachcomber'. He related that Mr. Hopkin enquired, 'What is bebop?'

'For us in the dock, for whom bebop was something of a musical religion, providing a definition would have represented a fairly daunting challenge. But Chief Inspectors learn to take these summary queries in their stride: 'A queer form of modern dancing - a Negro jive', he answered with brisk authority.

WHISPERS, MURMURS & ASIDES

DISPUTED TERMINOLOGY

Britain's Tin Pan Alley was in Denmark Street, off Charing Cross Road and song-pluggers quickly latched on to this new jazz called bebop or rebop. Their rising star in the idiom was the nineteen-year old Ronnie Scott. In the sixties, I showed Ronnie this advert and he grunted in annoyance as he and many of his colleagues of the time objected to the onomatopoeic phraseology, 'bebop'. The early publicist for the new jazz, Steve Race, pleaded for the term, 'Minton's Jazz' as a more dignified description, but bebop/rebop persisted.

After all, 'bebop/rebop' was no more an outlandish phrase than other terms, including 'jazz' itself, that emerged throughout the entire history of the music. There are many others such as 'boogie-woogie', 'stride', 'funk', and indeed 'swing'.   J.G.

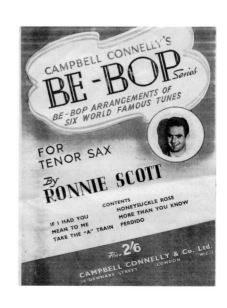

HERBERT COOT LETTERS

(The correspondence between Herbert Coot and Ronnie Scott, with apologies to The Henry Root Letters by William Donaldson)

10th January, 1984
Dear Mr. Scott,
I am devout fan of yours. I wish there were more like you. Not that it would have much effect on the younger generation if this were the case. My daughter Elisa is mad about Barry Manilow and she's twenty-four. My son, nineteen, also a Herbert, is into heavy metal bands, the volume of which 'would' — like one of Ted Dexter's off-drives — loosen a rhino's balls. I keep telling them they should go to Ronnie Scott's Club and listen to some decent music, but all they say is — Ronnie who?

Sorry about this, but I have done my best. Now I have small complaint. I went to see Nina Simone and she glowered at me all night. Why? Was it something about my appearance? I would be most grateful if you would find out. She will remember me. I was sitting in the second table from the left in the front row on the night of Tuesday, 10th January. I was wearing my MCC tie.

Regarding your joke about the club steaks glowing in the dark, it would have been a good idea had mine been aglow. I wouldn't have had so much difficulty finding it! Talk about a minute steak! Regarding the intervals between sets, could you not book some dancing girls to fill the gap? Like the ample Roly Polys on Les Dawson's BBC show? I could gawp at them and not get the kick in the shin from Mrs. Coot, who doesn't appreciate that my interest in the young female form at the age of forty-nine is aesthetic and not carnal.

I read that you were having financial problems a year or so ago. I trust this is now sorted out, but here's a pound, anyway.
Yours sincerely,
Herbert Coot

12th January, 1984
Dear Mr Coot,
Thank you for your letter of 10th January. I am delighted to hear that you are endeavouring to put your offspring on the right path. If only there were more like you. Please forgive my ignorance — but who is Barry Manilow?

The Roly Polys above were a group of ladies who had been 'in the chorus', but in their mature years reassembled to appear in the highly popular Les Dawson show on TV. The leader, centre is Mo Moreland. Photo courtesy of Mo

Regarding the size of your steak, the chef we had then was a midget — a nice enough chap — but he saw things, including steaks, from a small view point. You will notice a difference in the size of your sirloin next time you visit us. Our new chef is a gorilla, thus we can claim that our food is untouched by human hand, and not many clubs can make this boast.

I don't like to be rude to a member, but you must have an almighty conceit if you think for one moment that Nina Simone was just glowering at *you*. Regarding the Roly Polys (of whom I am a keen fan) we had a word with our architect, who advised that we couldn't possibly book them unless our band-stand was reinforced with RSGs — Rolled Steel Girders — to take the weight, and with things as they are at the moment, this is an expense we can't afford. You have no idea just how much your pound was appreciated. It was a life-saver. You wouldn't have any more to spare by any chance, would you? There would be full acknowledgement in our house magazine and in the national press. I have friends in Fleet Street.
Yours sincerely,
Ronnie Scott

WHISPERS, MURMURS & ASIDES

DEFINITIONS OF JAZZ

That inveterate harvester of jazz definitions, *JARS* versifier Ron Rubin, has sent me a few items, which I run for the edification of my readers.

'Jazz is obviously a curious use of rhythmic resources, and moreover, what a terrible revenge by the culture of the Negroes on that of the whites!' – Ignacy Jan Paderewski, who doubled as concert pianist and Prime Minister of Poland (1919).

'Jazz is the cacophonous warbling of an inebriated cockatoo.' — Earl Winterton.

'That vulgar, raucous, discordant abomination sometimes inaccurately called music, the proper name for which is jazz!' — Judge Tudor Rees.

Probably the most profound utterance about the music came from that distinguished drummer, Ringo Starr. His definition was, 'Jazz sounds like rats running on a tin roof.'

PAUL PRY

Slawkenbergius

I'd heard rumours that our venerable editor had changed watering holes, that the hostelry at which he now takes the edge off the pain was Three Greyhounds, on the corner of Greek and Old Compton Streets, where the hostess is one Roxy Beaujolais, who was 'on the door' at Ronnie's in the seventies.

I bearded the lion in his new den. He looked up — a trifle apprehensively, I thought. The sight of contributors doesn't always bode well for the editor. We creative artists get a little tetchy when our profundities are mauled by unfeeling editors, or marred by misprints.

'No problems with your copy in the current issue, old son?', he enquired — somewhat nervously, I thought. The guy's only human after all...

'No, except that you cut it by half'.

'Had to, old son, but I know how you feel. All we hacks are the same. What we have to say is highly significant and has to be said at length. There's one character, a lovely chap — always so enthusiastic about our music — but he'd cheerfully have me fill the entire mag with one of his album reviews. Otherwise you were happy? That's good. Well, I don't mind if I do, old son. You're a gentleman and a scholar. A drop of the amber-coloured fluid...'

'I know! It takes the edge off the pain'.

DOZZY GILLESPIE

'You're quite right, old son. I don't know what I'd do without it. Especially when the goofs rear up and kick me in the teeth after publication. I over-looked the misspelling of Wally Houser's surname, and he's only a Director of the Club and its lawyer! He wasn't thrilled, old son, but in his recollections of Dizzy Gillespie 'Dizzy' somehow became 'Dozzy'. Mercifully, I had it corrected in the nick of time, but can you imagine the fun the boys would have with that clanger? The phone would have rung in that ominous fashion and I would hear, 'Oh, it's only a small point, Jim, but who is this *Dozzy* Gillespie? I don't seem to find him in the reference books. Has he made any records?' That dedicated truffler for goofs, Kevin Henriques, would have been beside himself with joy. It makes a fellow feel absolutely parched, merely thinking about it. Why, that's uncommonly decent of you, old son. Make it a large one, there's a good chap.'

'When checking proofs I overlooked 1933 appearing instead of 1993, for the last Havana Jazz Festival. As you know, Ronnie's partner, Pete King, organised this and as he was born in 1929 he would have been a precocious genius at the age of four to have run this in 1933. And in doing the right thing by acknowledging Mark Gilbert in *Jazz Journal* for our piece on Bob Berg, Mark somehow became Martin. Picked up the pedants, of course, but, let's face it, old son, we're all the same. Dog is constantly eating dog in this game. Even yourself, old son.'

'Only in the interest of the higher truth.'

'Of course, old son. I was forgetting.'

The editor rummaged in his briefcase — actually, it was an Augustus Barnett carrier bag — and presented me with a cutting from the august *Times* sent to him by Jazz FM presenter Keith Howell, which I reproduce below:

Small specialist insurance magazine, which publishes a number of experts' contributions, seeks proofreader with the ability to enhance gramar and style. Fax essential.
About 3 hours per month.
Please reply to Box No 1929

Yes, dog eats dog...

At that moment the actor-manager, fresh from slaying 'em at the Civic Hall, Crosby, in a revival of *The Chocolate Soldier*, walked in. 'Ah, laddies...'

'We know, we know!' The editor and I cried in well-oiled unison, 'It's only a small point, and mine's a large Bells.'

The actor-manager spluttered over his silk cravat and departed.

Dizzy Gillespie by Richard Cole

26

DO YOU PLAY REQUESTS?*
RON RUBIN rubinates on a pianist's occupational hazard

'Only if they're asked for!' is the usual merry rejoinder we musicians like to make. But when we follow up with: 'What would you like to hear?' we can find ourselves in deep, or at any rate murky, waters. There might be a request for some obscure bossa nova, an old film theme or Victorian ballad, or something from *Top of the Pops* (i.e. the bottom of a barrel). Or perhaps 'something by Elton John' (to which the only proper reply is: 'I am sorry, I only play grown-up music') and of course there's always some clever dick who will ask you to play Rachmaninov's Third Piano Concerto…

Then there's that curious phenomenon which every cocktail pianist (though I hasten to add that I am of the Scotch-and-soda persuasion) has experienced: a request for a number you've just played. In my salad days I thought they must be taking the mickey, and would retort: 'I've just played it!' That's when they thought *I* was taking the mickey! The explanation is, of course, that all too often people only hear music subliminally, and don't know why a particular tune has surfaced into their consciousness. Over years — nay, decades — of being at the blunt end of all manner of requests, I got into the habit of jotting down the choicest items. Here are some of them.

GETTING THE TITLE WRONG

The most forgettable title of all time must surely be *As Time Goes By*. I've had it requested as *You Must Remember This, Play It Again, Sam, Casablanca, A Kiss Is Just A Kiss, As Tears Go By* and even *The Fundamental Things*. At the Pizza Express in Dean Street, a request for *Half Past Five* turned out to be *Opus Five*, and at another jazz club Miles Davis's *So What* somehow metamorphosed into *What's What*.
In a Munich piano bar, a gentleman asked me to play *Under The Rainbow*. When I pointed out the correct title to him, he replied, with stunning Teutonic logic: 'Oh, no — I think it is impossible to go over the rainbow; the title must be *Under The Rainbow!*'

I've had requests for *Besame Macho, The Vulgar Boatman* and *On Blue Dolphin Street*, and a colleague told me he was once asked to play *Nineteen Girls Sang in Berkeley Square*.

LOST IN TRANSLATION

'Can you touch Erroll Garner for me?' asked a young man in a Spanish piano bar. Well, I can think of one or two others I'd rather lay hands on, but I did manage to work that one out: the Spanish verb *tocar* means to touch, or to play a musical instrument (cf.Italian toccata). And when I made what I thought was a straight translation of Junior Mance's *Jubilation* into the Spanish *Jubilación*, a customer burst out laughing and said he'd never heard such a silly title — *jubilación* is the Spanish for retirement, or old-age pension (cf. our jubilee).

Working in Spain for several years, it was useful to know the Spanish titles for many of the standards. Some are translated literally- On the street where you live is *La Calle Donde Vives; Round Midnight* is *A Eso de la Medianoche* and so on – but *Night and Day* for some reason becomes *Dia Y Noche* (Day and Night). Others, presumably following the new lyric, can be mystifying, e.g. *I've Got You Under My Skin* is *Dentro De Mi, Begin the Beguine* becomes *Volver a Empezar, The Surrey With the Fringe on Top* is *La Calesa de Amor, 12th Street Rag* turns into *El Trapero,* and so on.
Unless planning a long stay in a non-anglophone country, it would be far simpler just to get the requester to whistle the first few bars…

THE RIDICULOUS

At a private party (something to do with the BAFTA awards), the host said: 'After the speeches will you please play some jiggery-pokery music' (I still haven't worked that one out!) And in a Covent Garden restaurant, a reasonably sane-looking chap presented me with a lengthy questionnaire of his own devising, which he asked me to fill in during the interval (no, I didn't). It included such gems as: 'I drink two and a half bottles of gin per week. Would you classify me as an alcoholic?' and 'I have been in the same job for fifteen years. Do you think I should seek a change?' There were many other questions, about his sex life, politics and God knows what else.
At another private do (in a village near Henley-on-Thames with the unlikely name of Bix), late in the evening when much booze had been consumed, an ample lady of the dowager type decided that she was going to sing *Rule Britannia* with piano accompaniment. I'd never played the ditty before, but thought I'd better have a go at it. Just as we launched into our duet, some of the over-refreshed guests decided what a topping idea it would be to re-enact a foxhunt. Taking down a variety of hunting horns which were displayed on the drawing room walls, they then proceeded to career around the grand piano on each other's backs bellowing 'Yoicks!' and 'Tally ho!' myself and the stout lady at the epicentre of all this, our musical efforts, now happily inaudible.
At Kettner's one night, a young chap wanted to hear a blues which was a great favourite of his. 'I can't remember the title', he said, 'but it starts like this: 'I woke up this morning…' Nice to be given a carte so blanche.
One of my favourites happened to a fellow pianist. A waiter at the establishment where he works came up and said: 'There's been a request for *Come Rain or Come Shine* — either will do'.
* Only if they're asked for...

INTERVIEW...
Ronnie the Punter

I entered Mr. Scott's office for this 'interview' page to find him gazing intently at TV. He, looked up to say 'Good afternoon, young man' (it's a dimly-lit office) and resumed his scrutiny of the screen. The event he was witnessing related to a long-standing arrangement he has with Mr. John Manley, a bookie — sorry, Turf Accountant, in Frith Street, a deal whereby Mr. Scott frequently calls on Mr. Manley to hand him sums of money, in return for which Mr. Manley hands Mr Scott a small piece of paper with the geographical location and time and event involving quadrupeds of the genus equine mounted by diminutive males in peaked caps, an arrangement that many would hardly regard is equitable, but, apparently, it satisfies Mr. Scott.

DARKEST SOHO

Well, perhaps not always satisfying him, but he never shows any signs of cancelling the deal. He is joined in this exercise by many other citizens of darkest Soho (Motto: 'The Lord 'elps 'im that 'elps 'isself'), whose general demeanour, cast of features and turn of phrase hardly suggest a willingness to part with cash very likely obtained by arduously shinning up and down the drainpipes of mansions, or bravely retrieving goods that unaccountably keep falling off the backs of lorries.

'Move your effing self!!!'

Illustration: Monty Sunshine

But, like Mr. Scott (Motto: 'Whilst I breathe, I hope'), who works hard for his money cracking the world's oldest jokes and playing the tenor saxophone at his club and in places like Cockermouth, Sale and Scunthorpe, they appeared to be happy with the arrangement, although there are occasions when the results of events had been greeted with rather crude observations, the more printable of which include, 'E got nowhere, the cowson, did'e?', 'Didn't'ave a turn of foot did'e?, the baalamb,' or 'E lacked a turn of toe, the effing bitch,' these outraged clients randomly mixing genus and gender in their disappointment.

But this disgruntlement in no way deters them from handing over more money to Mr. Manley the next day, or, indeed, that very same afternoon. True, there are some occasions when the owners of the bits of paper presented these to Mr. Manley, who hands them back their money and more, but usually to take it back again in exchange for yet another piece of paper, an arrangement eminently satisfactory to Mr. Manley (Motto: 'Several enter Frith Street every minute, and thank God').

COLONEL TALCOTT COVINGTON-HEMPHILL

Mr. Scott is assisted in his all-absorbing hobby by a Lt. Colonel Talcott Covington-Hemphill, a tipster— sorry, Turf Informant — who operates his 'Sure-Fire Winning System' from Suite 15, Blenheim Mews, London NW10, the Colonel despatching his selections for a financial consideration he sensibly insists on receiving in advance.

In truth, the Colonel is really one Abie Samuelson, but if you're an informant in the sport of kings, Lt. Colonel Talcott Covington-Hemphill sounds a trifle more impressive. As for his address — well,

he shares an office with a distributor of morally dubious literature (sent under plain covers) at the back of a totter's yard in Kensal Rise, NW10, where the law walks about in threes. That's if they are undermanned. More, if up to strength. The Colonel gets quite uptight about cynics who ask questions like — 'If his system is so sure-fire, why doesn't he keep it to himself and make a fortune?' In his adverts, the Colonel rebutts these snide questions, claiming that it would be untypically miserly of him not to share his knowledge with like-minded 'sportsmen', especially as this sharing made him a lot of nice friends, whom he advised to keep their bets to 'sensible' proportions, so not to upset the turf accountants — and with regard to dealings with the latter, it was also his advice that clients spread their bets far and wide, as turf accountants took a jaundiced view of consistent winners. He doesn't want his clients to be found 'uneconomic'.

The Colonel further asserts that should the time come when his sure-fire information affected starting prices, then, in all conscience, he would quit the game but, meantime, clients are urged to act on his advice, but quick. The Colonel was a little anxious when Mr. Scott, barnstorming in Cockermouth, Sale and Stockton, didn't send in his subscription and phoned Ronnie at his office. He eagerly enquired after Mr. Scott's health, promised to bring a large party to the club and spend a pound or two, adding, 'I just love your trumpet, bhoy,' which didn't please saxophonist Scott too much, but then, he didn't avail himself of the Colonel's services for that worthy's musical insight.

NOBLE PASSION

Mr. Scott's preoccupation with events on the TV that afternoon obviously precluded any chat with me and although normally a most taciturn person (to put it mildly), he became quite animated as the horses were being eased into the stalls and he displayed considerable agitation when one of them, Noble Passion, showed a marked reluctance to enter the stall assigned to this filly.

Eventually — to Mr. Scott's patent relief — the animal complied with the jockey's urging, and a moment later, all the horses shot out. All, that is, except Noble Passion, his immobility causing the usually graven Mr. Scott to jump up and down and wave his arms as if he were doing an imitation of Shirley Bassey.

'Move your effing self!', he roared at the screen, and after a few searing moments, Noble Passion actually took off. The commentator, seemingly taken by an attack of the hysterics, screamed the names of the animals as they raced down the track - Pipe Dream, Sweet Substitute, Sir Lester, Duke Ellington, Nick La Rocca and many more, but, alas, no further mention of Noble Passion, NP apparently not that keen to reach the finishing post, causing Mr. Scott to lose that composure normally associated with the proprietor of a sophisticated and world-famous night club that has enjoyed the patronage of royalty.

It was painfully clear to me that I wasn't going to get much out of Mr. Scott that afternoon, especially when he asked partner Pete King (Motto: 'If they don't come in voluntarily, chuck 'em in'), for a handful of 'readies'. It was obvious that Mr. Scott's disappointment at the failure of Noble Passion wasn't going to upset his arrangement with Mr. Manley, and clutching the readies reluctantly supplied by Mr. King, he departed.

HOPE SPRINGS ETERNAL

I hung around in hope of getting an interview, but the moment Mr. Scott appeared clutching another piece of paper from Mr. Manley, muttering that the animal ('Hope Springs Eternal', I believe), was an 'absolute cert', I knew I might as well go home, which I did — my departure quite unnoticed. As I left, I pondered on easier ways of earning a living and wondered if there was an opening in the business which Mr. Manley conducted so successfully. By renting a small room, and having bits of paper printed, I could perhaps have got Mr. Scott to pay me instead of Mr. Manley the money he earns in Cockermouth, Sale and Stockton, and, of the two, surely I am the most deserving. Yes, the next time I 'interview' Mr. Scott, I'll put this to him and the state of jazz can take care of itself, although I am not too optimistic about Mr. Scott accepting the suggestion.   J.G.

Slawkenbergius

NUDGERS AND HOGGERS

I own to having a saintly nature; I claim to be the epitome of tolerance, the personification of goodwill, the acme of bonhomie. I am so much in demand I've had to compile a waiting list — and everyone in their turn — for my presence at parties, weddings, hunt meetings, barmitzvahs, seances, soirees and various other social activities. You name it, and I'm wanted to set the seal on the occasion.

I'm not boasting, mark you. I attribute my beauteous soul to genetic inheritance. Some of us have it; most of you haven't. It's one of the distressing facts of life that nature is random, not to say quirky, in the distribution of her favours. A shame, really, but that's the way it goes.

However… There are occasions when my saintly patience is sorely tried, when my all-abiding faith in the essential goodness of man (and woman, come to that) is put to severe test. To wit: bar-hoggers and nudgers, and particularly those who frequent the Club bars! Now me being a 100% nice guy would stand back if the bar was crowded, and allow others to get served. I'm like that. As I say, I'm cast in the saintly mould.

Not so with the hoggers, though. They will have you stretching over their shoulders to catch the attention of Kiwi Floss in the main bar and Scottish Liz in the bar downstairs. Not will these huggers budge when it's indicated by word or gesture that they move aside. Thus the ordering of drink, proffering of money, acceptance of beverage, giving of money and talking of change becomes a neck-stretching, juggling, balancing exercise I can well do without in my pursuit of happiness juice. And those nudgers! A plague on 'em! Those who seem oblivious that their legs, arms and bums are irratingly impinging on one's physical consciousness. Alas, they are never young, beautiful, nubile females — in which case the physical proximity would be acceptable, indeed welcome, not to say an event. On the contrary, the offenders are middle-aged, fat and bulky, or lean and spiky males. Some, dammit, blow their horrible cigarette smoke in your direction.

Others, I am sorry to say, are half-drunk. As W.C. Fields said, 'I hate drunks, they give us drinkers a bad name.'

I had to suffer one of these nudgers during a Panama Francis season. True, I could have left the bar, and sat a table, but I would have lost my place and, I confess, I like to lean on the bar and sup up when I'm listening to jazz, and why not? And I had to throw a fellow a few hard looks… Eventually, he departed. And what a sweet relief it is when your nudger has gone…

Now, you hoggers and nudgers, take heed! Slawky has spoken!!

JOHN DANKWORTH
alto-saxophonist, clarinettist, composer, arranger, tutor and leader

John by Mike Hatchard

I first met John Dankworth in 1949 when I was editing *Jazz Illustrated*, published by Bert and Stan Wilcox, who also ran a band agency. One of the bands they represented was the newly formed Johnny Dankworth Seven led by the 22 year-old poll winner Johnny Dankworth.

He wrote an article in *Jazz Illustrated* outlining his aims, and we ran pictures of the band comprising Johnny, Jimmy Deuchar (trumpet), Eddie Harvey (trombone), Don Rendell (tenor saxophone), Tony Kinsey (drums) Bill Le Sage (piano), and Eric Dawson (bass). The band was booked by Les Perrin, who became the firm's press agent (and later, on his own account, his clients included Frank Sinatra and the Rolling Stones) but when *Jazz Illustrated* folded, I, without any previous experience, became the band's booker. I had to stumble my way through the agency jungle and, initially, at least, not too successfully. I got used to Bill Le Sage, the band's manager, walking into the office and looking at me more in sorrow than in anger. Nearly half a century later, I had the genuine pleasure of interviewing John in the basement bar at Ronnie's. This was the first time we had spoken at any length since the Wilcox days, although we had a brief conversation when the BBC filmed the Club Eleven Reunion at Ronnie's in 1984.

In our preliminary chat, John told me that he and his wife Cleo Laine were on their way to the Wigmore Hall to hear pianist Peter Fisher and violinist Alvin Moisey performing John's composition, *Mariposa*. J.G.

JG: John, that's a far cry from the frenetic young be-bopper at the Club Eleven nearly fifty years ago, and the time I was your novice booker at the Wilcox office in Earlham Street, with a whelk stall and a gay bookseller at his barrow outside.

JD: And the cafe next door, a real greasy spoon establishment! The proprietor, an Italian, used to gravely take one's order and yell down the hatch, 'Mario! Two eggs and chips-SOIGNE!', as if these had to be very special egg and chips. Funny how trivia sticks in the mind.

JG: I have another memory of that cafe. You were in the office when you remarked that you had to go there, to meet a young girl singer and you were already two hours late. The girl was Cleo.

JD: I don't remember that.

JG: I bet Cleo does! Do you recall the hostility between the jazz camps ?

JD: Oh, yes. You were either a Traditionalist or a Modernist, and one wasn't allowed to be anything in between.

JG: You were a pioneer British bopper, but you were once a sort of traditionalist, playing with with Freddy Mirfield's Garbage Men, billed as Britain's answer to Spike Jones.

JD: Someone gave me a copy of that 78 recently. Phew! But I was genuinely broad in my tastes. Joe Venuti and Eddie Lang, Louis Armstrong Hot Five and Seven, Clarence Williams and his Washboard Band, Artie Shaw and Benny Goodman, but once I got into be-bop I found myself on one side of the ideological struggle. I made some comment in the musical press and Humphrey Lyttelton wrote that I should be smacked over the wrist with my clarinet.

JG: That was before HL 'discovered' modern jazz. Such was the intensity of feeling, the social as well as the musical life was separate — in clubs, pubs and cafes and although the war is no more, the partisanship still remains. I recall that you tyro boppers were very forthright about the mouldy fygges.

JD: Yes, that attitude did exist.

Remember that be-bop was one of the biggest watersheds in jazz. It suddenly asserted itself with a very big bang. There was little metamorphosis to it.

JG: It was then that a group of you formed the Club Eleven to play that new jazz. Before that there was no one. You were indeed pioneers.

JD: The whole thing started in Archer Street, which, as you remember, was the open-air social club and unofficial employment exchange for professional musicians. We went to Archer Street because not many had telephones in those days. And some of us were working on the Transatlantic boats. We would get to New York, immediately make for 52nd Street and listen to the be-bop giants in the flesh. Not records they made months previously. We would be listening to them on the Thursday, dock into England on the Sunday and be playing the latest Charlie Parker licks on the Monday at the Club Eleven. We were important in the process and wanted to impart the truth to others. We had no thought of commercial possibilities. We were all young and idealistic and the thought never entered our heads, but of course, it caught on and it wasn't too long before we had lovely little Harry Morris collecting half-crowns at the door.

JG: You then formed the Seven and got some flack for prettifying the music, like playing waltzes — *Haunted Ballroom*, for instance — and using vocalists singing pop tunes. In *Jazz Illustrated* you wrote, 'British modern jazz is being represented by two schools, neither of which I condone. The raucous 'bebop' school, with its eye to physical excitement at the expense of musical value and the 'progressives', with their unblushing Impressionistic emulation of the symphonic world.

They may be commended for attempting to bring better music to the Tin-Pan Alley-fed populace, but their only progression seems to be away from the roots of jazz'.

JD: Did I write that!?

JG: Yes, John, and here's the evidence.

JD: It would have been suicidal to have a completely bebop policy. Alright for the critics and our minority fan club, but they didn't have to pay the wages, the coach or our agent to see us through even moderately successful nights at, say, the Casino Ballroom, Warrington, with a guarantee of £25 against 60% of the door take. We had to compromise. As it is, we ran into trouble with dance hall owners and managers. One of them, Gerry Cohen, harangued the audience for jitterbugging and, at one gig, even had us starting the session with a waltz. You can imagine how that went down with the dedicated jazz fans, however few there may have been.

JG: Quite unintentionally, you were responsible for a fight between Les Perrin and myself.

JD: Really ?

JG: You decided to refuse

Back row: Eddie Harvey (trombone), Don Rendell (tenor sax); Middle: Bill le Sage (piano), Johnny Dankworth (alto sax), Jimmy Deuchar (trumpet); Front: Eric Dawson (bass), Tony Kinsey (drums) circa 1950

a BBC 'Jazz Club' broadcast as you didn't want to be typed as purely a jazz band, but nobody told me, and I was taking such a booking on the phone when Perrin, anxious to publicise this startling refusal from someone who was a multiple jazz poll winner, instructed me not to accept it. There was an argument that resulted in a flurry of fists, sheaves of paper billowing into the air and and the telephone cord strung around my neck. Balmy days! I remember those low guarantees on gigs but at the time it was all one could get. Often they only met the coach fare to get on the first leg of a tour. I also remember that you recorded on clarinet with Joe Daniels, he of Hot Shots fame.

JD: Did I ? I can't recall that.

JG: I ribbed you, the fervent be-bopper doing a Dixie, and you tartly replied, 'It's work,' with a meaningful look at the booker who hadn't filled your date sheet. You probably got about three pounds for that Daniels session. In 1951 you left Wilcox to be represented by big agent

Harold Davison and the band took off, to the point when you were doing some 250 gigs a year, but in 1953 you broke up the Seven to form your big band.

JD: Davison persuaded me that this was the right step and, true, the Seven had run its course. There was no bad feeling, but we had been elbow to elbow for three years, and realised it was time to move to other things. With the big band there were twenty one of us on the road, and with it all the hassles. I became a sort of father confessor to guys older than myself with domestic and marital problems although I was single myself.

JG: If the economic and artistic situation were to suddenly revert to the forties and fifties, would you fancy piling into the coach to do a few more thousand miles leading a big band?

JD: I still get a thrill out of working with a big band, like, say, NYJO, or the Generation Band with my son Alec. But these occasional exercises are not like having a regular band,

Dame Cleo Laine and Sir John Dankworth
Illustration by Mike Hatchard

with the spontaneity we got playing night after night. It was truly a communal thing, and a newcomer could put in something that would make an old arrangement sparkle. Often, too, our best performances were when we were all dog-tired, after a long road journey or a flight from Germany or somewhere. But, in answer to your question — no, I don't think I'd fancy Belper, Warrington, Ashton-under-Lyne or Darlington again.

JG: You brought in Peter King, a highly acclaimed alto-saxophonist. This raised a few eye-brows.

JD: Yes, I was beginning to realise that I am really a writing person, even though I was one of the first saxophone players in the country to play bebop, which requires technique and know-how. I had no illusion of grandeur about my playing and I couldn't think of anyone better than Peter King to come in with us.

JG: John, you often made the headlines, but there was one occasion when you wish you hadn't, and that was when you shouted 'What about playing some jazz?' at a Lionel Hampton concert at the Royal Festival Hall in October 1956.

JD: I was afraid you were going to mention that, but at least I stood up to be counted, in what many people thought to be a most

unsatisfactory performance, especially as it was specifically advertised as a jazz concert, as opposed to Hampton's rock-and-roll show at the Empress Hall the previous Sunday. Although I came in for a lot of criticism I feel on reflection that I, a paying customer, was entitled to object.

JG: Going back to your big band, is there a particular record of yours which you remember with especial pleasure?

JD: I can remember Bugle Call Rag, with great solos by Keith Christie on trombone and Eddie Blair on trumpet.

JG: How many recordings of yours have you got?

JD: Only those which have come out on compilations. Musicians tend not to be collectors. Records, generally, seem to collect me rather than I collect them. People give you them to research some particular project. For instance, when Cleo did an album of Duke Ellington tunes for RCA, I said to the producer in New York 'You must have a great many Ellington records that I should be listening to and he said, "Have I?" I had to remind him that the Duke made some of his greatest recordings for RCA Victor and in due course I was presented with some fifteen CDs'.

JG: Typical that he wasn't aware of the masterpieces in his archives! Can I return to my

question about you going on the road. Would you find the musicians you want?

JD: No trouble at all! There's such a plethora of young players who have all got so much to say and once they get the diarrhoea tendencies out of their system — that is, playing five hundred notes to the bar — they have extremely interesting new ideas.

JG: Would you, a senior citizen, feel any incompatibility?

JD: Not really. I think they would listen, as they do in the Generation Band. The standard is infinitely higher than in my day. Most of them have had a thorough training, which is far more effective than being on the road with a dance band. Then there are the jazz courses, which never existed in my day. I used to smuggle my saxophone case into the Royal Academy of Music and told them it was a bassoon. Had they suspected it was a saxophone the word would have got around and some professor would have been outraged at the very presence of such.

The above interview first appeared in *JARS* in March-April 1996. In early 2006 John was knighted and by way of a tribute for this honour we re-ran this interview in *JARS 159*, March-April 2006, with the following heading, alleging the Queen's comment: 'Arise, Sir Johnny and keep swinging. Just love your bebop!'

WHISPERS, MURMURS & ASIDES

FISH-EATING VEGETARIANS

It's always nice to see people one knows being mentioned in the lay press and I read Cleo Laine talking about her health and dietary habits in the *Evening Standard*, but I blinked a bit when I read that she and husband John Dankworth were fish-eating vegetarians. Eh? A few days later, in the letters column, an equally puzzled reader wrote, 'If they are fish-eating vegetarians, then I'm a wine-drinking teetotaller'.

'CAN YOU REPEAT THE QUESTION?'
DIGBY FAIRWEATHER considers the art of the interviewer

'It's a question', said Nick Freeth, my one-time producer at Jazz (sorry, 'Smooth') FM, looking at me keenly, 'of who'll play the interview game.' Nick was talking about our programming plan for my show, the 'Sunday Joint', for a weekly one-hour live interview with stars of the British (and sometimes American) jazz scene. And over the next eight years — first for Jazz FM, later for Radios 2 and 3 — I was to find out that my producer was right on the button.

It's funny how jazz musicians are frequently sharply divided between those who enjoy verbalising about their craft and those who just play but don't much care to talk about it. There's absolutely no guarantee that figures of excellence on the jazz scene see their music-making as a subject for deep intellectual post- or pre-mortems. Players as (ostensibly) diverse as Nat Gonella and Stan Tracey (both of whom I was privileged to interview down the years) definitely don't see the need to talk up a storm about their craft as well as to play one. Whereas others — from Michael Brecker to Richard Sudhalter — were, and still are, an interviewer's dream; able (given a — hopefully — intelligent question) to talk fluently, passionately and of course rivetingly through every available minute of airtime.

A FEATHER IN A WIND TUNNEL

One of the most intellectual and vocal of my interviewees was Artie Shaw. He'd come to London to conduct Bob Wilber through performances of both Mozart's and Artie's own clarinet concerto back in the l990s and I was fascinated to meet him, remembering the delights of The Trouble with Cinderella (with its marvellous account of an after-midnight rehearsal in chapter 39!) and respecting the intellectual decisions of his later career. When he arrived in the studio — looking remarkably like the latter-day Sean Connery — he greeted me jovially. 'Hey, Digby! I see we've really got some fair weather today! And I hear you play trumpet! Got a top G?' It seemed we were off to a good start, and on the whole

we were. Artie Shaw was as mentally bright as he had been fifty years before; in the midst of a day of intensive press interviews he was plainly in his element, and answered my questions willingly and at length. Indeed, one other reporter from a shiny colour supplement was to observe, later that week, that interviewing Shaw was 'like being a feather in a wind tunnel', and I was to benefit from that situation. If there was a problem at all, it was that, once or twice, I tended to pitch my own questions at the wrong kind of 'arty' level. 'Did being Jewish add a level of passion to your creativity?' I asked. 'Bach didn't need it!' responded the Master briskly before heading off at high speed to be interviewed on a live BBC show whose then-presenter I won't name here to spare his blushes. 'Did you ever play with Benny Goodman?' was his opening question and I'm glad I wasn't around to hear the answer.

EXPECTATIONS

It would probably have been better to let Artie know how much I loved his records, but if I did have a policy in those days it was to try, at all times, not to ask the questions that my subjects had (presumably) been asked endless times previously. Try, for a non-jazz example, to find an interview with the late Sir John Mills that doesn't instantly home in on Great Expectations — the film in which he was simply a (delightful) coathanger for the eccentric and irresistible cast of characters surrounding him. Many musicians have formulated stock answers to staunch the aggravation of parallel situations — in much the same way that, sometimes, they build frames for their solos.

I once asked Humphrey Lyttelton — Britain's greatest jazz polymath — if he would have been happy just being a trumpeter. He thought for a minute, replied 'no' and then paid me what for an interviewer is sometimes the ultimate compliment. 'You know,' said Humph, 'I don't think I've ever been asked that before!'

RONNIE'S JOKES

Over the years we've had some very attractive waitresses working at the Club. We had one girl who looked like Barbarella. Sir John Barbarella. Then we had a girl called Bonnie who came from Australia — which is a wonderful place. To come from. Bonnie was very modest. I remember she was so modest she used to eat bananas sideways.
Some of the girls are pretty but not very bright. I remeber speaking to one waitress once about books and I asked her if she liked Dickens. She said she didn't know, she'd never been to one. She also thought that Moby Dick was a venereal disease.
Then we had a very nice little girl who came all the way from India. She flew here by Air Bombay and she told me something about the airline which I never knew before. It seems that they only serve meals to the first class passengers. But they let the tourist class passengers come up and beg.
Of course we get all classes of people in the Club — some of them very high class indeed. Which is why Jeff Ellison, who was on the door at the Frith Street Club for twelve years, used to say that he was a doorman to royalty.

UNWIN ON THE SAX

Professor' Stanley Unwin, who died on 12 January 2002, aged ninety, was a master of verbal imagery – turning words inside out and imparting to them a quirky surrealistic edge which somehow heightened their original meaning. When Ronnie Scott's Club reached its thirtieth birthday, Stanley sent Ronnie a cassette in which he drew, in his inimitable way, the history of the saxophone. Ronnie was vastly amused and responded with a letter of thanks but the cassette was mislaid until now. It has been transcribed by Mike Pointon, a close friend of Stanley's, and we have great pleasure in publishing it for the Club's forty-fifth birthday.

I met Stanley but once and it was a delight to have a little 'tilty-elbow' (as he put it) with him.   J.G.

Unwin by Trog

This is a saxophorial historical to celebrate the thirty years of Ronnie Scott's speshlode in Frith Street or Sohothrall with gathery peoplode who have that joy to listen for these wonderful instrumolds that he has so manifepst. Ronnie Scott. Oh, yes!

Of course, it also celebrates the thorkus of the inventor of that instrument: Adolph Sax. Now he was born in 1814 and he deserves a speshlode mention consideration in that the merits of his father which refleps Adolph's own genius in the invention and development of the saxophone also refleps from the maternal side about which we know so little. It's well known that sons, more often than not so, inherit the characteristics of their mothers down through consanguinity through father, sorrell and son and revealed by genes and light brown hormones…

Now, having said all this, it is true that Adolph's father, Charles Joseph Sax, was born in 1791 — by the way that's the time that Mozart falolloped and died and flat on the bokus and a young Beethoven was playing the organ for the elector and emulating Vogeler's work at that time — Beethoven being so young-not so deaf and stuffin' of wax in his earoles at that time — he was working on the Rizzaballet for Count Waldstein.

HORMONES AND CLARINEPPERS

Adolph Sax invented the sax horn, or rather a whole range of sax horns in 1842. The versatile quality that he sought from the earlier hormones and the bass clarineppers made by his father required him to experiment but the time and finance for the dignit in the pockey was very difficult to come by. His popularity was enhanced by the thought of Berlioz, Halevy and others and he soon developed this instrument of joy: the saxophone.

Illustration: Monty Sunhine

SAXOPHOBIA

Of course, he registered it in 1846 and the inventive power producing such an unusual tone and quality aroused much jealously and ill-feeling in some of his contemporaries. But being a wise and deep thorkus in his mileode for attackfold he found help from powerful friends like journalists who trumpey-up his places in the newspaper and especially General de Roumigny who was the aide-de-camp to Louis-Philippe so that the French army bands has all saxophobia included. They jettisoned their obones, French hormones, bassooles — all gone! Oh, dear, never since Sousa and clarineppers Jimmy Noone and Bechet in the afterludy — oh, dear!

Now, the question is this — how did he manage to obtain such a remarkable tonal quality from his invention? I believe it was inspired by his love of the human singy voice in the larynx of the human beal starting perhaps with the soprano to emulate his own mother through the whole range down to the bassy-profundo or bass sax. He took the reed of the clarineppers but used a conical brass tube with above twenty lateral orifips, all covered by keys, three-fingered place for three fingold other hand huffalo-dowd — now there's an ambidextrold trickly-how! And of course there were two small holes or pippysqueakers which provided the scaley-shifters huffalo for that.

JAZZMOLDE

The range is generally considered from B to F upper toc-toc-toc — that's the high range-berr-tocker very high huffalo-dowd, therefore the super-soprano emulating the Jenny-Linders or the female voice who reachy-huf in the heavenly bode with the lark in the early maudie. But, of course, all the members of the family are frequently made with an extension of the bell for B-flabbers. After all, this is the most popular key for the jazzmolde, for people who twisty-ho, dance huffalo-dowder, break dance, jumpit'n'through — all those want that B-flabber.

So, what have we got? The oristot fingold-pluggery. This gives us the joy of the saxophobia as we have it today — Johnny Coltrane, Ron Scottie, Stanny Getzit. I think he does! Let's have it! Let's have it! Oh, joy!

Prof. Unwin had two occupations:
Engineering the Beeb's radio stations,
Then comic supreme,
With his whimsical stream-
Of-consciousness verbalisations.
RON RUBIN

ZOOT SIMS

In his book, *Some of my Best Friends are Blues*, Ronnie Scott says: 'If I had to name one musician whose playing perfectly exemplified the soaring spirit of free-wheeling, free-swinging, therapeutic jazz it would be John Haley 'Zoot' Sims. Ever since I heard him on record as one of the famous 'Four Brothers' saxophone section of the Woody Herman Band of 1947-1949, I had been a fan of his and it was a thrill to see him actually take the stand in my own Club.'

There is a story about Zoot Sims, who died on March 23rd 1985, aged 59, that truly reflects his approach to jazz. He was on a gig somewhere outside New York and the pianist was Roger Kellaway. Zoot, a most genial man, was however, quite firm in his instructions to the younger Kellaway.

'No extensions, Roger', he said.

'Extensions' here meant inversions or substitutions in the straight chord sequence. These would not have suited the totally uncluttered style of John Haley Sims, born Inglewood, California on October 29th 1925, who commenced swinging in the mid-forties and continued to do so right up to his death. In fact when he realised that there was nothing the doctors could do for him he remarked, ';I'm going to go on blowing until I die.'

The bad news that he had cancer became known last summer and then came the glad tidings that he was out and about, but there had been no remedial treatment.

RESPECTED

The sort of respect Zoot commanded was exemplified at a party held in New York, to celebrate his fiftieth birthday. A brass plaque presented to him bore the following very apt, inscription: TO JOHN HALEY SIMS, THE JAZZ MUSICIAN'S JAZZ MUSICIAN, a dedication that should be engraved upon his headstone. Fortunately, there are countless records that bear testimony to this tribute and, of course, there are the memories of those who had the privilege of hearing him in the flesh, such as his appearances at the Club.

I saw him at the revived, and the last, Beaulieu Festival in July 1977, blowing furiously in the company of Joe Newman, Joe Venuti, Teddy Wilson, Bob Wilbur, Bobby Rosengarden, and Major Holley in the jam session finale. Old Joe Venuti stood at the end of the line and, playing superbly, dominated the session. The crowd was with him, partly because of his performance, partly on account of his age, then estimated seventy-eight, but the player that really challenged Joe was Zoot.

VIC'S REMEDY

Amazingly, for immediately previous to this he had been slumped in the chair in the musician's tent, his tenor slung from his neck. He had taken one or two drinks over the top. Someone, I forget who, said, 'Hey, let's wake Zoot, he's on soon' and various attempts were made to stir the slumbering saxophonist, but to no avail. Trombonist Vic Dickenson chuckled and said, 'I know what to do', got up (rather unsteadily, for Vic, too, liked a drink) and grabbed Zoot by an ankle. Vic must have known just what pressure to apply, and where, to restore Zoot to consciousness. Zoot awoke with a start and still seated, immediately started blowing! He looked a little shame-faced at the laughter this aroused and immediately returned to the arms of Morpheus. Listening to him in that jam session you wouldn't have believed it possible, but he was one of the few exceptions to the rule that drink adversely affects performance.

It is a significant part of the Club's history that he was the first American musician to play a season (four weeks) in November, 1961, at 39 Gerrard Street, the beginning of a pageantry of US jazz giants that have appeared at Ronnie's ever since.

RONNIE AND ZOOT

Ronnie was particularly fond of Zoot, both as a musician and a human being, declaring that he had never heard a word against him and was very distressed to hear of his passing. He heard the sad news on the day of Zoot's death and knew immediately that he had to g fly to New York to attend the memorial service. It was a Saturday, the banks were closed, but he and Pete King managed to rustle up sufficient to pay the fare and just about sustain subsistence level during his four days in that expensive city.

Ronnie reports that it was a massively attended service held at St. Peter's Lutheran Church, Manhattan, and conducted by the Reverend John Gensel, the 'Jazz Pastor', and among the mourners Ronnie saw Joe Newman, Milt Hinton, Major Holley, Dick Hyman, Roger Kellaway, Joe Temperley, Tommy Flanagan, George Shearing, Dave McKenna, Ruby Braff, Scott Hamilton, James Moody, Mel Lewis, Benny Goodman, Annie Ros and Woody Herman.

He estimated that there were seven to eight hundred people present to pay homage. Rightfully, it wasn't a mournful gathering. Rather the opposite; the vibes were good and warm, and although it's a cliché to add that this is how Zoot would have wished it, still it has to be said. He would not have wished for tears.

He gagged right up to the end. One morning in hospital the doctor came into the ward and Zoot quipped, 'Hey, doc, you are looking a bit better today!'

Returning to the matter of his style, Ronnie tells a story that reflects his personality and lack of pretension. He and Zoot were in the Club office watching the moon-landing on TV and Zoot remarked, 'Jesus! They're walking on the moon and I am still playing *Indiana*.' Yes, *Indiana* is an old warhorse, but as with any hackneyed theme played by Zoot Sims it was transformed into a thing of joy. J.G.

Zoot at Ronnie Scott's, Gerrard Street (Jackie Dougan on drums)

UP THERE WITH THE CHAPS
An extra-terrestrial report of the great jam session in the sky by the late Slawkenbergius

Illustration: Hedley Picton

Well, I don't like to say I told you so — but I was right in claiming that I was destined for heaven. One October morning I had a sudden, excruciating pain in my chest and heavy metal bands pounded in my head. I thought, this is *hell,* but, within seconds, I was standing at the pearly gates being greeted by a benign old gentleman with a flowing beard and dressed in a white mantle.

'Ah, Slawkenbergius, we have been expecting you,' he said.

'Are you?'

'Heavens, no, he's very tied up. No, my name is Peter. St. Peter. You may have heard of me. I'm always on the gate duty — although, sad to say, an ungodly number go to the opposition. But *we* have a marvellous quota of jazzmen.' He snapped his fingers, gyrated his hips, wriggled his shoulders and tapped his feet. 'Yes, it's really cooking up here now. So much happening.'

I couldn't help but register my amazement at this renowned figure acting like he was Cab Calloway, and, spotting my reaction, he quickly reverted to his normal dignified mien, but putting his arm round my shoulder, opened up to a fellow spirit.

'I've been a fan since Joe Oliver's Creole Jazz Band. I must introduce you to King later. No! King *Oliver*, not the Almighty. He's not really into jazz. More your classical man. Understandably, when you consider the Haydns, Mozarts and Bachs writing those oratorios and the like in homage to his glory whilst the jazzers were extolling the virtues of hooch, coke, hop, and weed, and those female blue singers shamefully going on about big black snakes, and their babies rocking them in their big brass beds until their faces turned cherry red — I mean to say — is it any wonder that the Deity isn't too enamoured of jazzmen? I had to twist his arm to get some of them in here, I can tell you.'

'When will I meet him?'

'Not for some time. He's doing his best to avert the holocaust right now. He's working on a new project, realising that some of His grand design, particularly with regard to the behaviour of human kind hasn't worked out. Now, that would put a hell (whoops, sorry!) of a strain on me. As it is I work all the hours God gave me. But I mustn't bore you with my occupational problems –I'm sure you would like to meet some of the chaps.' He beckoned at me to follow him into a marbled hall and I gaped in excitement, joy and astonishment at whom I saw assembled there.

There was the New Orleans contingent headed by Louis,

The Duke by Pennington

of course, with Kid Ory, Red Allen, Ed Hall, Johnny Dodds, Albert Nicholas, Jimmie Noone, Sidney Bechet and Alphonse Picou. Near them were the whiteys: Bix, Bunny, Muggsy, Big T, Pee Wee, Miff, Adrian, Gene and Eddie. Opposite them — joy of joys — a full Ducal line-up — Bubber Miley, Rex Stewart, Artie Whetsol, Posey Jenkins, Tricky Sam Nanton, Juan Tizol in the brass, Johnny Hodges, Harry Carney, Paul Gonsalves, Ben Webster and Barney Bigard in the reeds and Jimmy Blanton, Sonny Greer, Fred Guy and the Duke himself in the rhythm. And there was Bird, Prez, Hawk, Don Byas, Bud Powell and Art Pepper, Paul Desmond, Al Haig, Django and so many more I've not space to mention.

It was all too much for me...

'Christ Almghty!' I exclaimed.

'Slawkenbergius!'my host snapped, 'You must not take *his* name in vain!'

'So sorry, St. Peter, but I just didn't expect to see some of those cats up here.'

'Oh, you mean their life-style *down there* — the drinking, smoking naughty-type African Woodbines, popping, inhaling, mainlining and — ahem — womanising. That was the work of Satan — the ratbag — but the music they played came from us, rather like God making the country and the Devil making the city. And don't be so sniffy, either. You only just made it here. Your earthly behaviour was less then exemplary. And we can do without your usual scurrility. No more upsetting lady journalists with gross chauvinism, no more those snide sideswipes at your old mates like George Melly in your column.' I ignored these last thrusts and, tit for tat, pointed to the sex segregation. 'Was this right in heaven?' I enquired.

'You can't expect the habits of a lifetime to be eradicated that quickly. In any case it works better stylistically. You should know that.'

A voice called out from one of the groups. Good God! It was dear old Bill Coleman, a great trumpeter and one of the nicest chaps I ever met on earth.

'Nice to see you Slawky — I always knew you would make it up here!'At which greeting I shot St. P a meaningful glance, but forgetting where I was, said, 'Lovely to see you Bill, let's have a taste'. Again, St. Peter took umbrage.

'Slawkenbergius! We don't drink up here.'

'You mean – Ben and Bix and Pee-Wee are totally on the wagon?'

'Utterly. We have no lushes. No money to buy the evil stuff. We ban the root of all evil.'

Ben Webster by Nemethy

Johnny Hodges by Pennington

'Doesn't Ben complain?'

'Bitterly, but he'll get over that in a millennium or so.'

'And Bird or Bud without a score?'

'Certainly, though both were naughty in seeking a connection on arrival, but we have no cokey Joes, reefer men, hopheads or vipers to supply them.'

'What about Duke and the chicks?'

'No, none of *that*, either. Oh, yes, he made his usual pass at a dishy lady angel, but was sent packing with his tail between his legs — so to speak. Like Ben — he'll have plenty of time to forget the weaknesses of the flesh.'

Well, well, I thought, things have changed. It suddenly occurred to me — 'Where are the Brits?'

There they all were — Tubby, Phil, Derek Humble, Joe Harriott, Keith Christie, Alex Welsh, Archie Semple, Sandy Brown and many more old faces, some of whom could barely have passed muster for admission.

Of course, one or two of them, no doubt remembering my odd criticism of them on earth, gave me a bit of the old lip. Remarks like, 'What are *you* doing up here?' were made. I gave them some of the old comeback — I'm not turning the other cheek with old drinking mates. No matter where, not me!

'I almost hesitate to ask in the circumstances, St. Peter, but where are the girls?'

'You must mean Billie, Bessie, Mary Lou, Sarah, Ella, Betty and Lil Armstrong, . Yes, they are here. You will be hearing them in due course. Now I must leave you to it. I'm wanted at the gates'.

Truly, it was all too much and I thought, a little drop of something would be just right when I remembered St P's stern words about the devil drink. Ashamed as I am to admit it I found myself mumbling about the place not being what it's cracked up to be, at which point I woke up. My ascent to Nirvana was only a dream, the result of too much ripe Stilton and a bottle of Côtes du Roussillion, and I am sure it will be an enormous relief to my legion of readers that I am alive, and well, as can be expected, and that you can read my usual homilies later in this edition.

Illustration: Hedley Picton

WHISPERS, MURMURS & ASIDES

FUNKY WAILING

Heaven forbid I should indicate that I am the overtly literary type – the sort of chap who walks around with a book under his arm. Nor would I wish to be associated with those writers, on jazz particularly, who preface, or interlard, their lines with quotations from Proust, Pope, Voltaire and Flaubert, but, yes, I am a bit of a bookworm.

Nothing too taxing for the grey matter, but eschewing the effluence of, for instance, that litigantly successful fakir Jeffrey Archer. I get through a lot of jazz literature, of course, reference books particularly. One I'm constantly dipping into is *Jazz: The Essential Companion* by Ian Carr, Digby Fairweather and Brian Priestley, and there I came across Ian's definition of 'funky'.

Some older readers will recall that 'funky' was much used by jazz critics in the fifties and sixties: that compère Tony Hall at the old Studio 51 and Flamingo Clubs was always on about the chaps' 'funky wailing'. Here is Ian's definition:

'This may derive from the obsolete English word funk — smoke, steam, stench. In jazz and rock the term 'funky' signifies music which is extremely physical and 'dirty' — the rhythms are strong, clear and hypnotic, and the phrasing of the melodic and chordal instruments is bluesy and very vocalised.

The whole musical idea of funk derives from the blues, etc …' This rang a bell — that I have seen a definition of funk in a reprint of a late 18th century lexicon — 'The Scoundrel's Dictionary, an Explanation of the Cant Words Used By Thieves, House-breakers, Pickpockets and Whores' called *The Dictionary Of The Vulgar Tongue* by a Captain Grose.

This read, 'to smoke: figuratively to smoke. Hence the reference to a session that is 'smoking'.

How odd that language of London's low-life two centuries ago should enter jazz terminology, three thousand miles distant and only fairly recently. Not one of the 16,000 songs listed in Brian Rust's *Jazz Records 1887 – 1942* has 'funk' in the title.

PAUL PRY

BENNY GOODMAN IN LONDON, 1949

In 1936, a spectacular clarinettist, with a somewhat unprepossessing personality, called Benny Goodman, born in a Chicago slum in July, 1909, became the 'King of Swing'. He led a band that in terms of creativity, as opposed to technical ability, was far inferior to the contemporary black bands, Duke Ellington, Count Basie, Claude Hopkins, Don Redman, Earl Hines, Mills Blue Rhythm, Teddy Hill, Edgar Hayes and Fletcher Henderson, but almost overnight Goodman became an internationally famed band leader.

He was undoubtedly a brilliant musician; a superb technician and massively inventive; at times, his playing was truly impassioned.

Buffs will dispute the claim that he was the world's greatest clarinettist, arguing that his black contemporaries — Johnny Dodds, Jimmy Noone, Sidney Bechet, Ed Hall, Albert Nicholas and, the ultra-traditionalists will avow, George Lewis, were infinitely superior. But among the white performers on the instrument, it was generally accepted that only Pee Wee Russell challenged his supremacy, but Pee Wee never made the big time financially.

PUTTING JAZZ ON THE MAP

Certainly, Benny Goodman put jazz in the public eye. More than Duke and the rest of the superior black bands and no one could take away from him his reputation as a supreme master of the clarinet.

Given this emergence as a major figure in the mid thirties, and remaining the King into the forties, he like the rest of his contemporaries, black and white, were denied appearance in the United Kingdom. The reason was a ban imposed by the Ministry of Labour on foreign musicians appearing here, ostensibly depriving British musicians of work. This embargo was at the insistence of the British Musicians' Union, chagrined by the American Federation of Musicians' refusal to allow British musicians to play in America.

On the surface, this might seem a reasonable tit for tat attitude, but the crucial fact was that we did not have any musicians to interest the American public. We had no Benny Goodman, no Louis Armstrong, no Duke Ellington, no Jack Teagarden, no Count Basie…

The Americans in the field of jazz had definitely more to offer, but stubborn insistence on spurious reciprocity prevented the British jazz enthusiast from hearing their idols in the flesh.

The ban on Americans was imposed in 1934, following the sensationally successful visit of Duke Ellington, but a few musicians breached this cultural Iron Curtain under the guise of 'variety' acts, to appear only in theatres, the Variety Artists Federation not having the same rigid objections to foreign artists as their brothers in the Musicians' Union.

BENNY GOODMAN REVUE

Thus, in July 1949, fifty years ago, Goodman played in Britain under the billing of 'Benny Goodman Revue' at the London Palladium. The bill comprised the Goodman Sextet – Benny, Buddy Greco (piano), Charlie Short (bass), Pete Chilver (guitar), Tommy Pollard (vibraphone) and Flash Winston (drums), comedian Herkie Styles ('The Jester'), Marcy Lutes ('Song Stylist'), Jean 'Toots' Thielemans ('Virtuoso of the harmonica') and the Skyrockets Orchestra, directed by Woolf Phillips, the band including alto-saxophonist Johnny Dankworth, and guest trumpeter Kenny Baker. The first part of the bill was the usual mix of variety acts, including the eccentric 'sand dancers' Wilson, Keppel & Betty, entitling their performance, *Cleopatra's Nightmare* and 'blue' Max Miller.

UNION INTERFERENCE

The Musicians' Union, peeved that a permit had been granted, goose-stepped in by forbidding two of the musicians (three, including trumpeter Leon Calvert booked to play with Skyrockets) to appear, as they were in arrears with their dues. Had they not complied, the Union would have 'blacked' the entire proceedings. Thus Laurie Morgan (drums) and Dave Goldberg (guitar), booked as part of the Goodman Sextet, did not appear. The farrago occasioned a banner headline in the *Melody Maker*, which had long been campaigning for selective entry on grounds of pure talent, the like of which we did not possess over here.

Editor Ray Sonin reviewed the show, somewhat unfavourably, rightly pointing to the sparse appearance of Benny Goodman, but using superlatives about his playing. Sonin also mentioned another maniacal aspect of this situation. Thielemans had been denied permission

BG by Richard Cole

This is part of the programme on sale at the Palladium during Benny Goodman's week. Keen-eyed readers will note that a member of the reed section was a twenty-two year old Johnny Dankworth whose clarinet Goodman 'borrowed' unbeknownst to its owner. Dankworth, listening to Goodman playing the instrument, thought to himself, 'Yes, it's my clarinet but I wish I could play like that'.

to appear as a guitarist, but not as a harmonica player! Balmy days!

Somehow, they were allowed to appear on the BBC's Hi Gang show, featuring Ben Lyon, Bebe Daniels and Vic Oliver, but were forbidden to appear in a setting far more appropriate – the BBC's Jazz Club, a half hour slot, the Beeb's niggardly allocation to jazz in those days. Plus ça change!

It was indeed farcical that a musician of Benny Goodman's calibre should make his British debut as a variety 'turn' and that the then Musicians' Union should deprive, for patently spiteful reasons, British players of the honour and experience of playing with one of the greatest figures in jazz.

The *Melody Maker* also reported that, 'On Monday there was a veritable meeting of the musical clans, for representatives of the profession turned out in force to greet Benny — including Maurice Burman, Sid Phillips, Stanley Black, Harry Letham, Harry Gold (and several of his band), Jack Nathan, Norman Stenfalt, Ray Noble, Cab Kaye and Ronnie Scott.'

FLASH WINSTON'S RECOLLECTIONS

A few years back, Cecil 'Flash' Winston submitted a piece to *JARS* recalling his appearance with Goodman at the Palladium, but we suggested to Flash that he wait until the 50th anniversary of the event. Alas, Flash died in April, 1998, aged seventy-four, and will not see his retrospective of a memorable, if at times unnerving, experience.

Flash recalls that Benny Goodman visited the Club Eleven and, these years later, it's still something of

Wilson, Keppel and Betty preceding the King of Swing in a 'variety' show

a mystery that Goodman made the visit. Perhaps he didn't know it was a club dedicated to music which, initially at least, he didn't like. There were many British musicians more stylistically in accord with Goodman than beboppers — pianists Gerry Moore and Eddie Macauley, vibraphonist Roy Marsh, drummers George Fierstone and Jock Jacobson, guitarists George Elliot and Lauderic Caton (the latter a pioneer electric guitarist in Britain and fervent disciple of Charlie Christian, one of Goodman's alumni), bassists Len Harrison and Jack Collier, but the honour of accompanying the great man went to the young modernists.

THE KING & I
by CECIL 'FLASH' WINSTON

It had got around that there was a lot happening at the Club Eleven, and we had various notabilities in the business dropping in to see what it was all about. One, to our surprise, was Benny Goodman, due to play a two week engagement at the London Palladium. He came along with pianist Buddy Greco, being allowed to bring only one musician.

To help him recreate the famous Benny Goodman Sextet, he booked Laurie Morgan (drums) and Tommy Pollard (vibraphone), both Club Eleven alumni, the Sextet completed by bassist Charlie Short and guitarist Pete Chilver, but both were in arrears with their union dues. Short, who was playing with me at the Stork Club recommended me as Laurie's replacement. On the opening night the Sextet began playing behind the curtains, which slowly arose to thunderous applause.

Warming to these hands across the footlights, Goodman started with a very fast *China Boy*, following this with an even faster *The World Is Waiting For The Sunrise*.

It was during the second number that I became the hapless recipient of the feared Goodman glare — 'The

Ray', the eyes turn to ice behind rimless spectacles and the object of this laser beam is invariably reduced to a heap of blubbering humanity, freezing the hands into immobility. Unfortunately, I had missed a beat in Goodman's encore and only after deep sedation and the smell of incense I was able to make the second show.

TEMPERAMENTAL MARCY

Benny's armoury in his autocratic ways was not limited to 'The Ray'. Singer Marcy Lutes (with Benny's Big Band in the States) was on the show and made a habit of phrasing behind the beat. Goodman, a martinet for the right value of crochet, would sidle alongside her and play every note exactly how it was written.

One night the temperamental Marcy stormed off the stage mouthing obscenities in a broad Brooklyn accent. Waiting in the wings, I managed to catch, just before she slammed her dressing room door, the memorable phrase, 'King or no fucking King. He ain't gonna fucking bug me!'

During the Palladium engagement, the King of Swing rarely engaged in pleasantries with lesser mortals. As one tiptoed past his dressing room, the sound of his clarinet playing the Mozart *Clarinet Quintet* in A could be heard. That practice makes perfect was demonstrated in every one of the shows. ▶▶

The one time BG did mingle with us was outside the precincts of the Palladium. We made a guest appearance on the BBC's 'Hi Gang' radio show, and after the run-through, Benny sat with us in the auditorium. Dispensing with protocol, he lethargically intoned, 'They seem to like our Sextet, eh, fellows?' This all-inclusive 'our' was a wonderful moment.

The two weeks I spent playing with Benny Goodman had its perks. Pictures of me were displayed at Drum City at very little expense to myself. Locks of my hair were kept by my barber, and a carton of chewing gum was sent from a famous kiosk whose manager implored my endorsement. Of course there were one or two poison pen letters, that I had deliberately forgotten to post Laurie Morgan's dues to the Union. That the only thing I could drum on were people's nerves.

Nevertheless, the resulting publicity I received silenced the libels, leaving me with the memory of an experience that any drummer would have given his paradiddles to have lived through.

The Sextet's appearance on 'Hi Gang' exists on Jazz in Britain 1919-50 *on Properbox 88 compiled by Jim Godbolt. Wastefully, one of the numbers has Benny singing, but he performed brilliantly on* The World Is Waiting For The Sunrise. *Unfortunately the rhythm section was under-recorded, and especially unfortunate as this was the only example of Flash on record, apart from him announcing at a Club Eleven concert in King's George's Hall, Adeline Place, recorded by Carlo Krahmer for his Esquire label in 1949, also on Properbox 88.* J.G.

WHISPERS, MURMURS & ASIDES

BG AND THE BEGGARS

I am reminded of two tales of Benny's character. BG was notorious for his meanness. He attended Ronnie Scott's Club one evening, ordered a sandwich and left without paying. Another story was of him having a small group rehearsal at his apartment in New York with singer Peggy Lee. It was a winter's day and Miss Lee remarked, 'Benny, it sure is cold in here.' Benny replied, 'Yeah, you're right,' and left the room, presumably to turn on the central heating. He returned wearing a heavy sweater, the central heating switch undisturbed.

Ronnie loved to tell the story of an untypical Benny giving money to a Moscow beggar, during his 1962 tour of Russia. Victor Feldman, who took his cine-camera with him, was in the line-up and photographed this singular action. When he later showed the film to the band, Benny not being present, Victor reversed the film to make it appear that Mr. G was the recipient, much to everyone's amusement. Apparently, each had a beef with their martinet leader, as indeed the history of BG and his sidemen is littered.   PAUL PRY

Al Hirschfeld's famous cartoon of Teddy Wilson, Benny Goodman and Gene Krupa, from *Benny – King of Swing*, published by Thames & Hudson.

RONNIE'S JOKES

As the years went by the quality of the food we served at the Club improved tremendously. And today we never get complaints about the food. We get a few people throwing up, but no complaints.

You've probably gathered by now from these little interludes between sets that I'm not a professional comedian; but we do have a fantastic professional comedian at the Club. We call him the chef. He's rather an unusual guy-he's half black and half Japanese and every 7 December attacks Pearl Bailey.

He got married three weeks ago, and already he can hear the patter of tiny feet around the house. His mother-in-law's a dwarf. And she's very ugly. It seems her husband took her on a very expensive holiday round the world rather than kiss her goodbye.

Which reminds me of that dramatic day in March 1965 when we kissed goodbye to our veteran piano. Nobody reported seeing Stan Tracey wipe away a fugitive tear...

GIGS FROM HELL
Cornish Capers
by CAMPBELL BURNAP

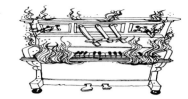

Although the English get misty-eyed about Cornwall, the Cornish people don't return the sentiment. After all, they are Celts in exile and still aspire to independence from Westminster. The English find all this very romantic – while aspiring themselves to owning a holiday cottage down there in the south-west. Thatched roof, ideally. And, of course, there are the remote smugglers' coves to bang on about, as well as the abandoned tin mines, pony trekking, pasty-eating, and floral-dancing on every corner.

Globe-trotting trumpeter Keith Smith — a Londoner – put some temporary roots down in Cornwall in the late 1970s. Unfamiliar with half measures, Smith acquired not one dream dwelling with picturesque thatching, but three, which he converted into a single, much envied home. Within no time he was applying his entrepreneurial confidence along the south Cornish coast, and a healthy little jazz scene began to emerge.

In 1979 Keith invited pianist Johnny Parker, clarinettist Dick Charlesworth and myself down to play a gig in the area. It was in the pretty harbour town of Looe, and he'd booked us into a tiny B & B in a nearby village. Dick and I shared a room, while Johnny took the single. The landlady, Mrs Hulker, fussed around to make sure we were comfortable. Tea and biscuits appeared, and as she prepared our pre-gig meal she giggled about how nice it was to have 'show biz people from London' to stay. Her husband would enjoy meeting us too, she said. He drove a gravel lorry for the local council, and we would see him in the morning. Johnny had Mrs H blushing when he remarked on how nice her hair looked… 'Had it done locally?' he asked. The compliment was generously answered with complimentary glasses of Liebfraumilch from the sideboard, and she assured us that a late breakfast would be no problem. She also invited us to use the dining room if we wanted to unwind a little after the gig.

As we drove off to work I mused wistfully about the literary connections this part of Cornwall could boast of: Sir Arthur Quiller-Couch had been Mayor of nearby Fowey, and his friend, Kenneth Grahame, conceived his immortal *The Wind in the Willows* during idyllic summer holidays messing about in boats on the local river. Dick was in reflective mood, too. 'Rural hospitality,' he said, 'there's nothing quite like it.'

RURAL IDYLL SHATTERED

The muffled thumping was alarmingly insistent, like the Flanders artillery bombardment I'd heard re-created at the Imperial War Museum. My head swam, and I was aware of the drumming of heavy rain. Then a bang, and a rough sergeant's voice barking, 'Bastards, get up, get up — bastards, bastards!' I jolted upright and found myself looking at a huge man framed in the bedroom doorway. His apoplexy could have graced an H. M. Bateman cartoon, while his forearms resembled those of Popeye's adversary, Bluto.

It was Mr Hulker of gravel-lorry fame. The time was 7.35am and by 7.36 he had laid out, first, his predicament, and then (much more menacingly), ours. He had just discovered the surface of his polished dining-room table destroyed by a repeating pattern of white onion rings – stains left by whisky glasses after Dick and Johnny had finished off half a bottle in the early hours. Unless he was paid £40 immediately (a hefty sum in 1979), he would call the police. In the meantime, he had parked his lorry across the back of my car, and he assured me that he wouldn't hesitate to use a 25-pound sledge-hammer on it if we didn't meet his wishes. I protested that I had gone straight to bed and was therefore free of guilt. He was mildly understanding. 'Fuckin' bad luck, that,' he said.

The commotion had gradually woken Dick in the next bed. Deeply hungover, and oblivious to the conversation, he peered at his watch, then at the stranger in our bedroom, frowned deeply and said, 'It's a bit bloody early for breakfast, we were told we could have a late one.' Hulker was about to turn volcanic, but I interjected in time, explaining the problem about the table.

A little less aggression from the aggrieved householder, just a touch of contrition from the culprits — then we might have negotiated a mutually-agreeable solution. But Johnny with Dick also resented their rude awakening and dug their heels in. The police were called and two grey-haired London jazzers with hangovers were driven away to Looe police station in a squad car for questioning. Although completely innocent myself, I thought it wise not to ask for breakfast and spent the next four hours sitting in my immovable car listening to the incessant rain on the roof.

Early in the afternoon the still-stubborn pair arrived back, this time with Keith Smith who played a diplomatic role, paid a reduced amount of damages to the family and then persuaded Bluto to move his gravel lorry from behind my car. As we drove out, the two Hulkers and their equally massive son lined up on the doorstep. Their goodbyes were of the good-riddance variety, and the very last Cornish phrase I heard was, 'Filthy London scum, we're going to write to Esther Rantzen about you lot.'

My two colleagues fell asleep instantly, leaving me to handle the 300-mile drive back to London. I was hungry, frustrated, and furious with both of them. Forty minutes up the road there was a stirring from the back seat, and then Dick's voice:
'Oh, fuck!'
'What is it now?'
I rasped.
'I forgot to sign the guest book.'

Johnny Parker by Trog

41

A CHAT with THE CHANCELLOR
The Rt. Hon KENNETH CLARKE, talks about his enthusiasm for jazz

Kenneth by Trog

One afternoon in February I received a telephone call from the Treasury. Well, one does, doesn't one? Actually, it was from the Treasury Press Office, responding to my letters to the Rt. Hon. Kenneth Clarke, QC, MP and Chancellor of the Exchequer, and jazz enthusiast, requesting that he granted me an interview.

Press Officer Steve Bird gave me a date and time I could see Mr. Clarke — 5.45 p.m. on St. Valentine's Day, and in a force six gale, rain lashing down. I pressed my way down Whitehall, reflecting on the Evening Standard placards screaming, 'Valentine's Day Massacre Of The Pound', I'd seen from the 29 bus to Trafalgar Square.

It wouldn't have surprised me to be told on arrival that Mr. Clarke was otherwise occupied. More things on his mind than talking about jazz.

The Treasury building isn't marked as such. It doesn't have a big neon facia saying THIS IS WHERE WE SPEND YOUR MONEY, or anything like that, to indicate its situation, and I met up against a sequence of closed doors. I got a little panicky about not making my appointment on time — assuming it was still on after the 'Valentine Day's Massacre', but I found an open door. I announced that I had an appointment with Mr. Clarke and a uniformed commissionaire took my name.

Trouble here. After several stabs, including 'Gob Bold', he got it right, but more name trouble cropped up.

'What initial Mr. Clarke, sir?', enquired the commissionaire.

'K', I replied.

'K?' He look puzzled and ran his forefinger down the list of names.

'It was K you said, sir, wasn't it?', looking up, and still bemused.

By now, I'm wondering if I'm in the right building or in a bad dream, and it's 5.45 p.m..

He turned to his mate. 'Bert, do you know a K. Clarke?'

'Can't say I do', said Bert.

A further look, a sudden gasp of realisation that I was there to see THE Mr.Clarke, and a sigh of relief from this now apprehensive hack. I was led to the reception room through endless corridors of power by a young man who informed me that there were fifteen miles of these in the building, It seemed that I'd done five of them when, exhausted, I was ushered into the Chancellor's vast office. Standing behind an enormous desk and smoking a cigar, he greeted me affably. I had a feeling of total unreality. It's not every day of the week one chats to the Chancellor of the Exchequer. When one thinks of the billions upon billions he handles, some of it my money, and when I thought of what I'd got in my Post Office savings...

A little hiccup with the Walkman, but the interview got going.

J.G.

DANCING SLIPPER BALLROOM, NOTTINGHAM

JG: Were you interested in music in your childhood?

KC: Not really. I went to the sort of school that, nowadays, no doubt teaches music sensibly, but then singing in unison from the *Oxford Song Book* was about the sum of it all. In my early teens I developed the usual interest in pop music, but soon switched to jazz.

JG: Did your parents listen to the dance bands of the thirties and forties on the radio. I mean names like Jack Payne, Jack Hylton, Ambrose and the like?

KC: No. And we didn't have any of their records about the house. My introduction to the music was when I was old enough — or looked old enough — to go to places with bars where I heard traditional jazz. One of the first places was the Mapperley Tea Rooms, which didn't sell tea and had a quite dreadful trad band.

JG: I was an agent in the 50s and constantly booked bands into the Dancing Slipper Ballroom — in Nottingham. Did you go there?

KC: I was a positive fixture at the Dancing Slipper. If anyone wanted to see me they knew I'd be there.'

JG: 'Did you know the promoter, Bill Kinnell?

KC: No; I was one of the regular customers, but I didn't know him.

JG: We used to call him 'Fu' Kinnell. (*I don't think the Chancellor got the meaning of the nickname or maybe he didn't think that someone in his* *position should recognise such a crudity...*) Did you go to the rival club, the Nottingham Rhythm Club run by Ken Allsop?

KC: Yes, I did. That was at the Trent Bridge Hotel. I listened to them all, Chris Barber, Kenny Ball, Acker Bilk, Ken Colyer, Sandy Brown and Humphrey Lyttelton with Wally Fawkes. That started my interest in the wider aspects of jazz and I got into jazz literature. I bought books by Hughes Panassié, Brian Rust, Alun Morgan and, later on, your own histories of jazz in Britain. I haunted the second-hand record shops for jazz records. The first record I bought was an LP by Louis Armstrong's Hot Seven, which made me realise how different it was from the trad I had been listening to.

KEN A JIVER?

JG: Were you a jiver on the floor?

KC: Yes, but not a very good one. Throughout my life dancing has been fairly catastrophic. But, yes, I got on the floor.

JG: You then had a conversion to what is known as modern jazz?

KC: Yes, I would regard myself as a modernist nowadays, but I like jazz of all kinds. I was an avid reader of the magazines — *Jazz Monthly* and *Jazz Journal* and I still subscribe to *Jazz Journal*. I must be one of their most loyal customers. I was quite fanatical about jazz.

JG: Do you still play records?

KC: Yes, but not enough. I mean what has driven jazz to the back of my life is the sheer lack of time. When I was a junior minister I was a regular visitor to Ronnie's, but when I became Secretary of State For Health I was far too busy to stay up late at night. And playing records is precluded by the enormous amount of paper work I have to get through. My jazz listening nowadays is in the car — on tapes – driving to and from my home in Nottingham.

JG: Do you play jazz records late at night at No 11 Downing Street?

KC: No.

JG: You might get a complaint from No 10 if you did?

KC: No, that's far enough away, I'm glad to say. I just don't have the equipment to play records at No 11.

BIX BEIDERBECKE

JG: You mentioned Brian Rust earlier on. He's a propagandist for white jazz; Bix Beiderbecke, Red Nichols and the like. Do any of those players interest you?

KC: Funnily enough, I was playing a Beiderbecke tape, one of those re-vamped in stereo cassettes by Robert Parker only yesterday, driving down to London.

JG: Obviously, you have broad tastes, and I got the impression that you were strictly into modern jazz.

KC: Yes, nowadays, it is more likely to be bop or hard bop I play. But I have very eclectic tastes and Beiderbecke I much enjoy.

JG: Perhaps I shouldn't ask a politician about the middle ground. I refer to what is known as mainstream – Count Basie or Duke Ellington of the thirties and forties, for instance.

KC: Yes, I can listen to any kind of good jazz. Lester Young with Count Basie, an example. I'm not one of those people who keep up the feuds of my youth when you were either a trad man or a modernist. I went to hear Basie many times when the ban on American musicians was lifted. I thought that ban was a disgrace. I know you covered that extensively in your book.

JG: Do you have any jazz conversations in the House? Are there any other fellow spirits?

KC: There are a few. The person who is the most quoted is John Prescott. And David Steel. I was constantly bumping into David Steel at Ronnie's.

JG: I gather there's not much jazz conversation at Cabinet level.

KC: At Cabinet level?! I don't think there's anyone round the Cabinet table who would recognise a jazz record if you played it to them.

LOW-LIFE MUSIC

JG: In one of the interviews you gave, you mentioned that jazz was regarded as low-life music and although it has become quite respectable, what with obituaries on jazzmen in the quality dailies and occasional spots on Radio 3, the stigma still exists. Do you have people expressing disbelief that a Cabinet Minister should be so interested in this so-called low-life music?

KC: I think all that attitude is dying out. But you will know as well as I do that most people who hear that you are interested in jazz have only the haziest notion of what it sounds like and have a curious view of what you mean. No, I don't often get that sort of query.

JG: I know I'm interviewing you, but perhaps I could mention a personal experience that illustrates the opinion of many about the music. The postman, intrigued by my interest in jazz, which he deduced from seeing letters addressed to the editor of *Jazz at Ronnie Scott's* and handing over LPs, enquired, 'Aren't you rather old to be interested in jazz? I mean, I was listening to Ted Heath and that when I was eighteen...' From that I assumed he had gone on to higher things. Like Mantovani...

KC: There was a time, in the eighties, when the jazz audience was getting rather elderly, but having gone to a few jazz concerts of late, I see many younger people present.

MOLE JAZZ

JG: Do you frequent the specialist jazz shops?

KC: My record collection in the later years was built up from

Illustration: Wally Fawkes 'Trog'

Mole Jazz. I used to be on their mailing list. For every record I bought over the counter I must have bought 50 by mail order.

JG: Do you have any particular favourites in pre-bebop jazz?

KC: Yes, I like Jelly Roll Morton, and, of course the Armstrong Hot Fives and Sevens, and you have discovered that I am still a subscriber to *Jazz Journal* which, as you know, isn't devoted entirely to modern jazz. Far from it.

RONNIE SCOTT'S

JG: I would like to ask what attracted you to Ronnie Scott's Club?

KC: You can listen to good jazz!

JG: But isn't there something about the ambience?

KC: Of course, it is now a great place to unwind. I now claim I don't go there because I am too busy, and there is something in that, but it's actually because, partly, I am getting older. The Club used to fit in very well with the House of Commons which usually starts packing up at 10 o'clock, and if you had a vote at ten, you would get to Ronnie's by the time it started to warm up and used to be able to stay to the end. But I'm too old for that, although I did regard it as Mecca. One of the great things about being a member

of Parliament was being near to Ronnie's, which wasn't the case when I was a barrister in the Midlands. When I was a Junior Minister, I would have to wind up a debate and the adrenaline was flowing. One couldn't sleep for a few hours after that and it was a total relaxation to go to Ronnie's.

JG: One of the things about the club, if I may say, is that notabilities, and personalities, are not given the 'big hello' treatment and have the spotlight shone on them.

KC: I would be driven away by that. I used to go alone, I used to pay, and sink into the darkness. Often on my own. Get into a corner, have a drink and enjoy the music and not being descended upon by some idiot wanting to talk about politics. I shall be along there shortly to hear the National Youth Jazz Orchestra.

I liked Mr. Kenneth Clarke, even if he is a politician... A nice sense of humour. He laughed when I told him he had an identity problem at the front office and when I thanked him for seeing me, and adding that I realised he had a few problems on

his mind, he joked, 'Yes, the pound, for instance.'

As he was such a pleasant chap, one almost forgot how much he whips off my miserable pittance every six months.

Following the publication of this interview I received a letter from Mr. Clarke, which read:

Thank you very much for persevering with your attempts to get me a copy of JARS with your interview with me and Trog's splendid drawing. This has now arrived safely at my Nottingham home and I will eventually get the drawing framed and put on my study wall.

I hope we bump into one another in a not too distant future'

The issue of *JARS* to which Mr. Clarke refers was no 92 (March/April, 1995) and, naturally a copy was sent to him addressed to No 11 Downing Street, his official residence, where, conceivably, an official, disturbed at seeing the front page of a jazz magazine through the see-through envelope, ordered a minion to shred it and be quick about it, my man! On the other hand, Royal Mail failed to deliver, as they have with cheques for this poor hack from the Premium Bonds Office, Vernons Pools and the National Lottery.   J.G.

Typical Ronnie Scott's members giving the Club a rest so as to discuss solutions to the country's economic situation–would you believe?

HERBERT COOT LETTERS

(The correspondence between Herbert Coot and Ronnie Scott, with apologies to The Henry Root Letters by William Donaldson)

24th January, 1984
Dear Mr. Scott,
I am writing to register my objections about the nature, not to mention the length, of your jokes. Mrs. Coot had led a secluded life and, frankly, I prefer to keep it that way. This may sound unacceptably Victorian in this permissive age (the spirit of which you are doing your damnedest to promote with your morally dubious funnies), but I don't really feel that an evening's entertainment should be ruined by the aftermath of my being pressed by Mrs. Coot for an explanation of the following gags: the prudish girl who eats her banana sideways; the Antipodean lady called Roxy Beaujolais who does tricks with wallabies; the waitress who thought Moby Dick was a venereal disease.
Regarding your query in your letter of April 12th if I have any more pounds to spare, as I have made my pile in fumigated feathers and can't bear to see anyone skint, here's another pound, but let that do you for the time being.
Yours sincerely,
Herbert Coot

8th February, 1984
Dear Mr. Scott,
I am sorry you have not replied to my letter of the 24th January regarding the dubious nature of your jokes. I still think the Roly Polys a better interval bet and a lot more wholesome with it, too. However, I am now writing about another matter. I went to see Lou Donaldson and what with the dimness of your lighting and the colour of his skin I did not actually see that much of him — just a blurred outline. This is not on account of my eyesight, which is quite good for a man of my age, but the combination of Stygian gloom and Donaldson's pigmentation was such that had I seen him walking down Putney High Street the following morning I wouldn't have recognised him.
If you have to keep the lights so dimmed because you owe the LEB money, here's a pound.
Yours sincerely,
Herbert Coot

10th February 1984
Dear Mr. Coot,
Many thanks for your letters and my apologies for not replying sooner. My secretary, Bonnie Blair, doesn't always feel like typing and I have to wait until the mood takes her, which isn't very often. There is nothing I can do about this as I, with every other employer in the land, are bound by the various acts relating to Sex Equality and Racial Discrimination, although Miss Blair is white. At least, I think so. It's difficult to tell with the lighting we've got here Regarding our lighting; we are running a night club, not a floodlit football match.
About my jokes; I would be happy to explain them to Mrs. Coot in the nicest possible way.
Many thanks for the pound — I am most grateful. I hope the day will soon come when I can do you a favour. In the meantime if you would like to cut out my signature on this letter and paste it in your autograph book — be my guest. It's the least I can do.
Yours sincerely,
Ronnie Scott

WHISPERS, MURMURS AND ASIDES

ANOTHER FINE (TYPOGRAPHICAL) MESS

Club regulars will be well aware of the Ronnie joke regarding conductor Sir John Barbirolli, but for those who aren't, here it is: 'We have had some very attractive waitresses at the Club. One girl looked like Barbarella. Sir John Barbarella.'
Apropos Sir John's wife, Barbara, I am obliged to Ron Rubin for sending me this gem from the *Reading Chronicle.*
In the audience were musical celebrities, such as Lady Barbara Olly, wife of the famous conductor.
What a joy are other people's boo-boos!

Melly by Trog

There was an old chap
from New Delhi
Who modelled himself
on George Melly
He'd the voice and the
smile and the sartorial
style
But couldn't quite
manage the belly.

Ron Rubin

INTERVIEW...
in between Ronnie answering the telephone

Perish the thought that I should bore readers with my problems — I'm sure you all have plenty of your own — but I do own to the fact that one of the problems connected with the — ahem — office I hold with this paper is the hard time I have trying to interview the man whose name graces the fascia board outside 47 Frith Street, W.1. and our front page. Name of Ronnie Scott, tenor saxophonist and raconteur. But try I do — continuously — and one bright April afternoon I bearded the lion in his den, that windowless cell at the back of the club, to grab at a few straws with which to fashion the bricks of this column. As usual he peered through the gloom, and with some degree of recognition, but showed no enthusiasm for the encounter. But he did remark, 'Oh, hello young man,' this indicating that he wasn't quite sure who I was, nor did his demeanour inspire me with much hope. In fact, he seemed more world-weary than ever.

'Anything wrong,' I asked,

Earl Hines by Nemethy

hopeful that my solicitude would perhaps make him a mite more conversational. He sighed heavily. 'Nothing really. Just a feeling of disenchantment. That coupled with ennui.' He sighed again. 'In truth, I'm becoming increasingly insular.'

'I had noticed. But for our interview to go in the next issue of the mag. Anything to tell me? Some recent experiences on tour, for instance.'

'Nothing, really. Went to Stockton last week, but it was closed. I know! That's an old joke, but the old ones are the best, I always say. Excuse me for a moment. Sharon! Have you done that letter for me? Oh, there's a good girl.'

'You writing a letter? I don't believe it!'

'Got to. Spot of litigation. Hate it, though. Letter writing, I mean: litigation, I've sort of got used to. But writing anything I find a drag. In fact, you know Jim — it is Jim isn't it? — I do like to get names right — I think I was born just to play tenor saxophone. And tell a few jokes, of course. Not much to show in a lifetime is it? Think of the epitaph on my headstone. Probably no more than, 'He played a few notes and cracked some jokes' — rather sad when you come to think about it.'

'Heavens, you do sound down. Have you ever thought of getting yourself a proper job?'

'Wish I had a pound for as many times as I've heard that question asked of jazz musicians. But what else could I do? Nothing! No, I shall have to carry on playing the sax until the day they find me recumbent and rigid, eyes closed and toes pointed upwards.'

'Perish the thought! At least while I'm working for you. I got some ideas for our chat from reading your book *Some Of My Best Friends Are Blues*-'

'Any good?'

'Oh, yes, I think they're very good ideas.'

'No, the book I mean.'

'Haven't you read it?'

'Can't say I have, and any queries regarding that you must get in touch with my ghost. Name of Mike Hennessey. Quite a nice chap for a jazz journalist. Ah, Sharon. You've got the letter. Thanks. Yes, you can go now. Don't forget to switch the telephone through. I've got to answer the phone for a while. My partner Pete King is off to buy another Porsche. He has to have a new one every year. Doesn't like to be seen in old motors.

Oh, dear, the phone's ringing already. Good evening. Ronnie Scott's. Tonight, sir, we have the world famous jazz pianist Earl Hines with his Quartet and Marva Josie together with the Bobby Wellins Quartet. Yes, sir, Earl has been around for quite some time. No, Bobby hasn't been around quite as long.

Four seats? Certainly, sir. You want a table as near to the bandstand as possible. So that the band can drown the chatter of your friends? As you wish, sir. Look forward to seeing you tonight. Goodbye, sir.'

You know — er — Jim — we get all sorts on this telephone. You wouldn't believe half the calls we get. I had someone ring up last week wanting 5,000 cartons of oats. Scott's Porridge Oats.

Geddit? Some idiot receptionist confused us with them! Wish I could have obliged the caller, though. Might have been a pound or two in it. Business hasn't been too brisk of late.' 'About the interview for *JARS*.' '*JARS*?'

'*Jazz At Ronnie Scott's* — your house magazine. I'm the — ahem — editor.'

'Yes, of course. I was forgetting.'

'Have you read the humorous piece I left you last week?'

'Fraid I have. I didn't think it at all funny. Very laboured, in fact.'

I thought: Bloody cheek! Here's this Grimaldi of Frith Street nightly parading jokes as old as the hills — so antediluvian that, in a geological sense, they'd defy the carbon dating process – and he's turning down my funnies! Had a good mind to tell him so, too, but you don't bite the hand that feeds you the occasional crust, so I merely replied, but with a hint of steel — 'I agree, but who are you and I amongst so many?'

'Like it! Next time I get a barracker — that is, should I ever get a barracker — I'll certainly use that. Excuse me, here's the phone again. Yes, sir, tonight we have the world famous jazz pianist Earl Hines with Marva Josie and the Bobby Wellins Quartet. We close at three, Sir. Have we a big menu? (Aside to JG: Big menu, but very little food) 'Yes sir, an extensive a la carte. Party of six. Certainly sir. Clothes? Yes, they should be worn. Only joking, sir. As informal as you like. Thank you, sir. See you later.'

'I know what you're thinking! I've used that clothes gag before but, as I say, the old jokes are the best.'

'Except, apparently, my old jokes.'

'Ah, but there are old jokes and old jokes. Now, if you'll excuse me...'

I knew exactly what he was going to do. Practise the saxophone. I knew exactly what he was going to say. It would be — 'Must get in some practice. Don't really have to, of course, but conscience compels me.' He picked up his tenor and said, 'Must get in some practice. Don't really have to, of course, but conscience compels me...'

I fled. I, too, was disenchanted. J.G.

Slawkenbergius

FAFFERS, FF & THE AM

It was a wet and windy December morning in Soho. No more tables outside the cafes; condensation ran down their windows as the denizens of the sinful square mile sipped their cappuccinos. I am on my rounds and bump into Fall-About Francis, his cognomen arising from his partiality for happiness juice, this severely affecting his equilibrium. Actually, it was he, having had a few heart-starters before lunch, bumped into me. As I have previously mentioned, the ravages of numerous drams do not affect Old Faffer's rheumy eye for errors of spelling, punctuation and grammar in *JARS*.

'Ah, Skawkenbergius! I've just read the new issue of *JARS*. 'You misspelt 'replied' in your column, tell your editor that 'harassing' has one 'r' and two 's's' — not the other way round, and Roland Keale's video review has superfluous words.' Tautology! Triumphantly baring his Benson and Hedged fangs (Benson and Hedged- geddit?), he reeled on his way. I was thankful we hadn't met in the bar, for here he would have blagged me into buying him a large Johnny Walker, downed it in one gulp, and departed. He's a guv'nor bar-blagger, is Faffers.

Shortly afterwards I spotted Feminist Freda, our Lady in Jazz, as strident a sister wot ever drew breath, who regards me, of all people, as a male chauvinist pig, and always gives me a hard time.

What had I done to upset this fearsomely militant female? Referred to 'man-hole covers' when it should be 'person-hole covers' or written about the jazz fraternity when — she avows — it should be community? Had I overlooked yet another exception to the rule, for whatever cosmic reason, that jazz is primarily a male activity? Whatever — I took evasive action and when it comes to avoiding FF I can move with agility of a young gazelle.

My next encounter was with the actor-manager. 'Ah, laddie, I've got a bone to pick with you - regarding me not taking you into the Groucho Club. It's not me, laddie, it's the door staff, they're just that wee bit particular, y'know. As I told you, they don't let any old Steve, Kevin or Brian in. And you just were that bit over the top, laddie.'

'They let Jeffrey Barnard in, and he's always sozzled.'

'Ah yes, laddie, but he's a famous drunk, whereas you laddie... well... not too put too fine a point on it, laddie... are just a drunk. Must be on my way, laddie, a rehearsal, y'know.'

A revival of *Sweeney Todd* for the Civic, Barnsley, I muttered to myself as, once again, I made my way to the French Pub in Dean Street, where they happily admit ordinary drunks.

Typical Ronnie Scott's members limbering up

THE MASSEY HALL CONCERT
A personal reminiscence by ALAIN PRESENCER

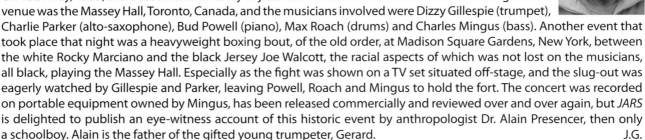

On 15th May, 1953, there assembled an array of jazzmen the like of which will never be seen again. The venue was the Massey Hall, Toronto, Canada, and the musicians involved were Dizzy Gillespie (trumpet), Charlie Parker (alto-saxophone), Bud Powell (piano), Max Roach (drums) and Charles Mingus (bass). Another event that took place that night was a heavyweight boxing bout, of the old order, at Madison Square Gardens, New York, between the white Rocky Marciano and the black Jersey Joe Walcott, the racial aspects of which was not lost on the musicians, all black, playing the Massey Hall. Especially as the fight was shown on a TV set situated off-stage, and the slug-out was eagerly watched by Gillespie and Parker, leaving Powell, Roach and Mingus to hold the fort. The concert was recorded on portable equipment owned by Mingus, has been released commercially and reviewed over and over again, but *JARS* is delighted to publish an eye-witness account of this historic event by anthropologist Dr. Alain Presencer, then only a schoolboy. Alain is the father of the gifted young trumpeter, Gerard.   J.G.

'A fool and his money are easily parted,' were my mother's words to me as I left my home on the balmy evening of 15th May, 1953, to make my way to the Massey Hall from the Toronto suburb of North York to hear Charlie Parker and Dizzy Gillespie in concert. I was fourteen years old, jazz mad, and this was to be my first live jazz experience.

In my pocket I had a one-dollar ticket, an extra dollar for the bus fare, a coke, and a notebook. I still have that notebook and although it's over forty years since that stupendous event, it's almost as if it were last night. Were I to live another forty years, I know the feeling will be the same.

NON-SMILING MUSICIANS

I was an hour early and walked up and down upside the hall reading the signs – 'JAZZ CONCERT TONIGHT'. Nothing else. I had paced up and down a thousand times and then stood outside the stage door and every time a black face went in and out I smiled, hoping I'd be noticed, but not one of them smiled back.

The show started a half an hour late and the hall about only a quarter full. (The next day the press reported – 'MASSEY HALL 3/4 EMPTY FOR BOPPERS'.) An usher pulled me from my dollar and pushed me into row four, dead centre, and that night, that magical night, remains forever in my memory, heart and guts. It was spontaneous, unrestricted, inventive and original and it was loud, really loud. (Since the audience was so sparse, we were all moved to

the front of the house and I quickly occupied a front seat for my dollar!)

According to my scribbled notes — the first half of the concert was 'Interminably dull', and I was bitterly disappointed. 'No Dizzy Gillespie and no Charlie Parker — only a sweaty, crouched-up pianist called Bud Powell'.

'BUD NO TATUM'

Someone near me said, 'He's no Art Tatum,' and although I had never heard of Tatum, I nodded in a knowing fashion. Many years later I heard Bud's contribution on the recording and he is superb! Like a man possessed, but the notes of a fourteen-year old read, 'Powell ain't no Tatum and the audience are talking about the Jersey Joe Walcott and Rocky Marciano fight, that Marciano hadn't a chance and the man next to me says that Parker has put a 100 dollars on Jersey Joe to knock out Marciano by round five, and I agreed with him.'

(As it happened, Marciano knocked out Walcott in the first round, but the absence of musicians on the stand in the programme's early part was because they were looking at the hour-long preliminaries before the actual fight.)

THAT PLASTIC ALTO

The second half began — exploding with *Perdido* — Parker and Gillespie, close together, in baggy white suits, Parker holding a mysterious white alto that, I later discovered, was made of plastic and borrowed from a local music shop, Heintzman's Music, Yonge Street.* Dizzy, with his hamster cheeks, distended like two great balloons, threatening to burst with each explosive blast, hurriedly left the stage to watch the fight on TV.

My notes read, 'I wish someone would switch off the TV, so I can hear when Bud Powell is playing.' I was rapidly revising my opinion on Bud, but I wrote, 'I don't

---

* This probably accounts for Parker's 'ownership' of the plastic acrylic alto manufactured by the Grafton Company in Britain in the early fifties, and could have been the instrument that fetched a staggering £93 000 when auctioned at Christie's in September, 1994

Charles Mingus by Pennington

think Parker and Gillespie think much of his playing as they talk loudly to each other during his solos'. There was a standing ovation at the finish of *Perdido* and *Salt Peanuts*, and after Bud's solo on *All The Things You Are*, I wrote, 'He's much better than Thelonious.' Obviously, I had changed my mind completely, and of Dizzy's solo on *Wee Dot*, I wrote, 'It was pure ice and fire.'

FABULOUS PARKER

I wasn't so impressed with Max Roach: 'He's good, but he'll never rival Buddy Rich or Gene Krupa, he's too loud and too hard. The speed at which Parker plays doesn't seem possible, you can't see his fingers move at all. His solo on Hot House was the end of the world until Dizzy came in and made a second ending. I must tell Dad'. (My father loved jazz, but my mother still holds to her appreciation of bebop, exemplified by her immortal question, 'What's Dizzy Gillespie supposed to mean?'

Night in Tunisia was the last number and from the outset of Parker's solo, the entire audience rise as one and swayed with closed eyes. My notes read, 'Oh, God, this is fabulous,' and to this day I can remember the tears that cascaded down my cheeks as Parker's tortured voice screamed and wailed each bloody phrase into shapes of liquid noise.

My last note ends, 'It seemed to me that all the endings were untidy, excepting *Night in Tunisia*', which wasn't a bad comment from a fourteen years old, even though I say so myself!

DISSENSION ON THE STAGE

All the musicians wore uniform white suits. Max Roach played on a white drum kit, Parker played on a white alto, (over all these years I have been mystified how a musician can leave his instrument at home when he sets off to play a gig).

My memory of this occasion is dominated by Mingus fiddling with his tape recorder and glancing around at Bud Powell, who refused to co-operate when Mingus (after *Perdido*) asked the somewhat askew Powell to raise the lid of the Steinway, Powell responded with what seemed to be a good-humoured riposte, 'Why don't you take a fucking flying jump at yourself?'

Parker laughed out loud, as did the most of the audience, but Max Roach, looking mildly embarrassed,

Left to right: Bud Powell, Charles Mingus, Max Roach, Dizzy Gillespie, Charlie Parker. Owing to the Marciano-Walcott fight being shown on television, at one stage only Powell, Mingus and Roach were playing

muttered, 'C'mon guys, cool it.'

Gillespie wasn't on stage. He was in the wings watching the fight on the box, the sound reaching the audience who heard Gillespie exclaim, 'Oh, shit, no!', at the unexpected spectacle of Marciano knocking Walcott out in the first round.

I remember, too, that Mingus addressed Parker by his surname. Mingus, then thirty-one, was a great hunk of a man, and during that evening it seemed as if he could only express relentless anger both verbally and musically and his playing was fierce and relentless. During the resultant applause from the sparse audience he responded with a scowl and then squatted beside his tape recorder to fiddle with the dials. In fact, I can still remember now that after everyone had left, the massive figure of Mingus coming back to the stage alone, to play back the tapes and pack away the machine.

The last sounds I heard that evening were tapes whirring as he played them backwards and forwards. But how marvellous that this limited equipment should have captured the sheer magic of that happening. I was a very lucky fourteen year old to be present when history was being made. Rumour has it that the organisers, the New Jazz Society, wanted Oscar Pettiford instead of Mingus. Would Pettiford, had he been booked, have brought along a tape recorder?

LETTER from MAX ROACH

Dear Editor,
I have just received your magazine with an account of the Massey Hall concert. It is, without doubt, the best recollection of that gig I have ever read and I have read some bullshit over the decades! This is jazz writing at its very best. Congratulations Ronnie Scott!
I hope Alain has changed his mind about my drumming over the years.
Best wishes,
Max Roach,
Mainz, Germany

The fourteen year old Alain and a seventy-five year old Max Roach. Main photo: David Sinclair

RON MATTHEWSON the bibulous bassist

Ron Matthewson, one of the world's leading bass players, enjoys a glass of AUNTIE'S INFERNO between sets, but also … ADORES Absinthe Ambrusco, Adnam's, Amstall's… anaesthetizes on Asbach… abhors abstainers. Must be something wrong with 'em', he mutters into his beer, which could be Burton, Benskins, Bass, Barley Wine, Brakspear's … bibulously bends an elbow for Benedictine, Beaujolais, Beefeater, Bloody Mary and Bacardi… bellows for Bells, belts down the Bulmer's… Bacchus his God, bacchanalia his goal. A boozy bod who… COPIOUSLY consumes Courvoisier, Chartreuse, Cointreau. Carling, Carlsberg, Canadian Club, Charrington's, Chateau-neuf-du-Pape, Campari, Cinzano… coos over Cockburn's, is Cuckoo over Curaçao, gets cut on Cutty Sark… DELIGHTS in Dubonnet, downs Dom Perignon, drains Dom Fernando, digs Dry Cane, dotes on Double Century, dwells on Dow's, dashes off drams of Drambuie. A great technician on the bass but many gasp at his draughtmanship… EULOGISTIC over 'E', ecstatic about English Ale, eagle-eyed when it comes to Everard's… eagerly examines restaurant menus more for their ingurgative than the ingestive items — if broke, orders the former and not the latter… FOND of Fosters, favours Fremlin's, flips over Fuller's.. Favourite terms — 'Bottoms Up', 'Down The Hatch', 'Here's Mud In Your Eye', 'Chin Chin' and 'Cheers'. Favourite tune — 'Lush Life'. Favourite film — *The Lost Weekend*. He GULPS Guinness, glugs Grant's, guzzles Gaymer's, goes ga-ga over Gordon's, gooey-eyed over Gilbey's … HARKS for Harvey's, has highs on Hock, hiccoughs on Heineken, this reaching the parts other lagers do not care to penetrate… Hawk-eyed when it comes to Haig — his vision a trifle hazy after a tot or two over the top of Highland Mist… INSATIABLY ingurgitates Ind Coope's, imbibes Irish Velvet, intense about IPA — you could say he was intoxicant-inclined… JOLLILY juices on jeroboams, jostles for Jack Daniels, junkets on Johnny Walker, KO's Kirsch and Kummell, gets kited on Kahlua… LOVES libations of Liebfraumilch, Lacon's, Long John's and Light Ale… laps Lowenbrau, lusts after Laphraoig… often lopes into the Dog and Duck for a livener … Loathes lemonade … MANIACAL about Macon, Midgal, Martlett's, Mead, McEwans's and Martini … gets merry on Merry Down … NEVER averse to a noggin, nutty about Newcastle Brown, gets newtish on Noilly Prat… nimble barwards… OPTS for Original Croft's… optic orientated … often has the hair of the dog… PENS paeans of praise for Pernod, gets pie-eyed on Pimms, plumps for Plum Brandy, has a penchant for Peroni Nastro Azzurro (he longs to be featured in one of their full-page advertisements in *Jazz Express*), pines for Punch, has been plastered on Porter, is Potty over Pils… positively prefers potions that pack a punch… QUAFFS quarts of Colespring, is a quotidian quencher… ROOTS for Ruddles, rhapsodizes over Remy Martin, raves over The Real Mackenzie, roused

Ron by Pennington

by Russian Stout — a real ale artiste… SUPS syllabub, slaughters Sam Smith's, sozzles Shepherd Neame's, savours Southern Comfort, swallows Smirnoff, seeks solace in Slivovitch. Strongbow provides the spiritoso in his playing — seen in many a saturnalia… TIPPLES Tetley's and Theakston's (especially their Old Peculiar) tanks up on Toby, topes Tia Maria, takes a taste of Teacher's, tranquillises on Tequila, gets tight on Tennants and tiddly on Truman's… UBIQUITOUS in bars, dives and drinking dens… VOTES for Vladivar Vodka and Valpolicella… WETS his whistle on Watney's Worthington and Woodpecker… wary of water — since reading that chemically polluted rain makes it acid he's made it a firm rule to detoxify H_2O with a little something usually of an amber colour. 'You've still to look after yer health', he says as he glowingly appraises the medicinal virtues of Glenfiddich, Glenlivet, Isle of Dogs and Glenmorangie. In truth, he's 'E' XTRA partial to the malts of his country — a roll call of their brand names sweet poetry to his Celtic soul, they keep him in the best spirits… YODELS for Younger's and yens for Young's — you name it, he's drunk it… ZOOMS in on alcoholic refreshments at parties, wakes, weddings, barmitzvahs, orgies, reunions and funerals. Yes, our Ron likes a drink, but is particularly fond of AUNTIE'S INFERNO available from all leading off-licences. J.G.

Slawkenbergius

THE DEVIL LOOKS
AFTER HIS CLONE

'It's a question of semantics, or of what construction you care to put on words', intoned our editor, James Charles Godbolt, as he accepted a glass of amber-coloured fluid from me one chilly February morning at the Three Greyhounds, Greek Street, run by Miss Roxy Beaujolais. He was referring to criticism of his contretemps with a certain motor spares salesman, in a cultural desert well north of the Watford Gap, who does a bit of hack journalism on the side, apparently for free, just to get his selective quotations, distortions and lies, and his name, in print.

'What they are implying, old son, is that such petty squabbles are quite beneath their dignity, but, should they be involved in disputes then these are legitimate contentions conducted from a high moral ground. It was always thus.

'My objections to this miscreant is not that he criticises my writings, but for his gross lies, but enough of him, old son, it's a dreary enough morning as it is.'

'But, how does he get away with this calumny,' I enquired.

'The devil looks after his clone,' JG replied.

I told the editor that I, too, had come under fire; a reader complaining about my jokes.

'That's the trouble with humour, old son. It doesn't always make people laugh. Ask Ronnie Scott how many times he's had to struggle before an audience of dead Greeks. Not a jot or a tittle of a titter. Tricky business, humour. Any fool can be profound, old son, but getting a laugh is an entirely indifferent glass of fire water.'

He stared meaningfully at his empty tumbler. I took the hint, and the ever attentive Miss Beaujolais gave him a refill as quick as you could say Johnny Walker.

'Yes, old son, come out with a profundity and it's accepted, or not, and life goes on, but when a gag dies, you DIE!'

I changed tack and enquired of Mr G. If he had recently suffered what all hacks fear most, typographical slip-ups.

'Need you ask, old son? In the last issue (JARS 91) I wrote a piece on the CD Officium with Jan Garbarek and the Hilliard Ensemble, advising that it had sold 35,000 copies. This, old son, appeared as 35 copies! — and with the rider that they expected to sell a few thousands more. After flogging only 35, they would hope so, wouldn't they? And after a near miss with The Brecker Brothers and *her* Musicians, we nearly had another gender bender with Norma Winstone appearing as 'Norman'. Mercifully, I spotted the goofs in the nick of time.'

'So we had an error-free issue?'

'You have to be joking, old son. I walked into Ray's Jazz Shop and got the big hello. Great, I thought, somebody loves me, but why were they so chuffed to see me? I'll tell you. They had spotted a boo-boo and couldn't get to a copy fast enough to joyously point it out. Quick to chide, slow to bless, might say. Human nature, old son. There's an awful lot of it about. It's everywhere. Not that we're alone in the boo-boo biz. Chris Parker reviewed George Coleman's recent appearance at the club in *The Times*, and wrote that the rythm section was 'fleet'. This appeared as 'bleak', quite a different connotation.'

I made my usual nod to Miss Beaujolais, but the editor demurred. 'No, old son, have this on me. No, really — half of Adnam's isn't it?' a combined entreaty and question that had Roxy doing a double-take that nearly ricked the poor girl's neck.

RONNIE'S JOKES

I remember once flying with my band to a date in Stockton and as we were approaching the runway, the pilot came on the intercom and said, 'We're about to land in Stockton - please set your watches back a hundred years'. Not many people know this, but they dropped an atom bomb in Stockton. It did £15 worth of damage.

Actually I spent a wonderful fortnight there one Sunday. We stayed at one of the cheaper boarding houses – the sort of place where you have to wipe your feet on the way out. I remember the rooms were very small – you turned the door-knob and it rearranged the furniture.

But the landlady was a nice old girl. She was Irish. Typical Irish - she had a green face. She used to do the cooking, and pygmies came all the way from Africa just to dip their arrows in her soup. It was the only place I've stayed where the sea gulls used to bring the guests bits of bread.

I remember the landlady said a funny thing to me when I arrived:

'I hope you have a good memory for faces.'

'Why?' I asked.

'Because there's no shaving mirror in the bathroom.'

A bit later on I saw the landlady and told her I wanted to talk to her about the ceiling in my room.

'What about it?' she asked.

'I'd like one.' I said, hopefully.

GEORGE MELLY
singer, modern art expert, author, critic, *bon vivant*, toper and roué

Melly by Trog

The following profile of the inimitable George Melly I wrote for issue No. 4, December 1979–January 1980, and knowing him as the agent for Mick Mulligan and his band that featured the outrageous Mr. Melly for twelve years. The booking of Melly at Ronnie's caused many eyebrows to be raised. He, after all, was a traditionalist immersed in the vocal style of blues singers, particularly Bessie Smith in the twenties.

In the mid-seventies, after a spell out of the business, Melly re-emerged as a singer and once again took to the road with John Chilton's Feetwarmers. Together they recorded for the Warner label; for one of the sessions Ronnie's Club was hired for an LP. The bar did a roaring trade, a fact noticed by Ronnie and Pete King who booked Melly and the Feetwarmers as a support for the stylistically opposite — very much so! — band led by pioneer bebop drummer Elvin Jones. They were so successful that they were booked for three weeks over the following Christmas and in December 2005, at the age of seventy-nine, he played his thirty third consecutive season at Ronnie's with his recently enlisted group, Digby Fairweather's Half Dozen.

I enjoyed writing about Melly; a rare character, the like which will not be seen again, and I did make reference to the time his early successes went to his head. He used to walk around wearing a T shirt with the word Mellymania stretched across his chest, blatant self advertisement not unnoticed by his critics, anything but... J.G.

An acknowledged expert on surrealist art recently visited Cleveland, Ohio, to make a film for American TV concerning an exhibition of surrealist paintings and followed this with a trip to Venice to make two more films, this time for BBC TV, on two painters famous in the genre, Max Ernst and René Magritte.

This travelling man of the media has published three books, two of them autobiographical and a serious study of pop music, is a prolific journalist, his outlets ranging from the up-market *The Times, The Guardian* and *The Observer* newspapers, the *New Statesman, New Society, Vogue* down to *Man About Town, Over Twenty One* and *Titbits*. A catholic assortment from a fertile pen.

He's appeared on many radio shows, these including *Start the Week, The Critics, World at One, Quote Unquote, Read All About It*, and TV appearances have included *Russell Harty, Michael Parkinson* and, a keen angler, *Angling To-day*. He likes a drink, is a *bon viveur*, and ladies' man, and one wonders how he finds time for these diverse activities in addition to an arduous touring schedule.

I am, of course, referring to George Melly who, with John Chilton's Feetwarmers, commences his now annual three-week season at the Club. It's a truism that everyone is unique but, to re-phrase George Orwell's immortal aphorism, Melly is more unique than most.

Born into provincial affluence, his father a Liverpool stockbroker, his mother from a musical Jewish family, he was educated at Stowe, a public school, did his National Service in the Royal Navy, electing for the Senior Service because he thought the traditional 'tar's' uniform with the 'dickey' collar and bell-bottom trousers, 'amusing', this reason for joining

giving a senior Naval officer apoplexy when George, on account of his public school education, was being automatically interviewed for a commission.

RUM, BUM AND CONCERTINA

The officer, not surprisingly, didn't consider him officer material and Melly served his time as an ordinary seaman. Well, perhaps not so ordinary, as his second autobiographical book *Rum, Bum and Concertina* reveals.

On demobilisation, he became a salesman at a Brook Street, Mayfair, art gallery specialising in surrealistic paintings, but in 1950 left to go on the road with Mick Mulligan's Magnolia Jazz Band, one of the many revivalist bands then emerging.

He was billed as their 'blues' singer and was the principal attraction of a band more renowned for their drinking and wenching than music making, although they cut many listenable records. George's vocal style, immediately recognisable and accompanied by a theatrical flamboyance came in for a lot of stick from the purist critics, some in Mulligan's band, even. In Melly's first book, *Owning Up* he mentions this, together with many other amusing tales (including scurrilous stories about myself, their agent) and particularly a comment by the band's clarinettist Ian Christie, now a film critic for the *Daily Express*.

One of George's numbers was *Organ Grinder Blues* during which rendering he imitated a monkey scratching himself. Christie, whilst acknowledging that the band's success rested largely on George, snapped, in his fashion, 'It's not very up-bringing for a musician to feel he can only get work because you imitate a monkey', a thrust that obviously wounded because George, these many years later still refers to it.

MELLY AND TROG IN DUO

When the Mulligan band broke up in 1962, George became a full time journalist, primarily writing the 'balloons' in Wally 'Trog' Fawkes's *Flook* strip in the *Daily Mail,* but also publishing *Owning Up* and *Revolt Into Style* (the study of pop) and film scripts. He lived in a large, elegantly-furnished house in up-market Gloucester Crescent, Regent's Park, with Jonathan Miller, Alan Bennett and Joan Bakewell, amongst other media people, as his neighbours. It was a milieu much to his taste. He patronised chic restaurants, revelled in the flim-flams of 'good eating': he dressed flamboyantly — wearing capes, wide brimmed hats and carrying a silver-topped walking stick. He frequently got himself into the news, particularly on the occasion he shouted abuse at the prosecuting counsel during the *Oz* 'obscenity' case.

In my book, *All This And 10%,* I got my own back on George, referring to him as a 'posturing exhibitionist', mentioning his 'declamatory bellowing in public places,' (which he still does), 'his considerable vanity hardly in keeping with an appearance that was never Byronic and showed no sign of abating as the girth and jowls increased.'

I recounted the occasion when we met on King's Road, Chelsea, where the 'Chelsea set', so called, paraded on Saturday afternoons. He incredulously enquired, 'What on earth are *you* doing here?', as though I hadn't the right sort of social and artistic credentials to use what, after all, was a public pavement. I showed him this (and, I must add, many favourable comments about him) before publication and he didn't ask that one unflattering word be changed. Extrovert and vain, he most certainly is, but honest with it and I gratefully acknowledged his help in preparation of that book.

MERLIN'S CAVE, KING'S CROSS

He made occasional appearances at jazz clubs, mostly at Merlin's Cave in Margery Street near King's Cross. His success in the media and the applause he received at these sessions rather inflated his already considerable self-esteem. In the parlance, 'he came on a bit heavy' and his old mates let him know it. When George walked into those haunts with familiar faces around him, his continuously genial grin was flecked with indication of apprehension when he spotted those contemporaries who are good at demolishing the uppity — Wally Fawkes, Ian Christie and Mick Mulligan. Hard men.

But the applause, whilst it didn't enamour him to many of the resident band, was sweet music to his ears, and he decided to give up his regular writing commitments and return to the road. After a shaky start, the package is now a very strong attraction and it is ironic that a man whose stage act is fundamentally the same as it was with Mulligan, and doing only moderate business, should, these many years later, be a big draw, and good luck to him. Although, again, not without his critics, Allan Jones, in the *Melody Maker,* wrote, 'George Melly's performance at the

Melly by Hedley Picton

Scott Club remains a spectacle at which the most sensitive will painfully cringe... his penchant for self-conscious displays of outrageous flamboyance and his Grand Manner... all sweeping gestures and husky asides, dahlings — do test one's sympathy and grate on one's nerves.

Then there's the rickety trad of the Feetwarmers; does there exist a more irritating form of music? I think not. The audience — helpless souls these fans of Melly — relished each smutty innuendo and crude aside. I mean, I've nothing against gratuitous filth as long as it's funny and the jokes not as old as the Feetwarmers.' A typically sweeping statement from a characteristically 'knocking' journalist and one who surely regards all pre-bop jazz as 'trad' but the opinions are not without foundation. George loves to shock.

However, this is an act the like of which is not to be found anywhere in the world and this intriguing combination of ham and intellectual is part of his considerable appeal, not the least at Ronnie Scott's Club.

GEORGE and JIM at the CLUB ELEVEN

The connection with Ronnie, albeit tenuous, goes back to 1949 when he and I, convinced traditionalists, nervously visited Club Eleven, the seminal modern jazz club in the UK, then at Mac's Rehearsal Rooms, Great Windmill Street. We were appalled by the strangeness of the music and the eccentric behaviour of the musicians and patrons.

Then, neither Melly, or anyone else, could have foreseen that he would become a household name, nor could anyone have visualised him making an annual three weeks appearance at a West End night club under the aegis of Ronnie Scott, also to become a household name, then one of the young men blowing that strange music at the Club Eleven.

Ronnie too, could hardly have visualised himself in his present role, and if he had, he would never have thought at booking Melly at a club he was running. In those days, the differences between the protagonists and players of the new and old school of jazz ran deep, the arguments bloody, the defenders of the old order including Sinclair Traill, editor of *Jazz Journal*, Derrick Stewart- Baxter, writing in that paper and Rex Harris in the *Melody Maker*.

Another magazine published at the time, edited by myself, was *Jazz Illustrated* which ran a brilliant reworking by George of Lewis Carroll's 'Jabberwocky', reproduced below. It graphically illustrated the difference in the ideologies, and for younger readers perhaps it should be explained that 'Titoed' is a reference to Tito Burns, accordionist band leader who played a modified bebop in dance halls with a sextet that at one stage included Ronnie Scott; that Johny Dankworth was one of the Club Eleven musicians; that a Mouldy Fygge was a traditionalist; that Cecil Gee was a gents outfitter in Charing Cross Road much patronised by the sharp dressing modernist, as opposed to the attire of the traditionalist with their Shetland Isle pullovers, corduroy trousers, duffel coats and sandals.

JAZZAWOCKY
'Twas bopping and the jivey toes
Did Gee and Cecil as they bopped
All bobby were the sex-a-glow
And the hairstyles outcropped

Beware the Jazzawock my son
the beat's that's two, the note that's whole,
Beware the jazz club bird and shun
the cornier Jelly - Roll

He took his flatted fifth in hand
Longtime the Mouldy Fygge he sought
So rested by the tom-tom tree,
and bopped a while in thought

And as in boppish thought he stood,
The Jazzawock with ties aflame
Came battling down the Sinclair Traill,
and Harrised as it came.

Do-Ba, Ba-oo and through and through
The flatted fifth stuck white and black
He left them high and Dizzily
He came Dankworthing back.

And hast thou 'sent' the Jazzawock?
Come to my arms thou boppish boy,
Oh, bopsters boast, you are the most'
He Titoed in his joy.

Twas bopping and the jivey toes,
Did Gee and Cecil as they bopped,
All bopped were the sex-a-glow,
And the hairstyles outcropped.

A delightful adaptation of classic nonsense accurately reflecting the critical and dress divisions of the fifties.

WHISPERS, MURMURS & ASIDES

JARS has made the national press–*The Evening Standard*. On 3rd May their Londoner's Diary, under the leading header — THE JADED PAST OF BLAIR AND ROCK PROMOTER, reported: 'Tony Blair's career as a student guitarist has been documented. I have discovered that in his youth he had another string to his musical bow. Before he went up to Oxford he was a promoter of a rock band Jade. This little known side of Blair's character is revealed by Adam Sieff, head of Sony music UK, in *Jazz at Ronnie Scott's* magazine.

'Apparently for the Fettes-educated Blair, the band contained several well- heeled public schoolboys, including Sieff, whose uncle was the long-standing chairman of Marks & Spencer and the drummer was James Lascelles, whose mother, the Countess of Harewood, allowed the group to rehearse in her house.

'He didn't stand out as an individual, but I remember being told that he was the guy who was organising everything,' Sieff tells me. 'He was very efficient selling tickets, booking the venues, that sort of thing. He put on a show every Friday night at a pub in Richmond. They were great days and they were his shows. I still have the posters. They say 'Please call Tony Blair.'

'I have no interest in politics, but I think someone should look into this aspect of the Prime Minister's youth. Perhaps my nephew Boris Johnson, editor of *The Spectator*?'

Your columnist phoned Mr. Johnson's office at *The Spectator* to check if he was following on Adam's suggestion, but got a curt negative from his secretary.

There's a jazz connection with the Harewoods. The Countess's' brother-in-law, the Honourable Gerald Lascelles, a cousin of the Queen, was a keen jazz fan, co-wrote a book with Sinclair Traill, founder of *Jazz Journal*, and was involved in an imbroglio with Louis Armstrong when Louis appeared in a ghastly misalliance with the Royal Philharmonic Orchestra at the Royal Festival Hall in December 1956, a fiasco of a concert which had conductor Norman Del Mar despairingly seated on the dias with his head in his hands, and no sympathy from the jazz-loving audience.

PAUL PRY

Members of Ronnie Scott's staff swearing total allegiance to Ronnie and Pete.

HERBERT COOT LETTERS

(The correspondence between Herbert Coot and Ronnie Scott, with apologies to The Henry Root Letters by William Donaldson)

14th February, 1984
Dear Mr. Scott,
I wish to protest, very strongly, at the manner in which I found myself at one of your tables last Wednesday evening. I was on my way to the Braganza in Frith Street for dinner with Mrs. Coot when, just as I was passing your club, I was seized by a fair-haired, barrel-chested fellow with the chin of a Henry Cooper and the tongue of a trooper, who bundled me to a table, at which point one of your burlier waitresses — a female who does a bit of mud- wrestling in Hamburg on the side, I shouldn't wonder — demanded an order with menaces.

Mrs. Coot, who was waiting for me at the Braganza, naturally got very worried, went home and called the police. By the time I was let out of your club and got home it was four o'clock and Mrs. Coot quite demented with worry, not to mention suspicious. It took me some time to convince her that I had been shanghaied into eating at Ronnie's and had to listen to your jokes, about which experience she appeared to be more sympathetic than the rough handling I received.

As you know, I normally enclose a pound, but in the circumstances, I don't feel so disposed.
Yours sincerely,
Herbert Coot

16th February, 1984
Dear Mr. Coot,
Thank you for your letter of 14th February. I am sorry you were so roughly handled and ever sorrier you did not enclose your usual pound. With things as they are I could really have done with that note.

I must explain how you suddenly came to be seated at one of our tables. We don't like to see a meagre attendance. If this happens, the word gets around to the Pizza Express, or Kettners — places like that – and if the attendance isn't up to, say, a dozen by 11 pm, we apply a long-standing house rule summed up by the dictum — 'If they won't enter voluntarily, chuck'em in'. My partner and manager of the club, Mr. Pete King, had to set an

Typical glamour at Ronnie Scott's

example to the door staff and you just happened to be passing. It's what we call the 'Enforcement patronage' ploy — needs must — although, of course, we would prefer that people entered voluntarily.

It's none of my business, of course, but has Mrs. Coot good reason to be suspicious?
Yours sincerely,
Ronnie Scott
PS. If you can afford to eat at the Braganza you can afford to send me a pound.

20th February, 1984
Dear Mr. Scott,
Next time I dine at the Braganza, I shall take another route or bring some of the boys with me. I have a good mind to report the incident to Esther Rantzen and have your 'Enforced Patronage' ploy, as you quaintly describe it, exposed on TV. No, I am not enclosing my usual pound. I have sent it to Peter Boizot at the Pizza Express instead.
Yours sincerely,
Herbert Coot

WHISPERS, MURMURS & ASIDES

Had a little chuckle at a Grouchoism I heard for the first time, which I've slightly varied.
Guest: 'I didn't come here to be insulted!'
Groucho: 'Oh, where do you usually go? Ronnie Scott's ?'
CLARKY TEWKESBURY

At Scott's there's a
bouncer outside
Who's seven feet tall
and as wide
He's actually paid
To drum up some trade
By chucking the punters
inside.

Ron Rubin

INTERVIEW...
Ronnie recalling a visit to Hong Kong

NEMETHY

It's my belief — and you can only avoid the following profound conclusions by not reading on — that people concerned with Club management and compelled to treat with a turnover of temperamental musicians, fractious staff and difficult customers — tend to view the human race with a jaundiced eye; keep, as best they can, a safe distance between themselves and other members of that race. And the longer they are at the game the more wary they become.

In the case of messrs Ronnie Scott and Pete King, their track record is lengthier than most — twenty years you may have read somewhere — and these two, as I can vouch, have cultivated a particularly telling expression (surely on a par with Benny Goodman's notorious glare known as 'The Ray') that indicates they'd be happy if you'd withdraw from their sight forthwith.

Correction! Mr King is often extremely direct—with a vocabulary largely consisting of words that comprise the succinct invocation 'F-Off!' Few I know can deliver these immortal words with such panache and conviction.

One of Ronnie's tactics is to pretend that the subterranean gloom of his windowless office prevents him from seeing too clearly. He continues close examination of the *Racing Times* or the TV set which (also a tactic) is continuously switched on. By use of these subterfuges he hopes that the visitor, like toothache, will go away. He's not rude. Just extremely cautious. This combines with him being an exceptionally private person.

For six months now I have been putting together the Club's house magazine and not the least of my problems is the almost impenetrable wall of silence from Ronnie and Pete. I'd sooner lead the proverbial horse to the trough and make it drink than try to extract information from either of these gentlemen about club happenings.

One murky February evening I ventured into the inner office and there was Ronnie. He still looks at me as though uncertain of my identity, and still gives me the don't-I-know-you-from-somewhere-look. He quickly tried one of his favourite ploys.

'Oh, hello-er-Jim, isn't it? Sharon and Karen will be back in a minute. I am sure they can help you — '

'Not unless they've recently been playing tenor saxophone in Hong Kong', came my quick-as-a-flash riposte.

Sort of trapped, he spoke.

'Well, it was a great experience. Wouldn't have missed it for anything. It's like the ultimate Petticoat Lane. Jam-packed! Every street literally TEEMS with jostling humanity. Something else! Quite incredible.

It's so packed people have to walk sideways. They sleep in layers there. But no aggro. No raised voices. The Chinese are truly a polite race. Good vibes, everywhere. Better atmosphere than Frith Street on a Sunday morning. We got there on a Sunday night — absolutely exhausted. We'd been in the air for a total of nineteen hours. God didn't give man wings, nor intend him to be in the air that long. But quickly the electric atmosphere of the place rejuvenated us. Like a shot in the arm.

We made a tactical error in our first choice of a restaurant. All the customers, Chinese, were eating western food with knifes and forks. Not the Ronnie Scott Quartet. We wanted the genuine article- chopsticks and all. We soon became aware that we looked like those funny Europeans who want to act native. Mind you, our chopstick technique wasn't all that hot, but neither was the food. I found myself wishing I was back at the Won Tin in Gerrard Street. But that dodgy meal was the exception. The rest of the food we had was quite delicious.

One evening we were the guests of Sir Run Run Shaw – the Sam Goldwyn of the Far East. He gave us 100-year old eggs. True, you can get these at any greasehouse on the M1, but Sir Shaw's were quite superb. Apparently they are sliced and pickled with lime. The ones you get on the M1 are pickled in DAZ.

Yes, I did happen to pop along to the races. We were the guests of the American Club at the famous Happy Valley racecourse. No, I didn't win anything as it happens. Horses are much the same there as anywhere.

Illustration: Monty Sunshine

Slow, uneconomic. Like the population they tend to move sideways. At least, the nags I backed….

No, no rides in rickshaws. We hardly saw one. But I did see trumpeter Jimmy Deuchar who played with my nine- piece in 1953. And tenor saxophonist Red Price, trumpeter Benny Perrin, ex-drummer and racing car driver Les Leston, now in business there. I had a blow with Jimmy and some Filipino musicians whose names are quite unpronounceable — even if I could remember them — which I can't. Good players, though.

Yes, the Quartet went down well. We were the only jazz band in a Festival comprising ballet, classical music, dance troupes from various countries and the like. We got good notices in the press—can't seem to lay my hands on them this very minute. No, I didn't crack any jokes. My Chinese is very limited. Actually, the audiences were mainly European. Only a few rather bemused looking Chinese. The mask of inscrutability dropped when we started. Unlike the Japanese they don't seem to dig jazz. Strange, isn't it?

Yes, we met quite a few people who had been to the Club. I only hope they didn't emigrate after the experience. I'd hate to think so. God knows we try hard to wow them here night after night but maybe we've lost one or two to the Empire. That's showbiz…

Excuse me, I must answer the phone. Who? Orthopaedic Beds? Oh, yes, I remember you now. What! Endorse your beds in an advert. No, I am sorry, I can't. It's three years since you sold me your product after a load of old chat, and nothing happened. I've still got a bad back. Oh yes, my wife likes the bed, but she 's got different springing. No, sorry – Good afternoon. The idiots! They sell me this bed three years ago and I am still suffering. It's probably due to all that bowing to ecstatic applause.'

'Or peering into the gloom to see if there's anyone there.'

'Oh, very witty — er — whatever your name is. You must stand in for me when I'm on tour. Can you play tenor as well? No? Well, it's not difficult, not according to some critics.

Back to Hong Kong… I wish I could go

back tonight, it was truly a wonderful experience. An assault on the senses. It makes Soho seems like Stockton on early closing day. I've never experienced such an atmosphere. Not even in New York, though, there's no sense of menace. As I say, good vibes. I'd like to record my thanks to Sir Run Run Shaw, Les Leston and Mr and Mrs Frank Chao for their hospitality and to Barbara and Bernadette and everyone connected with the Hong Kong Festival for their efficient running of the show for making us feel so much at ease. We hope to see them all again in the near future.

Now, er — Jim — isn't it — I really must make a note of your name sometime — I've got to get in some practice.'

I fled. As I've said before, anyone practising that instrument in a confined space is a dimension of hell. Out into Soho I, once again, had young ladies in doorways entreating me to join them for a good time, which is extremely hospitable of them, but I had to get home and write the column which, for the first time, actually justifies its title of 'Interview'.   J.G

Ronnie Scott's Big Band (1955): from left to right: Front: Pete King, Dougie Robinson, Joe Harriott, Benny Green, Ronnie Scott; Second row: Hank Shaw, Stan Palmer, Jimmy Watson, Dave Usden, Art Baxter (vocalist); Rear: Robin Kay, Jack Botterill, Ken Wray, Mac Minshull. Not shown are pianist Norman Stenfalt and drummmer Phil Seamen. This aggregation Ronnie called his 'aggrevation' band...

STAN TRACEY
interview with pianist, composer, arranger and leader

Stan Tracey by Cole

When I first rang Stan to fix this interview he wasn't in the best of tempers. 'Here I am, writing the notes for a CD with one of my compositions on it, and the pianist has screwed up the melody. Do I mention this in my notes?' But he was in fine humour when he and his wife and business manager, Jackie, came to my flat, or, to put in another way, he was genially acerbic. Two hours went very quickly. J.G.

JG: Was your family musical?
ST: My mother played on the clapped-out old piano we had. She played the black notes only. She also took up the violin and was artistic in so many other ways.
JG: What was your father's job?
ST: He was the general factotum in a club called Jack's in Orange Street. It was a watering hole for variety artists like Naughton and Gold of the Crazy Gang. He wasn't musical.
JG: Your first instrument was the accordion. Did you have lessons?
ST: The shop I bought it from gave lessons. I had a few, they were into tangos. I learned how to play *La Cumparsita*. It was my party piece.
JG: Would you play the accordion these days?
ST: No fear! No bloody fear!!
JG: Glad to hear it! I hope you don't mind my saying that I think your first instrument an abomination in jazz. I have thought so ever since I heard Cornell Smeltzer squeezing away on *Accordion Joe* with Duke Ellington. What a contrast between him and the rest of the guys!
ST: It's ghastly! It's bad enough being a second class citizen as a jazz musician, but the moment you strap on an accordeon you're a third class citizen immediately.

ENSA

JG: In 1943 you joined ENSA when you were seventeen. Any names with you then that we would know?
ST: No, ENSA was full of old variety acts who were grateful for the opportunity to work. It was a good war for them.
JG: When did you first start to play piano?
ST: One of the guys lugged a portable gramophone around and I heard 78s of Albert Ammons, Pete Johnson and Meade Lux Lewis. I was determined to be a boogie-woogie pianist. It was then I was escorted into the RAF.
JG: Escorted! I take it that you ignored that little note from His Majesty ordering you to attend a certain depot or barracks under pain of imprisonment if you didn't fancy it.

SELLERS, HANCOCK and MONKHOUSE

ST: Not quite. I gave my digs in Ashford, Kent, as my permanent address and it took them a year or so to catch up with me. I was in Carlisle when two RAF policemen heavily indicated that I went along with them. The ENSA manager persuaded them to let me see the week through. I was, after all, doing my bit playing the accordion for our brave boys. When I got to the RAF Station,

Padgate, I was given a grilling, but I wasn't punished. Apart from being in the RAF for two years, that is. I was supposed to be drafted to India as a telephonist, but I didn't fancy that and applied to join the Ralph Reader RAF Gang Show and ended up in Cadogan Gardens, West London, in the same office as Peter Sellers. He was the office boy, although he was in the RAF. Tony Hancock produced the show. We toured Egypt, Cyprus and Palestine. I played on a wreck of a mini-piano that was never tuned.
JG: That must have stood you in good stead for another wreck, at Ronnie's in Gerrard Street, from the late 1950s.
ST: Certainly did. It was in the RAF that I met up with Bob Monkhouse and accompanied him on broadcasts. I had chummed up with a baritone singer called Barry Martin and we intended to go on the halls as a double act - a sort of hip Bob and Alf Pearson. We went to every agent in the West End, including Bernard Delfont, but no-one wanted to know. By this time I'd heard Dizzy, Parker and Monk, but was still on accordion when I played with Eddie Thompson in 1950.
JG: With a gig fee of a pound, fifteen shillings or maybe two pounds?

ROY FOX

ST: Oh, I don't know about TWO quid. That was roughly what I was supposed to get when I went on tour with Roy Fox. The tour was a disaster. This one-time household name and millionaire was old hat, leaving a trail of dud cheques and not paying the guys. He would pay one of us a couple of quid, and borrow one of them back to keep another guy quiet.

JG: That was another world. You would have travelled on a coach which, with driver, cost 1/6d per hour. Digs 12/6d a night. Sometimes less.

(Here, Stan and I tried to recall if he and I had been in the same coach on a disastrous tour of Kenny Baker's Band with Tubby Hayes in the Borders in 1950/51. It was organised by a promoter called Duncan McKinnon — Drunken Duncan — the only man to have been carried into his own promotion, but our memories failed us. Perhaps, one day, Kenny Baker will refresh our memories.)

ST: I toured with Tony Crombie, then with guitarist Malcolm Mitchell, who billed himself as 'Merely Sensational', and Basil Kirchin, 'The Biggest Little Band In The Land'. There was talk of me joining Eric Delaney, but he'd heard that I then liked a smoke, and told someone, 'I wouldn't touch him with a barge pole.' A while later a cheery voice came on the phone asking me to join his band. It was Delaney. Quick as a flash,I enquired. 'Found a barge pole, then?'. End of telephone call.

In February 1957 I went on a tour with Ronnie Scott to America as part of the first Anglo-American band exchanges. We played in vast stadiums in a rock 'n roll show that included Laverne Baker, Fats Domino, Chuck Berry and The Schoolboys. We played one number every night - whilst people were looking for their seats. As Ronnie put it, 'They needed a British be-bop band like they needed a synagogue in Damascus'. Those exchanges were a farce. We were just tokens in the charade.

At our appearance in a genuine jazz club, the Blue Note, New York, the show started at nine. We were on at eight. We had to sign a piece of paper purporting that we received the same money as Eddie Condon was receiving in the UK. I've been living on it since.

TED HEATH

Later that year I joined Ted Heath. There wasn't a lot of solo space. It was OK financially, but stifling, and Ted was a very stiff and autocratic leader. For my solos I was presented with Frank Horrox's solos written out. I said, 'I can't read this flyshit', and, grudgingly, Ted let me do my own thing. He liked to hear the same solos all the time.

JG: You must have been reading music by then.

ST: I was reading by the time I left.

JG: Did you ever think of following the footsteps of Britishers Joe Saye, Ralph Sharon, Derek Smith, and Dill Jones by trying your luck in the States?

ST: Not for one minute! I realised how long it had taken me to establish whatever reputation here and the thought of starting all over again in a huge country where they already had one or two tasty players - no thanks.

JG: I'd like to ask how it was that Duke Ellington as a pianist influenced you. Most of the so-called modern school were into Bud Powell; very few found Duke a mentor.

ST: My first profound influence — once I had decided I wasn't going to be a boogie-woogie player — was Thelonious Monk, but it was not until I was in my early thirties that I cottoned on to Duke at the keyboard.

JG: Both The Duke and Thelonious are very percussive players, which is obvious in your style. Nobody could describe you as a pretty player.

ST: No, the world isn't like that.

JG: You became the pianist at Ronnie's, almost from the time it opened at Gerrard Street.

ST: Yes, I was the resident idiot.

JG: It has been well documented that you led the trio accompanying a succession of great US musicians, and that you had the odd tiff with some of them. Like Stan Getz, for instance. There was the occasion when Getz acted up, and your retort was 'Bollocks'.

The quizzical Stan. Photograph: David Redfern

Stan Tracey by Cole

ST: Oh, yes, quick as a flash. I got on well with most, especially with Ben Webster, Zoot Sims and Sonny Rollins, but not with Stan Getz, Lucky Thompson or Don Byas.

JG: You received a memorable accolade from Sonny Rollins, who said, 'People over here don't realise just how good you are'. You must have found that flattering.

ST: I was more surprised than flattered.

JG: The piano at Gerrard Street caused you a lot of problems.

ROLAND KIRK

ST: Yes, but not as much as it caused Steve Race the night Roland Kirk invited him to sit in, having heard that Steve had likened him to clown Charlie Cairoli. I warned Steve about the keys that didn't work, but, unintentionally, this compounded his floundering when Kirk deliberately gave him a hard time. He didn't like being compared to a clown.

JG: You were at the club for six years. Why did you stick it out?

ST: Because I enjoyed it. It was great playing with those giants, but very hard work. Six nights at the club, maybe a Sunday concert, and no holidays, and people were surprised that one took the odd — er — aspirin.

JG: Out of all your albums 'Under Milk Wood' has been the most critically acclaimed Are you still earning royalties on this?

ST: Very little. My belief is that three fans bought the original release and everyone else taped it. Seriously, it has sold only a few thousand copies in four issues. I've made a lot more out of other albums.

JG: The two with Acker Bilk, for instance?

ST: I got paid a straight £200 per session for these.

JG: How did you get on with Denis Preston, the producer? A hard, unfeeling man, in my view.

ST: I kept my distance, but I enjoyed talking to him about the Duke. He was very knowledgable about Duke. I got on a lot better with Acker — a very down-to-earth-no-bullshit guy.

JG: How did you feel about the phenomenal success of Trad, whilst most modern musicians at that time were struggling?

ST: No sour grapes. It was a fact of life then and you can't buck against that. But I liked listening to the uniforms!

JG: Talk about your drummer son, Clark. This may be difficult for you. You have been quoted as saying that you had been looking for a drummer that suits you all your life and there he was in your loins. Perhaps I can make it easy for you by saying that nobody would believe that you would have an inferior musician because he is your son. Nobody could accuse you of nepotism. Tell me what you like about his playing.

ST: He has great time, he swings, he listens, he embellishes, he underlines, knows when to let up, when to keep it simple. The only other drummers with whom I've been at ease are Phil Seamen, Tony Crombie and Ronnie Stephenson.

JG: I've just given you a cup of tea. Sorry I didn't take the tea bag out. Not into tea drinking. You refused a drink, but you were once a soak.

ST: Not because I liked the taste. I drank to get high, but not any more. I avoid pubs, they make me uneasy.

GERARD PRESENCER

JG: In the New Year, you are changing your instrumentation. Bringing in the young Gerard Presencer for Art Themen after all these years.

ST: I loved the years with Art, but I had to make a change, even though I'm old enough to be Gerard's grandfather. In fact, my grandson, Ben, Clarke's son, six years old, is nearer to Gerard's age than mine, but it's great to be working with such a fine young player. The records I made with him recently are being issued on John Jack's Cadillac label in March.

JG: You have received a number of awards.

ST: I'm afraid they mean nothing in terms of work, but it's nice to be recognised. Not quite the same as a full date sheet, but you can't have everything.

JG: Do you ever ponder on the difference between your talent and creativity and the financial rewards?

ST: What's the point? At my time of life I'm fairly at ease with what I've done, what I am doing and what I hope to do.

On this note Stan and Jackie had to excuse themselves. As is usual with chats as enjoyable as this there was much more said than we have space for, but some of Stan's comments, highly enjoyable, were quite unprintable. it was indeed a most entertaining couple of hours.

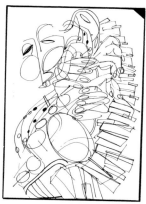

Illustration: Joy Johnson

RACE AGAINST (KIRK) TIME
STEVE RACE recalls a horrendous night at Ronnie's

Having read the interview with Stan Tracey I hastened round to see my old friend, the statuesque Ms Roxy Beaujolais, licensee of the Three Greyhounds in Greek Street.

'You look gobsmacked', she observed.

'The fact is I'm a bit baffled', I told her. 'You see, I once played one four-minute number at Ronnie Scott's old place. It was a third of a century ago but people still seem to be talking about it'.

'Because you were so good?' enquired Roxy.

'No, I floundered, to use Stan Tracey's apt expression. It was during Roland Kirk's visit in 1963. Kirk had a trick of playing three instruments at once, with an alto in one corner of his mouth, a soprano sax in the other corner and a clarinet in the middle, with a couple more blowing instruments slung around his neck as spares. At his waist he had a small hunting horn on which he used to go whoop-whoop at the end.

'Ye gods, quite the novelty multi-instrumentalist!', Roxy observed. 'Sounds like Charlie Cairoli,' she added.

Charlie Cairoli

'Funny you should say that. I'd described Kirk in a magazine as 'the Charlie Cairoli of jazz'. Someone read him my comments, with the result that Kirk rang me in my office in a towering rage. 'You called me a circus clown', he shouted (which incidentally I hadn't done). I tried to pacify him but he wouldn't listen. Anyway, a couple of nights later I slipped into Ronnie's to hear the man again, but someone tipped him the wink that I was in. He made an announcement about critics who think they're musicians, and called me out in order to make a fool of me. 'Come down here and play, Brother Race', he demanded.

'What did you do?' asked Roxy.

'I told him I'd rather listen to Brother Tracey, which God knows was true, but he insisted. So Stan moved aside from the piano stool, generously explaining to me which notes didn't work on the piano. (They included a whole octave around the middle of the keyboard). Roland Kirk announced that we would play *These Foolish Things*. He beat in a medium-four tempo and I played a suitable intro, whereupon Kirk came roaring in at exactly double the speed'.

'Ah, challenging stuff! What did you do?'

'I floundered. I was nervous, playing at no notice with such a great jazzman. Moreover, I'd had a fairly liquid dinner and was a trifle Godbolted'.

'Go on'.

'The following week I described the evening as fairly as I could in my *Melody Maker* column, and later in my autobiography. Years went by. Ronnie bought a newly-reconditioned piano. The club moved to its present premises in Frith Street. Stan Tracey wrote that marvellous *Under Milk Wood Suite* of his. And Roland Kirk died in 1977.

'So that was the end of it,' said Roxy

'You'd have thought so, wouldn't you?' I replied.

'Did you ever play play the piano at Ronnie Scott's again?'.

'No I never did. But sometimes I dream I'm there'.

'Accompanying Roland Kirk, you mean?'.

'No, Charlie Cairoli'.

Ronald Kirk

RONNIE'S JOKES

Roland Kirk was three of the most unforgettable musicians we ever had at the Club. The first time he came he introduced the nose flute. The second time he came he demonstrated the ear flute. Quite frankly, I couldn't bear to think what his next flute might be. But nobody slept while Roland was on. At other times we have had the odd person from Rent-a-Corpse and there are some audiences which amaze me by the way in which they control themselves.

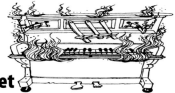

GIGS FROM HELL
The Scott's Club solicitor and alto saxophonist,
WALLY HOUSER, recalls gigs he'd rather forget

During my heyday as a musician (if I actually ever had a heyday) one could not afford to be choosy. The phone rang (if you were lucky) and some local exploiter of musicians — usually a non-playing band leader, something, I suppose, like the non-playing captain of a Davis Cup team — would offer you a gig. If you knew what was good for you, you accepted with profuse thanks.

Not for the likes of me were the gigs Ronnie Scott and Tubby Hayes got. These giants would be paid £10 or more. I was strictly a thirty bob man… two pounds if I was lucky and a fiver on New Year's Eve. I am speaking, of course, of the Fifties — almost half a century ago and positively medieval as regards the contrast with today's cultural standards. You never played a gig in anything other than a dinner suit (don't forget the black socks!) and you worked like a navvy. Take, for example, the Nantwich Hunt Ball in 1956. After 46 years, I do not know if it really was a hunt ball. It may have been a golf or cricket club dance, but it was held in a hall with dead animals' heads on the walls and the members were the sort of people I always instinctively hated — awash with self esteem.

SLAVE RATIONS
I was playing in a band run by a very nice man called Freddie Bracegirdle. He was a competent bass player and sufficiently socially aware to call the band Freddie Bamford and his Music. We left Manchester at 4pm and were expected to start playing for the reception at 5.30. At 7pm, we were allowed a 10-minute break and a glass of water (seriously!). We played through dinner from 7.15 to 9.30 at which time we were told that, after 15-minute break, dancing would commence until 1 am. All seven members of the band looked at each other with a wild surmise until the trumpet player rose, stepped off the stand, walked the length of the hall to the top table where he stood before the Master/President surrounded, as he was, by adoring fat ladies and sycophants.

Harry, the said trumpet player, fell to his knees: 'Please, sir', he whines. 'Me and the boys are hungry. Can we have some scraps?' He then stretched out with his forehead to the floor like a kowtowing coolie before the Emperor. After the embarrassment subsided, we were given food. Not the haunch of venison or the foie gras that the august assembly had enjoyed, but a small sandwich filled with some meat paste or other, which Harry reckoned was Kit-e-Kat… and a glass of water.

OFF TO THE SALT MINES
We actually finished playing at 2 a.m. By the time we got back home it was daylight. We had worked for more than eight hours for two pounds each. Five bob an hour and pay your own travelling expenses. A landmark gig.

The year before, I had been playing in Edinburgh at the musical equivalent of the salt mines of Siberia, the Mecca Dance Hall. For £12 per week, less tax, we worked every afternoon and evening, bar Sunday when the town was closed. We also rehearsed on Wednesday mornings and had a lunch hour session on the same day. Fourteen sessions a week for £12 less tax. Work it out!

However it was not a bad job by the standards of the day, but there was one unforgettable August night. The American fleet suddenly turned up in the Firth of Forth. About two thousand sex-starved Yankee sailors flush with money and testosterone came down like a wolf on the fold. About a thousand of them came into our dance hall, to the rage of the local yahoos.

The heat was intense, the atmosphere electric. It was clearly going to explode and at 10pm precisely, it did. The Edinburgh toughs are — or were — in a class of their own. They were fearless and deputed half a dozen of their number to guard the bandstand and protect the band. The free-for-all lasted about an hour. It was a large hall holding about two thousand people and the carnage was like one of those scenes in a Western. You know. People flying over bars, through mirrors, over the balcony. Smashed bottles everywhere. But it had none of the underlying humour of the film fight. It was bitter, brutal and bloody. The police stayed away. And the band played on… I was amazed no one was killed. It was terrifying.

These are just a couple of memories that stand out. There are many more. Maybe some time we'll revisit a few more which I have buried in my subconscious over the years.

Illustration: Pennington

A Day in The Life... of the Editor

I, the editor of *JARS*, sit imperiously in a high-backed executive chair at an enormous desk with a vast array of multi-coloured telephones through which I bark orders. I am situated in front of a large window from which the glare of daylight disconcerts those sitting before me. Hitler used this ploy when receiving visiting politicians. I find it most effective.

I call weekly editorial meetings at which I instruct my staff as to content, presentation, photos and cartoons required, usually to a chorus of total approval.

Occasionally, there are questions timorously raised, to which I permit myself an indulgent smile, indicating that Godbolt Almighty grants that young (well, youngish,) people should have their say, but usually I wave a dismissive hand, letting them know who's boss. Oh, the heady excitement of power! During these sessions, I am brought tea by the office boy, who apprehensively awaits my first sip to see that it has the required balance of tea, milk and sugar, all of organic origin, of course...

At the conclusion of these meetings, the staff respectfully bow out, murmuring incantations of appreciation as to how lucky they are to be under such inspiring leadership.

SWAMPED WITH ADVERTS

As for the vital advertising, I am daily — nay, hourly — inundated with calls from eager advertisers, some so anxious to book space that they call personally with a pre-paid cheque in one hand and a bottle of Johnnie Walker in the other, expressing the hope that I won't regard the whisky as a bribe, offensive to a man of my renowned probity. Their artwork is always the required proportion and delivered promptly to meet our deadlines.

PURE FANTASY

No it is not, and all the above is pure fantasy, although I devoutly wish it were true. *JARS* is produced in the work room of my flat on a table dominated by a computer and printer, surrounded by piles of drafts, jottings, press handouts, photos and letters. The 'in-house staff' consists of me and Chrissie Murray — she, alas, part-time. As for there being a commanding voice…

The truth is that Chrissie and myself have widely divergent views — as evidenced by her *Making Waves* column that encompasses contemporary events and me, in my *Flashback* features, recalling the giants, most now dead, who established jazz as the most potent music of the 20th century

TMM & QOF

Chrissie is TMM — Thoroughly Modern Millie — and I am QOF – Quintessential Old Fart — but, hopefully, from these opposite views emerges a magazine, now twenty-four years old, that reflects the present activities, history and ethos of the forty-five years old institution that is Ronnie Scott's Club, as well as mirroring the jazz scene generally. In this regard I am very lucky to have the services of Chrissie (as she constantly reminds me!) who has wide editorial experience working with such publications as *Cosmopolitan, Elle, The Sunday Telegraph, The Wire* and *Jazzwise* and in having (crawl, crawl) club director Pete King who, like Ronnie before him, lets us get on with the job and, mainly, approves our material.

As for advertising, vital revenue, I battle in a small, but fiercely competitive area, spend much of my time supplicating for this input, chasing the artwork and thereafter pleading with accounts departments for settlement of our invoices.

GODSBOIL – THE ULTIMATE IN SUPPURATION

The office boy..? That's me. I make the tea, empty the wastepaper baskets, hoover up, go to the stationery cupboard as bidden by Ms Murray and post the mail. Every Monday afternoon I deliver *JARS* to the specialist record shops in London's West End to ensure, for the benefit of our advertisers as well as the club management, that copies are on prominent display. All in all, I suppose I could be described as a space salesman, accounts chaser and office and delivery boy who does a bit of writing and editing in between.

Regarding the masses of paper on our desk, there are letters pointing to 'literals', and from PR ladies who appear to think we publish weekly, and one who believes that a rock 'n' roll concert in Barnsley would captivate our readers. One such communication I have before me is addressed to a 'Mr Godsboil', surely the ultimate suppuration. How many other editors can make such a boast?

But, please, I'm not complaining. I'm very lucky to have the job and regard the hassles a challenge, and without them the pleasure of having a good whinge is lost. Perish the thought!!

Apropos those accursed 'literals' that escape our closest scrutiny, there was a bloomer in the May-June issue. In one line, 'Big Boy' Goudie, in the review of the Django Reinhardt four-CD set on Properbox, is given as a tenor saxophonist, which he was. Two lines later he was a violinist, which he was not. 'Big Boy', by the way, isn't a reference to his height or weight.

Typical Scott members jumping with joy at the thought of hearing Ronnie's joke routine again

INTERVIEW...
the Editor compared with Barney Schatt

NEMETHY

Those who have read this mag since its inception will know what a harrowing experience it has been for me to wrest a word from the boss of 47 Frith Street, one Ronnie Scott, tenor saxophonist, raconteur, fancier of racing horses and inveterate watcher of TV. Squeezing blood out of stone or pleading with record companies for advertising has been a doddle in comparison.

Most bandleaders are only too keen to inform the populace about their activities. Not Ronnie. He didn't even tell me about assembling a large band, the first for many years, to accompany Ella Fitzgerald and Oscar Peterson for a season at the sprauncy Grosvenor House, Park Lane — where the tickets were a mere thirty quid a head — in July. A prestigious engagement that would have made nice copy for the June/July issue, but I learned of the gig reading the *Evening Standard*.

Peeved, I walked in his office to complain and — wonder of wonders — got the big welcome from Mr. Scott. 'Ah, Jim, how nice to see you. Please take a pew.'

I said to myself: Hello, hello, hello, what's all this, then?

Ella by Wally 'Trog' Fawkes

Normally when I enter his office he doesn't recall my name, has never asked me to take a seat, can barely take his eyes off the *Sporting Chronicle* or TV. I admit to having my suspicions. After thirty years in the business in a variety of roles I've acquired a certain wariness about mankind in general and jazz musicians in particular. Was it the sack? And the handshake would be anything but golden in these unsettled times. But, I quickly reassured myself — who else would do the job? Who else would battle with this solid wall of silence from the guv'nor and minions equally sworn to secrecy about their activities? There can't be another masochist of my ilk who'd grapple with such difficulties.

'Have a cigar, Jim. They're specially flown over from Havana.'

What is all this, I wondered? He may be hazy about my name, but knows I don't touch the pollutant weed.

'I don't smoke.'

'Well, pop one in your top pocket. They look quite impressive. You haven't got a suit?! Not even one for Sundays? I know we don't pay you very much, but this is ridiculous. Look, I've got one that will fit you. Haven't worn it since I bought it from Cecil Gee's twenty-five years ago — but judging from your usual style of clobber nobody will notice it's out of date.'

'Thank you.'

'Don't mention it. In fact, I've got something else you'll like. A really jazzy green eye-shade. Every editor should have one. This one is YOU. It belonged to my Uncle Barnet Schatt who edited the *Stepney and District Jewish Herald* just after the First World War. It's really a prized family heirloom but for *you…*'

'My Uncle Barney was similar to yourself, y'know. Strong and fearless in his approach to truth. Is that chair quite comfortable? Would you like a cup of tea? Sorry I can't offer you a drink — I know you like a glass — but the bar's closed.'

By now, I am truly worried. I voiced my suspicions.

What's all this solicitude about?

'I only wanted to say how noble it was of you to use that Steven Nemethy cartoon of you and myself in the June/July issue. He's caught my distinguished features admirably, but – heavens – he didn't half make you look a Mr. Nasty. He's made you practically bald, given you evil eyes and mean lips. I feel for you, though. Honestly, I myself have suffered — from Jak in the *Evening Standard*, Wally 'Trog' Fawkes of the *Daily Mail* and Richard Cole of the *Daily Express*. Mind you, the more I look at you, perhaps Steven wasn't that far out.'

'Thank you. But is this acknowledgement of my name, being offered a seat, cigar and a suit just because I published Steve's cartoon?'

'Just say it's my appreciation of you finding such a first-class draughtsman for the paper, but there is another matter I want to mention.'

I braced myself for the crunch. 'In Alun Morgan's excellent article on Art Pepper in the previous issue of *JARS* you overlooked half a sentence that bore no relationship to the previous or following paragraph. I'd be most grateful if you'd pay more attention when you're checking proofs.'

I felt immense relief. Things were as before. Ronnie, from whom I can barely get a word, who wouldn't put pen to paper even at gun point, is, nevertheless, hawk-eyed when it comes to errors in print — especially in this magazine. When I deliver each new issue I'm in a state of fear and trembling as to what errors I've overlooked he'll invariably notice. With a quite uncanny homing instinct his eyes immediately alight on the offending blemishes.

My relief that things were as normal

probably made me a little cocky, and I retaliated.

'It would have been nice if you, or any of your staff, had let me know you were doing a season with a big band at the Grosvenor House with Ella and Oscar.'

It's likely that my lips tightened, that my eyes glinted evilly, that I threw back my head enough for the 40 watt bulb in Ronnie's office to catch my receding hairline. The Guv'nor peered closely at me.

'Hmmm, I can clearly see now how Nemethy pictured you. Now, if you'll excuse me.'

'I know! You're going to say 'Must get in some practice. Don't have to, of course, but conscience compels me.'

'Jim! You're taking the words out of my mouth.'

'Ronnie, I know that spiel word for word, nuance for nuance but, don't worry, I'm off.'

As I've said before, anyone practising the tenor saxophone in a confined space is hard on the ears and, once again, I fled into darkest Soho, bumping into a bunch of swarthy gentlemen talking in Mediterranean tongues and, apparently, having nothing to do but to hang around the betting shop opposite Ronnie's but, more than likely, having a piece, so to speak, of those friendly ladies who speak so familiarly to one in these parts.　　　　　J.G.

Oscar Peterson by Richard Cole

Slawkenbergius

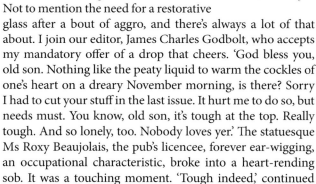

I have sworn, many times over, to summon up the resolve to pass the portals of the Three Greyhounds, 25 Greek Street, when I'm on my rounds in saucy Soho and its environs. But, resolve is one thing and habit is another. Not to mention the need for a restorative glass after a bout of aggro, and there's always a lot of that about. I join our editor, James Charles Godbolt, who accepts my mandatory offer of a drop that cheers. 'God bless you, old son. Nothing like the peaty liquid to warm the cockles of one's heart on a dreary November morning, is there? Sorry I had to cut your stuff in the last issue. It hurt me to do so, but needs must. You know, old son, it's tough at the top. Really tough. And so lonely, too. Nobody loves yer.' The statuesque Ms Roxy Beaujolais, the pub's licencee, forever ear-wigging, an occupational characteristic, broke into a heart-rending sob. It was a touching moment. 'Tough indeed,' continued JG, 'I've just been talking to Ronnie Scott . . .'

At the very mention of the name of our favourite OBE, the editor and myself bowed in obeisance, and were joined in this genuflection by Ms Beaujolais, who for seven long years, was on the door at Ronnie's. It was yet another touching moment. After this respectful pause, JG enquired, 'Do you know what he said?'

'Not being psychic, I wouldn't know', I countered.

'No need for that, old son. You know the question was purely rhetorical. If I may continue, I have read Ronnie's foreword to Tim Motion's lovely *Jazz Portraits*, and I said to Mr Scott, 'How come you write for other people, but I can't get you to write a word for your own house magazine. He said, 'Goldblatt, or whatever your name is, you couldn't afford me.' You could have knocked me down with a sledgehammer. But it's a line I'm going to use when those total strangers come on the phone for info. One doesn't mind scratching around for mates, but not for media researchers always on the cadge.'

'I know from the off they're after something for nothing, because they start with an enquiry after my health and the queries invariably go back to the mists of time. 'It's YOUR era,' they say, as though I'd just emerged from primeval swamps having just beaten off man-eating pterodactyls and dinosaurs. Why is this, old son?'

I hadn't the heart to tell JG that his antiquity was the reason and offered him a commiserative glass, which he sunk as if there was no tomorrow, and I continued on my rounds.

Talking of 'be-bop', some doughty veterans meet every Sunday lunchtime in the basement of the Kings Arms, Crouch End Hill, north London. The hard core of these gatherings comprises Club Eleven pioneer Laurie Morgan (drums), Iggy Quayle (piano) and Coleridge Goode (bass). Dancing, children welcome and the basement has its own bar.

PADDY'S PIANO

Have you heard the one about the Irish publican who was approached by certain musicians to get a gig at his pub? The pianist enquired, 'Have you got a piano?'

'Aye', said Paddy, 'and it's staying where it's safe — in the cellar.'

Roxy, Soho's grand dame licensee in her wedding corset, posed years after the happy event

65

Letter from Tchaikovsky to Ellington
imagined by JIM GODBOLT

JARS continues its tribute to the memory of pianist, composer, arranger and leader, 'Duke' Ellington, on the 20th anniversary of his death on 24th May, 1974, with an imagined letter (first published in *Jazz News*, 29th March 1961), to the Duke from Peter Ilich Tchaikovsky, on the occasion of Tchaikovsky's *The Nutcracker Suite*, reinterpreted, and movements retitled, by Duke Ellington and Billy Strayhorn and played by the Ellington Orchestra, recorded in May/June 1960, and now available, superbly remastered, on CD, Columbia Col 472 3562, in the Sony Jazz 'Passport' series.

Duke Ellington (piano) leading Ray Nance, Andres Meringuito, Willie Cook, Eddie Mullins (trumpets); Johnny Hodges, Paul Gonsalves, Russell Procope, Jimmy Hamilton (reeds); Juan Tizol, Lawrence Brown, Britt Woodman, Booty Wood (trombones); Aaron Bell (bass); Sam Woodyard (drums)

Overture; Toot Toot Tootie Toot (Dance of The Red-Pipes); Peanut Brittle Brigade (March); Sugar Rum Cherry (Dance of The Sugar Plum Fairy): Entr'acte: The Volga Vouty (Russian Dance); Chinoiserie (Chinese Dance); Dance Of The Floeradores (Waltz of the Flowers); Arabesque Cookie (Arabian Dance).

Dear Mr. Ellington,

Thanks to the miraculous system of music reproduction in your society and extra-terrestrial channels of communication, I have had the great pleasure of hearing my work, 'The Nutcracker Suite', as interpreted by yourself and your collaborator, Mr William Strayhorn, and I am writing to warmly congratulate you both on your orchestration and the excellence of your orchestra's performance. I am very happy to share my work with such talented musicians.

Since 1943, fifty years after my departure from mortal life, I, thanks to lapse of copyright control, have heard some monstrous plagiarisms of my compositions and I am particularly incensed by those 20th century song writers who have attached modern lyrics to these, but your orchestration and performance of my Suite impressed me for its exotic nuances, the very like of which I sought to achieve.

The more I listen to the dexterity of your scoring, the more I am amazed at the sense of form and breadth of imagination that animates you and Mr Strayhorn, and the technical agility and sublime ingenuity of the virtuosi who play those extraordinarily imaginative cadenzas.

The fact that these are tied largely to 4/4 time makes the skill of your musicians even more astonishing, and I perceive that no notation could encompass the shifts, phrasing and dynamics so displayed. The interweaving of your solo and orchestral parts intrigues me beyond measure. I am not familiar with the attachments to the trombones, but I am greatly entranced by the bizarre and exciting tone colours achieved with these devices, So many gradations of light and shade!

I notice extensive use of Mr Adolphe Sax's invention which was not much used in my day, and the tone and facility of your players, Mr. Harold Carney, Mr Paul Gonsalves and Mr. Cornelius Hodges, comes as a refreshing, and often startling, experience. I also commend the bamboo flute expertise of Mr. Russell Procope. The freedom extended to your virtuosi is something their counterparts of my day would have perhaps envied but, I have no illusions, they would not have been capable of such perfectly shaped improvisations and, in any case, the jazz idiom would have utterly confounded them as, I'm sure, it confounds most formal musicians of your time.

Your rhythm I also admire, and although mostly in common time, it achieves a remarkable elasticity and variety of patterns, and superbly buttresses your imaginative textures. If I have a criticism, it is that your percussionist, Mr. Samuel Woodyard, administrates his sticks a little too loudly for my ears, but I admit that unfamiliarity with the idiom could account for this unease of mine. Also, I am a little puzzled by the academic tone of the orchestral clarionettists I knew, and seemingly out of place with the

The Duke by Trog

timbre displayed by the rest of your musicians. It doesn't strike me as compatible.

But this is a minor criticism and may I continue my paeans of praise by complimenting you, sir, on your piano playing. Its harmonic subtleties and perfunctory aptness in the ensemble is a sheer delight.

I have heard that your critics, one a Mr. Max Harrison, have seen fit to accuse you of plagiaristic vulgarity, but you have my fullest support and to hell with your critics. They sound (especially, it appears, this Mr Harrison), very much like those of my generation – captious but without one scrap of creative ability themselves. As for plagiarism, may I say I am not the least offended that my themes have been used by yourself. In fact, I regard your interpretation as flattery of the highest order. I am also complimented that this is the first time you have devoted an entire recording session to another composer's work and I am intrigued by your retitling, especially the name you chose for my Dance Of The Red Pipes- Toot Tootie Toot! And The Volga Vouty! What, pray, is a Vouty and an Arabesque Cookie?

I suspect waggish associations. Obviously, you have a finely developed sense of humour. I conclude with praise for the strength, range and poise of your brass and saxophone sections, the sturdy resonance of Mr Raymond Nance, the ebullience of Mr Lawrence Brown and the animation of Mr Aaron Bell, but, if I have to single out one of your virtuosi for especial

Peter Tchaikovsky thinking about critics?

commendation it would be Mr Hodges, for his haunting tone and ravishing improvisation on Arabian Dance – sorry – Arabesque Cookie.

I look forward Mr Ellington, to further rearrangements of my works.

Yours sincerely,

Peter Tchaikovsky

Tchaikovsky and Ellington, of totally different cultures, living in different eras, were both superb tune writers and orchestrators. I like to think that had correspondence been possible, the above is what Tchaikovsky would have written.

Ellington and Strayhorn obviously approached their interpretation of the 'Nutcracker' with the utmost reverence. In their liner notes, the Duke is quoted as saying, 'That cat was it.' I feel that Tchaikovsky would have been equally complimentary about Ellington, although not, of course, in the argot of a twentieth century Harlemite African-American.   J.G.

WHISPERS, MURMURS & ASIDES

BATTLING ROBIN

Where did the England batsman Robin Smith go to relax after his courageous innings, facing those fearsome West Indian fast bowlers, that set England up for victory on the Saturday of the Lords Test? Why, Ronnie Scott's Club to hear Irakere. Talking of cricketers, club manager Pete King told me of the night that Imran Khan, the one who has married into the Goldsmith billions, came to the Club and the foyer was strewn with swooning females, much, Pete said, to the annoyance of husbands and boyfriends. What was it he'd got they hadn't?

RACHMANINOV AND THE HOSTESS

I heard a lovely tale on Radio 3. Oh, yes, it's yer culture output for me, despite its meagre allocation of time for jazz on a station existing for minority interests, but 'twas always thus .

Pianist Shura Cherkassy was the story teller. In 1919, or thereabouts, pianist/composer Sergei Rachmaninov was in New York and received an invite from a society hostess to attend a dinner and play for her guests. No money mentioned.

Sergei wrote back saying he would be pleased to accept her invitation, but would require 500 dollars, a small fortune then. She wrote back agreeing to the figure, but with the rider that he was not to mix with the guests. Rachmaninov wrote back —'In which case, I'll only charge 300 dollars.'

Like it. A fairly apposite story in the jazz world was the occasion in a Chelsea club when a certain pianist known for unasked hogging of the keyboard was at it. The club proprietor offered a certain saxophonist a tenner to go and break the pianist's arm.

'No, certainly not! Make it a fiver', replied the saxophonist.   TALCOTT MALAGROWTHER

DO YOU PLAY REQUESTS?*
RON RUBIN rubinates on a pianist's occupational hazard

LOST IN PRONUNCIATION

In Switzerland, a Bill Evans devotee asked for How My Heart Sinks, and in Germany and Austria I have had many a request for Stink (Sting — more properly, The Entertainer). Other garbled requests in Germanic territory have been 'Would You Like To Take A Wok', 'I Only Have Ice For You', and what sounded exactly like 'Veal Meat Again'. A fellow-musician told me he once had a request for what sounded to him like Sid James in Germany. (It turned out to be St James Infirmary…) Perhaps he was getting a bit Mutt-and-Jeff, as I am these days. (Did I really have requests for 'Chinese Stockings', 'Wonderbra', 'It's Hugh or No One' and 'London Derrière'?

THE HAZARDOUS

At a Zurich piano bar, back in the 1970s, I noticed a young fellow eying me across the lid of the grand piano (Heaped with fur coats, it doubled as a cloakroom). Shortly afterwards, a waiter came over: on his tray lay a large Scotch, a red rose and a request for 'Are You Lonesome Tonight?' (That'll teach me to segue from Mad About the Boy straight into The Man I Love…)
One night during the month I did at a hotel in Fribourg, Switzerland, a young girl who had been sitting between two rather sinister Mafioso types, both wearing shades, rushed up to the piano. 'Please help me!' she said in a hoarse whisper. My panic subsided when I realised that (a) this was apparently the name of a song (presumably in translation), and (b) she had one heck of a bad cold.
Also in the 1970s, at a US Officer's Club in Spain, I was constantly badgered to play Country music. I managed to convince the nice young pilots that Country & Western hadn't yet reached the UK. Then one evening they turned up with a copy of The Complete Works of Hank Williams — all 129 of the wretched things — which they'd found in the PX, and presented it to me with a rather touching dedication on the flyleaf. One of their number liked to tape the piano music on his reel-to-reel tape recorder. Well, if perchance ex-pilot Chuck Miller

of the VR-52 Det. Washington DC (C-118 Cruise) is still in possession of such musical gems as Your Cheatin' Heart, Hey Good Lookin' and Jambalaya, perpetrated by yours truly on the pianoforte, I'd gladly buy it from him. Just name the price, Chuck…

THE MADDENING

A request for 'something lively' just after I'd bashed out Honky Tonk Train Blues didn't put me in the best of moods. Neither did the two fellows in a Chelsea bistro who wanted to know: 'Where can we go to hear some jazz?' (I'd just played my Ellington/Strayhorn medley). But a request at Kettner's in Soho to play Trumpet Voluntary on the piano wasn't so wide of the mark. I later learned that the piece — falsely attributed to Purcell — was originally written by Jeremiah Clarke as a harpsichord solo.
Now picture this scene at the Bristol Hotel, Oslo: myself seated at the grand piano at the end of a long, elegant bar. At the far end of the room a party of noisy, drunk Germans. Every now and then one of them would bawl out: 'Play Beethoven's Fifth Symphony!'
Finally, I couldn't take any more. I walked across to their table and said, as sarcastically as I could manage: 'I suppose you are aware that there's no piano in symphony orchestra?' The loudest and the fattest shouted back: 'I don't care about that — just play Beethoven's Fifth Symphony!' I went back to the piano, and — if it's possible to play ironically — I ironically banged out those famous first eight notes. The whole bunch of them stood up and cheered, and I was force-fed aquavit and Scotch for the rest of the night. I decided there and then to memorise a few of the more popular symphonies for future use — just the first few notes, you understand…
In the 1980s I worked occasionally at a Zurich hotel bar which used to get so crowded late at night that a burly fellow was posted on the door to keep people out. I had one great fan who used to come in almost nightly. He always asked for Take Six and didn't seem to mind when I played in 5/4. When in his cups he would harangue the bemused customers, yelling: 'Pearls before SCHWEIN! Pearls before SCHWEIN!' He was eventually banned from the place, and I lost my one-man fan club.
The following exchange took place at a private party in a West End restaurant:
Punter: Excuse me — can you play any jazz?
Myself(somewhat testily): I'll have you know I've been playing jazz for over fifty years!
Punter: Oh, sorry — then you must be pretty fed up with it by now. I don't mind of you play something else…
Myself: No, no — you misunderstand me. I actually enjoy playing jazz. What would you like to hear?
Punter: How about Stranger on the Shore?
Myself: Say no more…
*Only if they're asked for…

'That's what not I've heard about band singers'
Illustration: Chick Jacob by kind permission of Punch

THE 'PRINCE OF DARKNESS' & 'BLACK LARRY'

In the 1950s, when Soho was a rundown area, where you could rent a room for fifty bob a week, it abounded in many Runyonesque characters, seemingly without means of livelihood, one of whom was Gypsy Larry, also known as 'Black' Larry, long-time general factotum at Ronnie Scott's Club, principally as a cleaner. In his book *Some of My Best Friends are Blues* (ghosted by Mike Hennessey) Ronnie recalled what must have been a riveting incident at the Club…

'One night Miles Davis came into the Club with his entourage — including his dentist, hairdresser, lawyer and a couple of very impressive ladies… There was much deferential bowing and scraping, much fluttering of waitresses and a constant hiss of stage whispers as customers pointed out the great man to one another.

'Miles, a slim, elegantly dressed figure with outsize dark glasses, sat through it all inscrutably. It was a momentous occasion, but it made no impression at all on Gypsy Larry. If he knew who Miles Davis was, he certainly didn't care, and when 3.30 a.m. came and Miles Davis and his party were still sitting at their tables, Larry appeared with his broom and unceremoniously turned them out. 'Come on, you lot — time to get out. I've got to sweep up here — come on, out of it!'— and Miles and his acolytes got to their feet humbly and drifted quietly away into the night.'

Pianist Johnny Parker writes: In the summer of 1953, I was living at 22 Frith Street, opposite where the Ronnie Scott Club now sits. It was next door to the site of the house where another pianist, Wolfgang Amadeus Mozart, lived, played and composed from 1764-65. One day I bumped into Gypsy Larry in Archer Street, which was the open-air social club and labour exchange for musicians, where I often used to see Ronnie Scott, Pete King and their cohorts. Larry invited me to his room in 'The Street, as the musicians affectionately called this little thoroughfare, just off Piccadilly.

He told me there was no electric light and it was 'a bit dingy', but the rent was cheap and it contained a piano, which he asked me to try out for him. We went round straight away and entered the room, which I can most kindly describe as squalid; the curtains had been up since the Old Queen died. Peering through the gloom, I espied the piano which was an ancient upright. A chair was provided and I sat down to play. My hand travelled up the keyboard and there, to my horror, I found what appeared to be a pair of human ears. They were plastic and sticky with adhesive.

'Don't worry,' said Larry, 'I'm sharing this pad with Ear'ole Jack and that's his spare pair.'

Ear'ole Jack had lost his ears in some fracas, but had obtained these artificial ones, which he stuck on before he left home. He was a bit sensitive about them and one day asked Larry if they were obviously false as people in the street had been giving him funny looks. Larry reassured him that they were fine, but then noticed that Jack had stuck them on… upside down.

This is the sort of idiosyncratic company that Larry loved to keep and it was a great pleasure to know him and, indeed, the many other Soho characters no longer with us.

Guitarist Diz Dizley's illustration of Gypsy Larry, who allegedly was born in a horse-drawn hansom cab at the turn of the 20th century.

MISTAKEN IDENTITY

Like all saintly hacks, I wouldn't dream of disclosing the identity of my informants. I desperately need their anecdotes and information for this column.

One of my chums advised that on a recent edition of University Challenge on BBC2, a question elicited the following response: 'Was it Screaming Chet Baker?'

Screaming Chet? The introverted sound of Chet's horn suggests more of a whisper than a scream, but what was the question?

My informant — tut-tut — had forgotten. I had to give the fellow a wigging, but help came from another source. The question was: 'What was the pseudonym used by Chester Burnett?'

I had to ask, 'Who is Chester Burnett?', and was told — Howlin' Wolf, my informant scornful of my pathetic ignorance.

Improbably, Chet Baker, who died in Amsterdam in 1988, also crops up in Schott's *Original Miscellany* (by Ben Schott, 2002). Under the heading 'Untimely Popstar Deaths', he appears in the wildly unlikely company of Buddy Holly, Keith Moon, Brian Jones, Sid Vicious, Tim Buckley, Jeff Buckley *et al*. Cause of death? Defenestration. DEFENESTRATION? That's a word that had me scrabbling through my OOED* after my newfangled computer's spellchecker told me it didn't exist. It means that Chet met his death falling out of a window.   J.G.

*Old-fashioned Oxford English Dictionary.

Jimmy Deuchar, Ronnie Scott, Gypsy Larry, Chet Baker and Tubby Hayes

HERBERT COOT LETTERS

(The correspondence between Herbert Coot and Ronnie Scott, with apologies to The Henry Root Letters by William Donaldson)

28th February, 1984
Dear Mr. Scott,

I attended your club to hear John Zaradin on Tuesday night and observed a tall, thin, haggard, cadaverous, shabbily dressed individual apparently chained to the bar for the entire evening. Mrs. Coot thought he had the most haunted eyes she has ever seen. It did not appear that the vast amount of alcoholic beverages he poured down his gullet improved his frame of mind. On the contrary, he appeared to become more and more morose as the evening went on.

It appeared that this individual is well known to yourself and your partner Mr. Pete King, the latter plying this unfortunate fellow with crude abuse on several occasions which I thought unreasonable as this chap didn't seem to be doing Mr. King any harm. I must, by the way, complain about the volume of Mr. King's abuse, this reaching the ears of Mrs. Coot who took exception, although, I have to admit, I was surprised she knew the meaning of Mr. King's expletives.

Since drink seems to be this person's pleasure, albeit taken sadly, I enclose a pound as my contribution towards a half pint of lager for him. Mrs. Coot and I would like to know who he is. He looked downtrodden enough to be a journalist or the like.

Yours sincerely,
Herbert Coot

Pete King and editor looking at the 100th edition of *JARS*. Note the sartorial splendour of the editor.
Photo: David Sinclair

15th March, 1984
Dear Mr. Coot,

Thank you for your letter of 28th February. The person you observed must have been Jim Godbolt, editor of our house magazine, a copy of which I enclose — sorry about the spelling and factual errors. The truth is we can't afford a top line man. Yes, it's a fact that life affords him little pleasure.

Regarding the pound contribution to the cost of half of lager (I can see you're quite a wag in your own little way) for Mr. Godbolt, Mr. King and I don't wish to encourage his unfortunate addiction and I thought this oncer would be better employed if placed on an absolute cert called Hooray Henry running at Newbury, the valuable information being passed onto me by Nino, my barber, when I was having my daily trim, and Nino is the Soho expert on gee-gees. I hope you won't mind. Naturally, I will cut you in on the winnings. Fair's fair.

Yours sincerely,
Ronnie Scott

P. S. Unfortunately the going at Newbury wasn't suited to Hooray Henry and it didn't get a place. In fact, it came in last. I'm letting you know this rather than it be thought that I'm taking you on, especially as you have been so generous with the quids, and may you continue to be so in the future.

April 30th, 1984
Dear Mr. Scott,

It was indeed nice of you to give me permission to cut out your signature on your letter of February 10th and paste it in my autograph book. I am most grateful and my friends are very impressed when they pop round for a sherry on a Sunday. I'm afraid I haven't the temerity to approach public figures for their signature, nor, once I am seated at your club, do I fancy my chances moving about in that Stygian gloom without doing myself a serious injury. Do you still owe the LEB money — even after the pound I sent you with my last letter?

I shall be bringing along my youngest son Wally next time I visit your club. I know I've mentioned my Herbert, but don't think I've told you about Wally. Actually, Mrs. Coot prefers to call him Walter — you know what women are like — always rooting for the formal – but the boy prefers to be known as Wally and indeed all his friends address him as such.

Talking of Mrs. Coot, the best day's work I ever did in my life was when I walked up the aisle with Emma, that's Mrs. C's Christian name, twenty five years ago. Ours is still an on-going relationship. Well, put it this way: she is always going on about something or other, and only the other day she was querulously querying why was it that I, a man who made his pile in fumigated feathers, and attaining the age of forty nine, should still be interested in jazz. She thinks I should have grown out of it by now. I argue that if a man of your age — fifty seven, I believe — continues playing then it's OK for me to go and listen to him, and on that count alone you can be assured that I will continue to visit your club despite everything — the food, the jokes, the lighting, not to mention being glowered at by your partner, Pete King.

In fact, I don't think you look at all bad for your age. Of course, I may be deceived by the lighting, and it may be the colour on your cheeks is what used to be called the night club tan, because I can well believe that you don't take that much healthy exercise, being the night bird that you are.

Thank you for that copy of *JARS*. I see what you mean about the errors. Can't you let someone at *Jazz Journal* or *The Guardian* look at it first?

Heavens! The front page had me wondering if the calendar that I get annually from my stockbroker was totally up the spout.

I enclose the usual pound. No! I'm making it two pounds. One for Mr. King. He truly looks as if he could do with a note.

Yours sincerely,
Herbert Coot

5th May, 1984
Dear Mr. Coot,
Please don't give my suggestion that you cut out my signature for your autograph book another thought. In fact, you can cut out the one at the bottom of this letter if you wish. You could always use it as a swap — for three of Humphrey Lyttelton's, for instance — or keep it in a safe place as a hedge against inflation.

I can assure you that a lot of people are after my signature — mostly on cheques — which leads me to enquire if you could up the pound contributions — by two or three thousand, perhaps? Then, we could pay the LEB, not to mention the fees for our editorial staff to attend evening classes — in English and proof reading. It will at least keep him off the drink for a few hours.

I'm looking forward to meeting your Wally. I hope he is as nice a lad as your Herbert, and has the price of a brandy (for me) in his pocket.

Thanks for your compliment — at least I took it as such —about my playing tenor at the age of fifty seven. In truth I don't feel any different now from when I was nineteen, bloody awful, but I know that when I get your usual pound I shall feel so much better.

Yours sincerely,
Ronnie Scott

Slawkenbergius

On a dank December morning, I popped into the Three Greyhounds, Greek Street, in sinful Soho, to find — surprise, surprise — our editor, James Charles Godbolt, taking a medicinal glass of amber-coloured fluid. As always, the proprietrix, Miss Roxy Beaujolais, late of the door staff at Ronnie Scott's Club, immediately refilled Mr G's tumbler and looked at me for the shekels.

I had a modest half of Adnam's, the lot of the minion. It was ever thus. Sigh, sigh…

As always, I asked JCG if there had been any near-miss disasters, typographically speaking, in the last issue of *JARS*.

'Need you ask, old son? We're constantly teetering on the edge of cock-ups. There was a beauty that could have appeared on the front page. A right clanger that would have had the boys frantically reaching for their quills, a humdinger that would have had Captious Kev actually lashing out on a first class stamp and sod the expense!

That boo-boo read, 'The Brecker Brothers and HER musicians'.

Oh, yes you can laugh, old son! Me, too, providing it was in any mag but *JARS*. And that wasn't all.'

STAN TRACEY

'Somehow, old son, STAN Tracey was transformed into SATAN Tracey? SATAN! Mind you, Stan often looks a bit

Satanic in some of the snaps I've seen of him. He's not one for the showbiz display of dentition, bless him. Lovely to see Satan- sorry, Stan — getting a lot of notices these days.

Satanic Tracey in Hades? Photo: David Sinclair

PERSONAL VIEW

JEWS AND JAZZ

I often get calls from people I don't know wanting information. At least this is an indication that *JARS* is known to so many, but it's also an occupational hazard. I'm too old in my tooth and long in my lobes to be surprised any more — the word 'surprise' left my vocabulary many, many moons ago, but, even so, some of the calls I get defy belief, and if the dialogue is prefaced by 'You don't know me, but...' I inwardly groan and say to myself,' No, I don't know you but I have an awful feeling I am going to...'

I've already mentioned the young lady who solemnly assured me she had a TV series lined up, the theme of which was the day black jazz took over from white jazz in this country — this, her actual phraseology, forever engraved upon my memory. I replied that this was news to me and she was shocked at my ignorance. Had I not written books about history of jazz in Britain?

A gentleman from Leeds commented on sleeve notes I had written for violinist Joe Venuti, and enquired was I really interested in Joe's work, or did I write the notes for money? I would have thought that the tone and tenor of my writing would have revealed a high degree of interest for Joseph Giuseppe, but my caller obviously had his doubts.

ARE YOU A JAZZ PERSON ?

A lady from a travel agency rang and asked me, 'Are you a jazz person?' I suppose that after donkey's years in the business as an agent, manager, club and concert promoter, author, journalist and editor in this little world of ours, I would qualify for such a description and at least she didn't enquire if I was a jazz 'fanatic' or 'fiend' or 'freak', and unusually, even got my name right.

The most recent lumber call I've had was from someone who rang to say, 'I have been commissioned to write an article on Jews and jazz and wanted information on the subject.' I was utterly dazed by the premise — if it can be called that, and what was the angle? A conspiracy of international Jewry to enter the world dominated by Aryans?

At that moment I was grappling with a technical problem on my computer and could have done without a call of this kind, and apart from expressing puzzlement at the premise, I told him I was too hard-pressed to answer his question, but he persisted, wanting me to point him in the right direction.

Three of the Jewish bebop 'mafia': drummers Cecil 'Flash' Winston, Laurie Morgan and Dave Davies

To where? To whom? His demands presupposed an area that had been researched. Not to my knowledge it wasn't, but then I've only been in the business for fifty-odd years.

What findings could possibly result from his investigations? All I could think of was that Jewish guys played jazz because they wanted to — as simple as that — and in case of Benny Goodman, Stan Getz, Paul Desmond and Ruby Braff for a start, praise be!

Further, I was immediately wary of talking about matters racial to a total stranger for fear of being misrepresented or misquoted, and rang off. Why did this man accept a commission about a subject of which he knew obviously nothing, but what was there to glean anyway?

No, my name isn't Goldblatt or Goldberg — although many correspondents and callers would have it so — showing undue sensitivity about possible anti-Semitism, but as someone in this day and age acutely aware of racial issues, I am, may I add, as wary of the rabidly politically correct as much as I am of the archetypal racist.

I further pondered on the non-question posed by my caller and mentally listed the number of Jewish jazzmen that came to mind, and realised how few there are, and these were not the numerous Jewish sidemen whose splendidly picturesque names pepper the discographies — names such as Rupe Briggadyke, Ducky Yontz, Gabby Buffato, John Kurzenkabe, Thurlow Cronzheimer, known to his friends as Ponzi Crunz, Marion Flickinger and Sammy Spumberg.

FRONT-RANK JAZZMEN

Of the front-rank soloists, I thought of reedmen Benny Goodman, Artie Shaw, Johnny Mince (Muenzenberger), Al Cohn, Stan Getz and Paul Desmond, trumpeters Red Rodney, Manny Klein, Shorty Rogers, Ziggy Elman and Ruby Braff, and vibraphonist Terry Gibbs. No trombonist, apart from Morey Samuel and Moe Zudecoff (who became Buddy Morrow) and these hardly front-rank. Undoubtedly there are others, and I can expect to be reminded of these! From the jazz correspondent of the *Jewish Chronicle*, perhaps?

In pre-war Britain we had trumpeters Max Goldberg and Norman Payne, trombonist Lew Davis, reedmen Billy Amstell, Harry and Laurie Gold, Sid Phillips and Nat Temple, pianist Gerry Moore and, post-war, saxophonist Ronnie Scott, Harry Klein, Bobby Wellins, pianists Victor Feldman, Lennie Felix, Ralph Sharon and Dick Katz, trumpeters Leon Calvert and Hank Shaw and very few on the traditional side — clarinettists Dave Shepherd, Monty Sunshine, Cy Laurie, Al Gay, trumpeter Benny Cohen and trombonist John Mortimer.

So, in a sense, I have answered my caller's question, for what it's worth, and, briefly — this is that Jewish people were attracted to jazz in the same way as were indigenous Scandinavians, British, French, Swiss, Italians and Russians.

The absurdity of the non-question led me to fanciful thought about adolescent Ronnie Scott, né Schatt, walking down Whitechapel, E1, one morning and saying to himself, 'There are so few Jews in jazz, I'd better go and buy a tenor saxophone and do something about it,' and coming across Tony Crombie, suggesting that he, another Jewish East End boy should take up the drums and help the cause.

Later, when Ronnie formed his big band, did he say to fellow-Jews Tony Crombie, Victor Feldman, Hank Shaw and Benny Green, 'We'll have to get some *goyim* in the band and I have in mind a tenor man called Pete King, and he'd probably make a good manager.'

Ridiculous, of course! Ronnie would never have thought along racial lines when it came to choosing his musical associates, but absurdity engenders absurdity and once again one wonders what is it about jazz that makes people, so patently ignorant of the music, think they can write about particular aspects of it? It's just not Kosher…

AFGHANS AND JAZZ

What next? An enquiry about Afghans and jazz? As I write I can almost hear the caller, 'Ah, Mr Godspell, you don't know me, but I have been commissioned to write a twelve part programme for Channel 4 about Afghans and jazz, and I was wondering…'

Knowing television companies and their approach to jazz, this wouldn't surprise me, but I am forgetting — the operative word has gone from my vocabulary.   J.G.

Slawkenbergius

As I step out of 47 Frith Street to commence my rounds, I say to myself, 'To whom can I bring a little cheer with a merry quip, a laugh and a joke, with a warm slap on the shoulder?' That's me. All heart. Always out to please. I just can't help it.

To a passing rozzer, for instance; 'Keep up the nick rate, son,' I say. The Soho boys in blue just love me. As do traffic wardens — when I enquire how many road hogs they have booked. 'Don't let them get you down, calling you 'Little Hitlers', I add. This always goes down well.

I was in such a benevolent mood one July morning when I neared the corner of Greek and Old Compton Streets where stands the Three Greyhounds, run by Miss Jenny Marguerite Hoffman, alias Roxy Beaujolais, from Sydney, Orstrylia, and loot collector at the door of Ronnie's in the seventies.

I happened to glance in, and there I saw our venerable editor, bowed over a glass of amber-coloured fluid, and patently in need of a cheer-up. First checking my wallet to see if I had the tin to sustain proximity with a toper of this calibre, I ventured in.

I offered him the mandatory, nay, obligatory, replenishment of his glass.

'Don't mind if I do, old son. Make it a large one, there's a good chap'.

'Anything wrong', I solicitously enquired, ready to offer a comforting word, and throw in a bit of crawling.

'Nothing much, old son. I'm too old in my tooth for surprises, but since you mention it, old son. There is something. I had a call from dear old Alf Lumby. Told me his local library had a clear-out and he got a book for 70p. It was *All This And Ten Percent*, my first book, old son. Sold for seventy effing P! Not a car boot sale, or a junk shop, but an effing library! 70p! You couldn't get a pint of Roxy's Adnam's Ale for that!'

'I am sure he enjoyed it'.

'At effing 70p so he should! You could enjoy Jeffrey Archer or Barbara Cartland at that price! Writing books about jazz is a mug's game, old son. A lot of sweat for SFA. I did OK for reviews by and large,, but I had some rubbishing from Captious Kev, Panjandrum Priestley, Slapsie Maxie Harrison, Snide Sam on the *Ham & High* and the Scurrilous Scouse'

'The one who described *JARS* as a leaflet?

'The one and the same. Slammed my second *History of Jazz in Britain* from end to end in *Jazz Journal*. Personal spite. He doesn't like me, old son.'

'How extraordinary'.

'Glad you see it that way, old son. Yes, personal spite. It stood out like a dog's balls'.

'Dog's balls! I've not heard that one before.'

'Neither had I until I started taking refreshment here, I got it from Miss Beaujolais. She's 'Strine, y'know'.

'The same effort got an awful drubbing in a mouldy fygge mag produced somewhere north of the Watford Gap. The editor, a Mike Hazelnut, or some such name, said that people had been queuing up with scalpels sharpened to review it, yet I gave their hero, George Lewis, the most expansive and favourable coverage. Those fygges are really hard to please.'

'But it's not only the critics, old son. Publishers! They hate authors and give us daffy females to handle the publicity. Ha ha ha! They couldn't put a book in a jiffy bag. They're all the same; Arabella, Lucinda, Fiona, Augustine, Petronella. They all think publishing a jolly wheeze between finishing school and landing a Hooray Henry in the country, and that's where they depart to, from about midday on Fridays, and not seen again until late Monday.'

'If you take my advice, old son, never write a jazz book, or you'll end up hearing the thousands of words you've sweated over being sold by a library for 70 effing p'.

I was so overwhelmed by this tale of woe, I felt obliged to offer a further replenishment of the editor's glass.

'That would be a little above my schedule for the time of the day, but for you, old son, I'll make an exception'.

That round proved extra expensive, for in walked the actor-manager, sartorially splendid as ever, but not his blooming across-the-footlights self. We thought he was wowing them at the Civic Hall, Crosby, with an extended run of *The Chocolate Soldier*, but not so.

'Unexpectedly vacant, laddies', said the AM, accepting a consolatory G and T. I got out before I had to further 'dive south' — as Miss Beaujolais, she of the trenchant phrase, would have put it.

RUBY BRAFF
interviewed by Jim Godbolt, himself uncomfortably quizzed by Ruby

Ruby by Trog

That very perceptive and admirably descriptive critic, Whitney Balliett, commenting on jazz trumpeters/cornettists, pointed to the diminutive stature of Louis Armstrong, Roy Eldridge, Bix Beiderbecke, Charlie Shavers, Ray Nance, Bobby Hackett and Miles Davis. 'The larger the lyrical soul, it would seem, the smaller its house', wrote Balliett. This was his introduction to a monograph on Ruby Braff; five feet, four inches and notorious for an equally short fuse.

I knew the stories about Reuben: his favourite tune is *Just Me, Just Me*, and that his favourite book is '*Mr Hyde and Mr. Hyde*'. Indeed, one of his albums was entitled *Me, Myself and I*, described in the *Penguin Guide to Jazz* on CDs, LPs and cassettes as 'Mainstream jazz at its very best', a tome Ruby obviously has not read, for him to be advised in what category he is generally placed in jazz literature.

Another tale concerning the forthright Mr. Braff was when he was appearing in a package led by festival organiser George Wein at Ronnie Scott's Club. Wein was the pianist, Ruby the cornettist and when Wein commenced a solo Braff, heard all over the room on the microphone, said to Wein, 'Keep it simple, George, don't try and express yourself.' Yet another story was record producer Dave Bennett enquiring of Ruby, 'Didn't you once share a flat with Kenny Davern?' And Braff's curt response was, 'No, he lived below me, where he *belonged*.'

My interview with him (and our very first meeting) at the Dean Street, Soho, flat where he was staying, didn't get off to a flying start. We shook hands, he howled in pain. He then introduced me to guitarist Howard Alden, grunting, 'If you are going to shake hands with him, please don't break his fingers, he needs them to play with me tonight.' And things got worse. Ruby doesn't look at you; he grimaces and glowers. He doesn't talk. He rasps, growls, grunts and grates. Emphatically so when he took exception to my opening comments, the thrust of which was that he was born in 1927, was very much younger than those who, seemingly, inspired him – Louis Armstrong, Bix Beiderbecke, Bobby Hackett and others of that ilk. Unwisely, I referred to him belonging to an older tradition.

J.G.

RB: What the fuck do you mean by an older tradition! I don't want to know about any older tradition! I've never played like anybody and nobody plays like me.

JG: Ruby, I am stating what people, like Whitney Balliett and Max Jones, and many others, have said about you.

RB: I don't give a shit what's been said about me. Most of it's inaccurate, anyway. I don't care about most people. I have nothing to do with most people. The best thing to do in an interview is to take it from the source.

JG: May I ask you, then, why, as a contemporary of, say, Fats Navarro and Clifford Brown, you didn't elect to play in the so-called bebop idiom.

RB: That's a fucking dumb question! Do they play like me? I don't play in any style but my own. Do you

go up to Johnny Hodges and ask him why he doesn't play like this or that guy? Would you go up to Teddy Wilson and ask him why he doesn't play like Lil Hardin or Bud Powell? Do you really wanna go on with this?

I had heard of interviews with Ruby that terminated suddenly, and this came very near to being one of them. I thought I would have to pack up my Walkman and walk. Desperately, I looked at my notes and my eye fell on the name of John Hammond.

JOHN HAMMOND

JG: Can I ask you about John Hammond?

RB: Sure. What do you wanna know?

JG: He was an interesting person from a wealthy socialite family, who did a lot for jazz in the thirties

and later produced those famous Vanguard sessions you were on.

RB: John has a very important place in musical history. OK. Those he championed, Benny Goodman, Count Basie and Billie Holiday, would have made it anyway, but that's not the point. His support brought them forward quicker.

JG: Those Vanguard sessions attracted the term 'mainstream'.

RB: There you go AGAIN! I don't go for all that shit! I don't give a fuck about mainstream, bop or what the fuck have you. These are novelty words to box musicians into categories. Commercial morons invented them! It's just music, that's all! You talk about mainstream. OK, we had Sir Charles Thompson, Vic Dickenson and Ed Hall. What would you have called those records had Charlie Parker and

Dizzy Gillespie been on them?

JG: I didn't invent the terminology, but had Bird and Diz been present I would say that the character would have altered considerably. Their conception was so much different and I think the term mainstream was helpful in identifying those who had been critically discarded in the traditional vs modern war of the late forties and early fifties, and, mercifully, were back in business thanks largely to people like John Hammond and Stanley Dance.

RB: Terminology doesn't mean a goddamn thing. I played with Bird and Dizzy and we never spoke in those terms. Bebop became a commercial word, and Dizzy exploited it. A load of baloney.

Here RB laughed. Well, more of a maniacal cackle, but it reduced the tension and I quickly changed tack.

ED HALL and PEE WEE RUSSELL

JG: I knew Ed Hall when he came over here and he was particularly sour about Pee Wee Russell, one of your heroes.

RB: Ed, a very nice man, didn't have the ear to understand Pee Wee. Ed was a rather banal player, very consonant, but he had a good spirit and a very good jazz tone. Of course he wouldn't understand Pee Wee. You had to be musically cultivated to understand him. When I first heard Pee Wee on the radio I thought it was someone with an electric saw cutting through a piece of wood, because I had been hearing Artie Shaw, Benny Goodman and Jimmy Dorsey, but Pee Wee was well ahead of them. He sounds contemporary today and always will.

JG: His death, and those of so many others you played and recorded with, must distress you. Two of the departed you recorded with were Coleman Hawkins and Lawrence Brown. Any comments about that session?

RB: Yeah, Coleman and Lawrence were not talking to each other, nor to me. I asked them to take off their overcoats, hats and gloves but had to use baritone saxophonist Ernie Caceres to mediate for me. A great baritone player, Ernie, A great mediator, too!

JG: I'd like to ask you about the session you recorded with Jack Teagarden

RB: I never played with Teagarden

JG (defiantly): You did, with Lucky Thompson and Ken Kersey and I've brought along a cassette of the record.

I played a Braff chorus from this cassette and Ruby grudgingly listened, grunted and waved a dismissive hand. Bravely, I persisted.

JG: How did this session come about? Such a mixture of guys

RB: There you go AGAIN! What mixture? They were MUSICIANS playing together! There was no mixture. Please tell me what you mean by 'mixture'?

JG: Well, you were stylistically different, although, unlike yourself, I thought the session came off very well, and I don't think you or JT had played with Lucky Thompson before.

RB: How do you know?

I was stymied. I didn't know, and at this stage Ruby launched into a vitriolic attack on the clarinettist and the organiser. To say that he was less than enthusiastic about them would be the understatement of the century. In fact, they were 'ass-holes' and their names henceforth were taboo. There were quite a few who came into the ass-hole category, including those whose music he admired, but there were also many he eulogised: Duke Ellington, Count Basie, Buck Clayton, Jack and Charlie Teagarden, Benny Morton and Emmett Berry. These were 'beautiful', but generally there were more ass-holes than beautiful people in the Braff experience of life.

SALOON BAR ENTERTAINER

JG: Ruby, you have been quoted as describing yourself as a saloon bar entertainer.

RB: Yeah. An entertainer with a bit of tin in his hand.

JG: And you don't expect total silence from your audience.

RB: No, they have the right to talk, to relax. I'm not playing in Carnegie Hall. I don't think they should shut up and drop dead. I love manipulating audiences.

I play them something soft and cerebral to make 'em listen, then give 'em something up-tempo so they can breathe again.

JG: There's a current wave of young British musicians who demand silence when they're playing

RB: If I were there I would demand my check and leave. Most of these guys haven't any talent anyway. Them and their so-called original compositions. Who the fuck wants to hear their compositions? Do they compare with the tunes of Gershwin, Kern, Berlin or Ellington? No, they don't!

JG: I recently wrote about the Duke at Fargo album where marvellous music was being played to animated chatter from the audience AND from the band, and how one of the engineers, a typical jazz buff, was horrified that Johnny Hodges engaged in conversation with Duke whilst Lawrence Brown was soloing.

RB: What would he have thought of Duke playing one of his extended works at Carnegie Hall when half the band walked off for a joint or whatever? I can't stand that keep silent attitude. If Duke and Count and the like can put up with chatter, so can I. Benny Goodman told me, as did Count Basie, that the worst thing to happen to jazz is that people no longer dance to it. I took it as a compliment when I got a physical response like dancing. It meant they liked what you were doing. I wished I'd been at the Savoy Ballroom when Chick Webb was playing to the coloured jitterbugs, but I was present one night at a coloured hall in Boston when Duke was playing and I vividly remember the SWISH of feet on the floor. Marvellous sound!

JG: And what a constellation of stars in one band – Cootie, Rex, Lawrence, Tricky Sam, Bigard, Hodges, Webster.

RB: Sonny Greer, Jimmy Blanton. The DELICIOUSNESS of it all. Thank God for giving us the phonograph so we can still hear that band and Count and the rest. I used to hear Duke and Cab Calloway and Benny Goodman on the radio when I was a kid in Boston. I even loved the Mickey Mouse bands.

JG: What! Sammy Kaye and his Swing and Sway Band?

RB: If I heard Sammy Kaye now after listening to some fucking rock crap I'd go up and kiss him. And Horace Heidt and Blue Barron and those cats. You had to be a musician to play in those bands.

BRITISH MUSICIANS

JG: I hear you think highly of certain British musicians?

RB: The greatest trombone player on the planet today is your Roy Williams. And Brian Lemon, Dave Green, Allan Ganley, Colin Purbrook, Simon Woolf, no one plays better than these guys. It's the British public who have an inferiority complex they would foist on musicians, and that's what's WRONG. Take Bruce Turner. I recorded with him in Belfast not long before he died. When I first came to Britain in 1826 — ha ha — it was John Hammond who told me to look out for Bruce, to make contact with him, and I did. He plays great. So musical.

Ruby wasn't buttering the parsnips, crushing them under foot was more in his line; his praise was genuine.

RB: Would you like to hear the record I made with Roy and Bruce? As you're a human being I'll play it to you.

A human being! Me! A hack in jazz journalism and an ex-band agent to boot! Heavens! No one has ever said this about me before! Good old Ruby, I say! To hell with his critics! Ass-holes!

As the cassette was playing (demonstrating, I have to say, the influence of Louis and Bobby Hackett in Ruby's eloquent playing), the conversation veered wildly, as it does among all jazz buffs — and Ruby Braff is the quintessential buff; nigh on 70 years old and still the juvenile enthusiast. There are indeed many sides to his volatile character. Somehow the chat moved to pianists ('I'm a piano buff'). Starting on a sad note, the brilliant Mel Powell, who recorded a great album Thigamagig, *with Ruby in 1954, is now totally paralysed.*

A PIANO BUFF

RB: It's awful! I just can't bear to think about it. So sad. Let's change the subject. Who are your favourite pianists?

I hadn't expected to be quizzed, and stumbled, but came up with Earl Hines, Teddy Wilson, Garland Wilson, Duke Ellington, Jimmy Reynolds and Nat King Cole, but in my confusion I omitted so many I liked – Joe Sullivan, Jess Stacy, Joe Bushkin and Randy Weston, but, thankfully, I remembered Count Basie.

RB: Count Basie INVENTED the rhythm section. Before him there was no such thing. You like a lot of good guys. So! Who else do you like?

Again I was nonplussed. Was Ruby trying to catch me out? Somewhere out of the recesses of my memory I came up with Claude Hopkins, not a name to conjure with, but I like his playing. A bullseye!

RB: Claude HOPKINS! I have the privilege and honour of being one of the few musicians who he didn't screw up. He was called 'The Assassin', and rightly so. He hated everybody, read a newspaper during their solos and deliberately played bum chords to throw them. Go on? Who else?

This time I responded with Una Mae Carlisle. Another bullseye!

RB: Jesus Christ! Fifty-five years ago I was playing truant from school, went to a friend's house and he played me a Una record with great Lester Young on it. 'Eyes' was in the title.

JG (proudly): Beautiful Eyes.

RB: That's it! [Ruby then sang, or rather burped, the Lester Young chorus.] After all these years I remember that chorus! Who else do you like?

JG (flattered by Ruby's interest): Nellie Lutcher.

To my astonishment, Ruby had not heard of Nellie, fine pianist as well as a most engaging singer.

JG: She made a few hit records

RB: That doesn't mean a damn thing. Who else?

JG (now emboldened, and taking chances): Jelly Roll Morton.

RB: Oh, yes. Fine composer and arranger, too.

That reaction surprised me a little. Ruby went on to praise many others, particularly Dick Hyman, Roger Kellaway, Hank Jones and Bob Brookmeyer. The conversation veered to favourite players generally. Indeed, we were like two old jazz buffs waffling away, and most enjoyable it was too. I warmed to Ruby for his enthusiasm.

JG: I haven't mentioned Bix Beiderbecke.

RB: A genius. Y'know, Miles Davis was a great admirer of Bix. He would seek out people who'd known him and ask them questions about him. You can hear a lot of Bix in Miles.

JG: I'd never heard that before.

RB: You ask me questions and you found out a lot of things, believe me. Miles was a very interesting guy. Played like no one else.

JG: What did you think of Frankie Trumbauer?

RB: Interesting player. Lester was much influenced by him.

Ruby turned his head to catch a chorus on the cassette of the Belfast session.

RB: Here! Listen to Roy Williams! What a musician! Listen to the noise the audience is making. I like a good noise when I'm playing. It makes for fun. Ha! Ha! Dave Bennett did a good job on the recording. He's a good man to have around.

JG: I've been listening while we've been talking. I agree with you and not for spurious patriotic reasons.

Almost inevitably we were back to Duke Ellington.

RB: I've still got a lot of Duke's 78s. 78s were great. Two and a half to three minutes of masterpieces. For a musician they concentrated the mind. You had to play good in those confines. Nowadays soloists go on and on when they shouldn't. Y'know, Duke, like a lot of geniuses, could cat nap, wake up and write a great tune on the spot, although how he managed it running a band, with all the hassles, the touring and the arranging, I'll never know. Louis was another great one for sleeping. So was Dizzy. He could sleep for a hundred hours on a plane. Maybe that's why he was a better trumpet player than me. I can't sleep.

Here was the patently modest Mr. Braff, but when the chat touched on agents, he was at his vitriolic best, especially about one British example. Then his mood changed with characteristic swiftness as he spoke wistfully of his trips of England not being the same since the deaths of Alec Welsh and sidemen Fred Hunt and Lennie Hastings, Sinclair Traill (editor of Jazz Journal), Doug Dobell, John Kendall and Max and Betty Jones who have died in recent years.

RB: I really miss those crazy people. Now, if you'll excuse me, young man, I've got to prepare a programme for tonight.

Young man! First I'm a human being, now I'm being addressed as 'young man'. A guy who can refer to me in such terms can't be all bad! Seriously, it was a most stimulating, unnerving, conversation. I'm so glad I lasted the hour-and-a-half course. Throughout our conversation Ruby doodled and played a word game, ironically, he started with the word 'charm' and got as many words as he could from it.

JG: I see that you are a doodler.

RB: Yes, I'm a Yankee Doodler Dandy.

JG: It's said that people can be judged from their doodles. I believe it's called Graphology.

RB: Ruby Braffology! Like it!

Indeed, Braffology would make quite a study. What would the investigative Braffologist discover? A disputatious misanthrope?

A man of the utmost musical integrity and supreme ability? An amusing and well-informed raconteur? An artist sure of his conception, but not of his identity? An utterly honest man who doesn't give a damn for social popularity? An impish character who parodies his own irascibility? I suspect that they will find, as have those who have already encountered (and that's the very word!) Ruby, the same extraordinary mixture of parts in the same unpredictable and disconcerting sequence. Trog's cartoons say it all. To the left, the quietly philosophical, avuncular Mr. B and to the right the admixture of the genial and the demonic. The demonic character who plays — and, when he feels so disposed, talks — like an angel.

Illustrations: Wally 'Trog' Fawkes

This interview first appeared in *JARS* 102, November–December 1996, and was reprinted in *JARS* 142 by way of an obituary of Ruby who died on 12 February 2003. I ended the latter with a note that this feature had received more comment than any other that had appeared in *JARS*. George Melly wrote: 'I express my pleasure, and recall the laughter I derived, from Jim Godbolt, known to have the odd moment of tetchiness, meeting up with the famously irascible Ruby Braff…'

A combative misanthrope, Ruby most certainly was, but there was a generous side to his nature. In the nineties, former *JARS* Associate Editor Cindy Hacker was an assistant tour manager for a Braff UK visit and was paid accordingly. A few weeks later, Cindy received a letter from Ruby, with an enclosure, thanking her for the 'enormous help' she had been. 'I don't think you knew how sick I was. I hadn't an ounce of strength. How fortunate for me that you were there. I am enclosing a small gift. Please believe me, it's not payment, because there is no money that could buy your output, but I would like you to treat yourself to a lovely dinner and some nice wine. Please think of me when you have that first nice taste.'

The enclosure was a 100-dollar bill.

Truly, Reuben Braff was a many-sided character.   J.G.

INTERVIEW...
Ronnie and the Rat Pack

On one warm, early August evening I entered Mr. Scott's office with notebook at the ready only to meet with his customary reluctance to talk. And, on this occasion I was faced with another dimension to his notorious non-communicativeness.

His thoughts were about going on holiday and he was awaiting a call from his travel agent. But this wasn't mentioned at the onset. In fact, Mr Scott told me he was going to Southend for his hols. Southend! I gaped at him in total disbelief. The Guv'nor of this world famed London institution, the haunt of royalty and stars of stage, screen, radio and TV, going to Southend?

'Yes, Jim, I like to get amongst the proletariat now and again. It helps to restore a sense of balance y'know. One tends to get suffocated rubbing shoulders with cafe society down here. I think it's imperative that one sees how the other half lives. I'm staying at Mrs Ramsbotham's Bayview Hotel. She does a smashing high tea. Her home-made scones and raspberry jam are something else. I can't tell you how much I look forward to that scrumptious tea after a dip in the briny, a stroll along the promenade,

a ride on the donkeys and a peep at what the butler saw. I keep away from the helter-skelter at my age, but I'm taking my sax along for a blow with the boys in the Kursaal band. I like to keep my fingers supple. Yes, Jim, I certainly recommend a fortnight at Bayview. You'll not find a tastier kipper for breakfast at any other resort, that's for sure.'

He kept the joke on the boil. He's good at the kid-stakes is Ronnie.

Apart from remembering my name, an occasion, he was in fact awaiting details of a flight to Corfu. 'I'd thought of going to Israel, Jim, but decided against it when I realised how many relatives I'd bump into there.'

So, no interview. Well, strictly speaking, there never is, but I usually manage to claw more than this from the taciturn Scott to fill this page. What could I do? My memory, creaking and getting worse day by day, fortuitously came to my aid. I recalled I had a drawing by Hedley Picton of the Club's Rat Pack, a rorty foursome who regularly turn up to heckle Ronnie during his joke-telling session and all joining in on Ronnie's punch lines.(Like thousands of members and guests they've heard

these a million times over and could recite them in their sleep which, in the case of this quartet, is during the day, their 'occupations' keeping them up at night).

Let's start with the charmer wearing the big hat to accommodate the size of his cranium, obviously — much to the amusement of his mates — giving the Guv'nor a sharp riposte. This is Jock Strapping. A scream! A laugh a minute! An absolute gas on New Year's Eve. Overfond of strong drink. A gold medallist berk! Should, in my view, be deported back over the border. Forthwith.

His occupation not certain, but allegedly a scaffolding erector, a calling that enables him to get a bird's eye view, so to speak, of other people's property.

To his right, absolutely knocked out by Jock's searing wit is Harpie Harry, from Kingston. Not that snug little town on the bend of the Thames in Surrey, but Kingston, Jamaica. Harry's occupation not clear — apart from 'managing' a certain kind of lady frequenting the Soho area, mostly late of night, and peddling certain substances regarded as highly dangerous to the human system by the medical profession, these activities attracting the attention of Old Bill, about which Harry bitterly complains alleging police brutality and racial oppression.

He's not mad about whitey and there's many a whitey not wild about Harry.

To Jock's immediate left is Giuseppe Fidlio Dodgioso, born Jubilee Buildings, Clerkenwell Rd (an 'Improved Dwelling for the Industrious Classes') but proud of his Sicilian family connections with Al Capone and fellow hoods.

By occupation he is a most industrious engraver and many a luckless shopkeeper has been the recipient of his craft, his specialities barely distinguishable from actual Bank of

Illustration: Hedley Picton
From left: Harpie Harry, Giuseppe Fidlio Dodgioso, Jack 'Bigmouth' Higso

England notes.

To his left, equally overcome by Jock's sally, is Jack 'Bigmouth' Higso, whose athleticism, acting on vital information from Jock, shinning up and down the drainpipes of Hampstead mansions is a byword amongst the criminal classes. His earnest pleas to various judges that he engages in these activities to feed a large wife and seven hungry children, leaving these distinguished worthies totally unmoved.

A right load of yobbos! Not too bothered about the environment; rather indifferent to the whale's fate; totally ignorant about jazz. You can't see any of 'em taking up Morris Dancing for a hobby. All have been guests of Her Majesty in the various institutions up and down the country designed and manned to keep them and their like away from society every so often, and what a good idea...

Note that they are not seated at one of the club's usual tables. A utility job from the staffroom suffices for them. Note the absence of glasses. Nothing, in fact, that they can throw at people. The bottle contains a vile firewater — their own brew, so unidentifiable that manager Pete King couldn't charge corkage.

All this is pure fantasy. No such persons would ever admitted to the club. If any of them, or their like, were to appear before door manageress Roxy Beaujolais, she'd surely strike terror into their craven hearts and they'd be fleeing in the Soho night in a trice, all as white as sheets, including Harry. I just had to fill a space and find an excuse for using Hedley's drawing.   J.G.

Slawkenbergius, the socialite...

In the no. 71 issue, I wrote of George Melly amongst the socialites, and his sundry other activities. Since then I have read, in the *Telegraph Magazine*, that he is an animal foster parent, and has adopted a fruit bat at Chester Zoo. The caption reads: 'I selected a modest creature', says the flamboyant jazz singer and modern art critic. 'They are rather endearing, hanging upside down in the dark.' Certainly more endearing than a fractious correspondent from Liverpool that I have.

At least, I think it's Liverpool he inhabits. (To be honest a Metropolitan cat like myself has trouble in sorting out those amorphous areas north of the Watford Gap.) He writes alleging that I'm jealous of Melly's popularity among society hostesses.

Too true I'm jealous! When you are stuck in a Kentish Town garret hacking out words to keep bones and soul together, with perhaps the odd trip to the off-licence for a bottle of happiness juice, a few invites from W1, SW1 and W8 would not come amiss, nor from N19 or N8, even...

As George Melly went to one as a fireman, what I pondered should be my get-up? I thought hard. I visualised the scene when the day came, of being ushered by a uniformed flunkey into a crowded room ablaze with the light of chandeliers, hearing 'MR. SLAWKENBERGIUS,' boomed out to the chattering glitterati and a hush falling as the name sank home.

It's not every day hooray society sets eyes on a Slawkenbergius dressed as a Viking, replete with helmet, breast plate and spear. The hostess, Mrs. Henrietta Fotheringay-Montmorency-Mortimer-Hetherington is seized by the Hon. Arabella Beaumont-Cockburn-Dyce-Innes-Lockington.

Arabella: (gushingly); 'Henrietta, my *deah*! You must introduce me to Mr. Slawkenbergius. He looks quite fascinating!'

Henrietta (icily): 'So that you can commandeer him all night, like you did George Melly at Bunty's party'.

Arabella (simpering): '*Dahling*, you know I only go for big game. Now do be an absolute sweetie and introduce me'.

Thus, holding a glass of vintage Dom Perignon in one hand and my spear in the other, I chat with Arabella. She throws out the names of dukes, counts, barons, and a rock star called Mick Hagger, or Magger, or something, and George Melly. I murmur that I, too, know George Melly, but she doesn't believe me.

Desperately, I seek a famous moniker to do my bit in this name-dropping exercise and — *eureka*! — I came up with one: Ronnie Scott! I claim to know him well, often having a laugh and a joke with him.

'Ronnie *who*?' enquires Arabella. (A pregnant moment; reminding me of the time Scottie took me aside and said, rather sadly, 'You know, Slawky, I am quite famous, but not many people know that.')

I am saved from claiming association with the famous by the sudden appearance of a Leticia who the ruthless Arabella uses to get shot of me.

'Leticia *deah*, how lovely to see you. You must meet Mr. Slawkenbergius!' Mercifully, it happens that Leticia is a nubile beauty who has a thing about ageing hacks who live in Kentish Town garrets, and we repair to the orangery to sit under an enormous palm by a pond teeming with exotic fish. I lean my spear against the nearest dowager, and Leticia and I sit and stare into each other's eyes...

Well, I can dream, can't I? In truth, I'm sitting in the garret chilled to the bone, taking sips — well, gulps, actually — of Australian plonk to warm my innards and wondering if I dreamt that I was in such high society.

Melly by Pennington

79

A Day in The Life... of the Editor

I am a great believer in the dictum 'Early to bed, and late to rise': in this increasingly dangerous world the longer one stays in the embrace of Morpheus the better, I say. But a call at 8 a.m. disturbs my slumber. It's from a bandleader who has spotted a goof in *JARS* about his personnel. I have repeatedly lauded this guy over the years and not a word of thanks. I am, after all, only a hack doing my bounden duty to praise a creative artist, but this one goof has him on the blower at his earliest. Roused from my blissful somnolence, the first job is to find my magnifying glass, as I am 'ophthalmically disadvantaged'. I imperatively need this artefact to see me (so to speak) through the day. Under which pile of drafts, magazines, letters and faxes is it? A frantic rummage. Having found it — breakfast! A cup of coffee, hoping the caffeine will kickstart this sluggish hack. I open the mail hoping for cheques, but usually finding numerous circulars from record companies, club and concert promoters and pharmaceutical companies. How do the latter know I'm a near total wreck needing their pills and potions?

CAPRICIOUS COMPUTER

With fear and trepidation I switch on the computer. That's the easy bit – how is this capricious brute going to behave? These wonders are miraculous provided you know how to handle the bastards, how to defeat their sneaky little ways of screwing up one's profundities, often making me wistfully yearn for the good old days of the quill pen and pewter pot of ink. You knew where you stood with these. Today, my PC is only moderately difficult and I hack away at this article.

ESMERALDA STRIKES AGAIN

Since that early-morning whinge, the phone has been silent and, as sudden prayers make God jump, the phone ringing makes Godbolt start apprehensively. As early-morning calls are inevitably aggro, the breaking of the telephonic silence invariably means more aggravation. And I'm right! It's from a PR lady who, it transpires, thinks that *JARS* is a weekly publication and that its editor is a Tim Goldstein. It depends on my mood at the moment how I react to these ladies who have not done their homework. Sometimes I say, 'Sorry, we don't have anybody of that name here,' and ask if Jim Godbolt will do, which I did on that day.

'How do you spell that?' she enquires.

'G-O-D-'

'Is that D for 'dog'?' was her rejoinder–cheeky!

'Yes, and the next letter is B – for 'bitch'.'

A PRICELESS TUTELAGE

In truth, I didn't make this riposte. Watching a succession of Ronald Colman films in the ninepennies at the Odeon, Halfway Street, Sidcup in my teens has ingrained in me the rudiments of being an English gentleman, and I was not to jettison this priceless tutelage in a moment of pique with Esmeralda. But there was more come-uppance to come.

'Can I have your surname?' she sweetly enquired.

Testily I replied that this was my surname.

'Is that *Mr.* Godbolt?' she queried.

'Hang on!' I said, reaching for my trusty magnifier. 'I'll check it out. It won't take me long.' Convinced, I told her she could use 'Mr.' as my gender designation.

RONALD COLMAN

(For those who don't know, Ronald Colman was an actor in Hollywood films from 1918-57 and is described in *Halliwell's Filmgoer's Companion* as a 'distinguished British romantic actor whose gentle manners, intelligence and good looks thrilled two generations'. This, in all modesty, I consider to be a pretty fair description of myself. *As Ronnie Scott would have said to a non-responsive audience, 'this is a joke'.*

A VEIN OF HUMOUR

After all this business, lunch comprising an apple and a glass of milk, then back to the PC. In all the years I've been editing *JARS* I've tried to maintain a level of humour, to perpetuate the spirit of Ronnie Scott's wit, but I have no illusions about the pitfalls in these endeavours. The trouble with humour is that it doesn't make everybody laugh. As for writing of any kind, someone — I can't remember who — claimed that it was easy. All you do is sit at the keyboard and open up a vein. I'm not complaining, since nobody twisted my arm to hack away for a living — of a sort – and the phone ringing is a welcome release from the lonely tedium. The next call is from an advertiser. As advertising is my income, my clients are precious to me, and, happily, they are people I truly like, as providers of jazz camaraderie. My caller is Cathy Gallagher from Cog, who had booked — and here we come to the minutiae aspect of my job — a half-page advertisement to be vertically positioned, but now requires it to be horizontal. This means rejigging the magazine, but for advertisers –bless them–one goes to extreme lengths to oblige.

JAZZ CAMARADERIE

An enjoyable part of my day is banter with the people who are essential to *JARS* – our advertisers – Peter, Martin and Maureen at Mole, Glyn and Mike at Ray's, Martin at Serious, Eddie at New Note, John and Hazel at Cadillac, Biyi at Joyful Noise, Adam at Sony, Nathan and Danny at Universal, Derek Everett at Jazz House, Mike and Angela at Chancery Cruising and Will and Steve at the Wenlock Arms. A further pleasure is shamelessly plundering the knowledge of collectors Brian Rust, Brian Davis, Mike Pointon, Campbell Burnap and Alun Morgan. It makes me feel privileged to be a part of this jazz fraternity.

WAR AND PEACE

I ask one of my musicians appearing at the Club for his biog and he sends me more words than you will find in *War and Peace* — reams dangle from the fax, which I cheerfully pass over to Chris Parker, my associate editor, who is utterly ruthless in condensing copy. I know, because he was the editor of both volumes of my *History of Jazz in Britain* when he was in charge of the jazz list at Quartet Books in the 1980s.

LINER NOTES

As in some mysterious way, early morning and sporadic calls indicate aggravation, it's a funny thing that evening calls are productive. It's 5.30, the phone goes and I know it's not Esmeralda. By now, she is in a Covent Garden wine bar telling her boyfriend of her encounter with a miserable old scrote who's touchy about his funny name. The call is from Dave Bennett, remasterer of 78s and LPs for CD compilations, asking me if I would like to do a liner note. I don't even bother to ask who the band or artists are — it's a welcome commission. Actually, the note was for a CD compilation of Ray Ellington's Quartet, and what a pleasure it was to hear these tracks, knowing that one of the musicians, Coleridge Goode — 86 — is still playing regularly. In all, the day passes very quickly with the writing, the research and the telephone calls, and I'm an extremely lucky guy to have the job, which brings me in contact with some very nice people. My day finishes at about 9.00 — time for a glass, or three, of vino.

RONNIE THE ACTOR
by ALAN PLATER

There's a well-worn line that runs: drummers and banjo players are guys who like to hang out with musicians. You can add writers to that list. Most of us wanted to be something else — in my case, Raich Carter in the winter, Bill Edrich in the summer, Jimmy James twice nightly and Duke Ellington after midnight. Nobody under fifty will know who the hell I'm talking about, the Duke aside; but writing plays was strictly a fifth best career choice.

The irony is that over the last couple of decades I've made a better living writing drama related to jazz than most people do playing the stuff: The Beiderbecke Trilogy, Rent Party, Misterioso and of course, the BBC film, *Doggin' Around*, starring Ronnie at the Club.

It was one of his few acting jobs — maybe the only one.

A quizzical Sott enquiring of his audience, 'What have you all been drinking? Cement?
Why not join hands and contact the living?'
Photo: David Redfern

He accepted it on condition that he wouldn't take his clothes off — 'unless, of course, the part demands it.'

His performance, as himself, was an object lesson. It included an impeccable piece of telephone acting. His dialogue ran, from memory, something like this:

'He's dead? (pause) Is it serious? (pause) Does that mean he can't play the tour? (pause) So tell me the bad news.'

The central character in *Doggin' Around*, a sardonic American pianist, played by Elliott Gould, says later in the movie; 'Life. That's just a fancy word we use for filling time between gigs.'

There was a lot of that in Ronnie, the way he stood at the mike, insulting the audience, the food and various ethnic majorities, saying to the world: take it easy. Folks, none of it is very important, apart from the music. And jazz by definition is a thing of the moment. If your ears blink, you miss it, and you miss it forever. That's why we don't talk when the band is on-stage.

The jokes were crucial. All compulsive joke-collectors (and it takes one to know one) are busy keeping melancholy at bay. 'We laugh lest we cry.'

There are dozens of moments to treasure. On an afternoon chat show, the totally admirable Mavis Nicholson commented on the fact that Ronnie was smoking. His immediate response was: 'My doctor says I need the tar.' Back in the 1970s he played with his quintet (the band with Louis Stewart) at our studio theatre in Hull to a 200% capacity audience. Somebody must have been chucking them in. It can now be revealed that over three hundred people crammed into an auditorium with 150 seats; the fire officer probably retired long ago.

That night Ronnie explained that the seagulls flew upside down over Stockton because there was nothing worth shitting on. I recycled the gag, substituting Gateshead for Stockton, for a play in Newcastle in 1995. It still works. That's the proper way to maintain our British heritage.

Alan Plater recounts his experience as an impresario in his book *Doggin' Around*, Northway Publications 2006

TONY CROMBIE a man of many parts

Recently I interviewed one of the great characters of British jazz. Tony Crombie, drummer, pianist, composer and raconteur. Puffing the while, he dragged his thirteen stone up five flights of stairs to my flat. Sorry, Tony, I should have told you there was no lift. He slumped, exhausted, into my armchair but rallied to spend two hours talking about his long and fascinating career in music. He is a very funny man.   J.G

My family lived in Artillery Passage, Bishopsgate when I was born on 25th May, 1925 and later moved to Wentworth Street, near Commercial Street. My mother was a pianist, accompanying silent films, and music, of one sort or another was part of my upbringing. I listened to all the dance bands on the radio. Most of the big band leaders — Harry Roy, Sidney Kyte, Lew Stone, Teddy Foster and Maurice Winnick, and their sidemen, came from the East End. The biggest name was Ambrose, and I was thrilled by his drummer, Max Bacon.

SWEAT SHOP

I was raised in a typical Jewish household. We were not orthodox, although my father, a furrier by trade, with an eye for business, often pretended to be. He got me into the trade, and I started as a 'nailer' — someone who nailed the animal skins onto a flat surface after they had been stretched and washed. I hated the job. It was real sweat shop stakes. I was paid 12/6d a week. The only escape from the Ghetto was through boxing or music. I had this old fashioned aversion to getting

The jiving that inspired Tony

thumped, so I chose music. I started at 5/- a night at the Stepney Youth Club in Whitechapel Road. Harry Robbins was on tenor, his brother Johnny on piano. My first big job 'tapping' was in 1941, at the Mazurka Club, Denman Street, off Shaftesbury Avenue, where I got seven pounds a week! Seven pounds! Twice what my father, skilled in his trade, was getting. Suddenly in the big time, I was wearing hand-made suits, black market shirts and ties and getting a cab from Whitechapel to Denman Street. 1/10 fare and a thrupenny tip for the driver. I was rolling in it! There were several dodgy moments in the air raids but being on the first floor you had no option but to keep going. One night we left the club to find that the Boosey and Hawkes shop a couple of doors away had been obliterated.

CARLO KRAHMER

I then worked with the near-blind drummer Carlo Krahmer at the Gremlin club, Archer Street. Carlo was an extraordinary man. He had club connections all over town. He must have been a secret Freemason — or member of the blind Mafia. He never used a stick to get around town and he humped his kit on buses. I bet the conductors loved him! All the gigs he fixed were blowing jobs. A jazz man's paradise. There were some wonderful characters in those dens. Like alto-player Jock Middleton — always drunk. He had no teeth and on his way to the gig he would pulp his cardboard bus tickets in his mouth, pressed them against his gums, and that was his embouchure! He played great. He's been around for a long time, playing at the Nest in Kingly Street and places like that before the war, Fats Waller raved over him. Another player I much admired was Alan Clare — a great pianist—and still is.

JITTERBUGS

There was a lot of jiving and jitterbugging in those days — introduced by the G.I.'s. I got a tremendous kick out of playing for dancers. I would follow them. The demise of dancing at jazz clubs was a terrible blow to the music. It's not as much fun, or as stimulating, playing for motionless people gawping at us. It was in Carlo's flat in Bedford Street, off Tottenham Court Road, that our little clique — Ronnie, Lennie Bush, Laurie Morgan, Pete Chilver, Dave Goldberg — and others — heard our first bebop records. Our first reaction was one of defensive/rejection. We asked ourselves — just what were these guys, like Gillespie and Parker trying to do? But, by then, it was too late. The seeds had been sown and were germinating in our minds. Ronnie and I took a very roundabout trip to New York to see and hear for ourselves. For both of us, it was the visual, as well as the aural, that mattered — to see just how those guys played. We practically starved at the end, but it was a wonderful experience. By the time we got home a few more bebop records had found their way into the country and it was Denis Rose who deciphered the codes. We would spend hours upon hours listening to those 78s until they were grey under the steel needles.

JEWISH INVOLVEMENT

Why were so many Jewish boys involved in this? Jewish people like aggravation, and bebop was aggravation! It was a challenge, and we had to find out how it ticked. It's funny, but there are now so very few Jewish boys involved in the business generally. Look at the bands that have appeared at Ronnie's recently — Jack Sharpe's and Tony Kinsey's — hardly a Jewish guy between them! I suppose it's because there is no ghetto to escape from anymore.

Ronnie, Denis, Pete and myself found ourselves in the Tito Burns Sextet taking bop to the people. We were a wild bunch and gave poor old Tito a hard time.

DUKE ELLINGTON

In 1948 I went on a British and Continental tour with Duke Ellington – Jack Fallon on bass, Malcolm Mitchell on guitar, trumpeter Ray Nance, singer Kay Davis and Duke. Duke had an enormous entourage schlepping about with him. He picked up tabs for everyone. One of the team was tap dancer, Harold Nicholas of the Nicholas Brothers. One night in Switzerland the tour manager forgot to tell me about a gig and I missed it. Harold took over the drums.

Musically, we jelled in no time. No, I didn't get to speak to Duke very much. He seemed rather shy in the presence of white people. I remember one night, in Edinburgh, when a local big shot threw a sumptuous party to which we were all invited. Duke included. A super grand piano had been laid on and although Duke was asked to play he kept saying — 'Later on, later on'. After a while Jack and Malcolm started to play and I sat at the piano — just comping. We played only a few bars when Duke edged me off the piano stool. To this day I don't know if it was because he couldn't stand my piano playing, or that I was stealing some of his thunder!

I joined Ronnie's nine-piece in 1953. We travelled thousands upon thousands of miles but we were young and enthusiastic and had a ball. One of the gigs we played was a concert with Max Bacon and his protégé Victor Feldman. It was a knockout listening to Max's Jewish patter. 'Good evenings, ladies and mantelpieces' was his opening line. That sort of Jewish humour isn't acceptable nowadays, but I always found it very funny. There's a musician I know whose Russian/Jewish mother never came to grips with the English language and she would say, 'Let's turn on the radio and hear that nice music from neuralgia' — meaning Geraldo.

Left to right: Duke Ellington, Tony Crombie, Malcolm Mitchell, Jack Fallon, Ray Nance. Kay Davis seated

Neuralgia! Like it!!

In 1954 I formed my own band and had some of the country's best in the team. At varying stages I had trumpeters Dizzy Reece, Les Condon, Leon Calvert, Jimmy Deuchar, saxists Joe Temperley, Derek Humble, Don Rendell, Bob Efford, Harry Klein and Bobby Wellins, pianists Harry South, Damian Robinson and Stan Tracey, bassists Ashley Kozak and Lenny Bush. Again we were constantly on the road and looking back I realize how tough it was in unheated wagons in pre-motorway Britain and playing all sorts of places — ice rinks, palais, drill halls, working men's clubs, etc, etc. In winter, we'd sit huddled up praying for the next roadside café to have a cup of tea.

ROCK 'N ROLL BAND

In 1956 I needed to make money — family commitments and all that — and I formed Britain's first rock 'n' roll band. It so happened I went to see the film *Blackboard Jungle,* and this being a cine-variety show, also on the bill was Billy Haley and his Comets. Once they came on, the place was rocking. I saw the light and formed the Rockets. Essentially it was a jazz band, but we played the rock and roll tunes and I laid down a heavy rock beat. The guys leapt about — Rex Morris, our tenor player, lay on his back and honked. I had a real old-timer, Lennie Harrison, who had recorded with Fats Waller, on bass and, no doubt about it, we were a riot. Full houses everywhere. I would be at the box office signing autographs for an hour after the show. One record of ours, *We're Gonna Teach You How To Rock,* got to number seven in the charts.

Yes, I came in for some stick from the guys in Archer Street. They asked, 'What were you up to?'

'This,' I said, bringing a pile of folding stuff, 'Would you like a drink?'

The Rockets peaked in about six months. In came the Cliff Richards, Tommy Steeles, Billy Furys, Dickie Prides — the solo acts. What was I do after this? Haunting Archer Street looking for gigs and it was my critics who were paying for the drinks. I went into Ronnie's Club with a band for a couple of years ▶▶

Georgie Fame by Pennington

was known in Britain and a year later he made his first appearance here. I like to think that my comments implanted the idea of him bringing a band here.

I have played with most of the big names including Lena Horne, Carmen McCrae, Tony Bennett, Jack Jones, Ben Webster, Paul Gonsalves, Jimmy Witherspoon and Coleman Hawkins.

Yes, Jim, I have been playing with a few trad bands lately- you've *heard*! But I'm relying upon you to act like a gentleman and not put *that* about.

and I toured with Ronnie. I wrote the music for several films including Spider's Web with Glynis Johns, Cicely Courtneidge, Jack Hulbert and Peter Butterworth.

MILES DAVIS AND HARRY SECOMBE

I have written tunes that have been recorded by Ray Nance, Paul Gonsalves, Stephane Grappelli, Blossom Dearie, Georgia Brown, Annie Ross, Peter Sellers, Spike Milligan and believe it or not, Harry Secombe who recorded my *Love Can Show The Way*.

Yes, that was a far cry from the Club Eleven. Miles Davis recorded one of my tunes, *So Near, So Far* in his famous *Seven Steps To Heaven* LP. I am still writing and arranging freelance, doing quite a lot with Georgie Fame.

BUDDY RICH

In the sixties I teamed up with organist Alan Haven and we were booked to appear at the Thunderbird Club, Las Vegas. Next door the Harry James Band with Buddy Rich was playing, and in the band was Red Kelly, a bassist whom I'd met at a US Army camp in England when he was with Woody Herman. He introduced me to Buddy. He seemed surprised that he

Buddy Rich by Nemethy

RONNIE'S JOKES

I want you to know that our waiters and waitresses will be very pleased to take you. Er, to take care of you.

And Martin, our maître d', will see that you are comfortably seated. Martin is also our sound man – the greatest sound man in the country. In the city... useless.

Actually Martin comes from Germany. He used to be in show business there during the war and had a very big following. Storm troopers, mostly.

Martin recently had a hair transplant. They took the hair from under his arms and put it on his head. And it looks great.

But it stinks.

He goes to a lot of trouble to keep looking young – hormone injections, plastic surgery. All a waste of money. There's only one way to keep looking young – hang around with old people.

Martin's a very well-educated guy, though. He took medicine at Oxford. Feels much better now. He once wrote a letter of complaint to the Tampax company, saying: 'I've been using your product for six months. Still can't swim, play tennis or ride a bike.'

A Day in The Life... of the Editor

This photo, of your editor, first gracing *JARS* in issue 111, provoked some uncalled-for hilarity. One young lady — well, youngish — all the ladies I know nowadays are of a certain age — certain age, plus, in most cases — remarked that she had never seen me smile, much less laugh, and enquired was

Photo: Johnny Parker

I drunk when Johnny Parker took that picture? Certainly not, as W.C. Fields once quipped, 'I smile every day. First thing in the morning — get it over and done with.' Mind you, there are times when one is uncertain whether to laugh or cry at some of the calls I get, the callers inevitably getting my name wrong.

MR GOBLIN'S INVOLVEMENT WITH JARS
One such only recently: a PR lady from a publishing house, who obviously hadn't done her homework, addressed me as Mr Goblin, and enquired, 'Are you still anything to do with Ronnie Scott's newsletter?' I let the 'Goblin' bit and the reference to a twenty-four page magazine as a 'newsletter' pass and meekly answered, 'Yes.'

Illustration: Gene Deitch

"GODBOLT? GODBOLT? — NEVER HEARD OF HIM."

Since repartee has been defined as thinking, days later, of what snappy response one could have shot back to a potty question, I realised I should have replied: 'Well, in a way I am sort of connected. I am the founder editor, have been doing the job for nigh on twenty years, I write much of the material, collate and proof all the copy, constantly chase contributors for same, hustle the management for booking schedules, grovel to record companies and retailers, publishers, festival and event organisers, etc, for advertisements, plead with them for their copy to meet our deadlines, and therefore supplicate on bended knee for payment. I keep anxious contact with plate makers, printers, finishers (who do the folding and stitching) and couriers who deliver the 14,000 to the club. Prior to publication I suffer badly from PPT — Pre-Publication Tension and PPA — Post-Publication Apprehension — waiting for the inevitable goof-spotter call.

I make the tea, empty the waste-paper baskets, stamp and post the letters and do a bit of hoovering and dusting. Every Monday afternoon I do my delivery boy bit, stacking the mag on the counters of the jazz record retailers in the West End. Yes, PR lady, Mr Goblin is still something to do with *JARS*.

HUMAN CHAIN
But, all this entails dealing with the human chain, and with it the vagaries of the human condition, a doddle it ain't. Anything to do with printed word is like galumphing through a minefield. There's a lot of aggro one way or another, and a day without 'ag' is a bonus day, and there aren't too many of those about. I can tell by the ominous fashion in which the telephone rings that I'm in for roasting — probably from a party who has taken objection to something written about him or her in the mag. (Conversely, if you were to praise them to the skies, you wouldn't hear a dicky bird. Strange, that.)

Now, dear reader, you can claim that the pitch of the telephone bell and the duration of the rings is electronically fixed, but I know differently, and the earlier the call, the bigger the aggro. Not that I am complaining. I love and I am proud to have, the gig, but at the end of the day I am more than ready for a glass, or two, of Happiness Juice.

Incidentally, this PR person wanted us to run a review of a new jazz book. She sent me a promo sheet, but no book.

SOMEBODY'S GOT TO DO IT
Recently, I was introduced to someone as the editor of *JARS*. On these occasions, one hopes for a comment, a suggestion of praise even. But here the guy looked at me as if I were the State hangman of yore, and said, 'Well, somebody's got to do it, haven't they?'

Typical Ronnie Scott Club members having an upmarket night out, for a change.

INTERVIEW...
Ronnie on the travails of leading a big band

Anyone wandering into Ronnie's early evening before the mob surges in might be struck by several things — one of them colliding with club director/manager Pete King — all thirteen stone of him — but what might puzzle the visitor most of all is the spectacle of people sitting separately and — apparently — not knowing each other and if they do — they're not talking. They're not members — as I say, the mob has yet to surge in.

The spectacle doesn't necessarily denote aggro. It just happens. Ronnie will leave the inner sanctum (probably because, at times, it resembles Grand Central Station in the rush hour), get himself a brandy from the main bar (he has a key). Light himself a fag and stare moodily into the distance, such as there is of it. And well he might sit there moodily. Running a jazz club is no joke, but then, it's better than working, I guess. Tony Coqueland, the club's book-keeper, has got himself a beer from the service hatch (he has an arrangement), has lit a fag and is staring gloomily into the same space from the other end of the room. Being a jazz club book-keeper and having to continually cook — sorry— adjust the accounts is enough to make anyone gloomy, but, then, he could always get himself a proper job if he wanted.

The dreaded Slawkenbergius might well be morosely hanging about in the hope that someone might offer him a drink. No particular reason for his moroseness. He's like that anyway.

FERROUS FRAGMENTISERS

There was such a night in late April. Being an outgoing and sociable sort of chap, although I say it myself, I didn't feel like sitting on my own, so I did a bit of eeny-meeny-miney-mo on my fingers and it came up that I sat with Ronnie. He glanced up, displaying no enthusiasm for my proximity. The brandy had yet to work its magic.

I went in head first. No messing about. To get conversation with Ronnie going one has to be daring.

I enquired: 'Ever heard of a company called Ferrous Fragmentisers Ltd. And would you know how to fragmentise ferrous?'

Ronnie showed no particular surprise at the question. He's been running a jazz night club for twenty three years and little surprises him any longer.

'I have no idea. Should I? I don't even know what ferrous means, or is.'

'Neither do I. That's why I'm asking. I saw this signboard outside their factory in Scrubs Lane, Acton, this morning and was intrigued. They were formerly Proley Cohen Limited. Does that ring any bells with you?'

'I'm Jewish, I know a few Cohens, but Proley Cohen I don't. Sorry, I can't help you.'

There followed an embarrassed silence. I'm accustomed to silence from Ronnie, especially when I'm trying to interview him, but this was an embarrassed silence, as though my mentioning Ferrous Fragmentisers Ltd (formerly Proley Cohen Ltd) was in the worst possible taste. This awkward hiatus was filled in — so to speak — by a torrid exchange of views between a member of the door staff and Slawkenbergius, the outraged former protesting that the spectacle of our calumnious correspondent's rusty old bike was hardly conducive to the club's image, that the sight of this heap would have the mob soon to be charging in hurrying back into Frith Street, a notion which Slawkenbergius testily rejected.

GOODMAN, SHAW & JENNEY

Somehow the chat between Ronnie and me got to those marvellously aligned saxophone teams that Benny Goodman and Artie Shaw used to have (this leading to Ronnie enthusing over Jack Jenney's trombone on Shaw's Stardust) but this serious appraisal of pre-war musical quality was disturbed by a new waitress — a very statuesque girl — who came to change the table cloths and replace the ashtrays. Ronnie, promptly dropping Goodman, Shaw, Jenney and me, took her hand and said, 'Dearest, if you play your cards right you can twist me round your little finger'.

To put it mildly, the girl looked alarmed. It transpired she was Dutch and spoke English very well. She understood the words perfectly, if not the vernacular meaning, but had no doubts about the carnal gleam in Scott's eye.

She gave him one of the biggest blanks I've ever seen a poor male receive, this silent rejection of such ardent overtures all the more poignant when you considered Ronnie had his name shimmering in neon lights outside the premises but, to be honest, was no chicken.

'She's a foreigner,' I said. Servilely trying to bolster the governor's bruised ego. 'One has to make allowances.'

He sighed. 'True, true, but this sort of thing has been happening too much lately, I've got to notice it.' He sighed. 'It used to be different when I was leading the big band.'

The conversation veered to this exciting but traumatic period in his life when he was the leader of a star-studded, temperament-wracked ensemble.

'Would you like to lead a big band again?' I asked in all innocence. Ronnie went a dreadful shade of pale. It transcended his night club tan even. Suddenly, it was as though his face had two different coloured layers of skin.

'The music was great, really great, although I say so myself. But, oh the aggro! Joe Harriott and Dougie Robinson, both superlative players, couldn't even agree on phrasing the arrangements; Phil Seamen was at loggerheads with Dave Usden. At Cheltenham one New Year's Eve —

a time of goodwill to all men — Phil and Dave were slugging it out during the waltz. I tried to look as if this were a normal part of the act. There was always bother of one sort or another. I walked out of a gig in Manchester one night and saw two birds rolling on the pavement trying to scratch each other's eyes out.'

'Didn't you try and stop them?'

'Are you joking? Try and stop two birds fighting?!!! I wouldn't be around to tell the tale if I had. Anyway, I looked up to see Joe Harriott lolling against a lamp post. I asked him what the hell was going on.'

'It's OK mun, they're fightin' over me, mun.'

'The ladies must have fought over you in those days, Ronnie,' I said, the old servility creeping up again.

He made a demurring gesture, but said, 'Well … now you mention it …'

'At Warrington?'

'Actually, not too much of that at Warrington.'

'Bolton?'

'Funnily enough, it was a fairly infrequent occurrence at Bolton.'

'Smethwick?'

'Ah Smethwick. That, too, was rather barren of females lusting after me.'

STOCKTON

'Stockton?'

'Stockton! What a comic you are! No-one, but no-one does it in Stockton. Not even the cats and dogs. In fact, Stockton'

'I know, Ronnie. It's always closed, it's a great town if you're a leper, when you go there by plane the pilot requests you to put your watches back a hundred years, three people standing around and they think it's a riot, it's got one set of traffic lights, they change once a week, people come out to watch, the night life finishes in the afternoon, you once told a cab driver to take you to the action and he took you to three old men fishing illegally, it's the kind of town that if you use your electric toothbrush the street lights dim, it's so boring the tide went out one afternoon and never came back, you went to the library and read the book, you had so little to do there you spent the day mixing LSD with chopped liver and took trips to Israel, the gulls fly upside down — there's nothing worth shitting on, they had to shoot an old man to start a cemetery, the local hooker was a virgin, if you turned the door knob you rearranged the furniture, the landladies didn't go in for ceilings and walls, or you needed a good memory for faces as they had no shaving mirrors, they screwed up the cornflakes… I know all that Ronnie, but what about the…'

'Jim! How on earth do you know all this? Have you played Stockton?' (For long I had harboured the suspicion that joker Scott is somnambulant — reciting his famed sing-along gags as if in a dream — now I know.)

He added: 'How can you? You haven't mentioned the atom bomb that was dropped on it. And did eight pounds worth of damage.'

'Ronnie, I've heard that spiel of yours a million times over; what I want to know is — in what towns did the chicks leap on you like they did Joe Harriott at Manchester?'

'Excuse me, I think Pete King wants a word with me,' and I was left like a spare member at a wedding.

Tony continued to look gloomily into space. Slawkenbergius, using vile language, removed his velocipede, Pete King looked expectantly at the door for sight of the hordes. Dramas had unfolded and the evening had yet to begin.   J.G.

WHISPERS, MURMURS AND ASIDES

YEAR 2009

Naturally, in this year of 1984, I congratulate that intrepid twosome, Ronnie Scott and Pete King, for keeping the world-renowned establishment known by most simply as 'Ronnie's' going for an impressive — nay — awe-inspiring — twenty-five years .

I've seen some of the congrats that have come in from 'the profession' (as the *Melody Maker* used to say) and am tickled by the one from Humphrey Lyttelton urging the chaps to 'Go for Gold'. If that were to be achieved the year would be 2009 and Ronnie eighty two.

I asked him how he felt about the prospect of being around then — and did he think he would be playing tenor saxophone? He shot me what used to be called an old-fashioned look. Ronnie, like a few more of us, is acutely aware of what could happen to us all in this dangerous world within the next quarter of a century, but it's a piquant thought that he might still be blowing. Like, for instance, Benny Waters, multi-saxophonist, born Maryland 23th January 1902; still very active, still touring the world. I saw him in Bill Lewington's instrument shop in Shaftesbury Avenue only recently. He looked marvellous. It can be done, Ronnie. Scientists and politicians allowing…

There's still quite a bit of life left in the guv'nor. I was talking to him at the Club recently when a young lady came up, kissed him and they both shot up to the bar, leaving me for dead. Charming!   J.G.

Ronnie's 'lit-up' in the 70s before total darkness became the practice

GEORGE MELLY
talks about his unique history and varied interests

Melly by Trog

From 1950 to 1962 I was the booking agent for Mick Mulligan and his Band with featured singer George Melly. George and I have met only occasionally since, and have had a few spats meantime, but this was quite a jolly conversation.   J.G.

JG: What shall we do, George? Have a nice cosy chat or a bit of aggro? **GM**: As you like. As you know, I have a skin like a rhinoceros. **JG**: Oh, I don't know about that, Georgie, I don't know about THAT. I've you seen you get uptight quite a few times, even with a cuddly old hack like me. **GM**: Well, we'll see, I'm sure you will put it to the test. **JG**: Our long association goes back to 1950 when you were one of a noisy team that plagued the life out of us serious jazz enthusiasts at the Blue Posts, near the London Jazz Club. You mention my antipathy in your first book, *Owning Up*. **GM**: I remember it well. You had a way of making your feelings known.

CHOCOLATE BISCUITS
JG: Thank you, George. I was also present at that youth club in Perivale, sometime in 1950, where the Mulligan band were playing and a boy put his head round the corner and yelled, 'Chocolate biscuits!' and the hall emptied. I've never seen such a stampede. **GM**: I don't blame them, do you? If it were a choice between chocolate biscuits in time of stringent rationing and listening to the early Mulligan band I would have done the same. That was the occasion when you, an agent, were asked by Mick to represent us and

you told him the best thing we could do was to pack it in. Then you were our agent for twelve years, until the band folded. **JG**: It seems longer. **GM**: Even longer to us. All those Drill Halls and Corn Exchanges, in unknown places from Land's End to John O' Groats. **JG**: You paid your dues in a cramped bandwagon and your fellow troubadours were not always the most congenial of chaps. In truth there can't have been a coterie who kept together for so long yet constantly savaging each other and, of course, their agent, particularly their agent. **GM**: Yes, some were less than loveable, but I'm told, I could be pretty insufferable. I suspect we were no different from any bunch virtually living in each other's pockets. Being on the road is a test of anyone's level of tolerance.

AFFECTION FOR MICK
Yet I retain an enormous affection — despite the rows — for Mick. There is something about him that is very magical. I ring him occasionally, and that personality comes over very strongly. An enormous magnetism. On tour now I still get people — those who bang on the beat with their Zimmer frames — coming up and telling me how much they recall the Mulligan band. In its way, it made a tremendous impact.

JG: The impact was more social than musical, perhaps? **GM**: Very much so, although Mick could have been a very fine trumpeter had he applied himself. But Uncle Alc wasn't that good for a trumpeter, and Uncle was always about. **JG**: I was listening to *Candy Lips*, made in 1950, the other day. **GM**: Oh, dear, that's a constant embarrassment to me. I seem to be singing on one note.

CLUB ELEVEN
JG: You and I were ardent traditionalists in those days and we nervously paid a visit to the seed-bed of British bebop, the Club Eleven, in that grubby basement in Great Windmill Street. It was an adventurous outing for us — consorting with the enemy in alien territory — listening to those far-out guys like Johnny Dankworth, Ronnie Scott, Tony Crombie, Flash Winston and a bass player called Lennie Harrison who, out of his skull on pot, was stomping about in his stockinged feet. I clearly remember manager Harry Morris, the eleventh man, greeting us with the words, 'Hello, *bhoys*, how nice to see you again', as he took our half a crowns. He'd never set eyes on either of us before. **GM**: I remember it very well. I thought the music appalling, but I suppose it was nothing more than sweet little be-bop. Nothing like to-day's free-form

fire-in-the-zoo music. Now I like bebop. Not as much as I like early Louis Armstrong and Jelly Roll Morton, but I can well see why Charlie Parker is such an icon. That tremendous invention. But, even then, I was fascinated by the bebop ethos. The guys in their sharp Cecil Gee suits, those marvellous East End girls with their beehive hairdos, tight pencil skirts and platform shoes, so unlike those art school types we associated with. They were all so smart and knowing. They were into the new thing. We were mouldy fygges harking back to the past.
JG: Funny you should mention the girls. At about the same time the Studio 51 in Great Newport Street was running modern sessions and one night, going to listen to Kenny Graham's Afro-Cubists, on entering I was preceded by two girls, and one said to the other, 'Oh, I couldn't listen to traditional, it would make me neurotic'.

DILL JONES

GM: Oh, very good. You know, Dill Jones, who loved, and could play both styles, was important in attempting to bridge the gap between the ancient and modern. *(Here George, the actor, gave a marvellous impersonation of the late Dill Jones, pianist, from Emlyn, Wales.)* 'Such a *pittie* that the beboppers don't appreciate Louis Armstrong and the traditionalists can't accept Parker.' What I remember most about the boppers was my horror at them smoking marijuana. Dill Jones pleaded for tolerance during the height of the Modern v. Traditional war in the late 40s,
JG: Overlooking the fact that you were half-pissed at the time.

GEORGE ON BENZEDRINE

GM: Not only half-pissed, but high on benzedrine, which you could then get from any chemist. I remember the Mulligan band played a gig in Holland, opposite a band led by Ronnie Scott, and we sat at opposite ends of the dining

table. Halfway through the meal our clarinettist, Pete Hull, loudly said, 'Pass the marijuana, old chap, if you will.' So embarrassing.
JG: I don't suppose at the time that you would have envisaged that years later you would be an annual feature at a club run by Ronnie Scott, and shortly to do your twenty-first consecutive season there.
GM: No, any more than you would have ever expected to be the editor of Ronnie's house mag. In fact, I was amazed when we played the club for the very first time. It was reported to me that someone came to the door and enquired who was on that week, and was told by the cashier, who obviously disapproved of the booking, 'Oh, it's some little Dixie band', (George imitating cashier Jeff Ellison.)

ARCHER STREET

JG: 'Dixie' was the term used by beboppers and dance band musicians who haunted Archer Street, their open air labour exchange, to describe traditional jazz.
GM: The ones that used to say 'Oh, yes, I can play Dixie, *bhoy*', and very few of them could. They were superior musicians in most ways, but had no grasp of the idiom.
JG: Did you ever go to Archer Street?
GM: Only for anthropological reasons. I would never have expected to get a gig there.
JG: Its demise as a social centre as well as a place to get gigs was a great shame. Such a colourful atmosphere. Now that you are more broad-minded in your tastes, have you many so-called modern jazz records in your collection?
GM: Not many. A tourist's lot, really. Some Gillespie, the Charlie Parker Memorial Album, some Thelonious Monk and Charles Mingus. I like Mingus. Very earthy. My collection comprises mostly vaudeville blues — apart from Bessie Smith, of course. I have all her records.

JOHN CHILTON

JG: George, despite your long association with jazz musicians, I think it would be true to say that you are not historically or discographically minded. You wouldn't, for instance, be able to converse with your *éminence grise* and partner, John Chilton, with whom you live and breathe on the road, who is very much up on both, being the erudite author that he is.
GM: That's true. I wouldn't, for instance, be able to talk about Coleman Hawkins, even though, of course, I have read John's book on the man.
JG: About the multiplicity of your activities; I mean, almost every paper or magazine I pick up, I see your name in some context or another. There was a quiz on Classic FM the other night and someone had to guess whose voice it was and, by George, it was yours. I read a feature on big bellies in one of the Sunday supplements and who should be an example of such, but you-know-who. You really are a most ubiquitous character. Famous, in fact.
GM: My wife, Diana, describes me as 'fat and fairly famous'.
JG: You have certainly made it from those days cramped in the Mulligan Volkswagen.
GM: Thank you for those few kind words, but I'm still in the bandwagon travelling thousands of miles a year.
JG: Yes, but the circumstances are very different. Your vehicle isn't a travelling dustbin like the Mulligan wagon was, and you no longer lodge in the likes of Mrs Mac's infamous doss house in Manchester.
GM: No, we stay in first class hotels, and I don't get out of my skull every night like I used to with Mick. It's rather sedate in comparison.
JG: It's no longer imperative that you tour, is it?
GM: I would be hard-pressed without band work. True, I have a house in town and one in the country, but if

I were to pop it tomorrow I doubt if I would leave much money. Property and paintings, yes, but little money. JG: But if you were earning enough from journalism and telly appearances, you would still go on the road, wouldn't you? You need the applause. GM: Yes, that's true. Without it I'm like an alcoholic without booze. When I was working in Fleet Street I hardly sang from one year to another, but like the alcoholic who gets a whiff of sherry in the trifle I was on the bandstand without a great deal of urging. It was those Sunday lunch-time sessions at Merlin's Cave, Kings Cross, that started it all off again. The band is my basic interest. JG: Are you thinking of retirement? Not that I'm suggesting that you should. GM: Yes, I thought of doing so after I nearly died with a burst ulcer about two years ago, but I didn't think about it for long. You're right. I do need the applause. And to prove myself. I've always been popular with the public, but rarely with the critics. JG: And that obviously rankles. GM: Yes, I own up, it does. The critics say, 'Oh, yes, he's a funny man, but he can't sing'. Max Jones used to say about me, 'There's a funny cat,'

but I think I can sing. Only recently a young critic in *The Times* warmly praised my singing. If you hang around long enough someone will stop copying what the others say about you. I think I sing with good time and in tune, and so did that young critic. JG: A lot of the criticism thrown at you is because of your posturing and posing, which is very much a part of your off-stage as well as on-stage persona. This gets up some people's noses and, quite illogically, they have a go at the singing as well. People have said... GM: I like that 'people have said' device to have a go at one. JG: Well, George it's true, isn't it? You have got up people's hooters. I mean, look at the time you were swaggering down the Kings Road, Chelsea, one Saturday afternoon in the mid sixties, with a similarly preening bunch of Chelseaites, when you looked up, saw me, and exclaimed, 'What are *YOU* doing here?' It was, after all, Georgie, a public pavement, but, obviously, not one you thought I should be treading. GM: Yes I was an arrogant little puppy. I hope I'm not as arrogant these days. JG: In these interviews, I always ask the subject his or her views

on Ronnie Scott's Club. Say what you like.

RONNIE SCOTT'S CLUB

GM: All these years after that Club Eleven experience, I am still very much aware of the bebop ambience at Ronnie's. You've got to be cool. You don't show emotion. Life has to be looked at through dark glasses. I loved that story of the occasion when Liza Minnelli came to the Club and the maître d' rushed in to inform Ronnie Scott, who, totally unimpressed, continued goggling at the TV in his office.

Over the years I've got to like Pete King and Ronnie Scott very much indeed. They have established the Club's ethos, and that they have been going for so many years is a tribute to their endeavours and personalities. I don't know if you should print this, but on my last appearance at the club I ran up a considerable drinks bill and paid by cheque. I saw Pete and he growled, 'Is this yours?,' he enquired. Puzzled, I said 'Yes', and he forthwith tore up the cheque. It was his way of saying, with one of his famous glowers, thanks for what had been a very good season. That was a very decent gesture. Now, Jim, I must be on my way.

That interview lasted for an hour and the above is but a part of our chat. As Max Jones said, he is a very funny cat; a one-off job, in fact. George Melly was on the road with Mick Mulligan for thirteen years before a further thirty on his own account accompanied by John Chilton's Feetwarmers and then Digby Fairweather's Half Dozen.

Melly was to achieve prominence as an author, TV celebrity, his louche way of life attracting attention of the media, details of which appeared in his many obituaries.

The Mick Mulligan band arriving at a gig, portrayed by Trog. Left to right: Frank Parr, George Melly, Ian Christie, Mick Mulligan surrounded by a bevy of admiring traddie groupies.

GIGS FROM HELL
Unnatural Functions
by ROY DAVENPORT

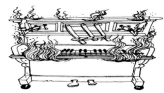

The following satirical poem, by the late Roy Davenport, will ring bells with many a musician who could tell a similar tale. Roy 'wrote' this in his head, driving back from a fraught gig

It's one of those gigs that you wish you'd not taken
But money speaks louder than pride, so you bite
Better judgement's dispensed with, ideals are forsaken
You kid yourself it'll be right on the night

The drive is a nightmare, you turn up last minute
The bandleader's tutting and itching to start
Too late it dawns on you, it's hell and you're in it
The drummer counts in — you can't find the first part

As is the tradition at small town Masonics
They've eaten their fill, and they won't leave their chairs
But sit there morosely and down gin and tonics
Whilst fixing the bandstand with baleful glares

The Worshipful Master is swaying
His Worshipful Lady is saving
'Is this the Veleta they're playing?'
You try to look cheerful and smile

The drummer is starting to slumber
The pianist is playing a rumba
The saxes, a quite different number
And their intonation is vile

The singer can't seem to remember
What rhymes with From May to December
The trombone begins to dismember
The next sixteen bars of the tune

The trumpet chats to the girl singer
The bandleader's wagging a finger
He's warning you not to malinger
You pray for an interval soon

The first set has lasted a lifetime already
The Worshipful Master is looking unsteady
His Worshipful Lady is saying, 'Now, Freddy,
You'd best not fall over again like last year'

The MC is angrily waving his fist
The Worshipful Master is even more pissed
His Worshipful Lady is cringing with shame
And her friends shake their heads as they mutter
'Dear, dear'

The barn dance and tango achieve scant approval
The waltz and the fox-trot go down much the same
The crowd starts to press for the band's quick removal
The bandleader's wondering who he can blame

The floor fills as soon as the disco starts pounding
The band makes a dash for the pub just next door
It takes fifteen minutes to get the first round in
You've time for two pints, so of course, you drink four

Then it's back into battle with all the guns blazing
The bandleader calls all the crap in the pad
The crowd whoop it up, the response is amazing
The MC swears blind you're the best band they've had

The barrel is scraped of the dregs from the 50s
The worst of the 60s exhumed and laid bare
Your musical taste buds are stripped of all feeling
You're playing bum notes and you don't even care

Then it's quarter to twelve, and the Worshipful Master
Is bidding three cheers for 'our musical friends'
A quick Auld Lang Syne and the National Anthem
And your private functional purgatory ends

You pack up in silence whilst telling yourself
That it's not just the money that makes it worth playing
Then the bandleader offers you two more next month
And your brain can't believe what it hears your mouth saying

'Yes, those dates are fine, shall I ring to confirm?
It's always a pleasure', you ooze with fake charm
With an external smile and an internal squirm
As the thin wad is pressed in your cold, sweating palm

You drive home while swearing you'll cancel tomorrow
From now on it's strictly for music, not cash
But the thought of the gas bill just adds to your sorrow
You just can't afford to say anything rash

And the following Friday, you're back counting junctions
On the M-fifty-something, in nose-to-tail haste
The hard shoulder's full of discarded compunctions
Condemned to a life of unnatural functions
A resident gig in the graveyard of taste

Typical Ronnie Scott's members tripping the light fantastic to a Charleston beat

MADHOUSE ON WHEELS
by TONY CROMBIE

Tony Crombie, (drummer /pianist /composer /wit /antique connoisseur) born Bishopsgate, London, 27th August 1925, died London, 18th of October 1999. His mother played piano for silent films, father was a furrier. He began working in the fur trade, took up drums and commenced playing local gigs beginning a long and distinguished career in music that included touring the UK with Duke Ellington in 1948. He, along with Ronnie Scott, was a founder member of the Club Eleven. He later toured with many famous American musicians and his compositions were recorded by musicians as diverse as Miles Davis, Stephane Grappelli, Paul Gonsalves, Blossom Dearie and Annie Ross. Tony contributed many highly informative articles for *JARS*, one of which was his recollection of touring with Ronnie Scott's Big Band.

Illustration: Monty Sunhine

It is 1942, approaching seventeen, and I was working in a wholesale tobacconist's warehouse in Houndsditch. Also on the staff was Harry Morris, jazz fan and live-wire. He frequented all the East End Jewish youth clubs, and after becoming acquainted with the fact that I played a bit of drums, combined with his knowing about Ronnie Scott's first tenor sax doodlings, set up a meeting between Ronnie and myself, which may not otherwise have taken place at that period, as Ronnie and I belonged to different clubs. Due to trumpeter/pianist Denis Rose's suggestions, I visited several West End nightclubs (The Cuba, The Jamboree and the Bag O'Nails) and Ronnie was the next to be initiated. Because of the war time shortage of musicians, I was able to secure a gig at the Mazurka Club, Denman Street, with Joe Rubini on piano, and that was the complete band! The clientele cared nothing about music. Ronnie, being rather shy, was talked into bringing his sax and having a 'blow'. From there we would go on to the Jamboree Club, where Carlo Krahmer held sway with a fine band. We sat there breathless with excitement listening to the likes of George Chisholm, Jimmy Skidmore, Tommy McQuater, Harry Hayes and the terrifyingly prodigious Freddie Crump, whose power and speed at the drums unfailingly left musicians and audiences completely wiped out. Ronnie was later to join Freddie and Denis Rose in the highly prestigious nine-piece band led by trumpeter Johnny Claes.

One evening, during an air raid, whilst playing at The Mazurka, there was a tremendous explosion and the Boosey and Hawkes showroom about ten yards down the road from us was obliterated.

BAG O'NAILS

I decided to seek employment underground, which I got at the Casablanca Club, a good place for visiting musicians, in as much as all were welcome. Another gig that came about was as drummer in Ray Ellington's band at The Bag O'Nails (Ray liked to 'front' the band with his brand of jive talk), producing many visits from Ronnie, as one of his early idols, Reggie Dare, was on tenor sax. After work, about 4am, most of the musicians in the West End would make their way to Lyons Corner House, Coventry Street, which was open all night and was absolutely packed with customers, requiring new arrivals to queue in the street until tables were vacated. All this with bombers overhead and fire engines and ambulances screaming in all directions. Eventually, we discovered a side door guarded by a Lyons official, an exact replica of the towering bully used by Charlie Chaplin in *Easy Street,* one of Charlie's classics. (Scottish actor Eric Campbell - Ed.).

By dropping half a crown into his ready palm, this gent could be humoured into opening the door, letting us into the delights of a warm restaurant and hot food. Those hours between 4 and 7am were magic. It was Archer Street, the open-air musicians' unofficial labour exchange and social club, transferred to the Corner House, with the added attraction of the many club hostesses who also gathered there.

GEORGE SHEARING & STEPHANE GRAPPELLI

Sitting there one morning with two old hands in the person of Denis Rose and Ray Ellington, the two greenhorns (Ronnie and I) were thrilled to see George Shearing and Stephane Grappelli walk in arm-in-arm and looking for a table. To our amazement, Ray pulled up a couple of chairs, gave Stephane a shout and the two of them came over and sat down. Denis, of course, knew them both, so Ronnie and I were introduced as two up and coming musicians, but were too awe-struck to say a word. Stephane and George were very kind, but did not pull rank on us. After a while, Ronnie must have asked Stephane about Django, who we all greatly admired. Stephane, whose English was somewhat rudimentary at that time, must have heard it said that smelly people 'hum', and he said, with an attempt at mental translation, 'Django 'ees a great player, but 'ees feet are really somesink to 'ear.'

We nearly choked trying to suppress our laughter. Another occasion I remember well was when Denis rehearsed Ray, Ronnie and me separately to sing a few bars of a popular tune so it would hopefully come out as four-part harmony. We shakily belted out the first phrase of *I'll Never Smile Again* in this full restaurant and nobody paid us the slightest attention except our waiter, a lugubrious type, who came over and whispered something in Ronnie's ear, causing him to fall about laughing. When he recovered, we asked him what had transpired. Apparently the waiter had said 'Scuse me, what do you blokes do for a living?'

The Ronnie Scott band bus – the 'madhouse on wheels'. Left to right peering out of the window: Jimmy Deuchar, Derek Humble, Tony Crombie, Pete King, Barbara Jay. Benny Green standing

US NAVY BAND

At that same establishment, Harry Morris, who had an uncanny knack for unearthing musicians, strolled in one early morning shepherding John Best, Conrad Gozzo, Frankie Beach, Ralph La Polla and Rocky Collucio, all members of the famed Artie Shaw U.S Navy band, now being led by tenor saxist Sam Donahue. Greetings were exchanged, meetings were arranged, and the very next night the American stars showed up at The Nuthouse Club and, moreover, sat in with the house band provided once again by the ubiquitous Carlo Krahmer. What a night to remember! Ronnie was extremely impressed by Sam, who not only achieved perfect hush in a steaming club with his rendition of 'Body and Soul' but also played driving, up-tempo numbers, which jelled wonderfully with the current tight four-in-a-bar work of the rhythm section. Ronnie played in that mode for a good while.

ARCHER STREET AND CLUB ELEVEN

Ronnie and I came together again at the Club Eleven, Great Windmill Street, managed by Harry Morris. We were a bunch of young Turks determined to play the new jazz called bebop, and didn't give a fig if no one came to see us. As it happened, it caught on. Firstly, mostly out of curiosity, but people became enthusiastic — we got press coverage, and British modern jazz came about.

Naturally, Ronnie and I met up weekly at Archer Street and what a great institution that was! Thronged day by day with musicians looking for gigs, especially on Mondays, and if you didn't get a gig, you were never short of a chat.

In Archer Street there was a café called Harmony Inn, where we would sit for hours over one cup of coffee. Here Ronnie's famous nine-piece band was conceived, following the departure of Ronnie and several other musicians from Jack Parnell's Big Band. This was in 1953, and the nine-piece, travelling thousands and thousands of miles on one-night stands, spread the gospel of modern jazz.
I wrote several arrangements for the band, e.g. *Stompin' at the Savoy, Flying Home* etc. specifically designed to feature Ronnie playing at fast tempos, and he came up with the goods. He was an exceptionally exciting soloist. And a very funny man. A gifted mimic, he could do amazing things with his face known as 'gurning', combined with astonishing bodily movements. He would often sabotage my drum solos, especially when I got on the tom-toms, much in vogue then, by holding his sax above his head like a spear, and performing a war dance that would have done credit to a Comanche medicine man. These gyrations would render me helpless with laughter, and the audiences enjoyed it. Other people's embarrassment always goes down well.

MADHOUSE ON WHEELS

That group was an experience — a revelation! Travelling from place to place, the atmosphere in the band bus resembled a madhouse on wheels. Verbal quizzes and the composing of risqué limericks, punctuated by shouts and roars of laughter, animal noises, some imitated, others natural, Ronnie running up the aisle in various comic impersonations, Derek Humble polishing up his ability to open locked doors, electric meters, etc, by practising on the mechanisms of his sax case, Benny Green looking solemn, doing *The Daily Telegraph* crossword puzzle, Ken Wray and Lennie Bush having hysterics about nothing in particular, manager Pete King staring straight ahead, wondering how this enterprise could ever pay its way, and Jimmy Deuchar working on an arrangement, figuring out the notes by talking to himself, and fingering in mid-air the valves of an imaginary trumpet.

Our vocalist, Art Baxter, a really wild character, when passing through a small town or village and feeling generous, would sometimes favour the local population by dropping his trousers and pressing his rear end against the window, whilst the rest of us peered out with deadpan expressions.

FAST TEMPOS

On stage, things were very different. Ronnie was extremely proud of the band, and demanded and got a consistently high quality performance. He really loved fast tempos, and to this end would rehearse the band on certain arrangements, gradually increasing the speed, until eventually we were playing jazz at tempos previously unbeknownst to Western civilisation (around 104 bars per minute) and equalled only by street musicians in Calcutta, but they had the added spur of playing whilst hopping barefoot on red-hot coals.

When the nine-piece band folded, we went our various ways, but with the opening of Ronnie's first club in Gerrard Street, I was invited to join his sextet which played there frequently, and once again he'd whipped together a formidable group — Deuchar, Humble, Bush, Tracey, myself and Ronnie leading on tenor. In recent years, with the transfer to Frith Street, he provided me with the opportunity to accompany many of the great jazz stars, for which I am deeply grateful. It was a privilege to know Ronnie, and to be considered a friend as well as a musical colleague.

TRIBUTE TO TONY

It is a melancholy part of my job to report the deaths of people in the business – musicians, writers, record producers – and particularly upsetting if I knew them personally, which is the case with most British musicians. One death that upset me more than others was that of the multitalented Tony 'The Baron' Crombie. The following poem by Ron Rubin appeared in JARS 122 together with a tribute to this very warm human being.　J.G.

A GREY DAY IN GOLDERS GREEN

First of all, let's set the scene:
A dismal day in Golders Green;
A bunch of jazzmen, mostly grey –
And women too – assemble, they
Are gathered to pay homage to
An eminent musician, who
Was pianist, composer, wit,
And master of the drummer's kit.

We file into the Chapel, where
Music percolates the air;
Friends and family stand and speak
About a man who was unique;
Stories, poignant, droll or sad
Bring to mind times good and bad;
And as we reminisce – or pray –
The coffin slowly slides away.

Outside, under leaden skies,
Smiles break out, and soon the guys
Are busy swapping anecdotes:
'Remember when we worked the boats?
And you and me – and was it Pete? –
Heard Bird on 52nd Street…'
Another voice says, 'Blimey, Heaven
Will soon look just like Club Eleven!'

No music was demanding as
What once was labelled Modern Jazz;
When Bebop burst upon the scene,
These were standard-bearers, keen
Young lions who prepared the way
For you young men who play today.
And one there was whose genial roar
Will, grievously, be heard no more.

But, friends, we cannot raise the dead,
So let's salute a life instead –
A full life, lived rewardingly:
Tony Crombie, R. I. P. 　　　*RON RUBIN*

POOR OL' DRUMMERS

It's a crying shame that poor ol' drummers are the butt of so many cruel jokes. The poor sods have to lug enormous amounts of equipment to gigs, they have to be on the job — so to speak — from the beginning to the end of the session, and when everyone else has gone home, they are still packing up, but the jibes persist.

One of Ronnie Scott's favourites was as follows:

Son: Dad, when I'm grown up I want to be a drummer.

Father: Make up your mind, son. You can't be both.

Clarinettist Wally Fawkes, a past master at the crippling one-liner, remarked: 'Playing with a drummer I once had was like walking through a minefield.'

Another joke was a conundrum:

Question: What is the difference between a drummer and a drum machine?

Answer: With a drum machine you only have to punch the information in once.

Yet another conundrum:

Question: How do you define a jazz sextet?

Answer: Five musicians and a drummer.

Alto saxophonist Peter King likes this poser…

Question: Why is a drum solo like a premature ejaculation?

Answer: Because although you know it's coming, you can't do anything about it.

Indeed, poor ol' drummers, but where would jazz be without them? They are the nerve centre of the rhythm section and whilst there are exceptions to the rule, a drummerless section is simply not a rhythm team. An example of this was the Sidney Bechet and Muggsy Spanier pairing on disc in 1940 with just guitar and bass. Whilst the music is fine, it lacks the propulsion that a drummer can provide. The entertaining limerick below, accompanying Derek Hazeldine's delightful cartoon, was penned by our poet laureate, Ron Rubin.　　J.G.

Some drummers get quite a big kick
From showing off every new trick.
They love to hold 'clinics'.
Which prompts certain cynics
To ask, Are the blighters all sick?'

JOKES I HAVE LOVED
Jokesville Press, 47 Frith Street, W1V 8TE

In 1979 Ronnie in association with Mike Hennessey, with a coda by Spike Milligan, published his *Some of My Best Friends Are Blues*, the title a play on the cliché 'Some of my best friends are Jews'. The book inspired me to write a spoof appraisal of other volumes by Scott. J.G.

The world's leading suppliers of jokes, quips, one-liners and *bon mots,* guaranteed to provide customers with the necessary material to make them instant funsters, are proud to announce the publication of a superb collection, *Jokes I Have Loved*, by Ronald Scott, on the occasion of his twentieth anniversary as a club owner.

This is a side-bursting compilation of prime gags for which the author is known from Smyrna to Sidcup, Omsk to Oban, Cockermouth to Corfu. Naturally it includes many tried and tested favourites. Not a single Joe Miller amongst these gems.

Included is a totally new variation of the 'Japanese Rabbi' standard; this a nugget of wit and brevity never before published or even used by the author in person in his own club. Mr Scott was adamant that it should first appear in this volume, resisting earnest entreaties from his partner, Mr. Peter King, that he resort to a winner of this calibre one night at the club when the atmosphere suggested a funeral party in its death throes.

Jocosophiles the world over will relish this magnificent collection that, given the reader studies it properly, will make him a riot at weddings, barmitzvahs and beach parties.

A RANGE OF TITLES

In addition, we announce the issue of a separate set of volumes by Mr Scott, the subject matter perhaps surprising for someone usually associated with the playing of tenor saxophone and running a nightclub in seamy Soho. The titles reflect a wide range of interests: Church decor; Sanitation; French coinage; Vegetable growing.

Consistent with Mr Scott's first published work, *Some of My Best Friends Are Blues*, the titles follow the *'Some of My Best Friends'* format and are listed as follows:

Some of My Best Friends Are Pews
Some of My Best Friends Are Loos
Some of My Best Friends Are Sous
Some of My Best Friends Are Q's

These volumes will assuredly become prized beyond price among bibliophiles and, moreover, we are more than proud to announce publication of a uniquely rare document – the facsimile of a hand-written essay by the author when only a schoolboy at Jews' Infant School, Aldgate, in 1934. This gem, the original happily retrieved from the dustbin after it had been thrown out in a heap of a domestic bric-à-brac, reveals that Mr Scott, even at the tender age of seven, had an exquisite turn of phrase and a proper regard for local ecology.

The background of this fascinating story is that the Stepney Borough Council cut down a tree that had become a favoured landmark in this dense concentration of bricks and mortar. Why the tree was severed isn't known, but the young Scott wrote an impassioned objection to this officially inspired desecration, and this protest kindly providence has enabled us to reproduce for grateful posterity. Ron Schatt, as signed,

When does Ronnie Scott start his jokes?

These are the jokes now, dear...

Illustration: Mel Calman

entitled this essay, *Some of My Best Friends Are Yews.*

All these volumes are printed on high quality art paper, the text set in handsome Times Roman, the covers in buckskin and the titles embossed in the finest gold leaf. As this is a limited edition — only 50,000 copies have been printed — all are personally signed by the author — maximum one collection per person. Price per collection only £250 (post-free). Postal orders only. No cheques. Personal callers with cash welcome.

This was meant to be humorous, but such are the pitfalls of attempting humour, a young lady many years later reading this exclaimed: 'I didn't know Ronnie had written so many books!' So much for humour…

Ronnie Scott wooing the ladies with his horn

INTERVIEW...
RONNIE SCOTT, O.B.E. –
The Editor recalls a visit
to Buckingham Palace

I got wind of a certain person's visit to a rather large and plushy pad in SW1, at which establishment a certain regal lady would bestow on that person's person an award called the O.B.E. Not that this certain person told me, the editor of his house magazine, about the visit, even though I'd previously hinted, heavily, that I might accompany him. But then, this certain person, one Ronnie Scott, never, as I've previously lamented, tells me anything about his activities. Now, I don't really believe in royal awards, but if there's one going begging I wouldn't say no. If an O.B.E. helps me earn a crust, why not, I asked myself, and this would be the opportunity to drop a hint or two in the royal ear.

I decided to wear the gongs I've already got. For what, you may ask? Well, I don't like to go on about it but — alright — it was for keeping the sea lanes clear during the war; the last war. No, it was nothing really — something that any red-blooded patriot would have done for the old country in its hour of peril and I still have a memento of my four years as Seaman J.C.H. Godbolt, LT/JX 317404. It's my demob suit which a grateful nation gave me once I'd sorted things out. They also gave me fifty pounds. Wish I had that now. Could have bought myself a pair of shoes with leather soles to go with wearing this suit for such a special occasion.

Alas, that demob outfit looked rather shabby, not to say dated, alongside the chic splendour of Mr. Scott's sartorial arrangements — courtesy of Moss Brothers Clothes Hire. By gum, he did look smart. Really natty.

No, I'm not suggesting he normally looks like a scruff-bag — let's just say that his normal dress is on the casual side as befits (whoops!) a rather non-conformist character who's been a bit of a wild jazzman in his day...

Mr. Scott gawped in astonishment and horror at either the spectacle of me or my demob suit, perhaps both, and hastily stepped into an elegant Daimler limousine — courtesy of Godfrey Davis Car Hire — to transport him to Buckingham Palace.

I went along, too — in the 25 bus, Mr. Scott's hasty entry into the swank limo was assisted by a snooty,

Snooty chauffeur, the investitured Scott and tetchy Godbolt on return from Buckingham Palace vividly portrayed by Nemethy

liveried chauffeur with a handlebar moustache and a fruity voice, who quickly closed the door to bar my entry. By the time I got to the Palace all the awardees were inside the gates and I was denied the chance of telling Her Majesty how tough it had been keeping the sea lanes clear — her old man being a Lt.RM she'd surely understand — and perhaps she'd bear me in mind for a gong to add to the War Service Chevrons 1941-45 and AS/MS silver badge I was proudly wearing. Drat!

The sartorially splendid and now fully investitured Mr. Scott came out wearing his award and graciously nodded to the hordes of camera-men as they took their snaps. I got some of that action, quick-sharp. Oh, yes, and I don't mind admitting it. I've no compunction about basking in reflected glory if there's likely to be a shilling or two in it sometime.

Mr. Scott was quick in re-entering the limo, but the chauffeur was not and there I was seated next to this toffee-nosed upstart. God — don't these jumped-up minions give themselves airs! He looked at me like a Royal corgi would glance at a Stoke Newington street hound. I paid the fellow no heed and addressed Mr. Ronnie Scott, saxophonist, wag, club owner and now, O.B.E. I enquired how he'd got on with the Queen.

'Oh, I told her a few of my classic funnies and she fell about laughing. She was so overcome her tiara slipped.'

I thought to myself — after Prince Philip's notoriously dreadful jokes even Ronnie's chestnuts would seem hilariously funny, not that I said so. I don't bite the hand that feeds me. Indeed, I fawn at the feet of the hand that feeds me...

'Which ones did you tell her?'

'Oh, the one about the Japanese Rabbi and Stockton being atom bombed.

I invited her to the club. Said she needn't bring along food-taster as our food, being cooked by a gorilla, was untouched by human hand.'

'Oh, very funny, sir,' said the liveried minion at the fur-covered wheel, prolonging a false laugh no doubt in hope of increasing his tip. This kind of person is prepared to go to any insinuating lengths to get money from you. Oh, how I hate his sort! Thank God my job doesn't require me to be servile to anyone – excepting advertisers and Ronnie Scott, that is.

I asked Ronnie if Prince Philip had been present.

'Oh, yes, he popped in to say hello and we cracked a few jokes together.' Bloody hell! That must have been a battle of the giants! Jumping Jokesville!! I was mentally picturing this slog-out when the snotty-nosed chauffeur, stepping out of his station, as his kind do, turned to me and enquired: 'Excuse me asking, sir — the 'sir' rolling off his tongue with all the superciliousness his kind are so good at conveying — where did you get *that* suit? I can't say I have seen I suit like *that* before. I hope you don't mind me asking, *sir.*'

Pointing to my gongs I put this fellow in his place, telling him he should be grateful to me for keeping the sea-lanes clear, making England safe for the likes of him to sit at be-furred wheels of limmos as if they owned such.

I resumed conversation with Mr. Scott.

'Will you be wearing your gong at the Club?'

'Only if creditors arrive. No one would dare slap a writ on an O.B.E.'

'Will you incorporate the award on your letter headings?'

'Only if writing to creditors.'

'Will you be wearing it on tour?'

'Only to silence the mob if they get out of hand or to get a dodgy promoter to pay up.'

We drew up outside the Club, smarty-pants chauffeur nipping out smartly to open the door for Mr. Scott, his other palm cocked upwards, to receive the tip he expected, and woe betide even an O.B.E. if *that* part of the charade wasn't forthcoming.

This achieved, he resumed his seat. I pressed a 50p piece into his oily palm saying, magnanimously, 'Get yourself a brown ale, my man.'

The cheeky coxcomb quickly reached for a duster and ostentatiously wiped where I had been seating.

Touche! But then, his sort constantly driving Hooray Henrys about town, are always picking up points on lifemanship at which Hoorays are so good. Various Soho work-shies

Illustration: Monty Sunshine

''E' said 'e'd be back in ten minutes'

lounging around Frith Street bowed as Ronnie regally entered the Club; minions at their labours inside genuflected as he strode to the office at the rear of the Club but, alas, Mr. Scott's newly acquired eminence didn't seem to have impinged on his secretary Mary Daly from Homerton, (prononced Om'e'ten) East London.

'Eyah, Ron!' she chirped in her rich Cockney accent. 'A geyser from Joe Coral's betting shop rang to say he was sorry the horses you backed didn't win, but will you pay up your account, and soon...'

They say no man is a hero to his valet, or, in this instance, his secretary, but it was a memorable day and as Ronnie has pointed out the honour is as much a recognition for jazz than one man's contribution to that music.

WHISPERS, MURMURS & ASIDES

OH! PLAY THAT GOOSEWING THING !

I am obliged to Anne Piombino for cuttings from the *Daily Telegraph* apropos the beginning of Mankind (sorry, Personkind) and our stance, physically, locomotively, speaking, as determined by computers, and, it appears, we were in step, six million years ago. No doubt, as now, out of step in all other respects, human nature being what it was and still is. Sigh, sigh...

In that same feature a column headed 'Blue Notes in the Jazz Age' read: 'Prehistoric man appears to have been a jazz buff who liked 'blue notes'. We found jazz-type scales on instruments dating to 20,000 years BC', said Dr. Graeme Lawson of the Archaeological Institute Research at Cambridge.

'Prehistoric and medieval man used goosewings and sheep shinbones to make pipes with three to five holes. Examination of the wear on pipes suggests notes were played using half-open holes, and our ancestors may have used a sliding action to bend notes in a way similar to jazz musicians'.

We've heard of Mouldy Fygge types who devoutly believe that jazz stopped in 1929, but the notion that it started 20,000 years ago is more than the old brain can take, it being a bit late at night as I write, and preparing for my cup of Horlicks and an Arrowroot biscuit before retiring.

CLARK 'CLARKY' TEWKSBURY

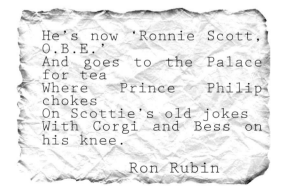

He's now 'Ronnie Scott, O.B.E.'
And goes to the Palace for tea
Where Prince Philip chokes
On Scottie's old jokes
With Corgi and Bess on his knee.

Ron Rubin

HERBERT COOT LETTERS

(The correspondence between Herbert Coot and Ronnie Scott, with apologies to The Henry Root Letters by William Donaldson)

25th September, 1984

Dear Mr. Scott,

I am writing to offer my congratulations on achieving your 25th anniversary and to tell you that my son Wally visited your Club recently with some of his young friends.

He said it was an experience he would never forget; he's never been amongst so many old people before and found what he called the 'geriatric ambience' most instructive. He was particularly intrigued, if not amused, by your jokes and asked me if they were part of the ritual of listening to what he called 'that old stuff'.

He added that it didn't appear that your customers were enjoying themselves that much, but admitted it was difficult to tell in the gloom.

Sorry that he was not more enthusiastic, but he's heavily into heavy metal and I fear his ears are permanently addled; it, heavy metal, also drove our cat Tiberius mad. We had to have poor Tibby put down. I urged this Wally of mine to grab your jokes while he can, explaining that they are gems of unrivalled antiquity and, in later life, he wouldn't want to be walking about regretting having missed the opportunity when it was there – like, alas, I did with Max Miller when he was around. I told Wally that having a memory of your banter would be tantamount to owning a brass open-horn wind-up gramophone, or a bull-nosed Morris.

Now, as you know, I have made my pile in purified feathers and as it is your 25th anniversary I am sending you a fiver instead of the usual pound. Please don't bother to thank me – it's a trifle. I don't think I've mentioned this to you before, but previous to involvement with purified feathers I was into suspended ceilings, but if you've seen one SC you've seen 'em all — not that it's much different with feathers.

I expect you have the same feelings about a sea of faces in front of you. One sea of faces the same as another, etc.

Yours sincerely,

Herbert Coot

30th September, 1984

Dear Mr. Coot,

It's a long time since I've played to a sea of faces. A small pool of dead Greeks, perhaps, but sea of faces – no. Not since I opened at the Astoria, Nottingham, with my big band in 1955. Someone had boobed with the advertising and people turned up thinking it was Ted Heath. Not that we got any more money for playing to a full house, but that's showbiz. I often think about the moolah that was rightfully mine when I have my cosy little chat with the bank manager every Monday.

I am grateful for that fiver. It's gone on a dead cert at 100 to 1. That will keep a small wolf from the door.

Sorry about your Wally, who seems well named. Where did you go wrong? Can you tell me how to get into suspended ceilings or purified feathers? Either must be a better earner than running a jazz club.

Yours sincerely,

Ronnie Scott

10th December, 1984

Dear Mr. Scott,

Thank you for your letter of 30th September. Regarding your query of whether I have an opening in my fumigating feathers company for yourself, I'm sorry to inform you that we had to abandon our over fifties entry scheme as we discovered that you can't teach old dogs new tricks, especially in the ticklish field of fumigated feathers. Sorry, but I will have a word, if you wish with my old colleagues in the suspended ceiling business and see if they can hang a job on you.

I was delighted to see that your 25th anniversary had a good press and even more delighted to note, in the *Daily Express*, that you have come up with a new joke, e.g. the one about you having a bad back because of bending over backwards to please Stan Getz. Could this, hopefully, be the beginning of a new era in the history of Scott the joke-teller? I certainly hope so, because, quite frankly, you have given your other gags a dreadful flogging over three decades and some new material would be more than welcome, especially if your stuff is less salacious and I can bring Mrs. Coot along without fear of embarrassment. I believe I have mentioned before that Mrs. Coot has led a secluded life and I would prefer to keep it that way.

That a veteran like Ponzi Crunz — he's ninety-three isn't he? – should send his congratulations on your Jubilee and express a wish to play for you, I find most touching. I look forward to seeing dear old Ponzi on your bandstand. My son Wally would certainly come along if you booked him. He's very struck with the geriatric ambience of the club and has been telling his friends about this place where old chaps perform for their contemporaries, although I tell him not to laugh — I remind him that you're young today and old tomorrow.

Yours sincerely,

Herbert Coot

P. S. Does your partner Pete King ever crack a joke, or laugh, even? I get the impression from seeing him at the door he does neither.

15th December, 1984

Dear Mr. Coot,

I am so glad that you like my new joke. Actually, it's not that new. I started to get pains in my lumbar region from the first time we booked Stan Getz, but if you think it's new, that's OK by me. As for dropping my beloved Joe Millers, I wouldn't dream of doing such a thing. What was good enough for my dear old Dad is good enough for me. I don't think I want to get hung up on suspended ceilings, thank you. It's not really me.

You are quite right about Mr. King, but running a jazz

night club for twenty years is no laughing matter, and in any case, it's part of our agreement that he leaves the jokes to me.

Yours sincerely,

Ronnie Scott

P.S. I don't really like to mention this, but you normally send me a pound with your letters…

10th February, 1985

Dear Mr. Scott,

Apropos the P.S. in your letter of December 15th, I sincerely apologise for not enclosing my usual pound. Purely an oversight, I assure you. I wouldn't want you to think of old Cootie as a meanie. I enclose a fiver; two pounds for you (thus clearing my arrears) one for your partner Pete King and two — why not? — for that poor man with the hang-dog look — your editor. I expect that expression of his is due to you leading him a dog's life. Hang-dog expression — a dog's life – geddit?

Yours sincerely,

Herbert Coot

17th February, 1985

Dear Mr. Coot,

Thank you for your letter of the 10th instant and what a relief to see the enclosure. Not that it's the money, you understand. It's the thought behind it and that's more important to me than filthy lucre. Going back to your letter of December 10th, I am puzzled by your son Wally's reference to our members and guests as geriatric. Why, only the other night we had a couple in who couldn't have been more than sixty. In fact, I think the lady was a bit younger; fifty-eight I'd say. All over each other they were, too. Nice to see this in a married couple. Mind you, I don't think they were married to each other, which may account for the lovey-doviness. Not that I'm passing moral judgement, mind you. They can get up to all the hanky-panky they want, providing they pay at the door and spend a few bob once seated.

Now, had your Wally been referring to our door staff I could see his point. True, they are getting on a bit, but I haven't the heart to sack them, nor could I do so. If I had luscious young dolly birds at the cash desk, for instance, we would have all sorts of young bucks with beastly carnal thoughts coming to the door and we're not that sort of club.

Yes, I got your joke about our editor with the hang-dog air. Nice to see you have a sharp sense of humour. If you don't mind I won't give our editor that two-er. He'd only spend it on drink. I'll put it on an absolute dead cert and, fair's fair, I'll share the dibs with you. Be assured of that.

Yours sincerely,

Ronnie Scott

WHISPERS, MURMURS AND ASIDES

A TALE OF TWO TEDS

In 1946 a barely 18 year-old Ronnie Scott got his 'first big break' — to use the terminology of the old *Melody Maker* — with Ted Heath's Band, then the biggest dance-cum-swing attraction in the country.

On Tuesday, 9th July, 1991 (Oh dear, some forty five years later — gosh, doesn't time fly?) Ronnie and his current ensemble were employed by another Ted Heath, Sir Edward Heath, Conservative MP for Bexley and Prime Minister from 1970-74, the gig being on Sir Edward's 75th birthday aboard the Thames pleasure cruiser Silver Barracuda.

I confess expressing surprise when I read of the engagement — in the national press — nobody at 47 Frith Street tells me anything. A 'modern' jazz band playing to a gathering of high Tories was a far cry from the Club Eleven in Great Windmill Street when the young RS was one of a gang of youthful rebels thumbing their noses at the musical establishment with their 'bebop', to an audience of all six people at half a crown a throw.

Artist Hedley Picton's impression of the proceedings below wasn't quite as it really was. Apparently, it was rather a sedate evening — not that I got much from Ronnie, who gave me the look he reserves for all journalists — one of overriding suspicion — when I tackled him about the night. All I gleaned was that a dowager-type lady asked them to play music appropriate to the situation and the gathering's age group. I enquired: 'So what did you play? *When You And I Were Young, Maggie, Time On My Hands, The Old Wishing Well, Have A Little Faith In Me, He May Be Old But He's Got Young Ideas?*'

Scott gave me what used to be described as an old-fashioned look, and huffily replied that, apart from the occasional complaint about the volume, the sextet went over very well and Sir Edward himself announced them as the 'finest band in the land'.

As for complaints about the volume — this is an experience known to bandleader Scott since 1953, when his itinerary with the famed nine-piece included such glamorous venues as the Casino, Warrington, the Gliderdrome, Boston and the Kiosk, Castleford.

Plus ça change!   LANCE FAIRFAX

Scott and Heath by Picton

A Day in The Life... of the Editor

God forbid that I should bore our readers with the background, the nuts and bolts, of publishing *JARS*. Undoubtedly, you all have problems of your own, but for those who are may be remotely interested, production is 10% inspiration and 90% organisation — preparation, investigation, collation, transposition and correction and the constant pursuit of editorial and advertising copy, to result, hopefully, in a readable balance of parts, the whole dependent upon the human chain. Therein lies another word that ends with 'ion' — aggravation — and a day without aggravation is a bonus day and there are not too many of those about.

Eventually, the type-setting and graphics are sent to the printer, but before publication I suffer from acute PPT — Pre-Publication Tension, and once it has hit the streets, from PPA — Post-Publication Apprehension — awaiting the inevitable calls that commence with… 'it's only a small point, Jim, BUT, you wrote…'

It's someone kindly pointing to a goof.

Advertising is vital to us — without it there would not be a *JARS* and I constantly grovel for this, supplicating on bended knee, imploring companies to take space, and a heart-rending spectacle it is, bringing my Associate Editor, Cindy Hacker, near to tears.

If I get a result, then follow my repeated phone calls, faxes and letters for copy of the right kind and size to meet the ever looming deadline.

Once published, then the almighty struggle for payment. It would be easier for me to walk to nearby Hampstead Heath, pick up the nearest pebble and squeeze blood from it. The 10% inspiration for the subsequent issue takes second place to the vital requirement of wrestling money from my debtors, many of whom appear mortally offended by the mention of filthy lucre, as if it were in the worst possible taste. And the lengths to which they go to avoid or delay payment! Such verbal juggling!

VOICE MAILS

Hiding behind those new-fangled 'voice mails' is the latest stratagem. They used to shelter behind a protective secretary lying through her back teeth about the presence or availability of her boss. Now, it's technology which shields the reluctant payer from his creditors.

If — and it's a big IF — one actually has voice-to-voice contact, they slip into automatic ambiguity mode. Such adroit manipulation of the language would be highly amusing if I were not on the receiving end — or rather, not on the receiving end of a cheque, leaving me fiscally disadvantaged.

Some examples: 'We don't appear to have received your invoice': (Send them a cheque and it will be 'actioned' (ugh!) immediately. Send them an invoice and their resident poltergeist nicks it): 'The accounts lady is at fire drill': 'Sorry, can't help you, our cheques are computer-generated and that's at the end of the quarter'; 'Our accountant is on holiday in Tenerife for three weeks.'

Others are plain cheeky: 'I see you have sent us an invoice for a subsequent issue. I like a man with a sense of humour'. The same miscreant once claimed that, owing to an industrial dispute the local post boxes were sealed and he couldn't post my cheque, adding how much this saddened him. They were not closed, but his seeing them when they were, earlier, planted an excuse in his head, to be used at a later date.

In the meantime, BT, the Post Office, Gas and electricity companies, stationers, the landlord, Ms Hacker and the off-licence (who supply me with the happiness juice to help deaden the pain of all this malarkey) expect prompt payment for service of goods rendered, and rightly so.

EDITOR'S FANTASY

I have sweet dreams of advertisers dispatching nubile young ladies — who lust after the mature kind of male — me for instance — to my office, with cheque in one hand and a bottle of fine wine in the other, preferably in a queue. I confessed this fantasy to Adam Sieff, head of Sony Jazz. Adam, quick to the point, as always, said, 'Jim, get real!'

I am very grateful to the few who do settle promptly. It would be invidious to name them here, but they know who they are, because each time they cheque me I thank them with tears in my eyes and my voice breaking with emotion. After a frustrating day chasing mazuma, the last thing I want is that phone ringing ominously. Now, you can avow that the ringing tone, timbre and pitch is constant, but I know otherwise. I can tell if it's one of those, 'Jim, it's only a small thing, BUT, you wrote…'

But I recently had a letter from the Public Lending Rights enclosing a cheque for royalties on my books obtainable in public libraries. Six volumes in all, circulating the length and breadth of the country.

My fiscal problems over! Advertisers! I don't need you! Wait a minute! Alas, no. The cheque was for the magnificent sum of £16.94 which will not noticeably change my way of life. Oh, well. Nobody twisted my arm to write these books and, advertisers, please may I continue to supplicate? *Please…*

Sometimes you just want to get up and yell 'Bollocks!'
Cartoon by Bill Stott

Slawkenbergius

S. WONDERFUL

It really is a shame that a concept as imaginative and bold as Jazz FM, and actually gaining the necessary franchise, should be marred by the presentation. You would have thought that they'd hire presenters who knew the music, not the like of that lady who — presumably reading from screen — pronounced 'S Wonderful' as 'S. Wonderful'. It's only the tiniest difference in pronunciation, but it represents a whacking ignorance. I don't blame the kids making these booboos. It's the management's fault for booking them. It's like putting a ballet dancer in command of battleship. Thank heavens, though, for Benny Green, Digby Fairweather, Campbell Burnap and Malcolm Laycock to redress the balance and it's good news that Keith Howell, late of LBC, is one more knowledgeable guy to join them.

WHY NO PONZI?

Now, a personal beef. There hasn't been a single note from, or mention of, Gubby Buffatoo, Eustern Woodfork, Ducky Yonce, Yoneg Hobespan, Rupe Briggadike, Moe Zudecoff, Tina Isgrow, Johnny Nadlinger, Joe 'Goggle' Eyes' August, Porky Cohen, Merrit Kenworthy, Ernie Intlehouse, D.S Barclay 'Horsecollar' Draper, Edgar 'Puddinghead' Battle, not to mention Perley Breed and Oliphant Chuckerbutty.

But— most galling of all — and this really hurts — not a sniff of trombonist Thurlow Cronzenheimer — Ponzi Crunz to you — whose sterling work graces *Tiger Rag* by Charles Dornberger on Victor, and *Hell's Bells* by Art Kassel and his Kassels-In-The-Air on Regal Zonophone, also released on the Gloria label as by Al Calman and his Hot Sizzlers - not many people know that.

You can get your 'Jazz FM Unfair to Ponzi' badges, banners, T-shirts and car stickers from me at moderately exorbitant prices. Send SAE for a list. I accept postal orders or cash. No cheques.

Of course, I'm only kidding. Few of the above were jazzmen, but they did actually exist. They can (except Oliphant) be looked up in the major discographical work, *Jazz Records 1897 to 1942* by Brian Rust, and it would be a good idea if Jazz FM were to invest in these two volumes.

But what would those presenters make of such picturesque names? Mind boggles.

'Hey there! I'm Jess Knownothing on the hoddest number in town — what a GREAT Sadderday it's gonna be. I'm

Illustration: Hedley Picton

gonna play yew now in a few minutes* 'Hell's Balls' by Artie Kossoff and his Cossacks featuring the GRATE Hunzi Hunz on trumpet.' Etc... etc...

Rumour has it that some of the criticisms have reached the Board and they're looking to improve matters. On the other hand there are stories of officials defending the indefensible, claiming that they are 'demystifying' jazz by presenters adopting the matey pop station approach and that the public are not concerned about the names, correctly pronounced or otherwise. Let us hope the former rumour is well-founded.
*One of my favourite Jazz FMisms.

WHISPERS, MURMURS & ASIDES

YOU, YOU'RE DRIVING ME CRAZY!

There you are, on a much publicised radio station; you are wearing padded earphones; are surrounded by state-of-the-art technology; faders, balancers, digital features, lights flashing; in fact, all the complexity of modern broadcasting gadgetry is at your finger-tips. You truly look the part. You are piped all over the building, including the foyer. You have lovingly and carefully put together a three-hour programme; done your research thoroughly, knowing only too well that if you make the slightest boo-boo the train-spotters will pounce; you hope that your informed commentary between discs will be of immense educative value; you believe your witty asides will have them falling about. But suddenly, the front-of-the-house security man pops his head round the door of your studio, and says, 'Ere. guv, can you tell me how to turn down the volume in the foyer. That noise is driving me effing crazy.'

This, I swear, was the chastening experience of Campbell Burnap at Jazz FM recently. The security man, clearly not into 'le jazz hot', was truly grateful when Campbell showed him what to do. 'Thank you guv,' he said,
'I really appreciate that.'

I'm a compassionate sort of guy, and I attempted to mollify a somewhat rueful Campbell. 'It could have been worse'. I said. 'He might have added that he couldn't stand the chat. Heaven knows what you were on about', but this wouldn't have gone down too well.   PAUL PRY

Editor's footnote

I recall a conversation with the founder of Jazz FM, Dave Lee. Prior to the station opening, *JARS* gave it extensive coverage and I, naïvely, was led to believe that I might stand a chance of getting some programmes on air, but when it came to the crunch, he said to me: 'There's no room for an *old* voice behind a Jazz FM microphone, not *even* Humphrey Lyttelton's.' Mercifully, my man Hoskinson was present and he trundled me home in my wheelchair, allowing me a few drops of restorative brandy in my bowl of bread and milk with me spluttering through toothless gums: 'Eat your heart out, Humph, eat your heart out.' Maybe if they had taken advice from the fraternity they wouldn't have gone out of business!   J.G.

PETE KING recalls the Club's history — and a unique story it is...

When I became a professional musician in Jack Olivere's Band I never envisaged that I'd become a band manager and then a club manager, but that's what fate had in store for me.

I met Ronnie when he was with Tito's sextet and then we met again when both of us were in the same sax section of Jack Parnell's band in 1953. That was a star-studded unit that included trumpeters Jimmie Deuchar and Jo Hunter, saxes Derek Humble and Harry Klein, trombonists Mac Minshull and Ken Wray, and drummer Phil Seamen, with Jack conducting. Although jazz constituted only approximately thirty percent of the book it was a great band to play in. I honestly felt privileged to be among so many very talented guys.

I don't want to dwell to much on my getting the boot, but the story has been sold many times that for Jack to make the band more commercial (or go under) he had to book a girl singer. He approached Marion Keene, a pretty girl and a good singer who had been in the Ambrose band. Marion agreed providing her husband, tenor man, Ronnie Keen, came with her, and out I went. Most of the guys gave notice to protest. In a way I felt bad about that (although of course, flattered in another respect) but on the other hand I wasn't unaware that Ronnie had a yearn to have his own band and that I might be in it.

HARMONY INN

There had been discussions over hundreds of cups of tea in the Harmony Inn, Archer Street, and when the co-operative nine-piece, with Ronnie unanimously elected the leader, came about, I found myself not only a playing member, but manager as well. I'd had no previous experience, but that's a job you learn day by day… the hard way!

When Ronnie formed his big band in 1955 I again was both player and manager. I can't say that doubling the job was easy, but I look back with a genuine affection on all the guys in both bands, although some of them could be bloody difficult, temperamental. To keep harmony among

Saxophonists Pete and Ronnie 'having a blow' at the Club's 30th

a bunch of guys virtually living in each other's pockets I often kept the peace when I really wanted to let fly.

Differences of opinion could rightly be expressed in a cooperative and expressed they were! Upsets were inevitable, given the financial circumstances. Ronnie and others were poll-winners, but that didn't mean the customers flocked in night after night; quite the contrary.

Then there was the grind of touring, this was before the days of the motorways, when it took eight hours to get to Manchester, one of our stamping grounds.

CASINO, WARRINGTON

The simple economics of the game then were that the well paid gigs were on the Friday and Saturday and a Sunday concert, and it was often peanuts time Monday to Thursday, but we had to take the scratch jobs to keep going. A few pounds at, say, the Casino Ballroom, Warrington, on a Thursday night, on straight percentage, might pay for the petrol that week and if we were playing the North east of Scotland we were glad of anything to help us get that far.

I shudder to think of just how many miles we covered, but we were young and enthusiastic and really had a lot of laughs. I mean it when I say I happily look back on those days, not that I (or any of us) would want to do it now. Naturally, it was the financial side that caused most aggravations — not too many, considering the personalities involved — but there all the same. If I paid out too much there would be nothing in the kitty; if I paid out too little I was a mean old skinflint.

It was in the big band I had temperamental problems; in the saxes with Dougie Robinson (who had left a very well paid job with Geraldo) and Joe Harriott. They were constantly at loggerheads about points of interpretation. Another problem was that trumpeter Dave Usden didn't exactly see eye to eye with Phil Seamen. In fact, they had a punch-up one New Year's Eve while the rest of us battled through Auld Lang Syne. Phil was a lovely bloke, but, at times, could get a little wild.

But, as I say, I look back on them all with affection and I wouldn't take back a day of those lovely times. It was certainly good training for running a club!

How Ronnie and I started the Club in 1959 has been told several times over, but not so widely publicised was the number of times we wondered just how we were going to keep going, but, somehow, we did, and are still here to tell the tale.

Looking back, if there's one thing I'm particularly pleased about is the result of our long negotiations with the Musicians Union to allow American soloists to play here accompanied by British musicians, staring with Zoot Sims.

HAROLD DAVISON

It was the succession of great soloists that saved us, and it was Harold Davison's loan that enabled us to move here to Frith Street and really establish a reputation, but in the early eighties we ran into serious trouble.

Business was bad and what money we had was to be paid out to musicians and others — suppliers and the Vatman —were put off. Our debts mounted and we had to get outside help. Someone — I won't mention his name-— came forward, and we agreed terms. It meant losing a degree of control, but we had no choice. To cut a long story short — on the day when we were to receive his cheque and sign contracts before solicitors, he reneged. On the very day! We were shattered. We had promised payment to creditors in anticipation of funds and suddenly — nothing!

(Editor's note: I looked into the office a few hours after the bad news and immediately picked up the vibes, but I clearly remember saying to Pete — 'This isn't the bad news you think it is. 'X' is a lunatic and the Club would never be the same with him here. Discussing that affair with Ronnie years after, I remarked that I couldn't have worked under such a man, and Ronnie said he doubted if HE would have survived the association — J.G)

Of course we had to have another meeting with our accountant, and he said, quite simply. 'There's no way you can continue in business, you must close'. Ronnie looked at me and asked, 'What do we do Pete?' I don't recall exactly what went through my mind in that dreadful moment, but I said something to the effect 'No, we're not going to close.' It wasn't just that my livelihood was threatened; it was the thought of losing something that was dear to me, and Ronnie looked up and said 'Well, if Pete says we're not going to close, then we don't.'

As we went home that night, neither of us had the least idea of how we were going to save the day, but, although we had deferred any action by the accountant to close us down, we, nevertheless, went into the hands of the receivers.

CHRIS BLACKWELL

It wasn't long after that when Chris Blackwell, boss of Island records, walked into the Club and asked questions about us. I had heard these dozens of times over, and I was a little short with him. It was bad enough to be in this situation without people prying into our problems. The conversation went something like this:
'Do you want your Club back?' he said
'Of course we do.'
'Will you be running it the way you always have?'
'We don't know any other way.'
'Fine', said Chris, 'Put me down for £25, 000.'

It was gut feeling that he wasn't kidding and I almost broke down. In fact, he wasn't kidding, and although £25,000 wasn't going to solve our problems it certainly was a tremendous help and we'll always be grateful to him.

Business improved, and we paid off our debts, but all the aggravations over the years and being at the Club for twelve hours a day five days a week took its toll. In April 1988 I had a heart attack. Quick thinking on the part of my wife Stella had me in hospital in no time, and I was in the care of a marvellous team of doctors and nurses at the Wellington, St. John's Wood. I was touched by the number of cards and calls I got, so many of the latter that Stella

Harold Davison and Chris Blackwell

had to put the block on visitors. I was very moved by the interest shown.

After working almost without a break for twenty-five years, quiet hospital life was a total change. It was another world, but one morning I got a knock on the door and looking up to see who it was, I saw only two fingers stuck up. It was Jim Godbolt, the editor of our house magazine. I was back in the real world.

LUCKY MAN

Ronnie was marvellous during my lay off. Not the most energetic of characters, he attended to all the business matters, and came to see me every day. Situations like this bring people closer. The staff, too, were marvellous and I had no worries as to how things were running, and since then I have taken things easier, as instructed. Nor do I get myself in a tizz when things go wrong. Although it wasn't his fault, Hugh Masekela didn't make his opening night at the Club in April 1989, the night the press are normally present, and we were fully booked, but I didn't let it rile me, contenting myself with the thought that over our thirty years history, our record for bands and soloists showing as advertised is very high. This considering the temperament of musicians, the visas and work permit hassles and flight delays.

In all, I count myself very lucky, in not only surviving the attack, but being able to look back on thirty years doing what I've enjoyed doing, and see no reason why we shouldn't carry on for a few more years yet.

A night punters didn't have to be 'chucked' into Ronnie's

CHARLIE WATTS

the Charlie Watts of the Rolling Stones interviewed in a swank Mayfair hotel

Charlie Watts by Trog

The meeting places for interviews I have conducted have been vastly different. With Pete Fincham of Mole Jazz it was on a cafe pavement table in New Row, off St. Martins Lane; with John Jack of Cadillac Records and singer Norma Winstone, it was the in the sylvan peace of Camley Natural Park in otherwise ghastly Kings Cross; with John Dankworth it was the basement bar of Ronnie's one afternoon when a stream of musicians were humping in their kit; with the Rt. Hon. Kenneth Clarke, QC. MP, then Chancellor of the Exchequer, it was in the rarefied atmosphere of the Treasury; with Sir David Steel MP., it was in his private chambers in Whitehall; with George Melly and Stan Tracey, it was in my flat four floors up and no lift. Both George and Stan puffed out on reaching my door.

Twice in hotels; once with Barbara Windsor in an upmarket establishment near the BBC but the setting for the interview I had with Rolling Stones drummer Charlie Watts was by far the plushest — the Forty Seven Hotel, Park Street, Mayfair and encountering the loftiest of minions who haughtily enquired my name as I entered the opulent foyer.

I often wonder what it is about the lackeys of the rich that compels them to take on such airs and graces.

After all, I was wearing my Ravers CC tie — no common or garden neckwear — and had washed behind my ears.

However, my ruffled neck feathers were calmed down by my first meeting with the extremely affable and forthcoming Charlie who, by virtue of his association with a certain rock group, is infinitely better known and considerably wealthier than any of my previous interviewees. J.G

JG: Charlie, you were a war baby, born on June 20th, 1941. What sort of music did you first hear? Were your family musical?

CW: Not really. We had records, mostly of Nat King Cole and Billy Eckstine, but I had an uncle, a drummer, who was a collector. He had all those Esquires, with Ronnie Scott, and Humphrey Lyttelton with Wally Fawkes and Keith Christie on Parlophone. He left me this collection, which I cherish. I often play them on my 78s record player, which my old friend bassist Dave Green got me.

JG: I hope you can find the steel needles and styluses. Recently I went to a Tottenham Court Road hi-fi shop and asked a young guy if they sold 78 styluses. Not tins of Songster soft, medium or loud needles, mark you, but a modern stylus. The look he gave me indicated that I was the nearest thing he'd seen from Mars that week. Which records first turned you on to jazz?

BANJO CHARLIE

CW: Earl Bostic's, then I heard Gerry Mulligan's *Walking Shoes* with Chico Hamilton on drums when I was thirteen. That got me interested in the drums. I met Chico about five years ago in the Blue Note in Chicago. He came up and said 'Hello'. It was frightening – like being a saxophone player and John Coltrane walks up to have a chat. Actually, my first instrument was a banjo.

JG: A banjo!?

CW: Yes. I had a record by the Johnny Dodds Trio, with Bud Scott on banjo with washboard and I thought I wanted to be a banjoist. But I got so confused by the instruction manual that I took the neck off and played brushes on the vellum.

JG: I think that it would be fair to say that had you persisted with the banjo your life would have turned out enormously different. Do you still retain an interest in early jazz?

CW: Yes. I have Dodds along with the very early Duke Ellington stuff, Creole Love Call, for instance, but I was soon with Charlie Parker with Monk and the record Bird made with Buddy Rich, which made me fall more and more in love with the drums, but I have always loved the Louis Armstrong Hot Five and Hot Seven. That music is timeless. When I was with my band in New York I went to the site of the Roseland Ballroom and thought how marvellous it would have been to hear Louis with Fletcher Henderson there in the twenties.

JG: I'm glad to hear this. Many seemed to reject the roots once they had latched on to more contemporary things. Who did you play with in your early days?

CW: Mostly with Dave Green, who lived next door. He on an old tea chest and me using brushes on the banjo. Dave has a recording of this group. We played at a pub called the Masons Arms, Edgware. I played a lot of Rhythm and Blues, mostly with Alexis Korner.

JG: And you have retained an interest ever since, despite having — ahem — associations far removed from jazz.

CW: I never lost my interest in jazz music. I've always loved going to jazz clubs. I still do, albeit, not as much now. I've always loved watching jazz musicians work.

JAGGER NO JAZZER

JG: Not so your colleagues, I believe. I was at the Marquee one night in the early sixties and I spotted a young man scowling heavily at a trad band, Dick Charlesworth's, on the stand. I had no idea who it was at the time, but when his face appeared constantly in the press, I realised it was Mick Jagger I had observed.

CW: That follows. Mick wouldn't have gone for trad. He would have been more interested in Joe Harriott, who was often at the Marquee, but he's not mad about jazz, anyway.

JG: Are any of your colleagues interested in jazz?

CW: Keith (Richards) loves Louis Armstrong, particularly him backing the early blues singers. He loves Eddie Condon.

JG: Does the subject of jazz come up when you are on tour?

CW: Only if a tape is being played. In the middle of our last tour Keith was raving about a saxophone player he'd heard on the radio and you can imagine what a wide field that is, but it transpired it was Joshua Redman on his album 'Wish'. Keith's not a Coltrane man. More into Coleman Hawkins and Lester Young. He's got very good ears.

JG: I wasn't aware he was interested in jazz, but, as you know, the jazz, rock and roll, R&B and pop worlds are very separate and we tend to stick in the areas we know.

CW: You are right, but I don't think those divisions mean much anymore. I mean when the music was splitting up in so many directions in the sixties it was very interesting. You knew that probably better than anyone when you were an agent booking all sorts and kinds. But it was great fun and a lot of good bands came out of it all.

CHRIS BARBER

JG: Did you ever read Jazz News in the sixties? That covered trad, mainstream and modern jazz, folk, R&B, skiffle, everything. It used to come out weekly. Heaven knows, how they did it, especially as they had Polish typesetters dealing with such esoteric subjects.

CW: Yes, I remember it very well, I used to read your articles in it. It was run by Chris Barber, someone I've a great admiration for. An amazing bloke.

JG: Oh, yes. In what is loosely described as the world of R&B, he is mentioned with great affection, if only because of the number of people he brought over to play with his band, including, wonder of wonders, John Lewis of the Modern Jazz Quartet. I'd love to know how Lewis enjoyed playing with a banjo. Chris also featured Joe Harriott — totally different in style. He is a very free thinking man.

CW: Very much so. He was the one who featured Alexis Korner and Cyril Davies. Pity about Cyril dying so young. Chris was much more radical than many a modernist. He created a broad base.

JG: I heard him talking on a radio programme recently and he claimed that it was by playing Robert Johnson records to Eric Clapton that Clapton first heard the blues

CW: Whether it's true or not, it wouldn't surprise me.

JG: Chris is a totally dedicated guy. He doesn't drink or smoke. Has never touched drugs. He has an enormous record collection, reputed to be worth half a million.

CW: I heard him with Lonnie Donegan on banjo at the Wembley Town Hall in the sixties. Perhaps you booked him there?

HALF A DOLLAR GIG

JG: No, I wasn't his agent then. I was originally, in 1950, when he didn't have a clue. Nor did I, being new to the business. It would have been Lyn Dutton who booked him. Jumping the chronology a bit, is there any truth in the tale that you had to be persuaded to leave your day job to join the Stones?

CW: No, I was persuaded by the money. I was working as a designer when I was playing with the Stones, mostly at the Richmond Hotel for Georgio Gomelsky. Then we used to get about three pounds a gig, but I remember one gig I did with Alexis, in Birmingham, the first time we played out of London, when my share was half a crown. Jack Bruce, Dick Heckstall-Smith and Cyril Davies got a pound each because they were professionals, but pianist Johnny Parker and myself got only half a dollar. That sticks in my memory.

JG: I understand you have done better since.

At this stage, Charlie launched into praise for a wide number of stylistically different British musicians — Wally Fawkes, Sandy Brown, Bruce Turner, John Picard, Mick Pyne, Bobby Wellins, Don Weller, Ronnie Scott, Peter King, Colin Smith, Bill Eyden, Jimmy Deuchar, Tony Coe, Evan Parker, John Stevens, Stan Greig, Johnny Parker and many others, and deplored that they were not more critically rated and better off financially.

JG: As you know, it's not the musicality that counts, it's the drawing power, and sadly, Brits don't draw crowds. Nothing would suit Pete King at Ronnie's better than to pick up the phone to Sidcup or Sydenham and book local guys. It would save him a lot of transatlantic hassle, but financially it just isn't on. A fact of life running a jazz club.

CW: Here I must say how much I bow to the efforts of Ronnie and Pete to bring in the great names after those dreadful barren years when they were only part of big tours or en route to another country. Then, suddenly, you could stand as near to Ben Webster as to see his bootlaces. It was magic.

I brought the conversation round to Charlie's Big Band that toured the US and played at Ronnie Scott's Club in 1985.

CW: We did two tours, including the Hollywood Bowl and venues in New York. And lots of other places I can't remember.

JG: With thirty-two pieces! An organisational nightmare.

CW: Sheri (Sheri Daly, his personal manager) saw to all that, but you were right, what with Ron Matthewson at one end and Don Weller at the other! (Prolonged

Illustration: Monty Sunshine

chuckles from **JG** and **CW**). But it was great. I only wish the band had been recorded. It showed just how good British musicians are.

JG: But, it's the truth, isn't it, that good as these musicians are they wouldn't have meant a thing in the US had your name not been on the billing? And the same would apply here, but good on you for getting them together. Did those trips cost you money? As an ex-agent, the economics interest me.

CW: It cost me money to play at Ronnie's. I always wanted to play at the Club, but by the time the band had been assembled I knew I couldn't ask the money to cover 32 musicians. But we struck a deal. Yes it was expensive, but worth it. It was great fun.

JG: And a miracle of compression on that bandstand! How come so many players, including two vibraphonists?

CW: Well, John Stevens picked some, I picked others – like Willie Garnett, John Picard and Colin Smith — and before long we had a monster team. It was somewhat ragged. A big band needs to play regularly to get precision. I wish I had led more from the front, but I was a bit messed up at the time and took the back seat. After all, John Stevens and Bill Eyden were there to keep things going.

PHIL SEAMEN

JG: It can be said you are the unique example of a rock star putting a lot of money into jazz because you love the music, and all credit to you. You mentioned having a bad patch. In what respect, may I ask?

CW: I was heavily into drugs and drink in the 80s, but no more. I was never very good at boozing anyway. I always remember seeing Phil Seamen drunk and I did the wannabe bit of drinking like him. But I did it all wrong and fell about.

JG: So did Phil!

CW: But he fell in the right places!

JG: The guys still talk about Phil with reverence.

CW: He was great! A shame he, too, went early.

JG: When you played those Richmond gigs did you envisage that your life was to change so drastically?

CW: No, as I had played in so many bands with a short life, I then gave the Stones a year. When we went big in America, I gave it another three, but here we are, thirty years later. In my case, I wouldn't have wanted the future laid out before me.

Sometime hereabouts in the conversation I admitted that I wasn't into the repertoire of the Rolling Stones.

CW: I don't think I would have been into Chicago blues unless I had joined them. Until then, the blues to me meant Charlie Parker.

JG: Let's talk about your latest CD, Long Ago and Far Away. Many have commented on the fact that singer Bernard Fowler is on every track. I hadn't heard of him until now.

CW: Bernard is a back-up singer with the Stones. A fine singer. But he didn't know these tunes before I played them to him. I wanted to do an album of the numbers I liked, things not played that often. I got them from my collection — Lee Wiley, Bob Crosby, Lucky Thompson, Serge Chaloff and the Duke. And I wanted to do an album with strings. Next time it will be a straightforward jazz album.

I told Charlie that the interview would be in the September/October issue of JARS, and he joined the company of fellow interviewees George Melly, John Dankworth, Spike Milligan, Stan Tracey, Sir David Steel, Barbara Windsor and Kenneth Clarke, Chancellor of the Exchequer.

CW: *THAT* Kenneth Clarke! Blimey! Is *he* interested in jazz? Kenny Clarke is my favourite drummer! I loved the Clarke-Boland band. Their album, *Volcano*, is one of my favourites. Ronnie was in that band, wasn't he?

At this stage Sheri Daly reminded Charlie that he had several other interviewers waiting to see him, and we said our farewells. He told me to 'keep rolling', the significance of which only hit me some time afterwards. As I reached the foyer, I had half a mind to press a 5p coin into the palm of the snotty-nosed minion with the words 'Here you are, my good man', but my nerve failed me and as I walked up Park Street I thought it somewhat piquant that multi-millionaire Charlie — the 347th richest man in the country, I read in the *Daily Telegraph* — should be selecting steel needles to play Humph Parlophones on his wind-up gramophone.

I much enjoyed my chat with Charlie. His doleful mien and dolorous tone of voice conceals a gentle sense of humour and I now understand why he is dubbed the 'quiet man' of the roistering Rolling Stones.

Ronnie and Charlie. Photo: David Redfern

Portrait of Slawkenbergius

It's now yonks since the 'Whispers, Murmurs and Asides' columnist Talcott Malagrowther was replaced by Slawkenbergius, and Ronnie Scott has asked me, Paul Pry, to write a monograph on your acerbic scribe. I have been instructed not to pull any punches. 'Truth must be served,' said Ronnie, and truth will be served, let there be no doubts about that.

Firstly, Slawkenbergius isn't his real name. If it were he'd surely do something about it. By deed poll. Nor can I reveal his proper name—on account of quite a few people he's written about wanting to do him serious injury. Age: not known and difficult to tell. After he's been on one of his benders he looks about eighty. If he's been off the sauce for a few days and standing in a favourable light, he might pass for sixty. Whatever, he's a person of some antiquity.

BENDERS

And those benders! When it's got about that he's giving it one, the door staff are firmly instructed to refuse him entry on account of him upsetting barmaids and waitresses with barbed tongue. All that guff about his modest half pints in the Dog and Duck is all my eye and Michael Horovitz. In short, it's about the human race's chances of survival in this arms-ridden world, he doesn't believe in tomorrows.

He's single, of course. No woman would have him. Not one in her right mind that is. This may seem unkind, but truth must be served.

Education? Minimal I would say—judging by the convoluted syntax he often uses, but the column's abrasiveness appeals to those who enjoy seeing others put down. They don't find it so appealing when they get a hammering, but that's human nature, I guess.

MISANTHROPIC

He's touchy, intolerant, paranoiac. His general demeanour is misanthropic. He's antisocial. Very much so. *Daily Express* film critic Ian Christie invited him to dinner. 'Who's let you down, Christie?' came the invitee's immediate response. At least he had no illusions that his name wasn't top of the list. It so transpired that his hunch was correct and Lord knows how many people Christie rang before coming to Slawky at the bottom of the barrel. In the late forties, both penniless, they roomed together in a seedy bedsit near Baker Street. Since then Christie has come up in the world, but Slawkenbergius...alas...

He lives in a Kentish Town garret, this habitat, if it can be so described, a scene of utter disarray. Books, magazines, newspapers, manuscripts, jottings, records, empty cartons of convenience foods, beer and wine bottles, form a tapestry of chaos. Cobwebs hang from the curtains. A camp bed, never made up, is the resting place for his old bones. A mouldering fried egg sits congealed in a thick layer of rancid grease in a blackened frying pan on a blackened stove. It's a life style in the true Grub Street tradition of impecunious hacks scratching a living from the pen. It's not a pretty sight.

SPIKED SOLILOQUIES

He rides an ancient bicycle muttering to himself as he pedals hunched over the handlebars, these soliloquies spiked with angry shouts at motorists, motor cyclists (particularly), pedestrians and stray dogs. (He has an overwhelming hatred of canine species; is constantly upsetting doggie owners.) He replaced the conventional bell—a mere tinkling device—with a loud motor horn that frightens the wits out of old ladies imprudently stepping off the pavement.

He's been known to leave his bike in the Club's foyer, much to the disgust of the door staff who bitterly complain that this ancient and rusty Velocette rather lowers the Club's image, and I suppose they have a point.

His wardrobe is somewhat limited and what there is of it usually concealed by a beer-stained demob mackintosh much frayed at the edges. I hasten to add that he's not one of the raincoat brigade. In fact, he's a bit if a puritan, although his quite unprintable objections to the proliferation of 'sex shops' in his beloved Soho is more a plaint against the disappearance of little shops and cafes he once patronised than a moral objection to those sleazy establishments run by patently nasty people.

Ladies of — ahem — easy virtue importuning him in Soho environs are given short shrift with a pithy Anglo-Saxon phrase I can't use in these pages. Mind you, business must be bad for harpies to think of approaching him, even for financial gain. I don't mean to be unkind, but he's no Ronald Colman...

He's totally apolitical. He vehemently asserts that all politicians are knaves and rascals and canvassers calling at his door are sent packing, their ears ringing with foul abuse.

His diet is frugal and occasional. I am talking about solid food. His intake of liquid refreshments is consistent and continuous. He gave up smoking some years back and with all the moral zeal of reformed whore ranting about the evils of sex he makes a great issue of coughing theatrically, clutching his throat, thumping his chest and waving away the offending fumes when someone lights up in his presence.

No, he's not Mr.Affable. Being on a desert island with him alone might be a little trying. He looks a little like Spike Milligan and not unlike our editor. This may seem unfair on Milligan and Godbolt, but truth must be served, and that completes my pen portrait of Slawkenbergius.

PAUL PRY

A trainee at Ronnie Scott's School for Waitresses practising the 'paying-up' procedure

BARBARA WINDSOR
a little known part of the famed Cockney Sparrow's history

Barbara singing one of her three songs nightly with Ronnie Scott's band.

I'm sitting in this roof restaurant, seventeen floors up. Next to me is a pretty hot cookie. She's… ahem — and I don't mean to be ungallant — of a certain age, but the electricity she's got will stay with her until she's eleventy. Sex appeal incarnate, transcending age factors and she still looks great. People are clocking us. Well, to be honest, her more than me. She's famous. But surely, I ask myself, they must be wondering who is this dude with the suave, sophisticated manner and the ready wit that has this beauteous chick falling about. (Alright, I own up, it was only a little giggle here and there, but you've got to pile it on sometimes, haven't you?)

I gave them a full frontal — facially, that is — so they have a good old gander at this high-flier with the worldly mien, a man-about-town whose expression clearly indicated that entertaining a doll like this among those high class rumpots was a twice daily experience. (I only wish it were true, by God I do…) OK, the peepers were on her, the males, particularly, having a gawp, Old Adam raising his ugly head as they lamped her charms, the birds looking at a honey like this as women always do, with that mixture of grudging admiration and tight-lipped envy.

As we talked, her tongue occasionally flicked those dewy lips, and my glasses steamed up. When, in a revealing mini-skirt, she crossed and uncrossed shapely pins and her deep green eyes fixed on mine, the handwriting in my note book became hieroglyphics. When she jabbed a finger in my arm to establish a point, my joints crackled.

Mercifully, in a way, that famous cleavage was under wraps. That would have had me totally goggle-eyed.

THE OLD COME-ON

Considering the time we were talking about — nearly four decades ago, mercy, mercy — this lady recalled real good. She answered questions straight from the lovely curve of her shoulders, recalling her stint as a chirpette with a certain British jazz combo in the early fifties, schlepping hundreds of miles a day playing strictly-from-hunger halls in Sticksville, mugging the mike for three numbers a night, working out at something like a hundred miles a chorus and for peanuts.

She recalled that the boss-man stuck her on the bandstand right next to the skin-walloper to whom a million shimmering decibels was pure joy, but not for this poor little chick. She has vivid memories of the guys who behaved like gentlemen and those who gave her the old come-on, but, she claims, she loved them all.

During this chit-chat she had a pot of tea, I had a lager. 'I'd join you, darling, but if I have one drink I want another… and another, and I've got more interviews to do.' When we left, the Maître d' addressed her as 'dear' — I had a good mind to put this clunkhead in his place, but this is the effect this charmer has on people. She exudes a genuine Cockney friendliness.

(With more than a nod to Damon Runyon, and Downbeat *of the 'forties, but I needed the* Oxford English Dictionary *to help me substitute a few of the phrases in Barbara's recollections, as* JARS *is a family paper).*

I had been interviewing Barbara Windsor at St George's Hotel, Portland Place, near the BBC… and her autobiography, *Barbara, the Laughter and Tears of a Cockney Sparrow*, recently published, refers to those days when she was a singer with Ronnie Scott's Band in 1953. It is a raunchy, racy, revealing read and although it has suffered some prurient editing, her down-to-earth character comes over very strongly.

P.S. Returning home to write up this interview I referred to Barbara's book, lavishly illustrated with photos and stills from her 'Carry On' films. One of the latter is from 'Carry on Camping', in which she loses her bikini top.

I'd written only a little when assailants crept up on me. One filled my legs with heavy metal. Another had a mule kick me in the small of the back, another tied my head to a pneumatic drill. A bug had struck and I retired under twenty blankets to do a five-day battle with the enemy. In my fevered brain, images of all kind crashed against each other in a crazy kaleidoscope, but… they included that still from 'Carry On Camping'. The delirium wasn't all bad.   J.G.

BARBARA RECALLS:

Sometime in 1953 I was working in cabaret at Monsieur Vincent's Côte D'Azur in 47 Frith Street, the same premises now occupied by Ronnie Scott's Club, and when that engagement finished I got a job in a Holloway Road shoe shop, but my agent, Peter Charlesworth, sent me for an audition as singer with Ronnie Scott's Band. I turned up to a rehearsal room in Gerrard Street where I auditioned with six other girls who all had better voices than me. I knew bugger-all about singing with a band, but I got the job. Years later I was on a Michael Parkinson Show with Ronnie, and there Ronnie told me I was chosen because I didn't elect to sing *The Lady Is A Tramp*.

I turned up in a long blue dress with forget-me-nots round my bust. When Ronnie saw it, he lifted his eyes to the sky. 'The dress is very nice,' he said, ripping off the flowers poor Mummy had stayed up all night sewing on, 'but these flowers are covering up the box office.' I didn't quite see what he meant then. I was still a bit of an innocent.

WHITE SLAVE MARKET

Mummy turned up to see me off on my first date with the band. She was quite convinced I was taken to be sold in the white slave market.

The first gig was in Southampton. Annie Ross had been singing with the band and she was a big name. The punters didn't know Barbara Windsor from a packet of Woodbines. I could almost hear the squelch of rotten tomatoes as I went into my first number. I was not only nervous, but my ears were ringing from Tony Crombie's drums. Both the vocalists had to sit on stage throughout the sets and Ronnie had put me near Tony. He's a great drummer, but I wasn't accustomed to such volume at close quarters. Ronnie was lovely. He stuck a pair of maracas in my hand and I was away. I sang three numbers a night.

I can remember many details as if it were yesterday but, apart from the opening night, the names of the venues and towns are lost in a mist. I do remember it was pre-motorway Britain and we seemed to be travelling endlessly and poor little me often bursting for a pee. It was even a pleasure to come across one of those roadside greasehouses the bands used then. Some of the hotels were really grotty, too, but I didn't care as long as I could clean my teeth and wash my parts.

Being a female I loved all the attention, even those knocks on the hotel bedroom door and, I'd say, 'Sorry, but I'm asleep,' I was actually quite dotty about trumpeter Les Condon who treated me like a thorough gentleman. I loved the way he respected me, but often wished he didn't. Typical female!

PETE KING

Pete King, the band's manager, I found rather frightening. 'So it's fifty bob is it,' he'd say, glowering as he came to pay me. He made me feel guilty about taking it. Fifty bob! And the hotel and agent's commission came out of that. I found Stan Tracey a little forbidding. I think that having to work out keys for vocalists over the years had given him, more than anyone else, the feeling that girl singers were just necessary evils. I found Benny Green a most interesting man — so well-read. I loved the black humour on those long journeys. Not that I understood it all. After my last gig we arrived in London at 6.45 in the morning, Les Condon helped me off the bus, and I caught the tube home.

LOVELY, HAIRY EXPERIENCE

Eleven years later I was working on the film 'Sparrows Can't Sing', and who should I see in the studio but Les, working in the band for the soundtrack. Although it was eleven years since he'd helped me off the bus and I'd become a star by then, I still went wobbly at the knees when I saw him. We had a chat and — big deal — I got him a line in the film.

I loved every second of that Scott experience. Of course, being the only girl among a crowd of horny men was a bit hairy. In those two weeks I learned more about men than at any other time. It was the first time in my life I had really gone off the rails. I loved the world and his wife after a few stiff G and Ts. At the end of the three weeks I went to see Peter. I had changed completely, my skirt hitched up, hanging out everywhere, chewing gum and coming out with sayings like 'Yeah, man' and 'Right on'. Peter decided that was the last time I would be allowed out on tour!

I often pop into the Club and get a warm welcome from Peter and Ronnie. I'm so glad they made such a success of the Club and it's nice to go in there, have a drink and listen to the music without the spotlight being put on you. I really love those two and, I say it again, I wouldn't have missed those few weeks with the band for anything.

'Gentleman' Les Condon, left, with famed Count Basie trumpeter, Reunald Jones. Les played with a number of bands including those of Ronnie Scott Tubby Hayes, Woody Herman, Tony Crombie and Humphrey Lyttelton. Les died in November 2007. He was a well respected musician and person. He was a much loved and respected musician and person

LADIES OF THE NIGHT...
recalled by FAIRWEATHER (DIGBY) drawing by FAIRWEATHER (AL)*

Illustration: Al Fairweather

When Jim Godbolt rang asking me to write about landladies experienced by musicians on the road, it was appropriate, for at the time, I was, in fact, a lodger, and my totally delightful landlady (and lord) were none other than Diana and George Melly. George and my band, the Half-Dozen, were completing our 2003 sell-out Christmas season (his thirtieth, our first!) at Ronnie Scott's, and staying with George and Diana in their wonderful house — filled with challenging modern art, discreet erotica, hatstands full of George's superb headgear; all guarded by small dogs known to my hosts as the 'yappies' — constituted, for me, 'Lovely Digs' (one of George's chapter titles in his classic *Owning-Up*).

OWNING-UP

Jim's phonecall also reminded me that George is probably the most observant and humorous chronicler of that (possibly dying) breed, the landlady. For everyone who ever read *Owning-Up*, Mrs Flanagan alone is etched in history. But the kind of formidable — or at least eccentric — figure regularly documented in George's 1965 classic seems somehow to belong naturally in the 1950s and 1960s; the kind of postwar figure of fun that turns up in British B-movies from Ealing. During that time I was first at school, then working for Southend Library. So what I was doing writing about landladies with such spurious authority I can't imagine. Most of my second-hand knowledge came first from *Owning-Up* and later — in the 1970s — from a valued association with Alex Welsh and his great band who, of course, had really experienced, and suffered, the real thing.

MRS FLANAGAN

Owning-Up's 'Mrs Flanagan' really did exist, but her name was actually George's tactful pseudonym for a legendary Manchester landlady who owned a boarding house well remembered by most senior members of the touring jazz fraternity. There are plenty of stories about Mrs Flanagan — tenorist Danny Moss once assured me that thick Manchester fogs regularly penetrated her upper dormitories — but many of the same sorts of hazard could be found anywhere on the road. Alex Welsh and his marvellous sidemen (almost as notable for their perceptively witty observations of the jazz life as their musical supremacy) catalogued many of them; the 'talking sink' in the corner of the room which burbled unaccountably just as sleep was approaching; the central heating radiator which did the same; the adjacent eight-lane motorway/railway/cathedral chiming on the quarter-hour — all putting paid to peaceful sleep as an option. Sometimes things could get more bizarre.

BRUCE TURNER'S JUMP BAND

My dear friend trombonist Pete Strange, who in the earlier 1960s played, recorded and toured with Bruce Turner's memorable Jump Band, recalls the entire group spending the night in a huge dormitory above a Lancashire transport café where the only bedspace available was mattresses hastily set between beds occupied by beefy lorry-drivers. Somewhere in the small hours an alarm clock rang prompting the convoy's collective departure and one huge man, setting feet to floor, nudged a toe into Turner's ribs. 'Time to go to work, mate!'
'Not going to work, Dad!' replied Bruce. As senior readers will know already, Bruce, apart from being (arguably) Britain's greatest swing alto-saxophonist, called everyone 'Dad', and said most things twice. 'Not going to work!'
'That's right, mate,' concurred his neighbour approvingly. 'Fuck 'em!'

THE PRO-ARACHNID LANDLADY

Later on I acquired a few first-hand experiences of my own. Once, in Swansea, a hairy spider's leg pulled itself under my pillow as I turned back the covers for an afternoon's pre-concert siesta. 'Now, there's unusual!' exclaimed my pro-arachnid landlady in her lilting Welsh accent as her startled semi-naked lodger bounded into the lounge to make a complaint. 'He's usually in the sitting room!'
Another time my long-time musical partner, pianist Stan Barker — a proud Lancastrian — and I found ourselves in Harlow New Town, billeted in what amounted to a doss-house. 'What about breakfast?' Stan asked. 'There's a toaster in the room,' said our

* Al Fairweather was trumpeter with clarinettist and fellow-Scotsman Sandy Brown, 1949–66.

hostess, 'and bread and cereals!' 'How about milk?' Stan queried. 'I'll leave it outside in the night,' she promised and disappeared. Next morning Stan opened his door and found a packet of Omo.

As British jazz moves valiantly forward into the twenty-first century, though, it would seem that things are changing. Nowadays you can get a Travelodge (pristine but characterless) for not much more than the price of digs, or of course a small hotel. These, however, offer their own set of inbuilt hazards, including the bitchy habit of sending the musician — laden with luggage — up five flights and along three corridors to his place of rest. The late Beryl Bryden was good at circumventing such tricks. 'Ground floor!' she would boom, while parking her luggage trolley at Reception, 'unless you've a lift! Nothing above the road or down a corridor! And no-smoking of course!' She even woke up one landlady on the Wirral at 2 a.m. to demand a feather-pillow! But of course there are standard ways in which staff get their own back. In *Second Chorus*, Humphrey Lyttelton recalled the army of vacuum-cleaners making premature invasion outside the bedroom door. But now it's quite usual to get a peremptory knock followed by the stentorian threat

—' I'll come back!'— from the task-force leader. Hotels can be great or awful. An infamous one in Birmingham, which I won't name, offers towels so thin that (in trumpeter Bruce Adams's vivid phrase) 'you could spit peas through them!'

HOSPITABLE LANDLADIES

Of course, not all landladies (or landlords) were — or are — horrible. Pete Strange recalls a Mrs Watkinson at Grimsby who, for seven shillings, would lay on a cheese-and-pickle supper after the gig and all the kippers you could eat for breakfast. She sounds lovely. But some landladies are more hospitable yet. This last story has been attributed to quite a number of jazzmen, but Jack Parnell assures me that it was in fact the famous accordionist Tollefson who struck up an intimate relationship with his hostess during a South Coast theatre summer season. One day the maestro came back to find his summertime love spread-eagled across the kitchen-table and bestraddled by the lead violinist of the company. 'Oh dear,' exclaimed the object of passion viewing her disconcerted inamorato from a horizontal angle. 'You must think I'm a terrible flirt!' His response — unlike his music — was never recorded.

WHISPERS, MURMURS & ASIDES

THE ROYALS ARE JAZZIN'

Cartoon by Hedley Picton

I'm a sucker for those tit-bits about the Royal Family's social life and was riveted by a report in the *Daily Mail* that 'A small jazz group booked to appear at a grand country home expected the usual crowd of Hooray Henrys and Henriettas demanding to be entertained from dawn till dusk, but imagine their surprise to discover that the family's only guests were the Queen, Prince Philip, Charles, Andrew and Edward and the Queen Mother. Even the servants had been dismissed for the night's occasion organised by the evergreen Dowager Lady Sybil Cholmondeley at her Palladian palace Houghton Hall, near Kings Lynn, Norfolk.'
One of the band said, 'They were all terribly relaxed. Prince Philip was stretched out on a sofa and everybody was helping

themselves to food and drink and the Queen Mother asked the band to play *Birth of the Blues*. I don't know why Diana wasn't there — perhaps she doesn't like jazz.'
Now, wouldn't it have been nice if the Queen and Consort had got up and had a little jive to the band. Here is artist Hedley Picton's impression of them cutting a rug, as we used to say back in the dark ages.

SINGERS OF YORE

A little gem from *The Standard Pronouncing Dictionary of the English Language* edited by P. Austin Nuttall LL.D. — 'Swinger, swing' — er, s. One who swings.' We all know that, I can hear you saying — but this dictionary is dated 1863! It's true, y'know, there's nothing new…
CLARK 'CLARKY' TEWKESBURY

'If I had it all to do over again, I would have liked to be the King of Swing.'

Cartoon by Dana Fradon from New Yorker, 1978

DUKE ELLINGTON IN ENGLAND
Duke Ellington's band made their UK debut in June 1933. A later notable figure in British jazz was in the audience...

A contemporary caricature of the Duke

Seventy years ago the greatest name in jazz played in Britain for the first time; a truly historic event. Of all the figures in the variegated history of jazz, none, in terms of sheer creative achievement, surpasses that of pianist/bandleader/composer and arranger Edward Kennedy Ellington and his piano playing was considered the least of his achievements.

But I, for one, believe that his chording was a vital spark plug and he was a fine stride pianist, up there with Fats Waller, Cliff Jackson, James P. Johnson and Donald Lambert. Since 'stride' piano is redolent of the Twenties, let it also be mentioned that Duke is on record with Charles Mingus and Max Roach, with John Coltrane and Elvin Jones, and with Louis Armstrong. But, then, the Duke crystallised almost every element of jazz in his succession of bands over an incredible five decades.

AN ARRAY OF GREAT SOLOISTS

No other bandleader – not even Count Basie – ever boasted such an array of great soloists... trumpeters Bubber Miley,

A banner headline trumpeting the great event

Freddy Jenkins, Artie Whetsol, Cootie Williams, Rex Stewart, Ray Nance, Cat Anderson, Clark Terry, Harold Baker; trombonists Tricky Sam Nanton, Lawrence Brown, Quentin Jackson, Julian Priester, Bootie Wood; clarinettists Barney Bigard, Jimmy Hamilton, Russell Procope; saxophonists Johnny Hodges, Harry Carney, Ben Webster, Paul Gonsalves, Harold Ashby, Al Sears; drummers Sonny Greer, Louie Bellson, Sam Woodyard, and Duke introduced us to that innovative bassist, Jimmy Blanton. Duke's arrangements and, later, those of Billy Strayhorn (often in collaboration), were designed to display the individual characteristics of his soloists. Duke wrote hundreds of superb tunes (with or without utilising themes of his sidemen) that are timeless in their appeal.

SECOND-CLASS CITIZEN

Duke died on 24th May 1974, aged 75, leading a band almost until the end of his extraordinarily productive life. He may have pondered on how he, a second-class citizen in his own country, had been acclaimed a genius throughout most of the Western world and fêted by royalty in Britain during his 1933 trip, long before the establishment acknowledged him in the US. And of all the many ironies attendant to the history of jazz, surely there are few as striking that the suave and sophisticated Duke, on his European debut, on Monday 9th June 1933 at the London Palladium should be on the same bill as Max Miller, the 'Cheeky Chappie' whose 'blue' humour had him banned by the BBC.

One moment there was Max, cracking his bawdy jokes, next the curtain rising on thirteen 'coloured' men performing magical flights of improvisation, interweaved in a rich tapestry of orchestral colours on tunes ranging from the plaintively melancholy to the lustily exultant. It was a supremely imaginative and superbly executed distillation of African-American culture, and for only 15 to 20 minutes. Duke's band was just a 'turn' on a variety bill.

The orchestra broadcast on the BBC's National Programme from 8pm to 8.45pm on Wednesday, 11th. In the *Era*, columnist Stanley Nelson challenged the fee the band received. He wrote: 'I cannot see for the life of me that the Ellington band, as good as it undoubtedly is, represents such a catch for the BBC. Its appeal is undoubtedly limited. They're lucky to get broadcast at all.'

The fee, which Nelson thought exorbitant, was — £30. No, not a misprint... *thirty* pounds (£30). For the entire band!

'THE THUNDERER' AND DUKE

The following, quite bizarre, review appeared in the august *Times* newspaper. Their 'Special Correspondent' wrote: 'Mr Duke Ellington, whose performance is the chief item in this week's programme at the Palladium, is exceptional and remarkably efficient in his own line. He does at once and with a considerable show of ingenuity what a jazz band commonly does with difficulty and often fails to do so (sic!). And the excitement and exacerbation of the nerves which was caused by the orchestra was the more disquieting by reason of their complete control and precision. It is not an orgy, but a scientific application of measured and dangerous stimuli…'

JACK'S DEFINING MOMENT

There can't be many people around who attended those six historic nights at the Palladium, but one who did is drummer/leader Jack Parnell, in whose 1951 band both Ronnie Scott and club director Pete King played.

Jack recalls the transforming moment at the Palladium in June 1933…

'I was nine. My uncle Val [Parnell], a director of the Palladium, took me to hear Duke's band. At that age I had no idea of their significance, but I was entranced by drummer Sonny Greer, seated behind a glittering array of kit, which I later discovered was a bass drum, snare drum, tom-tom, floor tom-tom, Chinese cymbal, Turkish cymbal, hi-hat cymbals, cowbell, tam-tams, tubular bells, woodblock, temple blocks, trays containing drumsticks, brushes, tympani mallets, a pair of tympani and vibraphone. It was awesome… a wondrous sight for a nine-year-old.

At that moment I was destined to be a drummer and, considering the great musicians, including Ronnie Scott, and singers I've had the privilege to work with over these years, I owe Sonny a lot!

The following year, I bought my first Duke Ellington 78, costing all of 3 shillings (15p). It was *Dear Old Southland* backed by *Daybreak Express*, which I still have, with many, many more Duke records prized in my collection.'   J.G.

Sonny Greer at his kit; photo: courtesy of The Max Jones Collection. Below, Jack Parnell, man and boy; photo(the adult) by David Sinclair

WHISPERS, MURMURS & ASIDES

PSEUD INDEED!

Again, I am obliged to Ron Rubin, who has a long proboscis for the absurd. He sent me the following classic, penned by Nick Coleman, writing about John Coltrane's 'Equinox' in *The Independent* and quoted in *Private's Eye*'s 'Pseud's Corner'.

'Bip- bip bop. Bib- bop… plank. The rhythm section forms itself into flat droplets, like drips from a tap plunging into a plastic watering can, hollow sounding and unresonant. It's a cyclical, potentially infinite pattern. Coltrane, on tenor sax, noses around the leak for eight minutes until he's satisfied that he's got to the bottom of the problem. Then he stops. Uncharacteristically, he is careful throughout, thoughtful and enquiring, not Herculean or ecstatic. This is the music that accompanied the birth of my son, and it will make my funeral a groove (Jazz, like life, is mostly plumbing).'

Oh, dearie me!   J.G.

A roving musician called Rubin
Liked black coffee with one sugar cube in;
But one night in Bombay,
At a topless cafe.
It was served to him white with one boob in.

Ron Rubin

113

A Night in The Life... of the Editor
with Ronnie, Spike, Ludwig and Keith

A conversation, of sorts, between Ronnie Scott, né Schatt, and *JARS* editor, Jim Godbolt, aka Goldblatt, concerning Scott, Spike Milligan and Ludwig Van Beethoven, including Keith Shadwick, on Burns Night, Wednesday, January 25th, 1995.

I had been laid low by influenza, made worse by the specifics, and, in my delirium had been visited by such well-wishers as Louis Armstrong, Count Basie, Duke Ellington, Ponzi Crunz and Ducky Yontz, who are no longer with us. Another solicitous visitor was Ronnie Scott — still about — who came bearing a large bottle of the best malt whisky, and with the comforting words, 'Get better soon, Goldblatt, we don't know how we'd get on without you and *JARS*. Fifteen years you've been doing such a grand job? Why it seems like only yesterday since you came into our lives, and praise be.'
I had been hallucinating...

ROBBIE BURNS NIGHT
And that night the radio was awash with tributes to Robert Burns, with readings of his poetry, in dialect, and live relays of wassailing Scots assailing my ears. I managed to doze off when the phone rang.
'Goldblatt? Schatt here. Which Beethoven symphony has a movement titled The Funeral March?'
I was still hallucinating. Ronnie Scott, jazzman, proprietor of a jazz club, asking me, an ancient jazz buff, such a question. Obviously, my condition was deteriorating. More aspirins and whisky? Or should I call a doctor?
'Are you there?' enquired a testy Scott.
'Yes, I'm here,' I replied, weakly, 'but I'm hearing things — I swear I heard you ask which Beethoven Symphony has a funeral march.'
'That's what I asked,' replied Scott. 'Which one is it?'
Here the peremptory Scott exclaimed: 'Come on man, jump to it. Time is money!'
I said I'd have a look in my reference books–*The Oxford Companion Of Music. Black's Dictionary of Music and Musicians, The Bloomsbury Dictionary*

What would Ludwig have thought of this conversation?

of Music. Oh yes, I've got these, and others, on my bookshelves. Prominently displayed. They lend a touch of class to a library otherwise concerned with low-life jazzmen, but now, half dead, I've got to actually read them.

KEITH SHADWICK
I couldn't find any reference to a Beethoven Funeral March, croakily rang Scott and suggested he try Keith Shadwick, who (with Robert Cowan) has a programme on Classic FM every Friday night.
'You know the guy, do me a favour and ring him.' This was phrased as a request, but the tone was commanding. Scott the boss. 'Now, please, it's rather urgent.'
'It's late, Ronnie, he's sure to be in bed, and why the rush?'
'Twelve o'clock LATE?' enquired a disbelieving Scott. 'And I can't tell you why', he added mysteriously.
Try ringing Ronnie Scott at twelve noon, and see what sort of frosty reception you get from someone who can't distinguish shapes until two p.m. Reluctantly, I called Keith, who was asleep. Or had been until I rang. He didn't know of a funeral march in any Beethoven work; Berlioz, Chopin, Mahler, Shostakovich, but not Ludwig Van B. I rang Scott and returned to sleep racked with phantasmagorical images, one of them the spectacle of a kilted Ludwig and Ronnie dancing a Highland reel to the wail of bagpipes, when, at about 12.30 a.m., the phone rang again.
'Schatt here. It's the second movement, the *Third Symphony, The Eroica*, please amend your reference books.'
When I awoke the following morning it took time for me to realise that the above conversation piece was not a part of my fevered images and rang Keith Shadwick, not only to apologise for disturbing him at such a late hour, but asking would he please amend his reference books.
You, dear reader, may be wondering why I got that call at the bewitching hour.

SCOTT, MILLIGAN AND BEETHOVEN
Well, some years ago, Ronnie Scott and Spike Milligan were in a box at the Albert Hall listening to Beethoven's *Eroica*. I'll repeat that for the benefit of those who are not able to credit such an unlikely juxtaposition. Ronnie and Spike were in a box at the Albert Hall listening to Beethoven's *Eroica*. Got it?
The funeral movement seemed to go on interminably and Spike, loudly, Milliganishly, cried, 'He must have lived an effing long way from the cemetery', and Ronnie cracked up.

(But he couldn't remember which symphony it was — hence the call.)

But why did he need to check? Because he had received a call from the BBC to attend a *This Is Your Life* programme, Spike the subject (hence the secrecy bit) and Ronnie intended to tell the Albert Hall story. But, in the event, the show over ran and Ronnie, rather like Gracie Fields who took her harp to a party and nobody asked her to play, was not called to pay his tribute to Spike.

So, all that kerfuffle for nothing- except that I, Ronnie Scott and Keith Shadwick now know that the second movement of Ludwig's Third Symphony is called The Funeral March. And, no doubt, many of you out there are now wiser. It's the sort of information that could come useful when conversation flags at a dinner party. Certainly, that call from Mr. Scott will keep my guests riveted for many years to come.

PERSONAL VIEW

I have often expressed my admiration for BBC Radio 3. It is, without question, an oasis of cultural value in an otherwise generally arid desert. I applaud the measured delivery and clear diction of their announcers and presenters. What I know about classical music I owe to R3 and its predecessor, the Third Programme. Long may it continue to provide its unique service. BUT, for a station designed, and heavily funded, for more minority interests, the jazz minority is scurvily treated by the operastes who dominate its programming.

Opera — sodden it is, and although opera is entitled to its showing on such a station, I often wonder how many of its listeners (and how many of them multilingual?) sit through those three to four hour marathons emoted in German, Russian, Czech, French and Italian. Perhaps controller Roger Wright has an answer?

And what a dastardly lot are the characters in these epics! Their antics involving murder, rape, infanticide, incest, backstabbing, treachery — gore galore, perpetrated by a truly amoral collection and invariably portrayed at inordinate length. In comparison, jazz people are the very essence of all that is pure, noble and upright.

COPULATION IN A COFFIN!

Radio 3 repeatedly trailed *Le Grande Macabre*, written by György Ligeti, (György who?), the announcer ecstatically delineating the unsavoury ingredients of the plot, which embraced all that is nasty in the operatic woodshed, he patently relishing one scene where, 'A young couple, desperate for a bit of peace and quiet from the mayhem around them, copulate in a coffin'. The entire phantasmagoria was described in the *Radio Times* as 'Evoking the grotesque fantasy world of Breughel and Hieronymus Bosch, a place of infinite corruption. The population is given to drunkenness and lust and the country is on the verge of political collapse — when Nekrotzer, *Le Grande Macabre* — announces the imminent destruction to the world.' Jazz people are accustomed to being described as 'fiends' and stories of their drink, drugs and sex peccadilloes eagerly taken up by the press, but there's not a self-respecting *fiend*, musician or fan I know, who would be seen dead — in a manner of speaking — having congress in a coffin, if only because the proximity of its rightful occupant would make a mockery of the R.I.P. headstone and — in a manner of speaking – put our fiend off his stroke,

Recently R3 ran a series of hour-long programmes on the 'Secrets of Orchestration' involving a writer, a presenter and the highly expensive services of the BBC National Orchestra of Wales playing snippets of great works to illustrate the commentary, and very educative it was, too. But why not a similar amount of time (at much less expense) to a series on jazz arrangers, such as Fletcher Henderson, Duke Ellington, Bill Challis, Don Redman, Gil Evans, Ernie Wilkins, Billy Strayhorn, John Dankworth, Buck Clayton and, for historical completeness, the early scores of Ferde Grofé with Paul Whiteman?

JAZZ FIENDS PAY THEIR FEES

I have to remind those opera-besotted planners at R3 that the jazz fraternity also stump up our licence fee, to help pay their salaries and our pleas for more airtime to jazz are fully justified. We don't expect this from the 'popular' stations. It's the minority appeal station from which we expect and deserve support. An indication of their attitude to jazz is that in the Millennium celebrations of the history of music over 2,000 years, they cancelled Jazz Record Requests on New Year's Eve. I am told that there is a jazz overseer at R3. What does he do all day long? The usual weekly allocation to jazz is Jazz Notes — four half hour slots late at night, a whole hour — whoopee! — for *Jazz Record Requests* at the civilised time,

6 p.m, on Saturdays, followed by a half hour for a series, and the late hour on the same day featuring 'contemporary' jazz. That amounts to four and a half hours from a station that is on the air twenty-four hours a day, seven days a week — that's a hundred and sixty eight hours! Indeed, the jazz allocation is criminally sparse.

There should be at least an hour a day devoted to jazz and this not just recorded material but 'live' performances from the host of British jazz musicians who could do with the money and the exposure, and such allocations of 'live' time spread stylistically, and not just for the 'contemporary' musicians unfairly favoured at present.

A few I could mention are Wally Fawkes, John Barnes, Acker Bilk, Diz Disley, Ron Rubin, Johnny Parker, Monty Sunshine, Mike Garrick, The Scott Legacy and Tommy Whittle. When did you last hear any of these on Radio 3? Whilst on this thorny subject, it appears that what few jazz presenters there are, arbitrarily choose who should be the interviewees. J.G.

INTERVIEW...
refuting a vile rumour

If the following lament has a familiar ring to it, please bear with me, but — and here it comes — this was supposed to be a report on the bi-monthly interview I have with Ronnie Scott and, usually — if I may make so bold — I manage to fashion some sort of brick from the few wisps of straw (conversationally speaking) I glean from these encounters, and this time it was my intention to enquire if there was any truth in a certain rumour that had reached my ears.

Not that I was hopeful of a reply, even if Ronnie had strong thoughts on the subject. In truth, Ronnie has many strong thoughts about lots of things, but getting him to talk about them is a horse of a quite different colour. You've got to catch him on the day when his metabolism charges the vocal chords and the mystery of that cycle in his chemistry I haven't yet fathomed out, nor do I think I've got that many years left to work on it.

Mind you, I have experienced his vocal side, but mostly when he's watching on TV those horses he'd backed showing reluctance to leave the starting stall or,

should they manage this, display an equal reluctance to beat the other gee-gees to the finishing post. On these fraught occasions Mr. Scott is frothily eloquent — and quite unprintable.

BLACK JAILER

On this day everything was loaded against discussion. The TV was on, volume full up; the phone didn't stop ringing; there was a stream of callers; a very noisy staff person with a beltful of clanking keys stomped about like a black jailer in a Hollywood period epic.

There were further complications when club taximan Joe Green walked in and queried a chess move he'd read about in a paper. Ronnie, to manager Pete King's disgust and despair, immediately spread his chess board on Pete's desk and set up to demonstrate its impossibility. Pete let fly a stream of obscenities.

As if this wasn't enough, Will Sproule, Ronnie's booker in the club's agency division, put his head round the door and enquired if Ronnie wanted to do a gig with his Quintet at the Pizza Express, Dean Street, W1.

'Where's that?' blandly enquired Ronnie as he lifted a Bishop.

Will, Irish, from Belfast, thought it was an Irish answer to a simple question. After all, the Pizza Express lies barely five hundred yards from Ronnie's, but if you're Irish and you believe in the little people you could be forgiven for thinking that Ronnie didn't know the whereabouts of the Pizza Express. He gave Ronnie the information.

'How do I get there?' enquired Ronnie, displacing a Bishop with a Knight. (At least, I think that's what he did for, I must confess, the game is totally beyond my intellect…)

Now, I'm not taken in by this

apparent artlessness. I know it's a trap for smarty-pants who try and come it — Ronnie is anything but simple. I also know that this feigned ignorance means extra effort on the part of his minions to get Ronnie to gigs and, therefore, less effort on his part in these exercises.

ART OF DELEGATION

Like Roger Horton at the 100 Club on the other side of Oxford Street, RS has mastered the art of delegation — meaning, in truth, heaping as much on the backs of others as is inhumanly possible. Both remind me of a classic line delivered by that buxom beauty of the silver screen in the thirties, Mae West, in one of her films. As she glided across the thick pile carpet of her sumptuously furnished apartment she drawled to a coloured maid, 'Beulah, peel me a grape.'

Both these past masters at delegation would have you peeling their grapes. But I digress. What was this rumour which, eventually, Ronnie vehemently rejected? It hurts me to talk of this calumny; of scoundrels and knaves who spread such heresy. I'd have them topped, so I would. I refer to the scurrilous tales being put about that Ronnie was changing his joke routine.

What sort of rapscallions are these so nefariously engaged? Come to think of it, topping would be too good for them, that it would. They must know the harm they'll do to the club spreading such stories!

Ronnie changing his routine, indeed! The very idea shakes me to the core. In this rapidly changing world — and not for the better, that's for sure — Scottie's jokes told in a rigidly unchanging sequence with undeviating inflection are something one can cling to — something rock-like in these turbulent times. One asks oneself what sort of life would it be without Ron's sing-along gags, each one we've known and loved for over

Ronnie, being addressed by the editor labouring a point, suddenly realises he has an urgent appointment elsewhere…

two decades.

But, bad news travels fast, and one evening at the Club recently a lady of a — ahem — certain age approached Roxy Beaujolais at the cash desk and (as Roxy sussed) while trying not to convey she was really of such antiquity as to have been listening to Ronnie's gags for twenty years, she gave the game away by owning up that these had amused her for that long and she wasn't paying good money to hear new jokes.

Relaxed by Roxy's gentle demeanour and winning smile she admitted that it was the cosily familiar that comforted her most in this unsettled society, that she was too old for change. Roxy, typically solicitous, emphatically scotched the idea that Ronnie would even consider, much less tell, new jokes. The lady, immensely relieved, paid her entrance fee. Who was actually playing music that night didn't seem to concern her.

Who was she? Perhaps a sad divorcee alone in her flat who wanted cheering up and what better cure for the blues than the Grimaldi of Frith Street's patter?

She's not the only one amused by the string of chestnuts delivered with the stomach-chilling nerve of a somnambulist blithely walking the rooftops at the dead of night, and I am delighted to report that record producer Jimmy Parsons recorded this spiel one April evening, and the intention is to later record Ronnie's Quintet and release an album with the tentative title of 'The Music and Wit of Ronnie Scott'.   J.G.

WHY DON'T YOU GET YOURSELF A PROPER JOB?
enquired MIKE GARRICK'S father

Mike Garrick, pianist, composer, leader and educator has, like most jazzmen, played all manner of gigs outside the jazz club and concert circuit, one of which, for the Arts Council, was at an ex-stately home. He pithily recalls the experience. Garrick reads this poem on the Vocalion DVD 'A New September'. Michael Garrick's New Quartet, live at Pizza on the Park

Here is a moment I relish;
You crawl up to a crumbling retreat
Complete with its ivy decked turrets
And echoes of once-marching feet.

The drawbridge might even be working
(The moat is still full to the brim)
And the blue British rain still a-belting down
Through thick, and through thinner – and thin.

You hop out at a huge oaken doorway
Which has shadowed the tall and the great
And lean on a white plastic bell push
And sit down for a ten-minute wait.

Emerges a pallid old jobsworth
Man and boy sixty year he hath been
'Just walk this way if you would, sir;'
Your eyes meet a riveting scene.

Priceless antiques all a-clutter
Wallpaper-thin and aloof
With a carpet to match and to top it –
A 40-watt bulb in the roof.

Oak carvings, fine brasswork & dustsheets
But where are we going to play?
On wind the corridors, stairways
and staterooms,
Vast tapestries now turning grey.

At last. 'Is there anything you need?'
Prays our guide with a clasp of his hands
'Some tea?' we enthuse politely
'And you don't have two music stands?'

The piano is noble but ancient
Tuned this morning but stiff with the damp
We unload, get warmed up, fix an order
And find there's no plug for the amp.

We change in M'Lady's last bedroom
Tea is served at the pull of a wire
White napkins, the best, with the family crest;
They even turn on the gas fire.

A knock on the door. In comes another;
The parochial Arts Person appears,
Bustling, purposeful, knowing,
'They're not really jazz fans', she fears.

'You'll play something they know?
O, splendid!
And of course I know you're not loud.
Time for a drink before starting?
I think we've got quite a good crowd.'

She's right. The bar's buzzing with locals
Then up looms a vaguely alien face:
'Remember the Bull's Head at Binley?
Whad' ya make o'this place?'

In we go. The standard lamp softens the darkness
The folding chairs' creak is but slight
We strike up — the acoustic is marvellous;
Ahead of us stretches the night.

Something old, something new, then some laughter
The rainstorm has vapoured away
And then, sure as fate in the interval –
'What do you do during the day?'

Then back to a warm, well-oiled welcome
We can hardly do anything wrong;
Confidence mounts, every last quaver counts
— We almost end up with a song.

For they like it, they're beaming they love you
You can hear the swart parapets ring
Yes, tonight you swung like the clappers
And tomorrow? It won't mean a thing.

IAN 'SPIKE' MACKINTOSH
English timber merchant, Louis Armstrong disciple

I don't know many timber merchants, white, middle-class, educated at a public school, devout believers in private enterprise and private education, with the unshakeable belief that Tories had the divine right to rule, who were officers in the Tank Corps, who played jazz trumpet as near to Louis Armstrong as any white man of any nationality ever achieved. In fact I know of only one — Ian 'Spike' Mackintosh, who died on January 18th, 1995 aged seventy-seven.   J.G.

Mackintosh by Trog

He was a much-loved man, although, frequently, his arrival at sessions with trumpet in hand was cause for alarm. It was no secret that he was very partial to a taste and after over-imbibing his playing was uncomfortably erratic. At his best he could uplift a session; at his worst, he could reduce it to a shambles.Short, dapper, with military moustache and a Hooray Henry accent — a gentleman jazzman, you might say — he was the most unlikely carrier of the Armstrong torch.

TWO OTHER SPIKES
Spike Mackintosh was born in London, on 9th February, 1918. He attended the City of London school where he developed an interest in jazz and took up the trumpet to emulate his hero Louis Armstrong. He admired the big black bands of the time — Duke Ellington, Count Basie, Fletcher Henderson, Chick Webb and Don Redman, and was particularly fond of recordings by Spike Hughes and his Negro Orchestra. He adopted the nickname of 'Spike' as mark of respect for the Anglo-Irishman who had travelled to New York in 1933 to make those historic recordings with personnel that included Red Allen, Coleman Hawkins, and Benny Carter.

Typically, Spike volunteered for the army at the outbreak of war, was soon commissioned in the Royal Tank Corps and saw action in France. Following Dunkirk, he was one of the few survivors of a troopship sunk by enemy action. He was picked up clutching his trumpet. He was again in action at El Alemein. Commanding one of the tanks assembled to launch an attack that proved to be one of the most decisive of the war, Lt. Mackintosh received his order to advance, but at that moment was listening to *West End Blues* by Louis Armstrong and his Savoy Ballroom Five from a Forces station and it was not until Louis had finished his majestic coda that Spike gave his order. Hitler — and Field Marshall Montgomery — could wait. First things first with Spike…

His tank was knocked out by enemy fire and German soldiers, believing him to be dead, stripped him of every possession, except his trumpet.

Later, in Naples, Spike was one of team of judges for a service dance band competition. One of the bands included gunner Spike Milligan on trumpet. Milligan, quasi-bitterly, recalled the contest in his *Where Have All The Bullets Gone?* one of his several very funny war memoirs. He wrote: 'The compère was Captain Philip Ridgeway. He was as informed on dance bands as Mrs. Thatcher is on groin-clenching in the Outer Hebrides. The other judges were Lt. Eddie Carroll and Lt. 'Spike' Mackintosh. Can you believe it? We didn't win! WE DIDN'T WIN!!! I wasn't even mentioned! Why were the 56 Area Welfare Services persecuting me like this? At the contest I had heard shouts of 'Give him the prize'. No one listened, even though I shouted it very loud. Never mind, there would be other wars.'

RENEGADE TRADITIONALISTS
On demobilisation, Spike Mackintosh returned to the family timber business and sat in at jam sessions, at the height of the Traditionalists versus Modernists war. He had no liking for bebop, nor for banjo-dominated revivalism. He found his musical, and drinking company with the mainstreamers, most of them renegade traditionalists. One of these was clarinettist/cartoonist Wally 'Trog' Fawkes, leading his Troglodytes. They recorded some twenty excellent sides for the Decca label on which Mackintosh proved just he had absorbed the essence as well as the phraseology of Armstrong. On some of these sessions the Troglodytes were joined by 'modernists' Eddie Taylor (drums), ex- Johnny Dankworth Seven, and Lennie Bush(bass), a founder member of the seminal Club Eleven where British Bebop started, and a member of Ronnie Scott's Ninepiece.

Spike was equally as authorative at a private party session in the company of veteran US saxophonist Bud Freeman, the set captured on portable equipment. He was not the least bit in awe of his distinguished session mate.

WILD BILL DAVISON

But he was not a consistent performer. On one occasion he moved, uninvited, to sit in with a band led by the brilliant Welsh pianist, Dill Jones. Jones, himself no stranger to the juice, quickly perceived Spike's condition and turned him away. Undeterred, Spike made his contribution from a seat in the audience. He had his insensitive side. He was at a party given in honour of the white US trumpeter, Wild Bill Davison and the tactful Mackintosh said to Davison, 'Ah, Wild Bill, my fourth favourite trumpeter.' 'Oh, yes,' growled Davison, 'and who are the other three?' Mackintosh replied: 'Louis Armstrong, Cootie Williams, Red Allen and Roy Eldridge. NO- you're my fifth favourite!'

Spike ran a weekly record session at the one-bar Drum and Monkey, Blenheim Terrace, St John's Wood, NW London. His fellow enthusiasts including Jack Hutton, ex-editor of the *Melody Maker*, clarinettists Ian Christie and Alan Cooper, trombonist Mike Pointon and pianist Stan Greig, dubbing themselves The Codgers. The rest of the clientele, whether they liked it or not, had their 'quiet drink' shattered by Louis Armstrong, Duke Ellington, Mills Blue Rhythm Band, and the like, at mind-blowing volume. They were also regaled with Spike vocally duplicating Armstrong's singing and playing. The irrepressible enthusiast! The landlord approved. His takings shot up at those sessions.

When Spike attended Ronnie's, the eponymous Mr Scott was treated to Spike singing (or rather gurgling) Louis's phrases. In fact, Ronnie used to do an imitation of Spike imitating Louis. Not many people know that.

Spike continued playing trumpet almost up until his death, sitting in with Wally Fawkes at the King Alfred, Marylebone Lane, West London. His thirst remained undiminished, and his 'lip' often faltered, but on his good nights the stirring resonances of Armstrong licks rang throughout the pub and well beyond.

One of the familiar aspects of these sessions was pianist Stan Greig, with a tense expression on his craggy features, his hands anxiously poised over the keys waiting to plunge them down for the resolving chord(s) to bring a Mackintosh coda spectacular to a triumphant finish, and when it finally happened there was a great sigh of relief from musicians and audience. Not all these climaxes came off. Spike's cliff-hangers were fraught occasions.

He was indeed a combination of opposites; the reiterative soak and erratic trumpeter when too deep in his cups; the amusing companion and fine player when he'd paced himself; the High Tory who was one of the chaps.

SHOULDN'T THAT CHILD BE IN BED

There are hundreds of stories about Spike, some of them undoubtedly apocryphal. One of them was when, totally legless, being apprehended by a policeman and solemnly telling the officer, in that public school posh voice of his, that any unsteadiness was due to the war injury, but my favourite tale concerned him at a party given by Wally Fawkes. Spike, well loaded, fell against a bamboo room divider bringing down the ornaments with a tremendous clatter. The noise awakened Joanna Fawkes, then about five, and in tears she stood at the top of the stairs leading to the drawing room. Spike, wiping bits of Italian pottery and trailus acanthus from his person, looked up and said, 'Wally, it's none of my business, but shouldn't that child be in bed?'

I can vouch for that tale. I was there.

He is survived by wife Diana, and three sons, Nick, Robert and Cameron, the latter a famous theatrical impresario and knighted.

RONNIE'S JOKES

Taking on bigger premises represented a big gamble, but, like my dad, I've always been a bit of a gambler and I must say I usually have a lot of luck. But mostly, I have been known to stop a runaway horse dead in its tracks just by putting money on it.

With the larger venue we engaged more staff. In 1966 we employed six waitresses and I believe three of them actually worked at the Club. On the whole our staff were pretty loyal and stayed with us, although we did have a lavatory attendant once who quit because he couldn't stand the smell of in the kitchen.

We also took a Hungarian waiter. He didn't understand the social security system when he started to work for us, and he used to stick Green Shield stamps on his insurance card. He got nicked for it and the judge gave him six months. And a tea set.

We also had a rather strange Italian waiter working for us briefly. He told us his previous job was road sweeper. In Venice.

But Luigi never got anything right. In fact, the only time he was right in his whole life was the one occasion when he thought he was wrong.

And I'll tell you, there were a lot of people who thought we were wrong - and insane- when we decided in 1968 to acquire the premises next door and redesign the Club as a three-storey entertainment complex...

HERBERT COOT LETTERS

(The correspondence between Herbert Coot and Ronnie Scott, with apologies to The Henry Root Letters by William Donaldson)

1st April, 1985
Dear Mr. Scott
I was hoping, after all these years I have been coming to your club (not to mention the quids I have settled into your palm) I could address you as 'Ronnie', but since I have to make a strong complaint about the service in your club, I will have to forgo this hoped-for familiarity. My beef is about that Amazonian female at your club, laughingly called a waitress, who threatened me and Mrs. Coot last week-end with — and I quote her own choice terminology — 'A thump up the bracket if you don't settle your bill here and now,' and when we were about to leave, your Mr. King physically restrained us. Mrs. Coot was very upset and made my life hell for days afterwards, accusing me of craven cowardice, asking why I didn't live up to the Errol Flynn image that made her accept my proposal of marriage twenty five years ago. I expect you've had the same problem yourself. All considered, I don't feel I can send you the usual pound.
Yours sincerely,
Herbert Coot

7th April, 1985
Dear Mr. Coot,
Considering the severity of your letter of the 1st instant I, too, will forbear to address you by your first name, but please accept my apologies for the incident to which you refer. However, you were wise not to take on Millie. Mad Millie, we call her and she's a tough cookie. You

Illustration: Hedley Picton

were right in your letter of 14th February last year in guessing that she engages in female wrestling, in mud, in Hamburg, and, as I recently discovered, she also does a bit, so to speak, of conventional wrestling. Last week she took on two SS men and gave them a terrible pasting. True, they were old SS men — well, they would be, wouldn't they? — and your ordinary roughs — no aristocrats — but they still remembered a trick or two. By the way, she recently won a knocker contest in the Reeperbahn. She went over really big.
Truth to tell, we find Millie is very useful dealing with difficult customers. If we're in trouble, she's our boy, if you get what I mean, and it's my belief that in the club's gloom she mistook you and Mrs. C. to be two of our prize bilkers, Mr. And Mrs. McLennan from Manchester. I'll have a word with Millie. Well, actually, I'll get Pete King to have a word. I can't stand the sight of blood, especially mine. As for people leaving before the end, this just isn't on. It looks so bad, as if the show isn't up to much and, as you know, this is never the case.
I do hope my explanation will make you feel happier and that you will send the usual quid with your next letter. Honestly, life doesn't seem the same without it. Nor does my wallet.
Yours sincerely,
Ronnie Scott
PS: No, I haven't had the same problem re an Errol Flynn image, but that's probably because I'm more the Ronald Colman type, like our editor.

Typical Ronnie Scott's members...

14th April, 1985
Dear Mr. Scott,
Thank you for your explanation, unsatisfactory as it is. In future will you kindly instruct your maitre 'd to spare us Mad Millie, or maybe drop me a note advising when she is sloshing about in mud in Hamburg or roughing up SS men. All I ask when I attend your club is some music, a glass of wine, a meal, your jokes, even, not a confrontation with MM. Against my better judgement, I enclose my usual pound and trust you will put this to meeting your electricity bill. Mrs. Coot likes to see what the other ladies are wearing.
Yours sincerely,
Herbert Coot

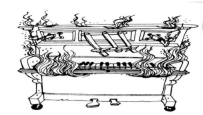

GIGS FROM HELL
Travels with Schatt O.B.E
by JOHN CRITCHINSON

Critchinson by Pennington

Life on the road with Ronnie was never dull — fraught maybe — but never mundane. He seemed able to create comic situations from almost anything, but the following happened and we just took part.

BARMY BLACKPOOL

Sometime in January-February early '80s we had a one-off gig in the Playground of the North. After a long drive through snow and fog, we arrived at the Venue — a sort of pub on the sea-front with function rooms above. Our gig was about three floors or what seemed like eighty-seven flights of stairs up — no lift! The room was a rectangle with a bar on one side and a very high stage, with a piano which had given its best at the end of the First World War. It was seriously out of tune and several notes did not work at all, or to be more precise in the words of Schatt — 'fucking useless'; Ronnie pointed out the terms of our contract which stated that a first class piano will be provided, tuned to A440 pitch on the day of the performance — to the somewhat reticent Promoter. His reply was, 'As far as I'm concerned, that is a first class piano and it was tuned this morning.' And that was it! Fortunately I had the Rhodes piano in the car and Martin Drew helped me carry it up the stairs; thus we were able to play the gig to a handful of people whilst the rain and snow pounded the windows and the Promoter disappeared. A suspicious Ronnie was relieved to see the Promoter appear at the end of the performance, but he only had about two thirds of the fee in notes. He again disappeared mumbling something about getting some more. After some forty-five minutes of total certainty on our part that he'd done a bunk, he appeared once more carrying several seemingly heavy bags which turned out to be the balance of the fee in coins of the realm which we then spent best part of an hour counting! We then went to load the cars and drove back through what was now a snow storm, and Ronnie gave the coins to Pete King to change into notes. Pete's comment unrepeatable!

VAL DE LOBO

A beautiful golfing complex on the Algarve where we knew we were to share villa accommodation during our two-gig stay. We arrived late on the Friday night before the gigs, and Martin Drew, Ronnie and myself were shown to a very classy looking villa although there was no sign of the promised self-drive car for our use. Ronnie noticed an unfinished villa next door and was assured that no building work would take place on Saturday; he was also promised that the car would be left outside the villa early next morning. At around

7.00am Saturday the building banging etc. started and still no car. An incensed Ronnie demanded the promoters attend his presence immediately, and very soon two ashen-faced guys arrived, and could only give feeble excuses for our problems. Ronnie then asserted that the whole organisation was a cock-up and issued the order, 'Martin, call the airport! Get us a flight home ASAP.' The already ashen-faced promoters turned a sickly yellow and one got down on his knees saying, 'Ronnie I beg you — don't go' and tears started to well. After some phone calls, the car appeared, the building work stopped and Ronnie relented. The two gigs were a success and we had a great time there. However, if we subsequently had problems with promoters or gigs, Ronnie would issue the magic words 'Martin, call the airport!'

RON MATHEWSON

In this business, it is a well know fact that when two jazz musicians anywhere in the world get together, they will end up talking about the legendary imbiber and wreckontour — Ron Matthewson. As Ronnie's most talented bass player for many years, I was privileged to work with him and enjoy some of his words of wisdom. We had driven to our gig in Hebden Bridge — Ronnie in the passenger seat and Dick Pearce and a sound-asleep Ron Mat in the back. When we arrived at the stage entrance we awoke a now snoring, head back, mouth wide open Ron who, after some stretching and head shaking said 'Ah, well, from one nightmare to another!' Another of Ron's classic lines was as he and I were driving to his flat. At a set of traffic lights in Chelsea, he suddenly stretched and said 'Ah well, nobody's perfect — and I include myself in that!' These are the words of a musical genius who is at his best when stretching.

LOVELY PUNTERS

We rely on people to pay money for whatever reason, to come and see us perform. Recently I had the good fortune to have two gigs at the Bulls Head, Barnes over a Friday and Saturday night. At the end of the Friday gig, one such gentleman said something like, 'I enjoyed it tonight. I'm not very fond of this modern stuff but tonight was good. I'm more into the mainstream stuff like tomorrow night here.' I told him I was doing a dep. for John Pearce that night. 'Oh — well I might come tomorrow then.' Saturday night at the end of a storming first set, I was making my way to the bar when my Friday punter caught me and said, 'See! I came here again. I'll bet you don't get too many people do that!' In the words of Duke Ellington: 'We love you madly.'

TUBBY HAYES

An appreciation of the late, great, Tubby Hayes by WALLY HOUSER

Here's a tricky question. Regardless of style, size or period, what's the best jazz group this country has ever produced? For me — no contest! It's the Jazz Couriers. Hands up those who remember the Jazz Couriers?

Formed in April, 1957, the personnel was one Ronnie Scott, the twenty-two old veteran Tubby Hayes, with a rhythm section comprising pianist Terry Shannon, bassist Phil Bates and drummer Bill Eyden. In fact, Phil was not the original bassist. Malcolm Cecil started with the band, but after one month it was P45 time and in May, 1957, Phil made up the quintet that was to last a good eighteen months and to become what, in my opinion, is simply the best home-grown jazz band of all.

MAGICAL

There was a kind of magic about it. The music they played would, I imagine, be now called hard bop. The band was influenced both as to its name and style by Art Blakey's Jazz Messengers and those of us who are lucky enough to have been alive when the Messengers were at their roaring peak (and that must be any jazz fan over fifty) are indeed fortunate.

In 1957 both Ronnie and Tubby were well established musicians. Despite his tender years, Tubby had been a bandleader before, as indeed had Ronnie who was then thirty, and their coming together seemed the most natural thing in the world. The arrangements, impetus and enthusiasm came, of course, from Tubby with his mile-wide smile (and mile-wide physique). Tubby, I think, was a genius (and I use the word advisedly) who, apart from his own limitless musical skills, had that rare ability to bring out the very best in others. This is not to suggest that Ronnie was in need of having the very best brought out of him. He has always been among the very best, but he and Tubbs were perfect foils for each other, musically and personality-wise. What Tubby was able to do in his playing, writing and sheer force of personality was mould all five musicians into one very cohesive and incredibly exciting unit with an authority and authenticity rarely known in this country.

Ron and Tubbs. Photo: David Redfern

SARAH VAUGHAN

I was living in Manchester at the time, but frequently travelled to London and saw the Couriers whenever I could. I saw them in Manchester on several occasions. I remember them at the old Bodega, and the Odeon when they were on the same bill as Sarah Vaughan who was touring here in 1958. I also saw them in London at the Dominion Theatre and at the Flamingo. Happy days!

The band was visually attractive. Five sharp young men in immaculate suits would come onto the stand and to hear them roar into Tubby's arrangement of Guys and Dolls or one of any number of Tubby originals or adaptations of Horace Silver tunes is something that will never be forgotten by those who experienced it. The band made a number of (sadly, too few) records.

I wonder whether any have been re-issued on CD. If not, why not? After all, the whole canon of the Blue Note recordings of the fifties and sixties has been re-issued. Most of them are wonderful, but many of them are very pedestrian indeed.

ENTHUSIASM EXHAUSTED

The band continued with the same personnel until about the end of 1958 when Phil Bates left to be replaced by Jeff Clyne, but for me it was never the same. This is not to suggest that Jeff was in any way inferior. Far from it, but I think by then Tubby had exhausted his enthusiasm. He felt that it had gone as far as it could, and Ronnie felt the same. The Couriers lasted for about another year.

It really is almost unbelievable to think that it is thirty six years or more since the Couriers disbanded, but no more unbelievable than to realise that is now twenty three years since Tubby died at the age (or, rather, no age) of thirty eight. His passing is a loss that can never be measured. At the time of his death he had been a professional musician in the public eye for about twenty two years and people had come to take his talent and presence for granted.

Along with a few others (Ronnie Scott, Peter King, Victor Feldman and George Shearing come to mind) he was one of the few British musicians who could hold his own in any company.

PRIVILEGE TO KNOW TUBBY

I had the privilege and pleasure of knowing him well, certainly in the last fifteen years of his life and although (and if he were alive today he would be the first to admit it) he could sometimes be a bit of a nuisance, what wouldn't I give to be able to walk into Ronnie's and hear one of his characteristic whoops of delight as he saw a familiar face. Those of us who remain have grown old or older with varying degrees of grace, but Tubby, of course, will never grow old and neither will his music.

TUBBS recalled by JACK SHARPE

The first time I can remember seeing Tubby Hayes play was at the 51 Club, Great Newport Street, off Charing Cross Road. A cherubic fifteen year old playing with enthusiasm and authority beyond his years. I was immediately captivated by his playing and outgoing personality, little dreaming that he was to become such a catalyst in my life as, in fact, many other people's lives also. I had just acquired my first taxi at the age of twenty-one, only to sell it a few months later without the slightest qualm when offered a place in Tubby's new eight-piece band that he was forming on leaving the Jack Parnell band.

TEMPO RECORDS

Signed up to Tito Burns, we cut our first recordings for Tempo Records at Decca Studios, West Hampstead, and embarked on our first one-night stands.

We couldn't, in fact, have chosen a worse time, although even if we had known, it would have not deterred us in the least. It was an end of an era when touring dance and jazz bands were on the way out. The day of the three-chord guitarists and rock-and-roll mayhem had begun.

Nevertheless, the eighteen months of Tubby's band was probably the best time of my life. The band, consisting of Dickie Hawdon and Dave Usden (trumpets), Mike Senn (alto) and myself (baritone and tenor), Harry South (piano), Pete Blannin (bass), Lennie Breslaw and/or Bill Eyden (drums) and Tubby with Bobby Breen (vocals). We played some of the most unlikely venues in the country. Percentage dates with about twenty paying customers on some occasions. But we had a ball, Tubby proving to be an excellent leader and extremely popular with dedicated fans who did show up at many of our dates.

'COMMERCIAL' BROADCASTS

In that 18-month period we passed our BBC audition and appeared on a teatime broadcast aimed at captive housewives. It was the custom to play very 'commercial', and there was no end of song pluggers around. Our offerings included *Rock Around the Clock, He's a Tramp*, and the epic *Yellow Rose of Texas*, the last introduced by a BBC announcer with an Oxford accent as 'One to set the teacups *rettling*.'

Despite our enthusiasm, the rigours of the touring had its effect, and after a particularly gruelling Scottish tour we were tired, hungry and demoralised, and decided to confront Tito Burns, our manager, to ask for financial assistance. As the coach pulled up outside Tito's residence in plush Maida Vale, Tubby and I were elected to be the spokesmen.

The door opened to reveal Tito resplendent in a silk dressing gown. He listened to our tale of woe, nodded as we protested that we were totally skint. He beamed us consolatory smile.

'Well, that makes all of us, doesn't it?'

We terminated the agreement there and then — fairly amicably — and the band broke up.

Of course, Tubby progressed from strength to strength, maturing into the great musician, composer and arranger, accepted worldwide, as we all expected he would.

Those early days on the road with 'The Little Giant' are etched into our memories to remain forever as a tremendous experience — for me, at least, a part of my life that I would not have missed for all the world.

His influence remains, and is perpetuated in our own Big Band where his compositions and arrangements, together with those of his contemporaries, are played, and like all great music, remains undated. The orchestra contains some young musicians who never met him. But all know his music and his genius inspires all of us still.

Tubby by Pennington

SCOTTIE THE RAKE

Ronnnie was seated before his TV when a programme called 'Pick of the Week', a round up of items from the previous week's programmes on ITV, came on, and saw a clip from an interview about the Club in which a Ken Andrew described the guv'nor as a 'womaniser, gambler, boozer and teller of immensely bad jokes.' Ronnie was put out: 'My jokes are *not* immensely bad. I wouldn't have been using them for thirty years if they were.'

'Er... , *ahem*, about the other allegations, Ronnie?' I gently enquired.

'Well,' Scottie replied with a massive show of casualness, 'Slawky, old man, you're a man of the world. You know that life isn't just playing a saxophone.'

'Quite,' I replied, flattered to be bracketed with this rake's progress, but, alas, knowing this not to be true. But I was suffused with envy at being in close proximity to such a rake-hell. Gosh! I wish I ran a night club.

SLAWKY

Ron by Hedley Picton

123

Slawkenbergius

On my rounds in exotic Soho I, perforce, look into the Three Greyhounds in Greek Street, run, as a pub should be ('No juke boxes, muzak or gaming machines here, sport') by Miss Roxy Beaujolais, from Sydney, Orstrylia. Nobody is perfect...

Inevitably, I see our editor taking the edge off pain with a 'normaliser', a glass of Invergordon's. Inevitably, I join him, and 'reach South', as Roxy, an expert on 'Strine', would have put it.

'That's very obliging of you old son,' said our Editor, adding that he wished me the very best of health, which was nice of him. I told him that certain people couldn't believe his story (*JARS* 85) that someone on a quality national had rung asking him to sing *Twist and Shout* over the telephone.

'Absolutely true, old son. I haven't the imagination to cook up a tale like that. I could have rendered them a reasonable *Muskrat Ramble*, had a stab at Bix's chorus on *Singing the Blues* and a slowish *Salt Peanuts*, but *Twist and Shout* wasn't really my glass of Invergordon's'.

The very recollection of all this had our editor agitatedly-draining-his-glass-and-thumping-it-on-the-counter-in-a-meaningful-way-and-having-it-immediately-picked-up-and-held-under-the-appropriate-optic-and-back-in-JG's-eager-mitt-by-the-sleight-of-hand-Miss Beaujolais-looking-at-me-for-the-readies-before-you-could-say-Ponzi Crunz-never-mind-Jack Robinson.

Yes, you pedants, I know this is exactly what I wrote in *JARS* 85, but the situation was an identical re-run, and no doubt, whilst I pop into this hostelry and the editor is present, there will be more of the same. It's the wretched lot of a minion hack. *Sigh, sigh…*

READY FOR THE RIVER

Our editor continued: 'I could have given them *Ready For the River*. With the way the world is going, old son, that's often the way I feel.'

He broke into song, only to be stopped after one chorus by Miss Beaujolais, who doesn't allow singing in her pub.

'I'm ready for the river
The rippling river
The river that flows down to the sea
I've made my will
Wrote some notes
Gonna keep on walkin' until my straw hat floats
I'm ready for the river
The river that flows down to the sea'

'You must know it, old son'.
I had to admit that I did not.
'Ah probably before your time, even. Mind you I wasn't surprised to receive that call. I'm always getting them. When Mr. Scott'— at that moment we both raised our glasses in obeisance to our Lord and Master — 'receives a call asking for information, he goes into automatic pilot.' 'Hang on, sir', he says with the speed of light, 'I'll give you the telephone number for the guy — a Jim somebody or the other — who edits our house magazine, he'll be sure to help you', and having imparted my number, quickly resumes goggling at the box in his office.'

HIRAM J GUGGENHEIM

'The Americans are the worst. My heart, and jaw, drops when I hear the accent over the blower. They're all studying something utterly abstruse, of no benefit to humanity whatsoever, on a whacking great grant, and bugging an impoverished hack like me.'

'Hi, I'm Hiram J Guggenheim, Jr. I'm majoring in sociology at Boston University, Mr-er GUDbolt, and I'm particularly interested in the absorption of non-indigenous jazz music into the cultural infrastructure of certain European countries, including your own, Mr-er-GUDbolt. I want to come and see you TO-DAY, Mr-er GUDbolt. Tomorrow I am off to MosCOW.'

'Yes, old son, that's exactly what Mr. Guggenheim said. The words are forever engraved in my memory. Obviously, he seemed to think that all I did in this quaint old country of ours was to sit about, perhaps listening to an old 78 of Ponzi Crunz, just pining for a call from someone like himself, waxing fat on a grant, to alleviate the utter boredom of my existence.'

'Mr. Guggenheim seemed surprised when I, in my best BBC English, told him I wasn't available at such short notice. Mind you, had Mr. Guggenheim offered me some loot for my valuable time I might have felt disposed to re-arrange my diary, but, surprise, surprise, Mr. Guggenheim didn't offer to dig into his grant. Not that he was totally deterred.' 'Whilst I have you on the phone, Mr-er GUDbolt, perhaps you would care to tell me about the sociological correlation of the number of Jews playing jazz in your country.' It's not often I'm short of words, old son, but that took my breath away.'

However, I recovered, and replied, 'Well, it's quite simple. They think it's better than working.'

'Heavens! If you published that you'd have the politically correct from N16 and N8 falling on you like a ton of old 78s.'

'Actually, old son, I funked it for that very reason. In fact, Hiram was well out of date. The number of Jewish guys in jazz nowadays is minimal. Not like the old days. All those kosher band leaders: Ambrose, Harry Roy, Joe Daniels, Harry Gold, Geraldo, Lew Stone — who all played some jazz — and the bebop Mafia of the forties — Ronnie, Tony Crombie, Hank Shaw, Laurie Morgan, Flash Winston, Norman Burns, Jeff Ellison, Lennie Breslaw and Leon Calvert, to name just a few'.

I left our editor further beefing about people, Americans particularly, taking up the time he could be taking the edge off the pain at the Three Greyhounds.

BRIEF ENCOUNTERS memories from the Club
by JIMMY PARSONS

I first visited the Club in Gerrard Street as a paying customer soon after it opened. I sat next to Mel Tormé (one of my early idols). I stayed late and missed the last tube home (there were no night buses then), so I had to walk to my home in Bow.

In the early 1960s I became an agent with an office in Denmark Street, W1, and my stable consisted of Blossom Dearie, Jimmy Witherspoon, Dakota Staton, Anita O'Day and Helen Merrill, all of whom I met hanging out at Annie Ross's club, 'Annie's Room', in Covent Garden. I first met Pete King in the Gerrard Street club in the mid 1960s with a view to getting my acts into the Club. We seemed to get on well from the start, and I found him very straightforward and honest — I liked him right away. During one of the many meetings we had, he revealed his and Ronnie's plans to move the Club to bigger and better premises in Frith Street; he said that after a short while — and if everything worked out — he might be able to find me a 'position' with the 'organisation'. True to his word, shortly after the opening of the new club, we met again, and he suggested we merge our interest as agents and form a new agency with Ronnie. Of course it would take time for this new venture to generate enough money for me to draw a salary, so I would have to work in the Club at night meantime. I was duly appointed cloakroom attendant (my 'position')! At the time, I was struggling to make ends meet, so I was very grateful for the chance to make any money at all.

RONNIE — THE FUNNY MAN

It was during that time that I got to know Ronnie really well. At night, he and Pete would station themselves at the front door, Ronnie meeting and greeting and Pete making sure that everybody bought a ticket! Ronnie was without doubt the funniest man I ever met, and he was a willing participant in every 'gag' situation created to raise a laugh. For example, he bore a striking resemblance to one of the late popes — Pius the something — so with the help of some props borrowed from the cloakroom, I dressed him in a long black coat and black wide-brimmed hat, and he stood in the entrance lobby blessing people as they came in, while I addressed him as 'Your Eminence'. Another time, he knelt on his shoes to make himself look very small and again put on a long coat and big hat, plus glasses, and pretended to be Toulouse Lautrec. He spoke gibberish French and pulled one of his funny faces. People seemed uncertain what to make of it all, but it certainly caused a laugh. Dear Ronnie; what a tragic loss.

I worked at night in the Club and during the day I ran the new agency from an office behind the stage. The objective of this new venture was simple: after the American artists had finished their seasons at the Club, we would then book them into any venue that could afford the fee. These venues tended to be universities or colleges, and so slowly, we built up a circuit around the UK and I was able to leave the cloakroom.

ROLAND KIRK

I have some good memories of being on the road with some of the giants of jazz. One of the first I toured with was Roland Kirk, and I remember being on a train with him and his band going north and going into a first-class dining compartment for lunch. It's worth remembering that Roland was blind and fiercely independent at this point, because, having taken everybody else's order, the waiter then turned to me and asked: 'What would he (Roland) like?' Roland barked back: 'Hey man, I'm blind, not deaf. Ask me!' To add to the waiter's embarrassment Roland then proceeded to order a starter, the main course and sweet to be served on the same plate and at the same time!

And how could I forget working with Coleman Hawkins — 'Bean' to his friends — small and frail with more than a fondness for Napoleon brandy (two or three bottles a day). I remember I was sitting in the dressing room at the Club one night while he ate his dinner, a bowl of soup, when Ben Webster called in to pay his respects. He and Bean had been friends for many years, and they were sat talking over old times when Stan Getz appeared — also to pay his respects. Imagine my surprise when Ben leaped from his chair, lifted Stan off his feet and pinned him to the wall, screaming abuse at him. I ran to get help to prise them apart, but I didn't find out the cause of the antagonism till later. It seems that Stan had once said something derogatory about Bean's playing in some magazine or other, and Ben had been waiting for years to 'straighten him out'.

RECORDING THE GREAT

I left the Club for a short while in 1970, and returned to take charge of the Club's music publishing and record production companies. At first, all was well in that department, and we managed to record albums by Buddy Rich, George Coleman, Louie Bellson, Arturo Sandoval and others, but sadly, Pye Records (who were funding our label) went out of business. This setback coincided with the crises the Club suffered, and so once again I returned to working in the Club at night — this time as cashier on the front desk, where I stayed until my retirement.

Following Ronnie's death, Pete asked if I would make the announcements from the stage — a terrifying prospect for someone who had quit singing years ago because of stage-fright! But I felt honoured to be asked, and determined to do my best. Janet, our sound engineer at the time, was a great help, full of encouragement and praise, as were Pete and Wally Houser, the Club's lawyer. I made many cock-ups, but hopefully, I didn't offend too many people.

I have enjoyed all the many years that I've spent in this great and historic club, but like everybody else, would have wished to have enjoyed Ronnie's company for longer. My undying thanks to Pete for his generosity and friendship. God knows what I would have done without him. My thanks, too, to all the staff for making the sometimes nightly 'grind' bearable. I'll miss their humour and comradeship.

SPIKE MILLIGAN
a very funny, very unpredictable, very controversial jazz enthusiast

Spike by Trog

One of the great comics of our time, Spike Milligan, was a keen jazz enthusiast and a one-time dance-band musician. His unique, surrealistic perspective on the world, allied to a strong sense of the absurd, combine to make him the very funny man that he is. One of the more famous manic-depressives.
About ten years ago I answered the telephone and a vaguely familiar voice enquired, 'Is this the dreaded Godbolt?'
'I don't know about the dreaded bit, but I own to the name. Who are you?'
'Spike Milligan'
'Oh, yeah, and who will you be next week? The Aga Khan, Mick Jagger or Charlie Chaplin?'
'If that's your attitude, I'll ring off'.
It hit me that the caller was indeed Spike Milligan and I spluttered my apologies. We had not met. A somewhat disjointed conversation ensued, myself rather in awe of a famous man and very surprised that he should call me. Since then, we have spoken over the telephone and corresponded several times but, recently, one of my letters drew the peeved comment: 'I had to read that in fucking instalments.'
Chastened I replied: 'Rgt lng ltr. Nr agn. J God'
In one of my letters I asked him for an interview to be published in *JARS*. Spike rang, but my phone was out of order. He not only sent me a telegram asking me to ring him, but also asked Ronnie Scott to ring me. I was flattered. As a hack and an editor, I am rarely flattered. More often flattened.
On a bitterly cold day in March, I took the train to Rye and was driven to Spike's lovely house overlooking the Sussex Downs by his charming wife Shelagh, who took me into an elegantly furnished lounge with an open fireplace and a log fire. She brought in tea and cakes. In walked a silver-haired frail figure with piercing eyes, who greeted me in a hoarse voice. It was Spike, now 78. He had had a triple-bypass heart operation three years previously, but, as I was to discover, his brain was quicksilver quick and his comments needle-sharp. Because I knew of his sudden mood swings and being rather in awe of him — a touch of hero-worship — I felt rather ill at ease, my unease increasing when we shook hands and he gasped in pain. Mind you, I think he put that on a bit. He peered quizzically at the sheaf of papers I had with me.
'I've been doing my homework on you, Spike.' I began fiddling with my Sony tape recorder and, worried that it might not pick up his faint voice, moved closer to him. I noticed how expressive his eyebrows were. 'Would you like to sit on my lap', he enquired, the voice mock stern, but those eyes twinkling.
I politely declined the offer and started my questions.

J.G.

JG: Spike, this is a lovely part of England, which you eloquently describe, as it was in 1940, in your book, *Adolf Hitler — My Part In His Downfall*, recalling the days when you were called up to the Army and stationed in Bexhill. Now, 55 years later, you're back, but in somewhat different circumstances. But I'd like to ask you about an even earlier phase in your life: childhood and adolescence in Catford, South London. Did you listen to the dance-bands of the day: Jack Hylton, Jack Payne, Ambrose, Billy Cotton and Lew Stone on the radio and 78s?
SM: Oh yes, and Paul Whiteman and the Rhythm Boys with Bing Crosby present. I was a great fan of Bing's. I won several Bing Crosby contests in such prestigious venues as Ladywell Baths and St Cyprian's Hall, Catford.
I played the ukulele and then string bass, carting that bloody great thing around on public transport. I would pre-empt jokes from bus and tram conductors with, 'No, I don't tuck it under my chin, no I don't know where it died, and I'm not taking it to be buried.' It's amazing how each of these jokers thought they were the first to make those cracks, falling about with laughter at their sallies. Or were about to before this prat put a stop to their fun.
JG: You then played trumpet with pianist Tommy Brettell's New Ritz Revels, a six-piece semi-pro band, which you describe as a bunch of spotty musicians held together by hair oil. Did you play any jazz in that band?
SM: Yes, all the standards — *Limehouse Blues, Rose Room, Lady Be Good, Bugle Call Rag* things like that. I took the solos. I admired Harry James, the hot Harry James with Benny Goodman, and Bunny Berigan. I tried to play like Bunny. We got ten shillings a gig.
JG: Did you ever envisage becoming

a professional musician?

SM: Yes, I was auditioned for third trumpet in Oscar Rabin's Romany Band at the Hammersmith Palais, but Adolf Hitler put paid to that. I was called up in 1940 — by force.

JG: In *Adolf Hitler — My Part In His Downfall*, you wrote some hilariously funny things about service bands and I would like to quote some of this material in the interview.

SM: Permission granted.

I took my trumpet to war. I thought I'd earn spare cash playing 'Fall In', 'Charge', 'Retreat', 'Lights Out', etc. I placed printed cards on the Battery Notice Board showing my scale of charges.

Fall In	*1/6d*
Fall Out	*1/-*
Charge	*1/9d*
Halt	*£468.0.0*
Retreat (Pianissimo)	*4/-*
Retreat(Fortissimo)	*10/-*
Lights Out	*3/-*

Lights Out played in private 4/- While waiting for these commissions I'd lie on my palliasse and play tunes like Body and Soul *and* I Can't Get Started. *It was with mixed feelings that I played* You Go to My Head *watching a hairy gunner cutting his toenails.*

JG: You attracted two jazz addicts, pianist Harry Edginton and guitarist Alf Fildes. You needed a drummer and you advertised in Part Two Orders: 'Wanted. House-trained drummer. Academic training an advantage but not essential. No coloureds, but men with names like Duke Ellington given preference.'

SM: No one applied, but one day I heard someone hammering a piece of Lease-Lend bacon. That's how we found a drummer, Douglas Kidgell. We hadn't a drum kit but we knew of one lying fallow under the stage of the Bexhill Old Town Church Hall and we 'requisitioned' it to prevent it falling into the hands of Germans.

SPIKE MACKINTOSH

JG: You were posted to Egypt, then to Italy, where you were wounded in battle. Here you were in a band that took part in a contest and one

of the judges was someone I knew very well: Spike Mackintosh, then a Lieutenant in the Tank Corps. He died only recently.

Again I quote from one of Spike's war memoirs, Where Have All The Bullets Gone?

'The compère for the contest was Captain Philip Ridgeway. He was as informed on dance-bands as Mrs Thatcher was on groin-clenching in the Outer Hebrides. The other judges were Lt. Spike Mackintosh and Lt. Eddie Carroll, a pre-war bandleader. Can you believe it? We didn't win! I wasn't even mentioned. At the contest I heard shouts of 'Give him the prize'. No one listened even though I shouted loud enough. Never mind, there would be other wars.'

JG: Did you speak to Lt. Mackintosh?

SM: Heavens, no! He was an officer and I was only a Gunner.

JG: Did you ever hear him play trumpet?

SM: No.

JG: A pity. He was a very fine player, I assure you.

Not surprisingly, given the nature and the history of the interviewee, and my nervousness, the conversation took some odd twists and turns. Somehow, pianist/composer Reginald Foresythe, son of a British barrister and West Indian mother, and active in the thirties, came up. He wrote pieces with titles like Dodging a Divorcee *and* Serenade to a Wealthy Widow. *Spike referred to him as Frederick Forsyth, the spy fiction author. Involuntarily, this old trainspotter made a correction. Those eyebrows tightened and I got the fish-eye.* 'Are you correcting me?' *he sternly enquired.* 'No', *I quickly replied.* 'For all I know Frederick may have also been a pianist', *an obviously feeble get-out. I speedily moved the conversation to Duke Ellington.*

SM: I particularly loved *The Mooche* by the Duke.

JG: I know. Last year I sent you a cassette of six versions.

SM: So you did. Thanks very much. Have another piece of cake.

In the amorphous nature of this

dialogue, the names o͏͏ ͏ ie Fields, Arthur Tracey (Th ͏ ͏et Singer), and Cavan O'Connor came up and Spike gave imitations of these worthies. I was treated to Sing As We Go *for Gracie, Marta,* Rambling Rose of the Wildwood' *for Tracey and* I'm Only A Strolling Vagabond, *for O'Connor. He likes a warble does Spike…*

I mentioned that I'd seen a reference in one of his books to 'Hooray Henries', and told him of my part in the coining of that term, but he didn't appear to be particularly impressed. I also made the mistake of telling a funny and got the I-tell-the-jokes-around-here look. Similar experiences with Ronnie Scott should have taught me this lesson.

BIX BEIDERBECKE and CHARLIE PARKER

JG: What were your reactions, given your musical background in the swing era, to the advent of bebop?

SM: I loved it — at once. Charlie Parker! The man was a magician! Such a flow of invention.

Here I was treated to yet another Milligan vocal rendering — of These Foolish Things, *although not quite with the Parker phraseology*

JG: When you returned home from the war you tuned into the battery-run Bakelite radio and found Harry Roy and his Tiger-Ragamuffins.

SM: Awful, fucking awful! Roy never could play the clarinet. Having heard Parker, Gillespie and Monk, it was so corny. Another awful noise was Billy Ternent and his tinky-poo band. It made me realise just how much music had changed since I'd been away and how the world I knew had changed too.

Spike talked of the musicians he admired: guitarists Eddie Lang and Charlie Christian, trumpeters Bunny Berigan, Louis Armstrong, Dizzy Gillespie, Warren Vaché, Doc Cheatham, Clifford Brown and Bix Beiderbecke.

SM: Beiderbecke! Such a pure sound. No vibrato. *I'm Coming Virginia* is my favourite Bix. Full of German angst, though.

JG: In your book, *Peace Work*, you

had a fantasy about Dizzy 'live' at your home in Leathwell Road, Deptford, South London:

'Dizzy lives at 3 Leathwell! Wow!
Sing Dizzy, blues
Hey there Dizzy playing at Leathwell Road!
Hey there Dizzy playing at Leathwell Road!
You play that music
A knighthood will be bestowed... oh, yeah!'

SM: I was then very much into modern jazz and sorry that I, a good swing player, was no longer playing trumpet with all these things happening. I was then on guitar with the Bill Hall Trio on the halls.

JG: Humphrey Lyttelton?

SM: Oh, I would have been a much better player than Humph, but my lip went.

Of the saxophone players Spike admired, he talked of Stan Getz, Coleman Hawkins, Gerry Mulligan, Bud Freeman and Ronnie Scott.

In contrast to his generous praise, I also saw the acidulous side of Spike Milligan.

JG: You wrote in *Peace Work* of going to a party and asking bandleader Tito Burns what did he play and he replied that he played cards.

SM: Yes — ho ho ho — and years later, when Burns was quite a well-known figure, I came across him and enquired, 'Are you still playing cards?' Revenge is sweet, Jim.

There were one or two more sharp comments. He was not a man to suffer fools gladly. He enquired about the economics of JARS and I told him that the Club pays me the cost of production and for delivering it to the specialist shops every week, that my wages came from getting the advertising, and

therefore I was primarily a space salesman and a delivery boy who did a bit of editing and writing in between. He seemed mildly amused by this reply. No more. It's hard work getting a laugh out of comics.

JG: Can I have your impression of Ronnie Scott's Club?

SM: The Club is fine, the music is fine, it's your fucking customers that are a bane. Noisy lot.

JG: *(Rather boldly)* But, Spike, you've been known to have the odd heckle. You barracked George Melly for instance.

SM: No I did not. I was cheering him on. I like George's act.

JG: I often see pianist Stan Greig who was in John Chilton's Feetwarmers backing Melly, and he tells me that, in 1979, you sat in on trumpet for three numbers and played — in his own words — very well. Do you miss being a trumpet player?

SM: Yes. There was a lovely euphoria about improvising on good tunes, but the lip and wind have gone, so I content myself playing piano.

ENTHUSIASM FOR JAZZ

JG: I'm glad to see that, despite your widely varying activities outside of music, you still retain your interest in jazz. You have written the prefaces to various jazz books, including Ronnie's *Some Of My Best Friends Are Blues*, and you championed the marvellous pianist Alan Clare, using him on your TV shows. In *Peace Work*, describing your experience on the halls, you added, 'I still let jazz music run through my head, always had and always will.'

SM: True. I see you have read my books, unlike some of my

interviewers.

I would like to have talked longer with Terence Alan Milligan, a man whose television shows and books have made me laugh so much, but I sensed he wanted to continue ravaging *Rebecca* and I took my leave, feeling all the better, despite the angst and the technological hang-ups, for making the journey Spike's enthusiasm for jazz was unquestionable, but he was somewhat hazy on jazz history. Bix Beiderbecke never recorded *Wolverine Blues* — Spike was confusing Bix being one of the Wolverines, nor, as he alleged, did Red Allen record with the Chocolate Dandies, but I held my peace. I didn't want another whack of those eyebrows.

I suddenly realised that the Sony wasn't running. I was choked. How much had I missed of this stimulating, if somewhat unnerving, conversation? I was apologetic, fearing that Spike would think I had wasted his time by not checking the machine out first — which I had.

He was very charming and considerate, told me to relax, was personally complimentary, and said I could ring him at any time to check points, a nice gesture from a very busy man. I asked if he had a tape recorder I could use. He emphatically shook his head. 'I have nothing to do with modern technology. I don't even have a typewriter.'

I was astonished. All this tremendous literary output — some fifty books — in longhand! Yet another surprising facet of this extraordinary man. He was writing, or rather, rewriting *Rebecca* by Daphne Du Maurier.

'I'm sending it up. I am a bit of an iconoclast.' The understatement of the century. Miss Du Maurier must be heaving in her grave.   J.G

RONNIE'S JOKES

Then there's the kitchen staff. Incidentally, the food here is great. Bit expensive. I think it's cheaper to eat the money, but it's great. Top breeders recommend it. We never get complaints about the food. After all three million flies can't be wrong.

'PROFESSOR' STANLEY UNWIN
spells out his unique view of jazz history

Unwin by Trog

When Jazz (how or what) came, is the dizziest of a fundamole. Not mark you of a Gillespeed fundamole, O no. There were no recorms vailabold 'til 1917; these by white perslode, The Original Dixieland Jazz Band. Maybe otherwise jazz handy down by fardles'n mothers 'til the first recorms in 1923 in a railside studio ramshackload by a black onsombly; Oliver's, 1923, with his Creole Jazz Band, which inclubed Louis Armstrong who strode with first fine second trumpy-blow. There's a start of a historical impaggers indeedy-ho! Early twenty yields the whiters band of Paul Whiteman, but with few jazz creaturals. These were some bar interjeps from Joe Venuti (catgut'n violin scrapey-joy, y'know) and Eddie Lang's guitar pluck'fretfolded; O yes. Mind you, there were hot solomes done by C Melody saxophobia from Frankie Trumbauer and Bix gave splendy cornet hot contribule too. O yes.

CHICK WEBBER A DRUMJOY
Contempries with these; big banders black were doing the jazz-play: Duke Ellingtones, Chick Webber of drumjoy, Charlie Johnson, Fletcher Henderstones, all of whom preceded Count Basics and Jimmy Luncefolder; all of this because peeplodes had a thaucus blacks could play this wild musicolly. But Whiters? Ahem. There were recorms jazz-pure by Hot Fido and several of Louis Armstrong. These with Jelly Roller of Morty fame are collector's classicool. Indeedy ho.

BEIDERWHILE
But what of smaller groupers gathery? Beiderwhile with Bixie-Gang and Frankie Tram C mellow saxifolder, then of course with Jean Goldkettle aboil before the Whitemold joinit. Next came hot interspurps with Casa'n Loma, leading to the Swing era of belly Goodmold, Dorsey'n Dorsey and Krupa drumset'n symbold. At the same toil there were white musicools like Eddie Condon of guitar'n pluck-it banjold and Bob Crosby's band. Later came-it the Dixieland Musee preservale from Muggsy Spanier's Ragtoil, leady-hup to a revivy-merge of obscury blacks from limbold quite suddly. George Lewis clarinebbers, trumplode of Bunk Johnson, Hunkydory trombslider, Big Bill Broonzy-bluesing and a fine leadermuxlewis of boog-it'n woog-it. Hey.

BE-POP PHENOMINAKERS
Concurry with this resurgey-ho came the blacklaunch sudlode of bepop phenomimakers. Out the window falolloped all most consef of jazzy joy as known-it then. Harmonic, tonefolders, rythmy. F-t! Down the cellar and no takers. Sollagommorra t'you lot and devil takers hindemyth. No thorks or hope of viabilly, but blieve it or not, woof. It was there. From now on it was nukkle dups'n fisticubbers tweel the fundamoles and the latest crabes. O dear. Young whites all passionale were 'toenails in the garters' for emulating Armstroder Louis and Jelly Rollers.

O joy for the real jazzy McCoydle. Eight in a bardle trumpey part, foot tabbers booflabber keychange, clarinebbers take-over. All these.

WALLY FAWKES
In 19 forty-fido it was protagger-tricks more than somewhat. I tell you. In England George Webb's Dixielanders, having Wally Fawkes's clarinebber, and in April of that year joined by Humph (ombooshoor for long ideas 'afloaty, tight libbers for high C's forceps) but in November he did a departy-ho. These Dixielanders managed by Jim who Godbolted the theme 'New New Orleans in Barnehurst Kent.' O deep folly! Nevertheleps, many musicools were inspirey to hup their instromolds'n form a galaxy of bandings like Crane River Jazzy-hocus, John Haim's King Jelly Rollers, The Cris Barbery Band-here's another fine tromslidery-ho-, Humph's early-early band of the traddy-genuine and later Ackery fine bilkers and Kenny Ball; that's London based for starters: Provincey-ho were Yorkshire Jazz Band, Merseysippi Jazz Band from Liverpole where as you know, the Liverbird did a wingflabber every time a virgin passed by. Also there was Second City Jazzmen from Birmygold and others to follow throom: O yes.

MODE OF BOP GRIP
At this mode of Bop Grip, Club Eleven began with Ronnie Scott, John Dankworthy — no less, and Dennis Rose to name a numbold. Scott and Dankworth took big bands on the road forthwold. Johnny D with the Cleo lady Laine vocal joyfold. Fine eppiglow mellow modulade'n fundamold. O yes. As in Yankyland — and I meanit the broadest sense of U.S'n stretchit — the big bands did a shrinkit in the sixties, trad jazz became commercial. In the UK, Ronnie Scott formed his own club spesslode in 19 fiftynile. Now in perpetyu-motion if you like, and extendy to Birmingold in the Midload. Then 'Free Form' emerged in the seventies with a frenetty metzoff. It made bebop a languid sound of light Sunday orchestrale by parison. Though not quite cuffalo teedy sound with two ploplumpers with the vicar. O no. However all this, the sixties pewkered forth a farrago of perslodes in the musey-world. Beatloders of Polly McCarton, who with Lennontones gabe forth Liverpuddly tunes of joy with Ringold of drummage; the Rolly-Stokers expressy fine hapload with Jagloads of mike in the lebbers swing'n jump huffalodown the stage and Willy Wymold of course lead guitar'n plucky, the King, Elvy Presloders, bent kneeclabber all rocky-jailhouses too. Evenso, the real jazz creators were, and still are, carrying the rythmold'n sound of self expressy-ho to infinny in the cosmos for sure. Deep Joy.

RECOLLECTIONS OF A JAZZ CLUB'S SOLICITOR
by WALLY HOUSER

Now where was I? I think when I last addressed you, I had mentioned Ornette Coleman and the pre-emptory dispatch of his manager from the Club by Pete King. I was thinking about this again and it put me in mind of the various encounters I have had with jazz musicians, famous and not so famous, during the thirty-five years of my association with the Club.

I was discussing this with our genial columnist Slawkenbergius only the other day. That sunny-natured scribe remarked that it must be one of the perks of the job, and of course one might be tempted to think so, since to spend an hour in the company, of say, Eddie Daniels or George Coleman, both gentlemen of infinite courtesy and amiability, would never be less than a pleasure.

PLEASURES COUNTERBALANCED

However, those pleasures are more than counterbalanced by the less rewarding side of dealing with the great and glorious. I recall one particularly harrowing experience. During the very hot summer of 1976, Art Blakey and the Jazz Messengers were passing through London airport en route to France, and two members of the group were found to be carrying minute quantities of various controlled substances. They were duly arrested and the full majesty of the law fell upon them. In the meantime, Art and the rest of the band went on to Paris. It goes almost without saying that this happened on the Saturday before the Bank Holiday Monday.

When else would such a thing occur? The two hapless hard-boppers were banged up in Uxbridge Police Station, and finding that escape was impossible, got in touch with the only name they knew in London, namely, Ronnie Scott. I was telephoned early on the Sunday morning by Mr. Scott (or was it Mr. King?) and told that, given my exalted position, it would behove me to hot-foot it to Uxbridge to spring the two prisoners from durance vile.

A GOODWILL GESTURE

I therefore left the bosom of my family, ignoring the blandishments of my wife and the tears of my children, and went to Uxbridge Police Station, where the Police, as ever, models of courtesy and helpfulness would have none whatsoever of my request to bail the two. I established that the court would sit the following day, i.e. Bank Holiday Monday, in Uxbridge Magistrates' Court, to deal with the matter. I therefore spent most of Bank Holiday Monday in Uxbridge Magistrates' Court explaining to the magistrates about how my clients had come from broken homes, were undergoing the rigours of being on the road, and in any case, had no intention of staying in the country. Both were sentenced to a mild fine and a severe wigging from the beak and both were off to join

Mr. Blakey in Paris. Without wishing to give myself a pat on the back, I had done a good job, and as a gesture on the part of the Club, did not make any charge to my two, by now happy, clients. A goodwill gesture, but it had an epilogue.

A BIT OF A CARVE-UP

Some moths later, Pete King asked me how much I had charged them, and I reminded him that I had made no charge, but the following facts then emerged. The two Messengers arrived in Paris to receive an even more serious upbraiding from Mr. Blakey than they had endured at the hands of the Uxbridge Magistrate, and when they were due to be paid later that week, they were docked $1000 each, on the grounds that this was what Mr. Blakey had paid me for their representation. At the time, I was rather distressed to learn about this, but later I found it extremely amusing. It was a very subtle use of the bandleader's right to 'carve' his sidemen. So much for the perks of my position.

BEN WEBSTER, 'THE BRUTE'

If I had to describe one thing as a perk out of all the multitude of experiences I have had over the years at the Club it would be the friendship that I developed with Ben Webster, and that began when he came to see me because he had his camera stolen from his hotel room in London. In he came to my office, the famous hat preceded by the famous belly. He told me what had happened. Apparently, he had been asleep in his room, which he described as very small, when somebody broke in and took his camera. He awoke. Now, to awake Ben Webster at 11 o'clock in the morning after he had a couple of drinks the night before, is about as sensible as waking a grizzly bear with an ingrowing claw from hibernation. He seized hold of the thief and threw him (and I mean *threw*) out of the open door. Unfortunately, this was not quite hard enough, because the thief legged it with the camera, and Ben naturally wanted to make a claim against the hotel, which we did successfully. When he came to my office

Ben Webster by Trog

to collect the cheque, he had his horn with him and I asked him to play something for me. A photograph of my son, Dan, was on my desk. I must be the only solicitor in London, or indeed, arguably the world, who has had the pleasure of hearing Ben Webster playing *Danny Boy* in his office. Sure, the perks are there.

HERBERT COOT LETTERS

(The correspondence between Herbert Coot and Ronnie Scott, with apologies to The Henry Root Letters by William Donaldson)

5th May, 1985

Dear Mr. Scott,

I am a methodical person: I keep all the correspondence and I note in your letter of February 17th, 1985 that the two pounds I sent for your editor (along with my usual pound for yourself) you placed on the 'dead cert' (rather than see JG spend it on drink) and promised to 'share the dibs' with me.

May I enquire if the horse (which you did not name) won and at what odds if it did, or (which is more likely knowing your percipience in these matters), if it managed to reach the finishing post at all. While I can only commend your concern for Mr. Godbolt's liver I thought at least you could advise me the outcome of the bet with his money. Not that the odds interest me. As you know, I made my pile in suspended ceilings and I'm doing well in fumigated feathers, but it's the principle of the matter that concerns me.

Yours sincerely,

Herbert Coot

25th May, 1985

Dear Mr. Coot,

I apologise most profusely on not advising you before now of that bet's outcome, and for the delay in replying to yours of the 5th instant. The reason for this is that I had some trouble pinning down that particular wager as being different in outcome from any other (for reasons which I will explain) I have placed in recent months.

I put that two quid on a treble—*C Jam Blues*, *When You're Smiling*, and *Who's Sorry Now?* Three horses with the names of jazz standards running the same day I thought to be a good omen, but adverse conditions prevailed. The spring sun got into the horse's eyes and only 'C Jam' got placed, but look on the bright side, Mr. Coot; better the money went to the bookie than helping to push Mr. Godbolt further down the path to a drunkard's grave.

I like a joke as much as the next man, but take offence at your unkind thrust regarding my 'percipience in these matters.' It's a known fact that I am very good judge of

Illustration: Monty Sunshine

a horse. I should be, after a lifetime's study of equine form. In fact, my bookmaker, Mr. Coral, frequently congratulates me on my choice of wagers and Mr.. Coral knows a lot about horses.

It's that damned sun getting into their eyes that has screwed things up.

Yours sincerely,

Ronnie Scott

29th May, 1985

Dear Mr. Scott,

I am well aware that you like a laugh and a joke, but not one of your revered witticisms had me falling about as much as the names of the horses you mentioned. With regard to *When You're Smiling* I should think this is rarely the case with you when the results come up, and *Who's Sorry Now?* must be the most apposite name of the horse you could back. Thanks for the laugh, and because I could do with a few ho-ho-hos I enclose my usual pound for yourself and one for your editor, though, no doubt, both quids will find their way to Mr. Coral. What, I wonder, will the name be of the next nag you back? *Someday, You'll be Sorry?* Or maybe *Where or When?* Ho- Ho-Ho!

Yours sincerely,

Herbert Coot

RONNIE'S JOKES

It was Ronnie Scott's practice to tell the audience about the future attractions and not getting any response he would say: 'You don't seem very impressed... Why don't you all join hands and see if you can contact the living?
Actually, you should have been at the Club last Monday. Somebody should have been here last Monday. We had the bouncers chucking them in. A guy rang up to ask what time the show started and we said, 'What time can you get here?'. The band was playing Tea for One and at the end of the number the audience was on its foot. It was two hours before we found out our cashier was dead. Mind you, years ago, when we first opened the Club, a dead cashier wouldn't have presented any problems'...

INTERVIEW...
whilst dining with an O.B.E.

Again I apologise to long-standing — and long suffering — readers of this page for reiterating that trying to interview that funny man, Ronnie Scott, is no fun. I don't know anyone so non-communicative, so clam-like, and here I was, once again, approaching the club, stomach sinking at the daunting task of getting him to give me a few words. I was also nursing a grievance.

I had just read in London's only evening newspaper, *The New Standard*, an interview with Ronnie by one Byron Rogers that took up nigh a full page. How come, I bitterly asked myself, this Rogers cat gets so much wordage from the guv'nor whereas I, editor of his house magazine, have to grovel for the privilege of a few muttered grunts from which I have to build a full page article?

AN INSTITUTION

In this *Standard* article I read that Ronnie is now an 'institution', and I firmly intended to have a few sharp words with this institution about unfairly preferential treatment to a Fleet Street journalist. I rolled trenchant phases round my tongue as I turned into Frith Street, but it was one of the two days in June when the sun shone, bringing the Mediterranean workshys out of their warrens to crowd the pavements in chattering and gesticulating groups, this so un-English noise and movement in a public place affecting me sharpening the trenchant phrases I was going to lay round Mr. Scott's ears. And — lo — who should I bump into but B C?
My cup of pain is now full and overflowing!
BC is a highly irritating, fully paid-up pest! A jazz buff who even managed to get himself the sack from one of the very few radio jazz programmes going. That programme's producer is one of the most tolerant men alive, but even he could take no more of this birk's crass loutishness.
'Ah-ha!' cried BC triumphantly, 'Talking to yourself, I see!'
'Yes, it's the only intelligent conversation I get!' I shot back, quick as a flash.
'You were repeating yourself, too'.
'Force of habit. Most of my contemporaries are rotten listeners. Good talkers — rotten listeners.' To which I meaningfully added, 'You, particularly!' I followed this sharp thrust with an emphatic 'Good-bye', and put a positive left foot forward in the direction of the Club.
I was in no mood to suffer his inane chat, nor to gaze upon his horrible physiognomy. True, his rodent-like features are not his fault, but I feel he should try and do something about his nauseous manner if he wants to see himself though a normal life span.
You will have gathered he's not one of my favourite chaps.
Now somewhat ruffled, I strode into Ronnie's office ready for battle. The institution was at his desk, as cool and composed as ever. There has been a flurry of press reports about the club suffering a rough patch, but you'd never think so looking at the institution whose name it bears.
'Ah, Jim. How nice to see you. I'm just going to have a bite. Please join me.'
I was taken aback. How can you have a go at someone — an institution at that — who asks you to dine? But I was puzzled. It was early evening — too soon for the club's kitchen to be operating. I mentioned this.
'Heavens, I don't mean eating here. We'll go somewhere nice.'
Well, what a lovely surprise! I wondered which famed Soho restaurant he'd be taking me to. Gay Hussar? Etoile? White Tower? Wheeler's? Gennaro's? Having had only a cheese roll and a half pint of bitter at the Dog and Duck that day I dwelt on what superb cuisine I'd soon be savouring. I'd start with the smoked salmon. No; I was forgetting asparagus was in season.

I'd have a dish of these succulent shoots with a freshly prepared Sauce Hollandaise, followed by Boeuf Stroganoff, with vegetables to include Pommes Allumettes and Petit Pois, finishing with a fine Stilton and crisp sticks of almond-white celery.

CHÂTEAUNEUF-DU-PAPE

All this to be washed down with a fine bottle of Châteauneuf-du-Pape, the presumption of which would delight, its charm amuse, its body sooth my tattered nerve ends. Or maybe a Mouton Rothschild claret where I'd be aghast at the price, even though I wasn't paying. Deferential, tip-expectant Meds would circle the table attending to our every whim and wish. Indeed, this was an unexpected bonus!
My expectations of wallowing in such exotica were dashed when I found myself walking into McDonald's Hamburger Bar in Shaftesbury Avenue. This was my first experience of such an establishment — probably because they are 'unlicensed'. (What a potty world we live in! People have to possess a licence to sell one of life's basic necessities!) In fact, I had only previously heard the name of this chain thanks to reading in the *Hampstead and Highgate Express* that a group of vociferous environmentalists successfully objected to a branch in trendy Hampstead High Street, and here I was dining in such a place with an institution. It's a funny old world.
He ordered a quarter-pound burger and chips. I settled for chicken and chips. After a day's repast of one cheese roll I couldn't look a gift horse in the mouth, but it's hardly your big deal is it? Not what you'd really expect from an institution who's also an OBE. Maybe a tinge of disappointment fuelled the grievance I was nurturing.
'I've got a bone to pick with you' I said.
'So, you got the wishbone. Lucky chap.'

'I'm speaking metaphorically.'
'Speak metaphorically if you wish, but not so loudly, please. People are looking at us like we're the odd couple.'
'I insist on asking why it is that someone called Byron Rogers gets a lengthy interview with you whereas me, your house mag editor, can barely get a bleeding word out of you.'
'I wish you wouldn't use bad language, Jim. The manager's looking at us.'
'Well, I'm upset. Peeved, in fact. In the last issue of JARS I wrote that under no circumstances would you consider using new jokes, yet I read in Byron Thingymmy's article that you're doing just that – like telling the customers to pretend they're on the Titanic.'
'Jim! Be fair! I have to vary my routine to keep up with events and those that were there enjoyed the joke.'
'Six people falling about doesn't compensate me for you making a mockery of my article. Furthermore in Rogers' article you said the club was somewhere you could eat for nothing. You know you never eat there, not with your aversion to steak and chips that glow in the dark…'
'Jim! There were eight people, not six and I've not bothered you with our financial problems. Not to put too fine a point on the matter, someone of your — ahem — age might be

hard pressed to get another job and I wouldn't want you to worry about that, not at — ahem — your age.'
Slightly mollified by such consideration, if hardly pleased at the reference to my years, I owned it wasn't only *The Standard* article that had upset me. I mentioned bumping into B C. Ronnie choked on his quarter pounder. He, too, had suffered that obnoxious person. We warmed to each other as we verbally tore him, and others of his ilk, apart. Animatedly discussing the many monsters who have plagued us over the years, we were in full agreement that BC picked up the most points for being the person you would last wish to be stranded with on that desert island.
Instead of the hoped-for Châteauneuf-du-Pape or the Mouton Rothschild, I had a milk shake. It had the consistency of hardening cement. I broke it into little pieces and risked my tooth chewing on them.
I thought Byron Rogers' article, called 'Frith Street Blues', and dealing with one or two problems the club is facing, was extremely entertaining; very well written and sharply picking up on Ronnie's quirkier traits. There were a couple of paragraphs I particularly liked:
'He (Ronnie) sat in a windowless office so dark that the rest of the spectrum,

Illustration: Picton

the blues and the reds and the greens, were just a folk memory here. He was dressed in black and every movement of his hands sent shadows streaming up the walls. Jazz musicians, like vampires, don't like the light.
He is a thin-faced man whose features owe more to geometry than anything else. Painters would love the triangles of shadows. He does not smile. There must be something about jazz that eases the expressions of its practitioners, for behind him on the wall was a collage of other blank and famous names.' I wish I'd have written that myself, and not a few days after enjoying this piece I saw another of Mr. Rogers' articles — about brass bands — in the *Radio Times*. Subject-wise this guy certainly gets around. I must try and meet him, to see if I can prise out the secret of getting a non-communicative institution to talk so freely.   J.G.

WHISPERS, MURMURS & ASIDES

CHAMPAGNE TOMMY

In the popular daily I buy in the hope of winning that million — which right now, would come in very handy —

I read some of the contents for my seventeen pence. One item that intrigued me concerned 'society' bandleader Tommy Kinsman, who was long active on the Hooray circuit.
According to this item Tommy was having a crafty gasper in a side room between sets when HRH, Edward the Prince of Wales (this was in the thirties) sneaked in with a giggling debutante and the

Kinsman and orchestra

sank (whoops!) on the sofa — to use the crude terminology of the lower orders — had it away, Kinsman undecided whether to cough discreetly or stay put. He elected for the latter, and who can blame him? It's not everyday you see a Royal at it…
It reminded me of another Kinsman tale. Leaving one of the stately homes after a gig he was bowing to her ladyship when a bottle of purloined champagne fell out of his pocket and smashed on the floor. Totally unperturbed, as would befit a lady of the quality, she immediately summoned a minion and said 'James! Get Mr. Kinsman another bottle of the Dom Perignon!'   TALCOTT MALAGROWTHER

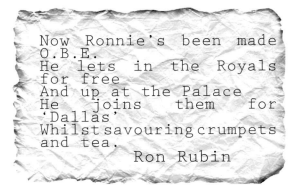

Now Ronnie's been made O.B.E.
He lets in the Royals for free
And up at the Palace
He joins them for 'Dallas'
Whilst savouring crumpets and tea.

      Ron Rubin

133

ALAN CLARE and BRUCE TURNER

It is with deep regret that we report the departure of two great characters whose music and personalities gave so much pleasure.

Pianist Alan Clare and alto-saxophonist Bruce Turner both died on November 29th 1993. Alan was seventy-two, Bruce seventy-one. It was a double blow for the jazz community, already saddened by so many deaths this year.

Both were just two of the highly talented and individualistic musicians the British jazz scene produced in the forties, who continued to lend colour to our lives right up until their deaths.

Alan Clare was born in Walthamstow, East London, on May 31st, 1921. He was playing piano at the age of three and it was his uncle Jack who introduced him to the records of Teddy Wilson, Fats Waller and Earl Hines. Because of his interest in jazz, uncle Jack was considered a 'bit mad' by the rest of the family. At the age of thirteen, Alan was playing in a local social club. He had to borrow his elder brother's long trousers to gain admission to licensed premises.

FATS WALLER

One of the highlights of Alan's life was at the age of seventeen, hearing Fats Waller at the Nest Club, Kingly Street, West Soho. He recalled: 'Watching that left hand I just gawped. I couldn't believe it. He used to come in and start it going, like an automatic reflex— the same way anyone would light a cigarette. It was independent of everything else he did, like shouting across the room and drinking neat gin with his free hand — straight out of the bottle, like we drink lemonade.'

In 1940 he was drafted into the army, but played with Stephane Grappelli and Sid Phillips on leave, and in the evenings. He became a member of 'Stars in Battledress', an entertainment troupe that included actress Janet Brown, later famous for impersonations of Mrs Thatcher. On D-Day plus five he was in the thick of action.

Alan Clare with the high priest of Goonery Spike Milligan

SID MILLWARD'S NITWITS

On demobilisation he did the rounds of clubs, including the Jamboree Club, where he was re-acquainted with early teenage friend, George Shearing . In their earlier days they would take out a rowing boat on the Battersea Park lake, near George's home.

Alan had an enjoyable spell with Sid Millward's Nitwits, a musical-cum-knockabout variety act. The comic in Alan revelled in the experience, but his subsequent career was more on the 'sophisticated' side, playing in hotels, restaurants and cocktail bars.

His first recordings were with Humphrey Lyttelton and Johnny Dankworth for drummer Carlo Krahmer, but never issued. His first issued recordings were from 1951, also for Carlo.

STUDIO CLUB

During the fifties, he had a long spell at the Studio Club, Swallow Street, off Regent Street, where Billie Holiday was a visitor. Alan's wife, Bloom, treasures the memory of Billie's hands on Alan's shoulders as he accompanied her.

I was a member of the club and recall how musicians, who would normally take the ability of their peers for granted, dropped in just to sit as near to Alan as possible as he spun out his improvisations. His friend Spike Milligan described his playing as 'silk-smooth'.

Alan recorded with Don Rendell, Jimmy Deuchar, Tony Crombie and many others, including Stephane Grappelli and Sir Yehudi Menuhin. He acted as well as played, in Spike Milligan's famous 'Q' series, and twice duetted with Oscar Peterson, on BBC TV.

When Frank Sinatra threw a party at the Savoy his choice of pianist was Alan.

Several of Alan's tunes (sometimes in collaboration with Tony Crombie) were recorded by the likes of Eartha Kitt, Cleo Laine, Annie Ross, Peter Sellers, Harry Secombe, and Stephane Grappelli. He wrote the music for several films, and made an appearance in a full-length version of 'Rising Damp', starring Leonard Rossiter.

It was a constant matter for wonder among the fraternity that Alan's fame was limited largely to musicians. He was a superb pianist with an astonishing harmonic sense, an acutely retentive ear, and deft execution, yet a large part of his career was spent in cocktail bars and restaurants playing what he laconically described as 'munch music'.

Aware that his music was being heard only subliminally he could dwell on his improvisations as though he were playing on his own, but should there be a request it was incredible how he nearly always went straight to the melody. His repertoire was enormous. It must have run into thousands of tunes.

HOLLAND PARK

With a slightly quizzical expression I got to know well,

watching and listening to him at the Studio Club, he was a master of dealing with those whose requests were vague or, worse, singing or humming a few bars of the tune they thought they wanted. He was a very witty man who told stories against himself. One, on the occasion of a Mayfair gig, when a lady, staring at him intently, exclaimed, 'Oh, so you're real! I though you were a tape!'

His widow, Bloom, to whom he was married to for forty six years, scattered his ashes in Holland Park near where they lived and, instead of flowers for his funeral, requested donations for the provision of a bench bearing his name in the park.

Bruce Turner was known as much for his eccentricities as the quality of his musicianship on the alto-saxophone and clarinet. He was a 100% vegetarian, non-smoking teetotaller and, in his youth, a rampaging womaniser. An unusual combination of parts but, then, Bruce was a most unusual person.

'FALSE CAMARADERIE OF THE SALOON BAR'
He never, ever, bought anyone a drink, partly because he was pathologically close with a pound, but also because he despised what he contemptuously dubbed 'the false camaraderie of the saloon bar.' Despite his 'health' regime, he compulsively munched his way through a prodigious amount of cakes and confectionery in his lifetime.

He addressed everyone, including his girl friends, two wives and daughters, as 'Dad'. It was a trait that presented him with the occasional difficulty: 'I met my father the other day, Dad, but didn't know what to call him, Dad'.
He assiduously presented a persona of vagueness,

Bruce Turner, Jim Godbolt and Wally Fawkes at the Six Bells, Kings Road, Chelsea

bewilderment and fragility, a sharply calculated front (Bruce was no fool) that acted as a buffer between himself and the smoky, boozy and carnivorous world he inhabited.

There were hundreds of stories about Bruce. One concerned the time he bought a motor car that quickly failed. Asked why he didn't consult someone he knew about motor cars, he replied, 'But, Dad, the man who sold me the car knew all about motor cars'.

Bruce Turner by Trog

MAINSTREAMER
Stylistically, Bruce was a 'mainstreamer', despite, when working in New York as a ship's musician on the Queen Mary in 1949, taking lessons from Lee Konitz. His models on the alto were not Charlie Parker and disciples, but Charlie Holmes, Benny Carter, Johnny Hodges and Hilton Jefferson. Yet his first gigs were on clarinet, with Billy Kaye, and then Freddy Randall's 'Chicago-style' band, with occasional private engagements, one such with bandleader Paul Heineman, depping for Vic Ash, or 'Wictor Hash', as Heineman put it, a mispronunciation that Bruce loved to mimic — with recollection of how much he was paid for the gig — three pounds! Another world!

GO HOME DIRTY BOPPER...
In 1952, Bruce joined Humphrey Lyttelton's then mainly 'traditional' band and outraged the purists' sensibilities concerning the despised saxophone — even though one of their heroes, Sidney Bechet played the soprano, but then, Bechet was from New Orleans, Louisiana, and Bruce was from Saltburn, Yorkshire. Bruce was born on 5th July 1922. Balmy days!

Just how balmy was illustrated when the band made an appearance at the Town Hall, Birmingham, and the moment he stepped forward to solo a bunch of crackpots unfurled a banner across several seats reading, 'GO HOME DIRTY BOPPER!'

In 1957 he formed his Jump Band, which pursued a financially hazardous course between the extremes of traditionalism and bebop. I can speak with heartfelt conviction about this period in his career — I was his agent. Finding work was difficult; as indeed he could be.

But his commitment to the sound he wanted, a homage to the 'Harlem' bands of the thirties — an extraordinarily fecund period in jazz — inspired this functionary to plead the case of the Jump Band. (Of course there was the financial aspect, and Bruce promptly settled his commission, a fact that would endear any parasitical ten per center to any bandleader!) Difficult as times were, the Jump Band kept going for five years.

In 1961 The Jump Band was the subject of a documentary, 'Living Jazz', directed by Jack Gold, shot on a shoe-string budget with the most limited of equipment, but for all its failings, reflecting more of the jazz musician than most all-glossy Hollywood bio-epics about jazzmen. Some of the footage was shot at the Six Bells, Kings Road, Chelsea, where Bruce had the hard core of the following.

We were both members of the Ravers CC, the jazzmen's XI and I vividly recall a game where skipper Robin Rathborne, placing the field, told Bruce to go to square leg. 'Phst, Dad', murmured Bruce, 'Don't like going anywhere that's square, Dad.'

In 1963 Bruce joined Acker Bilk's Paramount Jazz Band, helping, with trumpeter Al Fairweather (who also died in 1993) to change the once wholly traditional sound of the band, as he did with Lyttelton in 1952. He returned to Lyttelton twice after leaving Bilk in 1970, and went free-lance in 1988. Not one to push himself, he found himself 'scuffling'.

HOT AIR AND COOL MUSIC

In 1984 he published his autobiography, *Hot Air And Cool Music*, in which he railed against critics, cultists, and his one time agent! But we were good friends, and exchanged correspondence. He borrowed my *History of Jazz in Britain 1919-1950*, (in which, of course, he is mentioned) and in a letter to me, despatched second-class mail, he, sending up his own meanness, wrote: 'Confined to my bed with back trouble, I read *Jazz in Britain* from cover to cover. May I say I found it very fine. I nearly went out to buy a copy, but the spinal twinges precluded any such rash behaviour.'

He called himself the 'Jack Benny of Jazz'. He played at the Edinburgh Festival in 1991 with US clarinettist Ken Peplowski, who announced they were going to play *The Best Things in Life Are Free*, to which Bruce muttered, 'The free things in life are best, Dad', an observation that utterly confused Peplowski.

In November, I visited him in hospital with pianist Stan Greig, and sent him a cassette of tapes by Tab Smith, acknowledged in a letter where his illness showed in uncharacteristic typing errors. He told me to 'Tell the Dads that Bruce was on the mend', but an inoperable brain tumour was diagnosed and his end was near.

A benefit was staged at the 100 Club, Oxford Street, with Humphrey Lyttelton and Acker Bilk and their bands, George Melly and John Chilton's Feetwarmers and many other musicians giving their services free. It was an outstanding success, with queues stretching down Oxford Street long before the doors opened. Yes, the bill was strong, but stronger was the desire to pay tribute, and give support to, a dearly loved character.

Over a hundred people attended his cremation at Milton Keynes on 2nd December, to pay homage. His widow, Sandra, put a chocolate cake on the coffin, alongside which his four daughters placed a red rose. Humphrey Lyttelton gave an address, and his stories of Bruce's eccentricities had the mourners rocking with laughter. Which is as it should have been, as the occasion was a celebration of a funny man's life and the formal, solemn religious service would have been out of place.

I feel proud to have been associated with a fine musician and splendidly idiosyncratic character like Bruce Turner, and to have known Alan Clare.

Without doubt, they enriched the lives of us all in the jazz fraternity. J.G.

WHISPERS, MURMURS & ASIDES

OPERA AND JAZZ

It happens so frequently, that I didn't even bother to make a note of the last Wagnerian marathon on Radio 3, but, if my memory serves me right, it went on, and on, for something like four and a half hours — with breaks for characters talking about opera. It was on a Saturday afternoon and, naturally, Jazz Record Requests was given the heave-ho that day. O.K, I, in the spirit of tolerance for which I am famed, accept that opera is part of our cultural life, and, jazz 'freak' that I am actually enjoy some of it and, undoubtedly, it has spawned some great characters, particularly the prima donnas and the conductors, but, I ask, when did you last hear four and half consecutive hours of jazz on the station that is allegedly devoted to minority interests? Your answers, on a postcard, please . Bah ! J.G.

'I say, old thing, ai've got a notion that we pop down to jolly ol' Ronnie Scott's and partake a little of that rippin' hot jess'.
'Oh, Peregrine, that would be absolutely *sooo-pah*! They say Mr. Scott's jokes are frightfully amusin".
'Done, old horse, I'll get Parsons to call the *broo-am*!'

WALLY 'TROG' FAWKES
famous cartoonist compelled to cease his masterly drawings

TROG RETIRES

I was very sorry to read in the *Sunday Telegraph* in 2005 that problems with his eyesight have compelled famed cartoonist Wally 'Trog' Fawkes to give up drawing after sixty years at the top of his profession, during which he has received a succession of honours and awards. Happily, he retains normal sight, but to avoid further deterioration he has had to call it a day as an eye-punishing draughtsman.

For years he contributed a daily cartoon called 'Flook' to the *Daily Mail* and both George Melly and Humphrey Lyttelton were among the writers of the dialogue in the 'balloons'. It was a sharply satirical commentary on everyday events, social, musical and political.

ACUTE POWERS OF OBSERVATION

Wally is noted for his acute powers of observation, the almost uncanny ability to caricature features, facial and physical, yet the identity of his 'victims' was unmistakable and however seemingly cruel his caricatures were, many of his subjects urgently requested the original to display on their mantelpieces. To be 'done' by Trog was an honour.

One of these was Kenneth Clarke, QC, MP, and former Chancellor of the Exchequer, this image accompanying my interview with Chancellor Clarke at the Treasury that appeared in *JARS*. This was one of the many drawings that Wally has produced for us.

Although I have known Wally from our school days in the 1930s, and when he played clarinet with George Webb's Dixielanders in the mid-40s, I never approached him to contribute to *JARS*, but one Sunday evening in the early 1990s I received a call offering his services. I was delighted, of course, but only guessing at the fees an artist of his calibre could command, I had to say we couldn't

Wally and Melly

afford to pay him. Wally, typically generous, replied, 'That's OK. Make it a bottle.'

Wally is philosophical about the wrench of retiring after all these years, and he said, 'I can't complain,' — and here is the cricketer and musician talking – 'I've had a good innings and I've still got the clarinet.' (Wally, a classy batsman and a very pacy bowler, was a founder member of the Ravers Cricket Club – the jazzmen's eleven. A personal recollection: one of my memories of playing with him was, when fielding at second slip, making a reflex leap to pouch a catch off his fast bowling. (In my antiquity, I still revel in the memory of a thrilling moment of long lost agility). Wally doesn't recall that catch that for me has no price.

Wally played with Humphrey Lyttelton from 1948 to 1956, a partnership commonly referred to as 'Humph 'n' Wally'.

THE MAINSTREAM TROGLODYTES

On leaving Humph, he formed his Troglodytes in what became known as the 'mainstream' phase, when ardent traditionalists were dropping the chugging banjo and, as in Wally's case, employing 'modern' musicians such as ex-Dankworth Seven Eddie Taylor on drums, Club Eleven pioneer Lennie Bush on bass and Colin Purbrook on piano, resident at the Six Bells Jazz Club, King's Road, Chelsea, in the late 1950s.

The band he co-led, the Chilton–Fawkes Feetwarmers, saw the commencement of George Melly's re-entry into the music business, and these thirty years later George is still on the road and making his annual Christmas appearance at Ronnie Scott's.

Wally is a man of few words, but every syllable is charged with trenchant meaning. He was once a member of a band where the leader had left his wife to live with a much younger woman and this guy was banging on at great length as to how the lady was making enormous sexual demands on him, but he was coping. Wally, lethally, murmured, '*Mmm*... Would it help to talk about it?' Had I been present and seen the Fawkes' chin lifted, the eyes glinting, I'd have known this fellow was in for trouble.

The Trog drawing for *JARS* which I treasure most was made to commemorate our 100th edition, where I was the 'not out' batsman flanked by umpires Pete King and Ronnie Scott (page 14 of this book). Thereafter I was fearful of appearing in public, conscious of having elephant ears and almost non-existent chin. Talk about chinless wonders!

J.G.

Duke by Trog, an example of Wally's exceptional talent

THE CLUB ELEVEN RAIDED
by 'FLASH' WINSTON

In the mid-forties there came a great divide in jazz. Traditionalism flourished on one hand, and on the other, the new jazz, called bebop or rebop, was struggling to establish itself. In Britain, Humphrey Lyttelton, with Wally Fawkes on clarinet, was hitting the headlines, their mentors King Oliver, Louis Armstrong and Jelly Roll Morton.
At the same time, young musicians, their inspirations Dizzy Gillespie, Charlie Parker and Thelonious Monk, organised regular sessions at a grubby rehearsal room in Soho, calling themselves the Club Eleven. Drummer, pianist, raconteur and Marxist philosopher, Cecil 'Flash' Winston, a boyhood friend of Ronnie Scott's, recalls the formation of the Club. Allowing that he is relating events of nearly half a century ago, Flash's chronology is a little out of kilter. For instance, Ronnie Scott had been out of the Ted Heath Orchestra for over a year in 1948, but a little retrospective imagery is forgivable in so graphic a description of the then prevailing spirit.   J.G.

The spring of '48 sprang into motion, and the young lions watering at Harmony Inn, Archer Street, were guarding their loins. At one table sat Tommy Pollard, Denis Rose, Tony Crombie, and Laurie Morgan. Tom's fingers encircled a cup of tea, and through the steam rising to his clear blue eyes, he gazed prophetically into space. Rose added a note or two to a manuscript he was never without, whistled a few bars of Parker's Anthropology and looked imperiously around. Nearby sat Ronnie Scott, Johnny Rogers and Bernie Fenton, whilst Johnny Dankworth, Joe Muddel and Lennie Bush leaned nonchalantly against an adjacent pillar.

Crombie executed a two-fingered roll on the table top, and Pollard took the cue, his measured tones heard only by the 'Eleven'. 'What do you think of the idea of opening your own club?' he said. Morgan gave heed to Tom, 'I think it's a wonderful idea,' he breathed. I threw some dialect into his path, and putting the Indian sign of Sitting Tom queried, 'How?' Crombie finished a knuckled triplet and continued the party line. 'What did you have in mind, Tom,' he drawled.

Pollard gathered his thoughts and laid his cards on the table. The rumblings aroused the Gods, and the Olympians looked down and smiled at these mortals, who, having mastered the 'old men's music, were now looking for fresh fields to conquer. 'At the moment,' Tony said, 'we pay to play our kind of music.'

It was true. The gospel was practised in many an underground rehearsal room. 'If we pool our resources,' Pollard continued, we could look around for a large room and open our own club to the public.' Muddel's sharp features gave Bush a chiselled grin, Lenny stroked a grizzled chin and growled 'Gr-r-reat.' Crombie squared his broad shoulders, thrust his long legs under the table, picked his teeth and asked 'How do you see the set-up then, Tom?'

Pollards' answer had the simplicity of genius. 'Ronnie will have a sextet, Johnny can lead a quartet and 'Flash' will compère and link the groups.' Crombie balanced the chair he was sitting in back on its hind legs and called over to Scott. 'What do you think, Ron?' Tony asked, with a deference overshadowed by his cigarette holder. Scott, pondering the mysteries of life and Soho, remained preoccupied.

JEWISH PRUDENCE

Fortunately, a knowledge of 'Jewishprudence' allowed me the liberty of speaking for others in time of crisis. 'Don't worry about Ronnie, I said, 'He's tired of working for Ted Heath. He wants to front his own group'. Denis Rose nodded his head in pontifical affirmation and without further ado, assent became unanimous.

Following that Harmony Inn meeting, events moved with rapidity. I dropped in at Mac's Rehearsal Rooms, Great Windmill Street, where I had heard there was a room vacant. On my arrival, it was being swept by the caretaker, a half-breed of indeterminate race and allegiance. Dispensing with subtlety, I expostulated. 'How much does Mac want to hire this death trap?' His sunken eyes looked hastily for the exit, and then gazed at me with suspicion. Shaking his broom at my mohair, he swept the ground from under my feet, and spat surlily, 'You'll have to talk to Mac.' Tipping him the ash off my cigar, I left him to his gypsy incantations, and sought his feudal lord. Mac agreed to us having the room on a Wednesday night. We named the date, called the place the 'Club Eleven', after the number of its founders, and began preparations for blast-off.

RONNIE WHO?

A telephone call to Jack Marshall, associate editor of the *Melody Maker*, shattered his lethargy with news that the jazz world he knew was crumbling at the seams. Scott was leaving Ted Heath, Fenton severing relations with Oscar Rabin, and Rose, Dankworth, Crombie and Muddel were all abandoning Tito Burns. The diligence of this member of the Fourth Estate in carrying out his duties was admirable. 'Who did you say was leaving Heath?,' Marshall asked. 'Ronnie Scott,' I reiterated, adding as a sop to his erudition, 'bound for Elysian fields.'
To cut a long story short, and that's what Marshall did, the information I gave him over the hot line was mostly ignored. That the 'Club Eleven' would cement race relations, and that in six months it would be the new Jerusalem, attracting both priest and proselyte, the blue-pencilled Jack never printed. He did, however, splash pictures of the club's leading lights all over his front page. The rest, as they say, is history.
Broadcasts, recordings, and concerts came in quick succession and within three months, public acclaim was such as to to force us to acquire much larger premises in Carnaby Street, satisfying the legions of fans coming from all over the country to the by now famous Club Eleven.
The phenomenal rise of the club, though dependent on the new jazz music it embraced, owed much to the colourful and vibrant personalities of its founders. The quick-witted

'Water! For God's sake, water!' called out Flash from behind his cell bars; Illustration: Marta Rusin

and handsome Ronnie Scott, Johnny Dankworth, equally good looking, like Scott, cut out for fame, the ascetic Denis Rose, theoretical genius and a hive of musical energy and industry, Laurie Morgan, vitalised by a sojourn in the States, playing drums faster than most, the militant Tommy Pollard and socialist Bernie Fenton, the pragmatic Lennie Bush, the satirical Joe Muddel, and Tony Crombie, whose dark good looks and six foot frame caused many a flutter from the numerous beauties the Club Eleven attracted.

I was quite prepared to bow to the superior talents of Laurie Morgan and Tony Crombie as drummers, and act as a compère, though I was still very much concerned with the practice of music, playing till the early hours at Al Burnett's Stork Club. However, it was the Club Eleven that took precedence above all else as a laboratory in which our musical ideas were put to the test.

FROM SACK-CLOTH TO HASHISH

Meanwhile, back at the Club Eleven, certain manifestations of the permissive society to come were about to concern the authorities. The law regarding the use of stimulants had undergone radical change in the past. One recalled the prohibition of alcohol in America, and the dispensing of laudanum at the turn of the century to English factory workers. Addicted to the discipline of music and the concept of change, the founder members of the Club Eleven had a respect for the spirit, if not the letter, of the law. In consequence some were to indulge in a much milder drug than that imbibed by all classes — alcohol. In this case it was what was euphemistically described as 'naughty-type African Woodbines' — hashish.

What is common to most drugs is that they have the power to change one's frame of mind. Philosophy also has this capacity. However, whereas knowledge, understanding and wisdom, are slow cumulative processes, artificial stimulants are apt to give one an inordinate belief in 'instant revelation' and the law of diminishing returns often led to excess.

The mind-depending, mind-widening, call it what you will, effect of cannabis is undoubtedly dangerous. The inner world has its quicksands and pitfalls. Yet, no amount of moralising has ever prevented the young and adventurous from exploring unknown and forbidden territory. Long before the Beatles and the Stones aroused the apprehension of the Establishment, an identical alarm was evoked by the Club Eleven, and the repercussions were just as inevitable.

COUP DE GRASS

On the night of 15th April, 1950, the Club Eleven was raided. A line of constables marched resolutely across the floor of the Club Eleven, bringing to a halt the sound of music and the festive atmosphere. A uniformed officer told all to stop where they were and a task force that could have found the Holy Grail went about their business of search. A number of substances were located and docketed, their owners cautioned and then conducted outside to a waiting Black Maria. It was the first time I had travelled in this quaint conveyance. Placed in a tiny cubicle that allowed a minimum of movement and a modicum of air, it was an experience not without its traumas.

With a screech of brakes, the Black Maria finally came to a stop inside a courtyard of Savile Row Police Station. Released from confinement we were ushered into the station, charged, fingerprinted, and booked to appear in the magistrates' court first thing in the morning. The constabulary, not wishing us to be late for our appointment, insisted we stay the night. In the circumstances it would have been churlish to refuse, and we had no alternative but to comply with their request. Leading us to our rooms, a sergeant wished us goodnight and left, locking the doors behind us as a precaution against any intrusion of our privacy.

(Flash doesn't write of his theatrical contribution to the night's events, but the following was one of Ronnie Scott's favourite stories. Once 'banged up', Flash grasped the bars to the grille of his cell, and, echoing the Count of Monte Cristo imprisoned in the Chateau d'If, cried, 'Water! Water! For God's sake, water!' — the Editor)

'WHAT IS BEBOP?'

Stoically contemplating our sudden change of environment, we were rudely disturbed by one of the fellow prisoners rattling the bars of his cell, proclaiming his innocence, adding that if he was not given his asthma cure back, he would hold the police responsible for the consequences. His portrayal of injured pride was worthy of Sir Henry Irving at his most declamatory. Some ten minutes later he was released with apologies, handed back his herbal mixture and sent on his way to an asthmatical, but precious, freedom.

Early next morning we were again conducted to a waiting Black Maria and conveyed to the nearby Marlborough Street Magistrates' Court. Released on our own surety, and the promise to attend the parish inquisition two weeks hence,

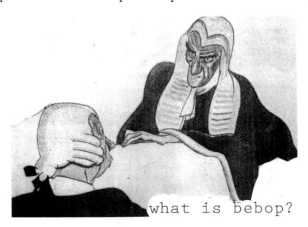

what is bebop?

we hurriedly left and made steps to prepare our defence.

The Club Eleven's landlords, no strangers to litigation, introduced us to a friendly lawyer willing to advocate on our behalf. Any apprehension we had left was added to by the fees he required and the rumour that he had once secured three months hard labour for a client charged with a parking offence.

It is only in times of stress that one finds out who one's friends really are. I shall always treasure the advice of numerous well wishers, but in the final analysis, I eschewed the loan of a crofters hut in the Outer Hebrides till things blew over and eventually decided to throw myself at the mercy of the court.

Justice Daniel Hopkin, presiding over our trial, had, we were told, a tendency to suffer from gout, and that the severity of his sentence often depended on the pain in his foot. There was little time to change our advocate for a chiropodist. All we could hope was the learned judge had got out of bed that morning on the right foot.

(An unexpected comic relief was provided by Mr. Hopkin when he solemnly enquired, 'What is bop?'. For once, the query was not typical magisterial facetiousness. It was, after all, a question that few in the jazz world could answer, much less a magistrate. A detective inspector replied: 'It is a queer form of modern dancing — a sort of Negro jive'. Mr Hopkin appeared satisfied with the explanation, although, no doubt, was none the wiser for it. (When the defendants took the witness box, they each gave reasons for their indulgence, Ronnie Scott claiming that his was for toothache. — the Editor)

Any levity we might have felt withered in the cold formality of the indictment. Pleading guilty to the charge, but with no previous convictions, we were released on the payment of a fifty pound fine. To the sight of relief from all concerned, we gratefully left Marlborough Street Court House and returned to the Club Eleven to resume activities.

DECLINE AND FALL

The news of the arrest, trial and conviction of some of the Club Eleven members occupied the front page of almost every national paper in the size and type usually reserved for earthquakes or war. Though this publicity did nothing to lessen attendances, the decline of the Club Eleven was only a matter of time.

Of course, there were a number of other factors contributing to the dissolution of an organisation that for the two years of its existence had a profound influence on its leading figures and devoted followers. Not least of which was the dichotomy resulting from the espousal of a music in which its English exponents, by their own admission, could never be considered first-rate. All believed that if Charlie Parker or Dizzy Gillespie were to play next door, the Club Eleven could forget it. Probably this self-effacement was the underlying cause for the use of stimulants.

To the Marxist, the contradictions lay deeper than the mystique of race and the inferiority of the white man to the American Negro in the field of progressive, and indeed, all jazz. The roots of the dilemma were entrenched in a music motivated by an unquenchable desire for freedom and individual expression, ideally manifested in the person of Charlie Parker. Political forces were preparing for the age of MacCarthy. After the demise of Parker at the messianic age of thirty-four, progressive jazz, like Christianity, was inevitably left to amorphous vagaries of so-called 'free-form'.

WHISPERS, MURMURS & ASIDES

THE MONSTER SAXOPHONIST

Ron Rubin found this cutting in a Majorcan newspaper in 1964 when he, on bass, and a tenor saxophonist called Ronnie Scott, played a season at the Indigo Club, Majorca. Author/poet Robert Graves was one of their regular listeners.

Ronnie recalls that Mr Graves had an urgent question to ask the young (whoops !) saxophonist:

'Ronnie, what's the pot situation in London these days ?'

Not many people know this aspect of a famous author. Keep tuned in to *JARS* for similar gems you will undoubtedly find handy when conversation flags over the dinner table.

HARRY MORRIS
THE QUINTESSENTIAL SOHOITE

Another conversation-livener is the tale of Harry Morris somewhere in central London in the late forties. Harry was the manager of the Club Eleven, Great Windmill Street, where Ronnie Scott, Johnny Dankworth, Denis Rose, Laurie Morgan and others launched 'modern' jazz in Britain in the late forties.

For what reason I don't know, but a group of them found themselves on a journey and at one point Harry, who had strict topographical parameters in his daily round, exclaimed, 'Guys! I've had enough of this! Let's get back to town.'

The 'guys' were at Marble Arch.

Another time Flash Winston approached Harry, who was also a street photographer, to take a picture of him 'Can you make me look less Jewish?' pleaded Flash. Harry replied, 'I am a photographer, not a plastic surgeon!'   PAUL PRY

Ronnie Scott, Harry Morris, Flash Winston

WHISPERS, MURMURS & ASIDES

COCK-UPS, GOOFS, BONERS AND HOWLERS

Deaths

McLEOD. — On August 18, peacefully in hospital, Joseph Phillip McLeod, loving dad of Joe, father-in-law to Gwen, loving grandad to Jane, Ian and Kelly. Sadly pissed.   15E

The Mail, Hartlepool

The above clipping is a classic example of a typesetter's error – but was it a mistake? Some of these setters have a waggish sense of humour and are well aware how easy it is for a harassed sub-editor to overlook a word similar to what was originally written — 'missed' in this case, for it is difficult to believe that the bereaved would have used the word that did appear — even though it may have been true that Old Joe liked a drop.

True, mistakes often originate in the typescript, these often compounded with a few of the typesetter's own. Of course this should be corrected in the galley proofs but, again, it's so easy to read what you think you are reading, especially like the howler in this clipping from the *Hartlepool Mail*.

BLUTMORES

These are but a few of the hazards attendant to publication involving the human chain. One weak link in that chain and… bingo… you've got your aggro. In the handling of the paste-up, material can fall away, leaving inexplicable gaps and mysteriously uncompleted paragraphs. There are further dangers in the production line. For those unaware, a printer's plates are sheets of metal on which the text is impressed via a film negative, both processed by one man and if he returns from the Rose and Crown after a lengthy lunch and his vision is impaired all manner of mishaps can occur.

I own up: I await each issue with trepidation for I know, by God I know, that any errors will be avidly seized upon and my telephone will ring (I swear) in an ominous fashion telling me, before I lift the receiver, that my caller is a Blutmore fulfilling his/her divine mission in life to advise where we have gone wrong, this immediately discernable from the tone of his/her first syllable.

Usually they are too late, because it's one of the facts of an editor's life that on receiving a new issue the first thing, the very first thing, that rears up and smites him straight between the eyes are the cock-ups. Why then, didn't he see them before actual printing? I don't know, except that Sod's Law is a constant in the print game…

Sometimes the errors are unimportant, but others could easily lead the publisher, writer and editor into the libel courts. Years ago, I reviewed the Capital Jazz Festival at Alexander Palace and commented that 'a somewhat introverted Tony Coe Quintet had — musically speaking – been given a kick up the backside by that exuberant ex-Basie trombonist Al Grey'.

The 'k' in 'kick' was replaced by the typesetter with an 'l', and you can work out for yourselves how that would have read. These years later I still get hot and cold thinking how near I came to grief — and much ribaldry from the Blutmores.

NEARLY ANOTHER CLASSIC BONER

In the No 45 issue of *JARS* I, again, stood on the precipice. Reviewing the *Vic Lewis Jam Session Volume 4* on Harlequin I concluded my piece by referring to 'six keen musicians', which, without doubt, they were. What the typesetter put instead (inadvertently?) was also without doubt, equally true, but not what I had written, and had it not been spotted by our Anne Piombino it might well have slipped my scrutiny and gone into immortality as another classic boner, giving rise to much hilarity and, inevitably, a spate of calls from the Blutmores.

I kept that piece of setting and reproduce it here:

Despite these track being home recorded the quality is excellent – a few clicks and hisses – but not sufficient to detract from enjoying the work of sex keen musicians whose official title was His Majesty's Royal Air Force Bomber Command Sextet

Now I hope that no smart Alec is going to quote this out of context. This would be very naughty.   J.G.

RONNIE'S JOKES

It was thanks to Pete's virtually giving up playing to concentrate on managing the Club that I was able to continue to run a band and do one-night stands around the country. Jazz was still very much a Cinderella music and we got to play in some pretty marginal places. I remember one town where all the girls were terribly unattractive. They had a beauty contest during the dance and nobody won. There was one girl who was so plain that she got obscene phone calls from a guy who reversed the charges - and she accepted them. It seems that when she was a kid her mother had to tie a pork chop round her neck before the dog would play with her.

But our bass player picked up a very nice girl. She was a redhead. No hair. Just a red head. I was told that she played Lady Godiva in a carnival once and everyone looked at the horse.

CECIL JACOB 'Flash' WINSTON

An early associate of Ronnie's was Cecil 'Flash' Winston, pianist, drummer, comedian, and author — as yet unpublished. Flash, from Globe Road, Whitechapel, in London's East End, was one of those arrested at the Club Eleven, Carnaby Street, on the night of April 15th, 1950, for being in possession of substances known among the profession as 'naughty type African Woodbines', or 'exotic cheroots'.

Inside the police cells in Savile Row, the waggish Flash crawled along the floor, gripping the door's bars and hoarsely cried 'Water! Water! For Godsake, water!' as if he were the Count of Monte Cristo incarcerated in the Chateau d'If.

The book Flash is working on is, he reports, a history of jazz based on the Hegelian concept of thesis, antithesis and synthesis: an interpretation which he feels will revolutionise the understanding of the influence that jazz had on his contemporaries and on the fabric of post-Second World War society. That's exactly how he put it to *JARS*.

Flash was very much a denizen of Soho when mob war was in its height and a job he had with gangster Jack Spot was hilariously related in a 50s *Melody Maker* and reproduced here as a flashback to a vanished Soho.   J.G.

I had just finished reading a biography of Jimmy 'Schnozzle' Durante. Much of his success, it said, came from playing for some of the toughest audiences in town — bootleggers, hoodlums and the like. If you can please a tough audience, it seemed, you could please anyone. So I listened closely to Joe Green.* 'You can play for Jack Spot,' he told me. 'He's opening a drinking and dancing club in Greek Court — just off Old Compton Street.'

Let's face it, at that particular moment I wasn't looking for glory or kicks — just cash: 'When does he open?' I said. I was a little flattered, too. Jack Spot — big man in his own line of business — knew of Cecil 'Flash' Winston. He'd heard me singing at the piano in a couple of clubs. And he wanted me.

*Joe Green, one of the club's present door staff and the club's transport domo.

BROTHERLY LOVE

Any first-year psychologist will tell you that, deep inside, we all yearn to be loved. I felt the stirrings of brotherly feeling for Jack Spot.

I was punctual on the opening night and before I could say 'Joe sent me', someone grabbed by arm. It was a gentlemen in an immaculately-cut suit and face to match.

'What do you want?' he demanded. The demand came from a gash pretty low down. I think it was his mouth. I told him that I was the pianist and grinned nonchalantly to prove that I'd been around. That foxed him. He sent for the boss. First through the door was a ten-inch cigar, followed by a man not unlike movie tough-guy Broderick Crawford. He threw an arm around my shoulder and hustled me into a long room half-filled with patrons and cigar smoke.

'Remember,' he said, 'if you've got a job with me, you've got a job for life.' Don't I get time off for good behaviour?' I ventured. It was the right tack. He roared his appreciation.

'That's what I like — a guy with a sense of humour.'

'And another thing: two tunes you just don't play here — 'Guilty' and 'Wanted'. He dug my ribs as cue. I laughed like mad.

*a long standing member of staff at Ronnie's in variety of capacities

After reading that Durante book the atmosphere of Spot's basement club was disappointing. Apart from a vague ominous feeling that something could happen, nothing much did. In fact, the boys were very much on their best behaviour — particularly when Mrs. Spot came. And Jack's peculiar conception of decorum insisted that hats should not be worn within the premises. There was no drunkenness, no gambling.

He was there nearly all the time — except when the big boxing promotions were on. He sat there and eyed newcomers with cold appraisal, a quietly-dressed moody man whose word in this little world was law. If he raised his eyebrows, someone came running. In fact one evening, I was halfway through the first number when the phone rang... didn't notice the hush that fell over the room till one of the boys came over and barked 'Stop!'

ALARM BELL PIANO

When the call was through, a wave from the boss signalled me to continue. The 'phone rang all the time and I obeyed it like an alarm beep despite protests from the artist within me. Musical tastes were strictly not hep. Requests tended to the maudlin side – *Heart Of My Heart*, *Shanty In Old Shanty Town*, *I Ain't Half Proud Of My Old Mum*, it might prove something to someone. Some of the characters would get up to sing, usually because Jack had told them to. If Jack asked for a song you did it. 'Touchy' might describe them. For

Rear: Lennie Bush, 'Ace' Rockman (a fan), Ronnie Scott; Front: Flash Winston, Jeff Ellison, Tony Crombie. Photo taken somewhere in Soho

Club Eleven associates of Flash: Denis Rose, Johnny Rogers, and Harry Morris

example. First listener was a stocky man very prone to depression. One night, carried away the music, I smiled, broadly. When I looked around, he loomed over me, glaring.

'What are you laughing about?' he snarled. 'Are you taking the micky?'

I talked very quickly and soothingly. When this boy was unhappy, everybody had to be unhappy. I was unhappy. Another shining light...proud of his slick appearance and way with women. His boast was that he had been given thirty days so often that the Government were thinking naming a month after him. He loved boogie-woogie. On the door, for any emergency, was a one-time pugilist. I sparred with him playfully one evening and I really had him worried. He thought he'd killed me.

EXCITEMENT

The patrons of the club ranged from strong-arm boys to effeminate types, but they included newspaper reporters, officers of the law, stars and quite ordinary citizens. All seemed to find a certain excitement there. And presiding over the scene was the enigmatic, unpredictable figure of Jack Spot. In my mind, he was written off as another frustrated entertainer. Urged by his associates, he would sometimes burst into song — and the lyrics would have stopped a prison concert party; the rest would be an anti-climax, for nobody could follow Jack Spot except possibly a bloodhound. I think he dreamed of starting an elegant Mayfair club, of rubbing elbows with the famous. And the first bid for star cabaret, I'm certain, would have got Billy Daniels. He idolised Billy. Certainly he took the Club seriously. When business was bad, he would pace the floor, his cigar at an aggresive angle. Not that he ran it as a money-making concern: it was merely a place where the boys could meet socially. I was there nearly a year when we fell out. I'd put a dep in and sometime before midnight I went to see how he was doing.

'Where have you been?' they demanded. Gratifying that they'd missed me so much but the very air felt cold and mean. 'We'll see you don't work anywhere after this,' they threatened. As I sadly walked up the steps, I had to admit that they had a point. My dep hadn't turned up: I was lucky I wasn't turned over.

10th November, 1989
Dear, Dear Ronnie,
Notwithstanding the considerable respect I have for our long acquaintance, I am obliged to take legal action against you for allowing my persona to be degraded in the 30th anniversary issue of JARS. In my article entitled 'Flash Winston', my intellectual criteria and attitude to the criminal classes were maliciously libelled and brought into disrepute by Jim Godbolt; a person I understand employed by Ronnie Scott Club.
I have never read a biography of Jimmy 'Schnozzle' Durante, nor have I ever felt 'the stirring of brotherly feeling for the gangster, Jack Spot', as your Mr. Godbolt indiscriminately and fallaciously maintains; adding further insult and injury by describing me as an 'author - as yet unpublished'.
I am told by solicitors that there is a law which holds an employer fully responsible for the actions of those within his employ at the time any offence to a plaintiff occurs. And as one must assume that Godbolt wrote the scurrilous article in question while subservient to your authority, so to speak, I am sure any judge would deem it just that you remunerate me for the defamation of character perpetrated as it were in the anniversary issue of your house magazine. However, in defence to the Old Boys Act, circa 1952, yet against the advice of my solicitors, I would be willing to settle the matter more or less amicably out of court. In short, if you are prepared to send me a cheque for

£5,000, I shall consider the issue closed.
P. S. If it is true, as is rumoured in certain circles, that you may find some difficulty in raising that amount of cash, I might accept
for eventual disposal at Christie's the marble bust of yourself by what's her name and your OBE with its fingerprints of the Queen. Both of which I am sure will fetch a tidy sum. But whichever way the cookie crumbles, or the ball bounces, it is imperative I hear from you one way or the other very quickly. Failing that we meet at Marlborough Street Court House, where, if memory serves correct, we both once brushed with a gout-ridden Justice Daniel Hopkin.
Sincerely
'Flash' Winston

Ronnie Scott replied:

Flash, getting on a bit, poor old chap, has got it all wrong. The article in the 30th anniversary issue (Sept-Oct 1989) was virtually a transcript of his article in a 1950s Melody Maker.
However, as the law is an ass and proceedings may develop, I am opening, following the example of Private Eye, a Ronnieballs Fund to meet the cost of litigation. Please make cheques out to me personally and not to Jim Godbolt. Cash contributions especially welcome.
Ronnie Scott

A FLASH OF INSPIRATION
by LAURIE MORGAN

A character of extreme complexity: born comedian, musically talented, diverse and hazardous to work with; devout Marxist and humanitarian. That was Cecil 'Flash' Winston: an extraordinary person, whom it was my luck to know, be outraged by, and to love.

His origins have already been recorded in jazz archives and his very funny articles about his life and the formation of the Club Eleven, have appeared in *JARS*...

I will remember him best for his unique contribution to London's emerging post-war jazz scene. For those who didn't know him, his appearance was that of a classical court jester: small framed, hook-nosed, piercing eyes; a puckish gnome.

We first became acquainted at the Fullado Club in New Compton Street, off Charing Cross Road. Here we discovered a mutual enthusiasm for a new music. A revolutionary music — bebop.

For Cecil, this New World clarion was a call to arms. He revelled in its controversial impact on the traditional scene. The setting for Flash's exploits were Soho's jazz and nightclubs. Exotically named venues — The Copacabana, Mandrake, West End Rendezvous — housed a Damon Runyon-like world of post-war rationing — black market shenanigans and gangsterdom.

Flash was compère-in-chief at the jazz sessions played in these salubrious surroundings, and it was at these times he did his thing. In full flight, when a following wind whipped up by his dedicated fans — including such future luminaries as Ronnie Scott, Johnny Speight and Marty Feldman — he would freefall into comic mayhem. Anarchy would reign, with everything sacrificed on the altar of comedy.

Anything not nailed down became a prop — chairs, tables, customers. Cavorting round the stage, smoking and flicking ash over everything in sight, Cecil brought to mind a certain other Marx(ist), one Groucho. More a happening than an 'act', his performance encompassed monologues, jokes, wisecracks and impressions, delivered at breakneck speed, accompanied by manic gesticulations. It would climax with a 'rendering'— meaning to tear apart —a funny song at the keyboards.

Picture this: A Punch-like marionette, hunched over the piano, fingers stabbing at the keys, prising out the notes. Elbows thrusting up and down in frenzied rhythm, all the while chanting strangled fragments of the tune.

Rarely was the house left standing. On at least one occasion — inflamed by the audience's hysteria — he leapt from his stool and ran up and down the length of the keyboard, before escaping, stage left: to wild applause.

COMMUNIST MANIFESTO

Eschewing all classical training, Flash took the Communist Manifesto as his songbook. This he studied avidly, whilst practising at the piano — no easy task! The uncluttered, minimalist style which resulted served him well in the clubs he later worked.

British bebop's guiding light, trumpeter Denis Rose, particularly enjoyed Cecil's accompaniment. As he put it: 'He didn't get in the way.'

Flash and I enjoyed two aborted attempts to gatecrash show business. On one especially bizarre occasion, we finished up in front of a full house at Mayfair's Astor Club, still arguing about what our act might consist of. In time it became clear that Cecil was unable — or unwilling — to bridle his rebellious spirit for the sake of what he called 'the gross of commercialism.' So we called time on our fledgling partnership, but stayed good friends.

To his ultimate credit — and our loss — Flash never compromised his deep-seated political and social convictions for fame and fortune. His heyday was fleeting. But in all his brilliance, Cecil was a Flash of Lightning, which pierced the gloom of the 1950s.

Laurie Morgan was born in Stoke Newington, London 4th September, 1926. Long associated with the British jazz scene, he was a founder member, with Ronnie Scott, of the Club Eleven in 1948. He often sat in at the Fullado Club, worked at Churchill's with Jack Jackson, society band leader, in 1947, and visited New York with Ronnie and Tony Crombie in 1947 to investigate the burgeoning bebop music scene.

FLASH IN THE PAN
by TONY CROMBIE

The year, 1950-ish – the place, Harmony Inn, Archer Street, Piccadilly, W1. Sitting around a table were five under-employed be-boppers, Flash Winston, Laurie Morgan, Harry Robbins, Lennie Bush, and the bloke whose photo glares out of my bus pass. 'We've got to get some work somehow,' said Harry. There followed a disconsolate silence. 'I've got an idea,' said Flash. 'Why don't we put a musical act together and try for some work on the boards?' (i.e. the Variety Stage). 'We only need to get a twenty minute spot organised, and that shouldn't be too difficult.' There was a dubious pause broken by a half-hearted, mumbled agreement to give it a go.

During the next week, having rehearsed for a couple of hours, Flash announced that he had secured an audition with highly successful Ted Heath, presumably for one of the 'Sunday Night at the Palladium' shows. Ted listened quite attentively to our efforts, at the end of which he suggested that as we sounded like a black band, we should black-up, a move he reckoned would bring us instant success, but he didn't actually offer us an engagement. Very odd.

Left to right: Roy Plomley (announcer), producer Charles Chilton, Denis Rose, Tito Burns, Alan Dean, Ted Heath, Tony Crombie, Pete Chilver, Jack Honeybourne, Ronnie Scott, Jack Fallon, Jo Muddel, the occasion being a broadcast of the BBC's *Accordion Club* programme

We decided to dilute the jazz content of the act and Flash then got us a further audition with an 'impresario' who was forming a show for a provincial tour. This gentleman, very confident in his soup-stained shirt and a jacket with the lining hanging down, thought we were OK, basing his judgement on years of experience, so he said, garnered in New York's theatreland. We were chuffed.

FIVE FLASHES OF RHYTHM

So it came about that with Flash as compère/comedian, Harry on tenor sax, vocals and violin (except that he didn't have one), Lennie on bass, Laurie at the drums and me on piano, we were ready for launching as 'The Five Flashes of Rhythm', so named by our director, Cecil Jacob Winston.
Opening date came around, away we went to the north of England to some crummy flea pit of a theatre, to take our first steps on the road to fame and fortune. Upon arrival, scanning the publicity posters, it became apparent that this was to be a nudist show; they were very popular at that time. Taken somewhat aback, Flash nevertheless made light of this news, saying, 'Well, maybe it's for the best 'cos our stage clothes are not up to much.' Harry Robbins was quite pleased, but then he was always a bit of a show-off. However, it was soon established that we weren't required to perform in the raw. Phew!! A relief.
First house Monday: 6.15 pm. About 20 people in the audience, most of them comatose. The Five Flashes standing in the wings waiting to do their spot. The first nudist tableau materialises in front of a tatty backcloth depicting a Norwegian forest during a snow storm. The star is the wife of our impresario; a lady of about 60 years of age, aided and abetted by four or five other models of similar vintage. We viewed this scene with mixed feelings – mostly horror and resentment. Gravity had done its work, and these ladies were living proof of same. Their act finished to ominous mutterings and groans from the ticket buying citizenry. 'Right, you're on,' hissed the stage manager, waking us from our trance. A C7th chord from the piano – unison vocals – 'When You're Smiling, When You're Smiling, The Whole World Smiles With You', then a little softer, and Flash steps

up to the mike. 'Good evening everybody' (everybody?), and from the Five Flashes of Rhythm, a big hello!'
'Goodbye,' shouts a disgruntled patron. 'Sorry Sir, no money refunded,' called out Flash exultantly. 'Well, we've just finished variety in the South, now we're here to finish it in the North.' We went into a popular novelty number of the moment — The Thing. 'I discovered a boom boom boom right before my eyes,' wailed Flash.
Next case. Laurie steps forward, mortar board on head to deliver the opus Professor Bop, during which an old crone seated in the front row rises, screeching. 'We don't know what you're on about.' And so it went on until mercifully the curtain fell for the end of the first half.
At the customary interval inquest, our 'Imp', formerly of Broadway, tells us how it should be and would be done in New York. Flash, by now getting fed up with all the references to these alleged American triumphs, mutters, 'Why don't you go back to New York and drop dead?', whilst nimbly ducking behind the two six-footers, Laurie and me.
Critics in the next day's local papers were lukewarm, with comments ranging from 'Save your money', to 'a nightmare'. Flash loved that kind of thing. Being an unrepentant Dada-ist ('You have to provoke, not pander'), his idea of success was to be booed off stage in a hail of rotten fruit and veg. We almost made it.

MAXIMILLIAN, MAGICIAN EXTRAORDINAIRE
One evening around mid-week, our featured illusionist 'Maximillian, Magician Extraordinaire', was being given a rough ride. 'Do something', pleaded the stage manager, propelling Mr. Winston by the seat of his trousers on to the stage. Dancing down to the footlights, Flash bawled out, 'Come on folks, give him a chance,' Jeers and fruity noises sounded in response. Scratching his head, Flash had a sudden inspiration — 'If you don't shut up we'll bring back the nudes.' Consternation! 'How dare you threaten us regulars!' said a customer, obviously a man of some taste, inasmuch he was attired in an orange-coloured Harris tweed jacket, a spotted scarf, topped off with a black bowler hat. Nevertheless, the gambit worked. A sullen hush descended upon the premises. 'That's better,' said our hero, striding self-importantly toward the wings, knocking over *en route* the magician's prop table, thereby releasing a cloud of dust and several doves, which, due to the shock of their unexpected liberation, flew wildly around, depositing the results of their most recent feed on the two front rows of the stalls, and the pit orchestra — piano, saxophone and drums, no less.
Saturday came, eventually, and in the interval of the last show of the week, the 'Imp' handed us our train tickets back to London, but during the second half of this extravaganza, he, accompanied by the aforementioned wife, skipped off without paying us.
There's no business like no business.

JACK PENNINGTON

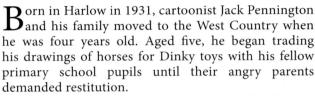

The work of cartoonists has featured in *JARS* from its inception in 1979, the artists including Wally 'Trog' Fawkes, Bill Stott, Codge (Barney Bates), John Byrne, Stephen Nemethy, Tim Holder, Humphrey Lyttelton, Paul Gonsalves, Richard Cole, Martin Litton, Monty Sunshine, Diz Disley and Hedley Picton.
Jack Pennington, who also had a long history of jazz promotion in the West Country, from 1952, booking all the great names of British bebop, including Ronnie Scott, died on 11th May 2006

Born in Harlow in 1931, cartoonist Jack Pennington and his family moved to the West Country when he was four years old. Aged five, he began trading his drawings of horses for Dinky toys with his fellow primary school pupils until their angry parents demanded restitution.

Pennington's interest in jazz was sparked when he was fifteen by Derek Watson, a semi-pro dance band tenor player who managed a very passable Lester Young-style tone during ballroom dancing classes at the local community centre. During National Service in 1950 he encountered a Stan Kenton-styled band at the NAAFI centre, the line-up including the equally young Ralph Dollimore, Kenny Napper and Bobby Pratt.

JAZZ AT THE ICEBOX

Pennington's interest in jazz intensified when he met the fifteen-year-old Tubby Hayes playing for Vic Lewis at a dance in Darlington. Tubbs suggested that he would willingly appear (for eight quid!) if Jack opened a jazz club after demob. The club opened in 1952 at the youth club in Corsham, Wiltshire, under the 'cool' name of Jazz at the Icebox, one of the first modern jazz clubs outside London. The resident pianist was the newly discovered John (Critch) Critchinson, who was paid one pound per session. The first 'guest' was Bill Le Sage, followed by Don Rendell, who became the Hon. Pres., then Jimmy Deuchar with Derek Humble.

PETE AND RONNIE

Following a grand punch-up at the youth club with the Pioneer Corps, the jazz club was swiftly relocated to licensed premises and Pete King became its London agent. Ronnie Scott became the first of a weekly procession of headliners over the next ten years, including Tubby Hayes (of course), Phil Seamen, Joe Harriott, Major Holley, Tommy Whittle, Buddy Featherstonehaugh, Vic Ash, Kathy Stobart, Dave Goldberg, Ronnie Ross, Jimmy Skidmore, Tony Kinsey, Terry Smith and Don Rendell's Roarin' Band.

This period of jazz promotions included five open-air sessions as part of the Chippenham Carnival (average 2,000 punters).

CARTOONING

In 1955 Jack married Pip, and their twin 'boys' are now aged forty-four. In 1957, his first cartoon was published in the *Bath Chronicle*. Despite receiving three guineas for his work, Jack earned his living in marketing, or commercial travelling as it was called at the time, as a commission-only agent for several furniture manufacturers, selling wholesale across the South of England. At the same time, his cartoons continued to sell and Jazz at the Icebox became nomadic in and around the Bath area.

In 1978 the *Bath Chronicle* offered Jack a freelance commission to supply a weekly jazz column with

Ronnie Scott's Quintet. From left: John Critchinson (piano), Ron Mathewson (double bass), Ronnie Scott (tenor saxophone), Dick Pearce (trumpet), Martin Drew (drums) here 'having a blow' on Ron's sax. Pennington's graphic impression of the band didn't meet with Ronnie Scott's approval, for some reason...

caricatures, as well as a Saturday cartoon — a gig that lasted until 1998 and the arrival of a juvenile editor!

JAZZ IN BATH

In both 1982 and 1984, Jack organised, under his own guarantees, a week-long Bath Jazz Festival and presented artists such as Harry Beckett, Danny Moss, Mike Carr, CDM, Ronnie and his various groups (including Critch), Stéphane Grappelli, Barbara Thompson, Al Cohn, Bobby Shew, Eddie Thompson, John Taylor, Norma Winstone, Alan Skidmore, Stan Tracey, NYJO, Shorty Rogers, Dick Morrissey, Gareth Williams, Andy Panayi, Alan Barnes, Humphrey Lyttelton, Art Themen, Don Weller, Jim Mullen, Peter King, Henry Lowther and Nikki Iles.

Pennington appeared with NYJO at festivals in Brecon, Bath and Soho, drawing projected caricatures for their top-selling Portraits suite.

About fifteen years ago he decided to make cartooning and illustrating a full-time occupation, targeting rather more lucrative outlets than newspapers. He was a member of the Cartoonists' Club of Great Britain and of the 'by invitation only' British Cartoonists Association. His caricatures are published world-wide.

J.G.

From **THIS** to..**THIS**

in only

70 Years!!

Right: Pennington by Pennington

DO YOU PLAY REQUESTS?*
RON RUBIN rubinates on a pianist's occupational hazard

The old memory bank (now somewhat overdrawn) has coughed up a few more recollections which could have come under the heading 'Getting the title wrong', viz… 'I Took A Trip On A Train' (meaning I Thought About You). 'It's A Quarter To Three' (meaning One For My Baby). 'I Like New York In June' (meaning How About You). 'The Way You Wear Your Hat' (meaning They Can't Take That Away From Me).

Drummer Kenny Harris recalled that when he was working on the Queen Mary, the band was nonplussed by a request for 'You Are The One'. It turned out to be Night And Day. Clarinettist Bernie Stanton remembers a Greek waiter at the Les Ambassadeurs saying there was a request from a party for 'some songs by George Gershpin and Cold Water'.

Speaking of Cole Porter — which he was, presumably -- someone once asked trumpeter Alan Elsdon for 'Cole Porter Stomp' (King Porter Stomp!) and on another occasion had someone request 'Teresa Green'. This turned out to be 'Trees Are Green', from It's A Wonderful World – geddit?!

I'M JUST WILD ABOUT HARVEY

A couple of others came in telephonically. At a Sunday jazz brunch in a West End hotel, the waiter said to the bandleader: 'Would you please keep the volume down — there's some people here trying to sleep,' and a vocalist was asked to sing I'm Just Wild About Harry, 'but could you please change 'Harry' to 'Harvey' — that's my boyfriend's name.'

Here's a rum one which happened to me in the piano bar of a Zurich hotel. An old lady said: 'I have this request, young man (those were the days) – Do your fingers ever get tired?'

What she meant, I suppose, was: I have a *question* (damned silly question, too…)

Finally, something which turned out to be a Non-Request: early one evening at the Bruselas Bar in Palma de Mallorca

where I worked for three years from 1969 to 1972, I noticed a middle-aged chap sitting on his own at the far end of the room. He seemed to be listening to the music with rapt attention. Ah, a jazz fan, I thought, and pulled out a few party pieces. After staring in my direction for some time, he got up and ambled towards me. Upon reaching the piano he leaned across and barked down my earhole in broad Yorkshire: 'What I like mysel' is a gud bruss bund!' and continued grumpily to the Gents.

* Only if they're asked for…

I SAID — I DON'T KNOW YOUR JODDAM "AS TRILLS THE GENTLE LARK AT DAWN!"

Acknowledgements to Chris Barber for the above taken from his Fan Club Magazine

DAVID STEEL
a jazz loving politician who, piquantly, recorded with 'loft' New York musicians

David Steel by Trog

The Rt. Honourable Sir David Steel, KBE, MP, formerly leader of the Liberal Party and co-founder of the Social Democratic Party, talks to Jim Godbolt about his admittedly peripheral interest in jazz, but the interview eventually yielded detail on an intriguing session in which Sir David participated.

On Valentine's Day in February 1995 I interviewed Mr. Kenneth Clarke, MP and Chancellor of the Exchequer, in the Treasury building, Whitehall. On an equally stormy day in March, I crossed to the other side of Whitehall and, politically speaking, to the other side of the House, to call at No. 1 Parliament Street, to interview the Rt. Honourable Sir David Steel. I was affably greeted by Sir David and fired the standard questions at him.   J.G

JG: Sir David, you were born in 1938. As a child and early teenager would you have been aware of your parents listening to dance bands on the radio – Ted Heath, Geraldo, Joe Loss, the Squadronaires and the like?

DS: No, I don't think they were very much into that kind of music. My father was a minister in the church and I was more influenced by church music than anything else. It wasn't until I came back from Kenya, where my father was working, when I was about fifteen, that I became interested in contemporary music. Not so much pop music — although I suppose there was a bit of that listening to Radio Luxembourg late at night. My interest in jazz came through watching the *Glenn Miller Story*. I went to see that about three times and became aware of Louis Armstrong who had quite a feature in the film. That was the foundation of my interest in jazz music.

THE SQUADRONAIRES
And there was a curious family link with the dance band business.

A cousin, once removed, of my mother, is Jimmy Miller, who was leader of the RAF Dance band, the Squadronaires, and Jimmy claims that he used to bounce me on his knee. I have several 78 records of the Squads, one I remember particularly was *Dolores*.

We talked a little bit about the Squadronaires, about trombonist George Chisholm's 80th birthday only the previous Wednesday, and that there were only four survivors of the original band, George, Tommy McQuater, Jimmy Miller and Harry Lewis. I mentioned that Jimmy Miller had told me what a hard time he had as titular leader of this bunch of wild young men, many of them hard-drinking Scotsmen.

DS: I didn't attend dance halls to listen to bands until I went to George Watson's College, and later, the University, at Edinburgh. I remember such local bands as Jim Baikie, and the Jazz Advocates. I remember the visiting bands — Humphrey Lyttelton, Acker Bilk and Kenny Ball. When I left University and worked in a quite humble job at the Scottish Liberal Party headquarters, I organised a short tour with Kenny Ball's Jazzmen to raise funds for the party and it was something of a feat for us to lose £800 with a band that was constantly in the charts. The reason was that we had an argument with the Edinburgh licensing authorities and we were not allowed to advertise the dance because we had a bar, and when we did advertise it, the licence was withdrawn. So nobody turned up at what was the main event of the tour. £800 was no small figure then and I wasn't very popular with the Party.

JG: What musicians or bands did you follow?

DS: In fact, I didn't attend a lot of jazz events. Although I am written up as a jazz fan, I have to say that my knowledge, and participation in the music is rather limited. When I embarked upon a political career, things like jazz came very low on the list of priorities, but I am an enthusiast, if not an expert. When I was in New York, as a young MP, I made it my business to seek out the Count Basie Orchestra playing in a restaurant, and more recently when I was on holiday in Florida, I sought out places where jazz was being played.

JG: Are you a collector of jazz records?

DS: Not in the strict sense. I'm a collector of classical records, but not that much jazz. I have a complete Glenn Miller set and a miscellaneous collection of people like Ella Fitzgerald, Louis Armstrong, Tommy Dorsey, Artie Shaw and Benny Goodman. And Fats Waller, of course. Very, very traditional. I'm not an adventurous jazz listener, and not really into modern jazz.

I once substituted for Humphrey Lyttelton on the *Best of Jazz* programme on the BBC's Radio 2 and played all my favourites. *Hearing Lyttelton's name, I told him of the trumpeter's connection, albeit tenuous, with the Scottish Borders. In April, 1947, Lyttelton joined George Webb's Dixielanders, of which I was laughingly called the manager, and Humph's first gig with the band was at the Town Hall, Hawick. It took fourteen hours in a raging snow storm to get there. When we got paid, the promoter, somewhat grumpily said, 'We thought you were going to be darkies' – the term 'Dixielanders' had unintentionally misled him into booking the band. A chuckle from Sir David —he is a very chuckly man.*

JG: Did you ever read jazz literature?

DS: No, not at all. I'm certainly not an expert. There are plenty of MPs who are. I just enjoy it.

JG: That's the most important thing of all. Although jazz has become respectable and featured in the so-called quality nationals and occasionally played on Radio 3, it still has low-life associations which may not seem a proper interest for a prominent figure in politics.

DS: I don't think it has now, although, I quite agree, it once did, and I remember that when I first went to Ronnie's some twenty odd years ago. I suppose it was regarded as a fairly risqué place.

RADIO BORDERS

JG: I mention the low-life associations because they certainly still exist. The drink and drugs and, unfortunately the bad reputation is not entirely unfounded. I still have people coming up to me and saying 'I hear you're a jazz *fiend*' or a 'jazz freak' I wondered whether a public figure like yourself experiences the same sort of reaction?

DS: No, I have no difficulties at all. For example, on my local commercial radio station, Radio Borders, I do a New Year show and I play nothing but jazz. On my show this year I played Ben Webster, Stan Getz, Miles Davis, Sonny Rollins, Count Basie and Duke Ellington amongst the chat, and no complaints. And this is the only jazz ever played on the station and it is in my constituency.

JG: Do you ever discuss jazz with other Members of Parliament?

DS: Yes, we have a jazz appreciation group, but I regret to say that I rarely attend because of other pressures.

JG: I'd like to ask you about Ronnie Scott's Club. I recall reading some unfavourable remarks you made about Ronnie Scott's jokes.

DS: Oh, I love Ronnie Scott's jokes. It's just that they are always the same and I may have made some disparaging references to that, but I like hearing them, and familiarity doesn't breed contempt. I think they're very funny.

JG: Of course, I'm biased, but I think the unashamed repetition is part of their enduring appeal, but Ronnie will assure you that his jokes have subtly changed over the years.

GEORGE MELLY

DS: I haven't noticed that. Indeed, knowing what's coming next is part of the charm. It's very good line of patter. I first started to go to Ronnie's to hear George Melly and John Chilton's Feetwarmers and I went almost religiously every Christmas thereafter. I'm a great admirer of Melly's act. There was a rather sad episode connected with Ronnie's. A group of us used to go, including my colleague, David Penhaligon, the MP for Truro, and the great advantage was that David was a teetotaller, so that if four or five of us went, he would drive us back to where we all lived in the Dolphin Square area. Sadly, he was killed in a car crash, and that sort of took the shine off visits thereafter and I haven't attended the Club as regularly as I once did.

JG: Are there any comments you would like to make, favourable or otherwise, about the Club?

DS: Ronnie and Pete very kindly made me an honorary member, so you would obviously expect me to be biased. It's very nice to be able to phone up and book a table.

JG: One of the things about the Club I may mention, something that other notable people, including Kenneth Clarke, appreciate, is that the spotlight is not turned on famous names.

DS: Exactly! That is actually quite important. You don't get the paparazzi. Compared with some other places, like the Talk of The Town, for instance. I found that very off-putting.

JG: There was a time when a new doorman rushed up to Ronnie to tell him that a member of Royalty was at the door and Ronnie, managing to look up from the television in his office, mildly enquired, 'So?'

DS: I noticed in the current issue of *JARS* that Kenneth Clarke in his interview said that he kept bumping into me at Ronnie's. That's a politician's gross exaggeration. I think I've seen him there twice. Typical politician's exaggeration.

(Laughter from JG here. An enjoyable touch of political acerbity.)

DS: The great thing for politicians is they can go to Ronnie's to unwind after a ten o'clock division. The timing is about right. I wouldn't say that the menu is brilliant. I mean, you wouldn't actually take someone there to eat.

JG: Well, Sir David, as Ronnie puts it–fifty thousand flies can't be wrong.

DS: Exactly, but if you've had a heavy day and you want a bit of relaxation, a couple of hours at Ronnie's is a great restorative, and the fact that one is left alone.

JG: I would like to ask you about George Melly. When I came into the business many years ago I was agent for Mick Mulligan's Band, with George as the featured singer. One of the flamboyant and entertaining figures of our time.

DS: Oh, yes. I've got several albums by George. On cassette mostly, for use in the car on my lengthy journeys between the House and my home in the Borders. I also have cassettes by Georgie Fame, whom I also much admire, especially as he started out as a pop singer.

JG: Are there any other artists you would care to talk about?

DS: Not really. As you can see I'm not an expert, but an enthusiast.
I'm not in the Ken Clarke league when it comes to jazz knowledge.

Here the conversation ended, Sir David politely escorted me to the lift, we shook hands, and I walked out into the snow.

However, re-checking on parts of our dialogue led me to a some truly surprising information, which certainly does not appear in any of the discographical works. On 29th June, 1982, a group of black musicians assembled at the Sigma Sound Studios, 1697 Broadway, New York, for a session conducted by producer/ vocalist Jesse Rae. They were Bernie Worrell (organ), Hiram Bullock (guitar), T.M. Stevens (bass) and Steve Jordan (drums), much sought after session musicians on the New York jazz/ funk/ rock/ crossover/ avant-garde scene, whose collective associates on a large number of albums include Carla Bley, The Brecker Brothers, Terri Lyne Carrington, Bill Evans, Gil Evans, Jaco Pastorius, David Sanborn, John Scofield, Lew Soloff and Steve Swallow. The session was a sound track for a video that didn't materialise.

There were two other performers on this session, both Scotsmen; producer Jesse Rae (vocals) who was attired in a medieval battle helmet, full plaid, kilt and sporran, and Mr (then) David Steel, Member of Parliament for Roxburgh, Selkirk and Peebles and leader of the Social and Democratic Party, singing, foot-tapping, and rapping. He, straight from an official engagement, was in evening dress, contrasting sharply with Mr Rae's apparel. The rest were dressed rather more casually.

As would be expected from the four musicians present, the production is a zippy, zappy, and rappy production and not one you would normally expect a member of the British Parliament and leader of a political party to be involved with, but there are more things in heaven and earth...

An edited version was issued on an EP on the Scotland Video label in 1982 entitled
DAVID STEEL - I FEEL LIBERAL – ALRIGHT! and on the back of the cover are instructions, with diagrams, on how to 'Dance The Steel-Step'.

Remember, *JARS* is the first magazine in which you have read of such a unique combination of parts, and I look forward to full, grateful, acknowledgement in future discographical tomes. I am obliged, not only to Sir David, but to his secretary, Jill Clements, and to Jesse Rae, for their ready co-operation.

HERBERT COOT LETTERS

(The correspondence between Herbert Coot and Ronnie Scott, with apologies to The Henry Root Letters by William Donaldson)

4th September, 1985
Dear Mr. Scott,
I was one of the lucky ones to get a ticket for the Club Eleven reunion. I had read so much about you and your activities in the late forties — I was only a schoolboy at the time — I just had to see you all re-assembled — so to speak.
Mrs. Coot fancied seeing herself on the telly in the audience and brought herself a new dress for the occasion. My young son Wally came along, and as we observed you all climbing up on the band-stand, I pointed out to him what an example you were; proof that growing old does not necessarily mean that one should look decrepit.
'Look', I said to Wally, 'not a help-stick or a pair of specs among them and they are all as old as God's Dog', and he was very impressed. I only hope I can show the same agility when I get to that sort of age.
I thought the music throughout was first class. Wally just could not believe that guys so old could play with such verve and enthusiasm. I am looking forward to seeing it on the telly. So is Mrs. Coot. She is quite convinced that the cameras roaming the audience lingered on her more than the rest of the ladies.
I enclose my usual pound
Yours sincerely,
Herbert Coot

7th September, 1985
Dear Mr. Coot,
Many thanks for your kind sentiments. I am deeply touched, but, between you and me, there was the creaking of old bones and a touch of the wheezes as we mounted the bandstand from some who haven't looked after themselves as well as I have. After the show I felt it my duty to warn a few of them about the dangers of overindulgence in tobacco and alcohol and they, Tony Crombie and Lennie Bush particularly, were very grateful for the advice.
Nevertheless, your comments are indeed welcome. It has long been a maxim of mine, and I am sure I speak for the other ten chaps present that, whatever one's antiquity, one should give one's all and that appreciation from the public, especially from someone as perceptive as yourself, is more important than money, and in any case, the gelt we get from the BBC would keep only the smallest wolf from the door.
I am indeed delighted to have been shown as a good example to one of the Wallys of this world. Talking about the money, thank you, of course, for your usual pound, but in the circumstances, I would have thought you could have made it a tenner, one for each of the geriatrics — sorry, I mean players. There's no need to worry about anything for Flash Winston — he doesn't need the money.
I'm looking forward to catching a glimpse of Mrs. Coot

when the film is shown and I'm hoping the camera caught my best side, the one that frequently has people confusing me with Ronald Colman.
Yours sincerely,
Ronnie Scott

AND IN RESPONSE... letter from Flash Winston

7th November, 1985
Dear Ronnie Scott,
It has come to my notice that you have grievously and gravely misrepresented me in a letter to Herbert Coot. As this correspondence of yours with Mr. Coot has not remained subject to private perusal alone but has been published for all to see in your Club Magazine, I feel duty bound, and in the light of the irreparable damage your misinterpretation may do to my persona, not only to protest most vehemently but to seek advice as to institution of further proceedings in the matter.
The canard in question, your categorical affirmation in print that Flash Winston does not need the money, with, I would add, its insidious inferences, is not only a gross dereliction in objective assessment, but could undermine both my standing with the Department of Health and Social Security and my credibility with the recipients of numerous begging letters I have recently despatched.
Unless an immediate recantation of this most reprehensible slander is published in your Magazine, I feel I have no alternative but to seek satisfaction from higher authority.
For the moment I shall remain yours in litigation.
Cecil (Flash) Winston.
PS. Of course, and in deference to our long acquaintance, if I receive some concrete intimation by return of post that your published slander is now negated, some surreptitious manifestation of your conviction that I do indeed 'need the money', I would be happily prepared to let the matter rest. The ball is in your court.

Typical Ronnie Scott's members having a musical night at home

CLUB ELEVEN REUNION
Britain's bebop pioneers reassembled at Ronnie's

I have often dreamt up ideas for a television show of a jazz character, and one evening, probably after a little too much vino, scribbled a note to contact Phil Speight, producer in the Arena BBC TV series suggesting the Club Eleven Reunion programme.

It was some days later that I had to disentangle my own hieroglyphs and, I have to say without nurturing much hope, I phoned Phil Speight to suggest to consider such a feature and, then capable of surprise, could scarcely believe he agreed. Nearly all the survivors of the original team were alive and willing. Not Ronnie. He, the forward-looking modernist, regarded this as an exercise in nostalgia. His Club Eleven colleagues pressed him to participate, he reluctantly agreed and I was the person to blame!

On the afternoon of the filming he was at his most difficult, tardily leaving his office for the rehearsal and pretending not to know the tunes they had played nearly twenty years previously. In the event, the show was a great success and its screening was highly acclaimed. All the musicians, including Ronnie, played with youthful verve and enthusiasm. There were many old faces, musicians and fans, present and the bar did a roaring trade. A warm and memorable ambience.

At the end of the filming, I was seated at the back of the Club feeling, if I may claim, pleasure that an idea of mine had come to fruition. I saw Ronnie walk from the bandstand, obviously making his way to the foyer, when he suddenly veered towards me. I even thought I might be in for a little praise. He grimaced at me and said, 'Are you satisfied now?'

However, a few months later I was standing with Ronnie at the Club entrance when along came Paul McCartney on the way to his office in Soho Square. He told Ronnie how much he had enjoyed the Club Eleven reunion film. Ronnie replied, 'Paul, meet Jim Godbolt — it was his idea', and I shook hands with a Beatle. OK, but I wished I had asked for his autograph. I am told this is worth a bob or two..

A HISTORIC REUNION

When the Young Turks of British bebop gathered to form the Club Eleven at Mac's Rehearsal Rooms, Great Windmill Street, W1, in 1948, there would not have been the least expectation that thirty seven years later — about half the biblical allotment of a life span — they would be reunited to play a session filmed by the television cameras. One of the Turks, Ronnie Scott, could not have foreseen that he would be celebrating his twenty-fifth anniversary as a jazz night club proprietor. But such a filming did take place, in Ronnie's Club, on

The Club Eleven bands at Ronnie Scott's Club, September 1st 1985. Rear: Joe Muddel, John Dankworth, Ronnie Scott, Laurie Morgan, Bernie Fenton, Norman Stenfalt, Henry 'Hank' Shaw, Johny Rogers. Front: Tony Crombie, Leon Calvert, Flash Winston, Lennie Bush Photo: David Redfern

Sunday September 1st and, truly, it was a magnificent occasion. It was good vibes right from the start when a queue formed long before the Club opened and once in the foyer, old friends, some who had not seen each other for twenty or thirty years or more, warmly greeted each other. The musicians on the stand were all surviving members of the original two bands, and of the founder members only Tommy Pollard and Denis Rose (and manager Harry Morris) had passed on.

The two bands were Ronnie Scott (tenor saxophone), Johnny Rogers (alto saxophone), Hank Shaw (trumpet), Tony Crombie (drums), Lennie Bush (bass), and replacing Tommy Pollard, Norman Stenfalt (piano) and the John Dankworth Quintet comprising John (alto saxophone), Leon Calvert (trumpet) Laurie Morgan (drums), Joe Muddel (bass) and Bernie Fenton (piano). The bands joined for the final session, playing 'Wee Dot' introduced by the club's original announcer, Cecil 'Flash' Winston.

The camera bulbs gave the club more light than it normally enjoys, catching the grey hairs and balding pates of some of the musicians, but they all played with youthful fire and spirit and with an expertise that comes of long experience. The Young Turks of yore are now seasoned professionals and whilst it was a nostalgic occasion, and nothing wrong with that, the music had the audience enthralled. They were held throughout, and, rightly, demanded an encore.

Apart from the footage taken on September 1st the complete programme includes interviews with all the musicians and fans, photographs from various collections, and some rare home movies of the principals taken during the time, December 1948 to April 1950, the Club Eleven was running. Producer Phil Speight is to be congratulated for accepting the idea that such a commemoration should be televised, and pressing for the necessary money to assemble such a project.   J.G.

STAN KENTON and RONNIE SCOTT

The appearance of Duke Ellington at the London Palladium in June 1933 was an outstanding event. It had jazz fans, musicians and critics reeling at such virtuosity. Another historic event was the appearance of Stan Kenton and his Orchestra at the Royal Albert Hall in the afternoon of March 10th 1956, the beginning of his English tour. Apart from Teddy Hill and his Band in the 'Cotton Club Show' at the London Palladium in July, 1937, Kenton's was the first band to perform in England since Cab Calloway and his Band played the Palladium in 1934.

After that appearance, the Ministry of Labour, bowing to intense pressure from the British Musicians Union, refused entry to foreign musicians, the ban on Americans of particular chagrin to the jazz enthusiast.

Kenton by Pennington

After continual pressure from the jazz press a reciprocal arrangement was struck between the Musicians Union and the American Federation of Musicians. Ted Heath's Band toured America and Kenton's visit opened the door to American jazzmen in Britain for the first time in twenty-two years.

That was forty years ago. Naturally, the high-powered Kenton Orchestra was a sensation. Ironically, the *Melody Maker* who had championed the entry of American musicians was not able to cover the event owing to a nationwide printers' strike.

Kenton appeared at Ronnie Scott's Club in 1972 and 1975, and during the latter visit their opening coincided with a power cut. They performed with only two spotlights powered by car batteries, playing to a candle-lit room. Manager Pete King recalls that this was the best natural acoustic balance he's ever heard.

The controversial Kenton, who died in 1979, left a legacy of great recordings and has a devoted cult following.

June Christy, Ronnie Scott, Zoot Sims, Frank Rosolino, Ken Wray, Conte Candoli, Jimmy Deuchar and Stan Kenton at the USAF base, Sculthorpe, Norfolk, in 1953 when Ronnie Scott's nine-piece played opposite Kenton on what was then virtually, American soil, and therefore not subject to the Musicians Union embargo. Alas, there are no survivors of this historic photo

RENDEZVOUS IN BRITAIN '96

In 1992 and 1994 Jazz fans from all over the U.K. came to pay tribute to 'America's Modern Man of Music' at the Daventry Hotel. The commemoration, titled

'Rendezvous in Britain '96', included, among others, Vic Lewis, Bill Russo, Lee Konitz, Milt Bernhart, Roy Reynolds, Buddy Childers and Jiggs Whigham.

PERSONAL VIEW

MOULDY FYGGES

A young — well, youngish — lady of my acquaintance was puzzled by Iain Ballamy's reference to 'mouldy fygges' in *JARS 133*.

Well, Emma, the Fygges first emerged as a species in the late Forties when the jazz world was split assunder by the almost coincidental upsurge of revivalism and bebop. The Fygges passionately, and volubly (and, occasionally, with fisticuffs), were on the side of the revivalists, their heroes being King Oliver, Jelly Roll Morton, Louis Armstrong, Bunk Johnson and George Lewis, all, as it happens, were from New Orleans. There were hundreds of young whites, particularly active in Britain, who followed in the steps of the masters. They deified trumpeter Ken Colyer, referring to him as 'the Guv'nor'.

When, in 1956, the ban on American musicians appearing here was lifted, the visitors, most of a certain vintage, were harried by the Fygges, who assailed them with a barrage of questions about their past and their contemporaries.

CORDUROY AND DUFFLE COATS

The Fygges loathed the saxophone — unless it was the soprano played by New Orleanian Sidney Bechet. They hated and derided bebop, scorning its unfamiliar structures, chord inversions and different tonality. They were distinguished as much by their mode of dress as their musical tastes. They wore tweed jackets and duffle coats, corduroy trousers, Fair Isle sweaters, sandals or chukka boots. Many smoked pipes.

Their modernist opposites wouldn't be seen dead in corduroys! Their tailors were Cecil Gee, of Charing Cross Road and Shaftesbury Avenue. Stove-pipe trousers, full-draped jackets and pencil-thin ties was 'the gear'. They regularly visited the hairdresser to give them the 'Duck's-Arse' style, whereas the Fygges were long-haired and bearded. The Fygges sank endless pints of bitter (or cider — Merrydown, a favourite), the modernists electing for the quaintly named 'naughty-type African Woodbine'. These opposites frequented different clubs and cafes, even though these habitats were only a few yards distant.

The Fygge is, of course, New Orleans jazz-orientated,

A Mouldy Fygge by Pennington

but most embraced in their record collections big bands, black and white, but usually recordings only up the Forties, including Fletcher Henderson. When, in 1956, the ban on American musicians playing here was lifted, one of the welcome visitors was master tenor saxophonist Coleman Hawkins, whose first records he made with Henderson in 1923, recordings he dearly wished to forget, and who could blame

Illustration: Selby

him? His solos are embarrassingly rooty-tooty and nothing like the majestic fluency he later exhibited.

But your Fygge was eager for recollections of Henderson's past and harried The Hawk. So much so, that he, seeking the nearest pub in concert intervals (he was fond of a brandy or three), would go to inordinate lengths to avoid the Fygges, referring to them as MFs, the acronym not for 'Mouldy Fygge', but for a description we can't possibly use in a family mag like *JARS*.

A depiction, above, of the Fygge by Smilby (writer/blues expert Francis Wilford-Smith) first appeared in issue No 7 of *Jazz Illustrated* (edited by the present editor of *JARS*), July 1950.

JI was one of the first mags to give coverage to bebop records, the reviewer being trombonist Eddie Harvey, a 'renegade traditionalist' (Humphrey Lyttelton's coinage), late of George Webb's Dixielanders, but then with the Dankworth Seven.

MIFF MOLE'S LITTLE MOLERS, ETC ETC

Your Fygge could, at the drop of a steel gramophone needle, reel off the personnel of Jelly Roll Morton's Red Hot Peppers, Louis Armstrong's Hot Five and Seven, the Charleston Chasers, Miff Mole's Little Molers, Broadway Bell-Hops, Chocolate Dandies, California Ramblers, McKinney's Cotton Pickers and the Bubbling Over Five. All this meticulously gleaned information can nowadays be culled from Brian Rust's massive *Jazz Records 1898 to 1942*, the Fygges' bible — and note the closing date of this epic volume!

There, Emma, is a thumbnail sketch of the Mouldy Fygge (and his 'cool' counterpart). But the days of this bewildered and increasingly entrenched anachronism, in a plethora of Cross-over, Fusion, Third Stream and World Music, are numbered.

This old fart, this 'anoraked nit-picker', will soon be as extinct as the pterodactyl, a prehistoric predatory raptor which many a Fygge resembled.

In his mid-seventies, he is due for dispatch to New Orleans in the sky, a fate he will consider his due as his jazz tastes have been so righteous in his mortal span.

A footnote, Emma. The feuding between the traditionalist and the modernist has, thankfully, long gone, but the dichotomy still exists. The funeral of pianist Bill Le Sage

Fifties' bebop jivers by Pennington

in November last was attended by some two-hundred-and-fifty mourners, principally bebop musicians. There were only two from the other side of the divide: saxophonist/clarinettist John Barnes — ex-Zenith Six, Mike Daniels Delta Jazzmen, Alex Welsh and Humphrey Lyttelton, and drummer Ron Bowden — ex-Crane River Jazz Band, Ken Colyer, Chris Barber and Kenny Ball.

When tradders pop it, you don't see boppers at the funeral. A fact of life in our still much-divided jazz world, Emma.

FASHION NOTE

Jack Pennington, himself a clothes-conscious young man-about-town in the Fifties, elaborates on the various fashion touches of his representation of 'bopping modernists'...

'Male dress shown is the style popular in the early Fifties, i.e. full drape-suited jacket (not to be confused with the Teddy-boy style which came later and was for 'Rockers'), two button, often in gaberdine, string tie (just replacing the wide and decorated), crêpe-soled shoes, soon to be displaced by the little black leather number, laced or buckled. Within a year, the charcoal grey 4- or 5-buttoned, 3-piece (Edwardian) had taken over. Pockets had flaps, including top and ticket, trousers were narrower with deeper turn-ups. The little black shoes survived. Hair, by Maison Louie of London, was a classic ten-bob 'D.A.' style and cut (including hair-netted/setting lotion application).'

Chrissie Murray, an obsessive student of fashion history,

adds the following observations about the modernist's lady's dress...

'War-time austerity of the Forties was replaced by unrelenting excess in the Fifties as fabrics came off ration. Fuller (often completely circular), mid-calf skirts, often yards of felt (and still celebrating Dior's post-war New Look) were worn on tiny, wide-belted, cinched-in waists, over layers of stiffened-net petticoats which swirled and rustled pleasingly as you jived. The classic 'Roman sandals' were popular summer wear and preferable to stilettos because they were easier to dance in. The not-always-flattering short, tortured hair style was the result of our heroine's frequent visits to Raymonde, the 'Mr Teasy-Weasy' school of ladies' Italian razor-cut — and every High Street had one.' My, my! *JARS* is now into fashion history… whatever next?

Writing about the war between the traditionalists and the boppers, I was reminded of Tom Ballenger's amusing cartoon that appeared in an early Fifties' *US Record Changer* during the height of this ideological conflict.   J.G

'Thus we conclude a round-table discussion on the subject, "New Orleans Jazz Compared to Bebop"…'

Cartoon by Tom Ballenger

RONNIE'S JOKES

Anyway in just a few moments… whatsisname will be back on the stand.   We   do,   as a matter of fact, have six very good waiters and waitresses in the Club. Between them they have a job opening a bag of crisps, but they're great. There's only one of our waiters moving. That's Enrico. Moving slowly, but moving.

Enrico's Italian — doesn't speak any English. He came to this country three years ago and couldn't speak a word of English. Took a job working for nothing in a Jewish restaurant. Thought he was learning English. Now he speaks great Yiddish and Italian. But no English.

You know, you can always tell Italians because of their pock-marked faces. It's from learning to eat with a knife and fork. And you can always tell a German. He walks as if he has a boil under the crotch.

RUBINERICKS
Bassist, pianist, poet RON RUBIN waxes limerickally about people associated with Ronnie Scott's Club and *JARS*

Ron Rubin born in Liverpool, July 8th, 1933. Educated at Liverpool College, and then dropped out of Law School. Played in the Cavern, Mardi Gras and other clubs. Moved to London in 1961 and played with musicians as diverse in styles as Sandy Brown, Lennie Best, Bruce Turner, Michael Garrick, Alex Welsh, Barbara Thompson and John Chilton's Feetwarmers with George Melly. He is featured on numerous albums.

Ron has contributed his verse and prose to a dozen or so anthologies such as *How To Be Well-Versed in Poetry, The Penguin Book Of Limericks, How To Be European, How To Be Tremendously Tuned Into Opera, How To be Absurdly Informed About The Famous And Infamous,* His own book, *Out On a Limerick — A Medley Of Musical Limericks* with illustrations by the late Tim Holder, published by New Millennium.

COLIN 'BARNEY' BATES
That affable cove, Colin Bates,
As 'Barney' plays fine 88s;
As 'Codge' he lampoons
The world with cartoons,
And as Colin gets pissed with his mates

THE RT. HON. KENNETH CLARKE, MP
When the Chancellor of the Exchequer
Came down to check out Michael Brecker,
He said: 'Where's Ronnie Scott?'
Sighed Pete: 'He forgot
To come back from a visit to Mecca...'

BRIAN DAVIS
Brian Davis, a critic astute,
Writes for JARS (it sure ain't for the loot!)
For him, Club Eleven
Was seven steps from Heaven
(But Scott's is a fair substitute)

LANCE FAIRFAX
'Slawkenbergius' has lately made room
For 'Lance Fairfax' – some chaps might presume
That it's all very odd
When a journalist bod
Hides behind TWO noms de plume...

WALLY FAWKES
Wally Fawkes could boast quite a biog. –
Clarinettist, and (alias 'Trog'),
Cartoonist; creator
Of Flook, illustrator
And cricketer...(one is agog!)

JIM GODBOLT
Says Godbolt, a cynical gent:
'As agent, my life was misspent';
But now he's a writer,
The world seems much brighter,
Though he misses the old ten percent...

CINDY HACKER
Associate Ed, Cindy Hacker
Is truly a bit of a cracker;
Some sexists can't credit her
With being sub-editor...
Growls Jim: 'That's no reason to sack her!'

WALLY HOUSER, LL.B
Wally Houser, tall, dark and urbane,
Is the Ronnie Scott Club legal brain;
He plays alto too,
And can wail on 'Jordu'
Or even 'Bei Mir Bist Du Schoen'

PETE KING
The club's 'gantze macher', Pete King
Takes everything under his wing;
His Scowl is severe,
But beneath that veneer
I suspect he's a kindly old thing

ALF LUMBY
Alf Lumby's a buff of long-standing,
Whose knowledge of jazz is commanding;
Though not quite so old
As dear Harry Gold,
He remembers Geraldo disbanding

ALUN MORGAN
Alun Morgan writes sleeve notes galore –
Two thousand-five hundred or more!
He quit architecture
Because (I conjecture)
He found life in a tin hat a bore

HEDLEY PICTON
Hedley Picton's a talented guy:
Cartoonist, ex-admin at the 'Y'
Now life is much calmer-
He's a Pembrokeshire farmer
But still hones his artistic eye

DAVID REDFERN
David Redfern (who's terribly tall)
Takes photos which grace the club's wall;
The great Buddy Rich
(Himself a mere titch)
Said: 'Redfern's the greatest of all!'

RON RUBIN
Plays piano. Writes humorous verse.
Used to play bass. Not averse
To a tincture or three
(A nice J & B)
Thinks wallpaper music a curse

RONNIE SCOTT
Ronnie's jokes are now getting so old
They seem to be gathering mould;
But still they beguile,
Well, it's all in the style,
And the timing with which they were told

A CLASSIC LETTER TO THE ED.

Like all magazines, we get letters asking for information. Glad to help wherever we can, but some of our correspondents seem to think that we are a full-time information service (or, in case of a lady from the picture department of *Time Out*, a supplier of free photographs, 'we don't have a budget for this'.)

One letter in particular, from a student at a South Coast Polytechnic, had me goggling and gurgling in amazement. It read:

' I am engaged in a course of study leading to the award of a MSc. Part of the course is to undertake a project related to Information Systems. My project is concerned with the creation of a database on jazz for use in a practical environment and to identify and analyse various attributes of style.

In particular, I wish to attempt an investigation of the following questions:

(A) What is style?
(B) Which attributes of style receive critical acclaim?
(C) Which proponents of style receive critical acclaim?
(D) Which elements of style are copied?
(E) What is the origin of particular characteristics?
(F) What influences has jazz on other musical forms?
(and vice versa)

To successfully design this database it is of paramount importance that I can model potential users conceptual schemes of the data. I would like to interview you, at any time convenient to yourself. Append a list of possible question areas, but any interview would be totally unstructured as your concepts and opinions would be of importance.

Do you have some form of discography?
Is it cross-referenced? How?
Is it up to date?
Is everything you want in it?
What information would you not want in an ideal discography?
What about biographical info? How do you keep this?
What do you see as the constituent parts of different styles of jazz?
How does be-bop differ from hard bop?
How does the new wave differ from the avant-garde?

What is the connection between jazz and blues, classical music, popular music, world events, or anything else?
What is it about two different players in the same style that makes them different?
What makes a player great?
How would you define jazz?
Do you think that jazz has any relevance nowadays?
Who/ what is the future of jazz?
If you have any doubts, queries, etc., please don't hesitate to ring the above number.'

Hesitate?! HESITATE to ring this out-of-town number. Not me, squire! He who hesitates is lost and sod the expense!

And what piddling consequence is my time? I could make a start at, say, 9 am one Monday morning, with maybe a break for meals and snatch a few hours sleep for as many months as it took. Perhaps I could allow myself a weekend off to do a little work on my own behalf, not being a student on a grant, nor aspiring to a MSc. That old database has just gotta be right! Of paramount importance. And the users get their conceptual schemes bang on. I was grateful that the interview would be 'unstructured'. Not mad about being structured. Sort of makes me edgy. Perhaps we have readers who could help this hopeful. Your answers, on a postcard, please...   J.G.

Typical Ronnie Scott members shaking a shoe to a few guys having a little tiddle-up

157

MUSIC AND MAIDEN OVERS
Vic Lewis with Tony Barrow (Chatto & Windus, 1987)

In this embarrassingly self-regarding volume there are an inordinate number of photographs of the author with almost everyone in the showbiz. That is, anyone who is anyone. Shots of Vic with royalty, too. Just falling short of her Majesty, but he's probably working on that right now.

There is Vic on a New Zealand glacier with Cilla Black; with Elton John in the director's box (where else?)at Watford Football Club; with Frankie Vaughan clearing snow off a New York Stret (!); conducting the Royal Philharmonic (!!) and playing trombone with Stan Kenton's Orchestra (!!!)

Whatever he was up to, or hob-nobbing with, a cameraman was fortuitously present. Here seen enjoying a joke with Duke Ellington, there in the company of Lester Young. 'I happened to bump into Lester', writes Vic. But... that omnipresent lensman was there, too, aperture ready for the click. There's a shot of him with clarinettist Pee-Wee Russell and cornetist Bobby Hackett from the same year (1938). Fair enough — he did record with these two and other famous jazzmen.

OK, it's only human to show that you have rubbed shoulders with the famous, but it's the tone of the text that sticks in the gullet; that's when one is not fighting to regain one's breath after choking on a particularly ripe chunk of *chutzpah*.

Vic doesn't believe in hiding his light under a bushel — far from it – and reading between the lines, and knowing much about his history, I can see that he's been a persuasive sort of chap in his time, obtaining many backers for his ventures, one of whom, Bert Wilcox, I was working for in 1950, when he was financing those disastrous 'Music For Moderns' tours with Lewis's 'Concert' Orchestra, but doesn't rate a mention. Not that everyone played ball. When financial backer Bill Benny died, Mrs. Benny most inconveniently shut off the cash supply; his one-time agent, Harold Davison, comes in for a lot of stick. 'A funny little man in a green pork pie hat,' writes Vic, who was, and still is, peeved that Davison, who master-minded the Anglo-American band exchanges in the early fifties negotiated for Ted Heath, and not Lewis, to play in the US in exchange for Stan Kenton in the first of the swaps, in 1956.

EXCHANGE RECIPROCITY

Lewis claims that he instigated this arrangement between the American and British unions. Whatever, Heath meant something in the US, Lewis didn't, and he forgets that it was Davison's entrepreneurial muscle that found the Lewis Orchestra many a prestigious engagement it would not have got otherwise.

He doesn't go much on the Beatles manager, Brian Epstein, who, he alleges, 'became decreasingly reliable'. (*Eh?*) He was miffed when saxophonist/fixer Ronnie Chamberlain 'allowed himself to be lured away by Ted Heath after twelve years with me.' *Tch!* Naughty, weak-minded Ronnie...

Vic's egotism is something else. 'I *accepted* (my italics) a long role in the film *Goodbye Mr. Chips*. He took arranger Nelson Riddle and son to Lord's Cricket Ground and 'when I went for a tinkle someone came up to them and said, 'Excuse me, but was that the *famous* (yes, my italics again!) Vic Lewis you were just talking to?'

He tells us he turned down a commission in the RAF, and was privy to details of D-Day long before the event, and that after a tiff with an officer he 'resigned' the service. This in war-time, mark you, but now I come to think about it, Vic probably did resign and got away with it.

There are many inaccuracies. Yes, I am aware how easy it is for these to slip through, but it's obvious that in this ego — trip the correct spelling of sidemen's and associates' names is incidental. Keith Christie, Art Ellefson, Jimmy Deuchar and Johnny Claes are given as Christy, Elefson, Duchar and Clays in the text, captions and index. In supposing that trumpeter Johnny Claes is now driving a taxi in New Zealand he is confusing him with saxophonist Derek Neville, and, anyway, both are dead.

All this, however, is nothing compared with the cricket section. That's quite breathtaking; a snap of Vic leading his team down the pavilion steps at Lord's onto the sacred turf, of him and Sir Frank Worrell opening the innings on another occasion; of the same Vic square-driving Worcestershire and England off-spinner Norman Gifford for four boundary runs.

VIC THE GREAT PRETENDER

True, he raised sums for charity with his teams of showbiz personalities and professional cricketers, but sad to say, Vic the cricketer was Vic the great pretender. He had no ball sense whatsoever, yet he says of himself while in the RAF... 'As the number of games I played diminished I degenerated from being a pretty fast-medium bowler to a pretty medium-pace bowler.'

By the time (late fifties) he made two memorable appearances for the Ravers CC (with whom I played for twenty years and know something about their history) his bowling had degenerated into minus-slow, was highly inaccurate and anything but pretty.

He is wrong in alleging that the Ravers came out of the *Melody Maker*. Only two of its staffmen, Max Jones and Bob Dawbarn, were regulars, with Max's son, Nick, making the occasional appearance.

Perhaps a clue to his expectations in life and his colossal *chutzpah* is in his admission that before entering the RAF he had not as much as cleaned his own shoes or made his own bed. Service life (though not, in this case, seeing action) must have been tough for someone from such a sheltered background, but since he was demobbed (sorry, since he *resigned*) from the service he's resumed being cosseted by backers, managers, agents, fixers and arrangers, leaving him free to gratuitously 'conduct' his bands and... to blow his own trombone.

The best part of the book is the excellent discography by Tony Middleton. A pity that author and 'ghost' didn't consult it when preparing the text.   J.G.

HERBERT COOT LETTERS

(The correspondence between Herbert Coot and Ronnie Scott, with apologies to The Henry Root Letters by William Donaldson)

10th December, 1985

Dear Mr Scott,

I saw the Club Eleven Reunion programme on the lantern and in colour, showing the nightclub tan of the principals very well indeed. Although I was present on the occasion, also in colour, it was a pleasure to see what a good job the Beeb made of it. Mrs Coot wasn't pleased though. They cut the crowd scenes in which she appeared and this after she had bought a new dress especially for the event. In fact, she was furious, particularly having told her friends she would be on the telly. I had to tell her; 'Emma', I said, 'You must not count your scenes before they are shown'.

I noticed on the night and again in the film that the age group of the audience was about the same as yourselves. I have heard that BBC ticket allocation department sends out blocks of tickets for OAPs for these outside broadcasts, but I hadn't realised how generous they are to our senior citizens! My son Wally, who got an O level in maths, worked out the aggregate to be some fifteen thousand years, give or take a century or two. I noticed how the technicians tactfully kept the St. John's Ambulance men out of camera.

I thought the interviews with yourself and your associates were jolly and liked your editor's tie, even though it looked as if it were the first time he had worn it for fifty years. I haven't enclosed the usual pound. As you are now a star of the TV screen such a trifling amount would be insulting.

Yours sincerely,

Henry Coot

15th December, 1985

Dear Mr Coot,

My commiserations to Mrs Coot. I, too, was disappointed. The camera didn't catch my best side — the one, I believe I've mentioned before — that has people thinking that Ronald Colman is still around — and they cut my best jokes.

Something to do with the morality code, whatever that is. I've written to the Director-General. I've a good mind to sue, except the BBC haven't got any money. At least, that's what they keep telling me when I get the occasional offer.

Between you and me, some of the chaps in the show have been showing off something terrible since it was shown, thinking they are Richard Arlen or Tyrone Power, which is ridiculous. However, should you know of a producer who's looking for a square-jawed, gimlet-eyed and clean-limbed chap to play the lead in a swashbuckling period drama…well, I can be found at the above address almost any night.

Oh, about your usual pound — or rather lack of it. Because my face was seen by millions doesn't alter the spondulicks situation one little bit. In fact as we were

Typical Ronnie Scott's customers hoofing

filming for the best part of two days it cost me a fortune in fags, especially with Flash Winston about.

Yours sincerely,

Ronnie Scott

PS. The editor's tie denotes membership of the Ravers CC, the owner giving the occasion the supreme accolade by wearing it. Round his neck, that is; normally it keeps up his trousers.

WHISPERS, MURMURS & ASIDES

THE PEAS MANAGER

There must be a word — and perhaps a scholarly reader can oblige — for the unaccountable recollection of names, places and incidents from the deep unconscious. Whatever, something must have prompted me to recall walking into Ronnie's office one afternoon hoping that he would not be too absorbed watching the television to notice my entry. In this instance, he was seated at his desk, but brushed aside a query I had, saying, 'I can't attend to you right now, I have to get hold of the peas manager.'

'The *what*, Ronnie?'

'The peas manager. Are you going deaf in your dotage, Goldblatt? I've got a letter before me here from a lady who enjoyed her evening at the Club, but thought the peas were well below standard. I've got to sort this out straight away,' and picking up the phone, he barked an order to his secretary, 'Bonnie, get me the peas guy immediately!'

Ronnie, of course, was joking but he had such a marvellous sense of the absurd. Peas manager, indeed!   J.G.

INTERVIEW...
was it a dream?

Those who have been reading *JARS* from its inception will, no doubt, be weary of my apologies for repeatedly mentioning how difficult it is to interview Ronnie Scott, but they must be as bemused as I am that a club owner should be so uncommunicative with the editor of his own house magazine. I tell you, it's a heavy cross to bear. You may ask — why do I masochistically endure this burden? The answer lies in one word; money. God knows, the rewards for this aggro are meagre, but enough to keep a small wolf from the door.

I was looking at the calendar and realised that the following day I was due to thread my way through the Mediterranean workshys thronging Frith Street to suffer the charade of an interview with the Guv'nor. I was also mindful of the fact that Ronnie was very forthcoming with one Byron Rogers in *The Evening Standard* in July. This still rankles.

There was a knock on the door. I was playing the superb Verve 'Back to Back' by Duke Ellington and Johnny Hodges recently re-released by Import Music Service. I have a neighbour who hates jazz — believe that or not — and I expected a complaint about the volume. As if music of this grandeur should be muted!

Or maybe it was the postman, but I quickly dismissed this quirky notion. It was Wednesday, I'd had a delivery on Monday and might be lucky if I got another on Friday. The postal service in NW5 is nothing short of hilarious — if you think having to collect your own post funny — and I kid you not.

FANTASIES

I fantasised about more enjoyable possibilities. Perhaps a record company executive pleading for three whole pages of advertising and pressing the cash in my willing palm. Maybe it was Alec Bedser, a chairman of the board of selectors for the English Cricket XI, wanting my advice on the team to tour India this winter.

He'd likely say: 'Jim, Ian Botham was particularly grateful for the tips you gave him on his batting stance, his bowling action and concentration in the field. Your wise counselling certainly made a difference to his performance. You could say it helped us retain the Ashes.'

I would say: 'Think nothing of it, Alec. Anything I can do for any of the chaps, just let me know.'

Perhaps it was Miss World (this year's title holder, of course) lusting after my body or, at least, my mind. I'd say; 'You can have either, darling, but preferably the former.'

I could go on. In fact, I will. I enjoy day-dreams about the rich, the influential and the beautiful knocking at my door. Maybe it was Cecil B. De Mille, epic film producer, famous for his Biblical extravaganzas. Alright, I know he died in 1959, but since then he's been researching God at close quarters and now reincarnated he wanted me to play him (God) in his (DeMille's) biggest production ever. I consider myself admirably suited to the role. Apart from my name (Godbolt — geddit?) I also possess the necessary spiritual qualifications — notwithstanding that these could go to hell (in a manner of speaking) if Miss World would have elected for the former option.

I'd say: 'Ready when you are Mr. De Mille.'

But, as it transpired, truth proved to be infinitely stranger than fiction. Why, bless my old cotton socks (to bowdlerise club director Pete King's favourite utterance) who should the caller be but Ronnie Scott! You could have knocked me down with a flatted fifth! Ronnie lives quite a distance from me and, truth to tell, he's not one to put himself out, not even for himself, and here he was at my door – this five floors up and no lift!

PLEASANT CHAT

Mahomet had come to the mountain. Or should it be the mountain had come to Mahomet? No matter; it was indeed a delightful surprise. Ron said; 'I know you felt a little peeved at me giving Byron Rogers a lengthy interview in *The Evening Standard* so I thought I'd pop in to make amends.'

We had a most pleasant chat — talking, first, about the chaps he heard and played with at the end of the war and just after — saxophonist

Illustration: Hedley Picton

160

Illustration: Hedley Picton

Reggie Dare, Harry Hayes, Rex Owen, Derek Neville and Buddy Featherstonhaugh. He expressed his admiration for Vic Ash, one of the first to essay the bop idiom on clarinet in this country. He told me a charming and rather touching story about Vic. His parents were totally deaf from birth but saw that the very young Vic wanted to play clarinet and although poor, and unable to hear their son's playing, bought him his first instrument.

Ronnie talked of the band, led by society maestro and occasional jazz trumpeter, Jack Jackson, at the swank Churchill's night club in Bond Street in the early fifties.

Ronnie was just one of the wild young beboppers in the band that also included guitarist Pete Chilvers and drummer Laurie Morgan. Ronnie had been generously allocated a sixteen bar chorus but decided to take more, and having taken off was explosively urged on by Laurie Morgan 'dropping bombs' in the be-bop fashion of the time. The dancers on the floor stood confused and outraged. Jackson, whose playing career started in 1925, and hardly one likely to dig bop, was drinking at the table of a Hooray Henry patron — as was the custom with bandleaders in those far-off days — when he became uncomfortably aware that things were getting out of hand.

He shot up to the stand and croak-whispered, 'What the hell's going on here!?'

'Schhh' cautioned Chilvers. 'Ronnie's got the message!'

'Give him one from me', spluttered Jackson, 'tell him he's got the sack!'

LOUIS

We laughed at this lovely tale of the old clashing with the new and somehow the conversation veered to Louis Armstrong, Ronnie enthusing about some Hot Five and Seven records he'd heard on a jukebox in a Fulham cafe. What? Louis on a jukebox in a Fulham cafe?

It hardly seems credible that music of such sublimity should issue from that accursed invention which usually spew out the yob's yowl. I wouldn't care if that caff wasn't Ronay-rated...

This led to chat about the great obbligatoists in jazz — Louis being one of these. We weren't talking about any old player who can 'fill-in' between measures, but those guv'nors who play a separate but complementary line to another soloist or vocalist and produce one of the experiences unique to jazz. I mentioned Lester Young and Jack Teagarden and Ronnie came up with Zoot Sims and Stan Getz.

It was indeed a nice and relaxed chat about music. Were my conversations with Ronnie always like this? I sadly reflected to myself.

I offered my guest a drink, He declined with a faintly dismissive gesture that somehow conveyed pity for someone who needed to drink such a poison. He offered me a cigarette.

I declined with a faintly dismissive gesture that somehow conveyed pity for someone who needed to inhale such a poison.

We talked of his touring days — I mean real touring — at least five gigs a week up and down the country. In those days I was an agent, often booking Ronnie's band from his agent, the legendary Harold Davison, now a multimillionaire and living in California.

'Did you end your days as an agent a millionaire, Jim?' he waggishly enquired.

'No.' I wistfully replied.

We vied with each other in reciting the names of venues once the stomping ground of innumerable touring bands. Most of these, like the bands, are no more.
'Casino Ballroom, Warrington!'
'Gaiety Ballroom, Grimsby!'
'Gliderdrome, Boston!'
'Palais-de-Danse, Stockton!'
'Rex Ballroom, Cambridge!'
'Samson and Hercules, Norwich!'
It was a strange litany for two middle-aged gentlemen to be reciting.

'Would you fancy leading a big band and doing that round all over again, Ronnie?' I innocently enquired. His face went white and reached for a fag and inhaled like a man who'd just heard that a debtor had died.

We got to talking about a TV programme on prostitutes and had a little ribald chuckle at one lady who formed a company called Personal Services Ltd. Ho! Ho! Ho! More guffawish laughter when we recalled another show on which was a clip, from Indian TV, of a lady announcer gravely informing viewers that a fifty year old ban on harmoniums in that country was now at an end.

'Let's go and have something to eat,' he said.

Now, I wasn't falling for that one again. The last time he made that invitation I had splendid visions of haute cuisine and fine wines in an exotic Soho restaurant, but found myself in McDonald's Burger Bar in Shaftesbury Avenue eating chicken and chips and finishing with a milk shake that nearly robbed me of my remaining tooth. In any case the nearest McDonald's in Kentish Town has a somewhat rough clientele not really suitable company for an OBE and his house magazine editor. I'm not a snob or anything, mark you, but one has to draw the line somewhere.

I said: 'As I'm host I'll rustle up a little something. Vegetarian gear do you? I can offer nut cutlets, jacket potatoes and spinach puree. Or would you prefer Aduki burgers with parsnip fritters followed by a nice cup of dandelion coffee? Very nutritious, Ronnie.'

To be truthful, he didn't look as if he fancied any of this wholesome fare, but he ate without comment, except to murmur that my home-cooked 100% wholewheat bread baked from organically grown stone-ground flour tasted like concentrated grit — actually he used a synonym for this word — and muttering words to the effect that vegetarian cooking might be OK for your health but it was f... hard on the palate and next time it's McDonald's...

FAG ADDICT

Characteristic of the fag addict he wanted — nay — had to have — the post-prandial inhalation of the carcinogenic weed the fumes of which pollute the air I had to breathe. But — panic! The packet was empty. Like some native of a vanished tribe playing through an ancient ritual his hands beat a rapid staccato on his side pockets in hope of finding another packet. Drawing a blank his expression conveyed utter despair.

'Don't you keep any?' he grunted, peevishly.

I must confess to permitting myself the prim expression of one who had given up the wretched habit and somehow conveying that it was a shame that others didn't exhibit the same sort of will-power.

'Gotta get some fags,.' he croaked desperately, and was out of my front door and down those five flights of stairs with the agility of a young gazelle.

It was the image of this unseemly scurry of an OBE down the stairs that woke me up. Yes, the old subconscious in hand with pre-sleep wishful thinking on the eve before I was due to see Ronnie, had produced this strange dream. The chat bit, however, was stored memory of fragmentary conversations in Ronnie's office — bits of dialogue interspersed between his chess moves, dealing with callers, answering the telephone and on the few occasions he could take his eyes off the TV.

Fully awake, I groaned realising that this was to be the day of the so-called interview. I turned over for further slumber hoping that my next visitant would be Miss World.   J.G.

RONNIE THE GURNER

I've previously acknowledged that editors are the most interdependent of animals, relying on information and copy from all quarters. Recently, I received a video in my post. It was one part of a series on Channel 4 regarding drug addiction called 'Hooked'. I had seen this listed in the *Radio Times* but, I thought, not for me, I get enough of that sort of thing at home, but I am grateful to Sharon Wagstaffe, once Ronnie Scott's secretary, for thinking the programme would be of interest and sending me the tape. Indeed, it was.

As could be expected, jazz musicians were featured, the central figure being Cecil Jacob 'Flash' Winston, a boyhood friend of Ronnie Scott and, with Ronnie, a co-founder of the Club Eleven, the launch-pad of bebop in Britain.

The programme included a familiar clip of Charlie Parker and Dizzy Gillespie (Parker an addict, Gillespie was not) and footage of British musicians, including Tony Crombie, Kenny Baker, Lennie Bush and Harry Robbins, but very funny was footage of Ronnie Scott, his features grotesquely contorted in apparent ecstasy puffing at a cigarette, whether an ordinary carcinogenic fag or a mind-altering joint I don't know, but in a programme like this the inference was clear.

Whether it demonstrated another of Scott's comic abilities — the ability to 'gurn', an example of which is in the adjacent picture, I've long said that it was a crying shame that the indolent Ronnie didn't fully exercise his considerable talents.

This is not the mere face-pulling of, say, Norman Wisdom, but a total and very comic transformation of features. I was unaware of the word 'gurning' before I read it in Tony Crombie's 'Madhouse on Wheels', a memoir of life on the road with Ronnie's Big Band in which Tony remembered Ronnie's skill at the manipulating of one's features, and it took me a while to understand what he meant.

Curiously, I saw the word shortly afterwards in an article about comedian Les Dawson, another classic gurner, but not one of my dictionaries included the word, not even Partridge's *Dictionary of Slang* includes the word.

Although no credit was given, many of the clips were from 'The Street', a compilation of 16mm film shot by trumpeter/pianist (and the guru of the early British beboppers), Denis Rose, in Archer Street in the 1950s, and was the companion film to 'The Club Eleven Reunion', shot at Ronnie's and shown on BBC2 in September 1984.

In 'Hooked', Flash eloquently and amusingly justified his drug-taking; a contentious issue (and there are drugs and drugs) but if I, personally, were to chose between a drunk or a 'smoker' give me the latter, and I have not touched a joint ever, but as someone who has more than a nodding acquaintance with Bacchus, I wholeheartedly echo that famous boozer, W.C. Fields, who rasped, 'I hate drunks, they give us drinkers a bad name.'   J.G.

Ronnie, gurning, lecherously

HERBERT COOT LETTERS

(The correspondence between Herbert Coot and Ronnie Scott, with apologies to The Henry Root Letters by William Donaldson)

10th September, 1987
Dear Mr. Scott,

I am writing to say how much I, Mrs. Coot and our son Wally enjoyed Arturo Sandoval when we visited your club. Mrs. Coot said his high notes sent shivers down her spine and it's a long time since she's said that about anyone, including me.

You may remember in our previous correspondence that it was Wally's suggestion that we Coots had an Old Folks Night, and no better place than your club, but he was astonished that so many young people were present. By the way, he hopes you don't take offence at his reference to your OFNs. He's a kind-hearted lad and takes the view that old folks have as much right to enjoyment as those of his own age, and thinks how noble it is of you to fulfil such a function.

Mrs. Coot was puzzled by the handwritten (by yourself, I believe) notices in luminous chalk on a board by the cash desk announcing that future attractions include Fay Wray, Hugh Herbert, Richard Arlen, Franklin Pangborn and Maria Ouspenskya.

Of course, none of us here at Duckham Mansions are old enough to be up on such names, but Mrs. C's old dad is – he remembers seeing some of them on the silent screen as a lad and used to collect their portraits on cigarette cards. He says that all those you mention are dead. How come they will be appearing at the Frith Street Fun House?
Yours sincerely,
Herbert Coot

PS. I must say that I admire your elegant script on that chalk board. When the time comes for you to get yourself a proper job it should be where such talents could be usefully employed.

17th September, 1987
Dear Mr. Coot,

Mrs. C's old dad could well be right about Maria Ouspenskya (if not, she's a hundred and one) and, true, it's likely that the others I have mentioned are no longer with us (nor indeed anyone else) but Fay Wray is still alive. I saw her on the box only the other night and my pulse raced, I don't mind telling you – though not as much as when I first saw her in a revival of 'King Kong' at The Regent, Stamford Hill (1939, I think), probably because this time round she was fully dressed and forty eight years older.

But in my youth she was a great passion of mine. Given half the chance I would have tackled Kong when she, half naked, was struggling and screaming in the monster's hand on the top of the Empire State Building.

Incidentally, what makes you think that all those who appear in the club are alive? Sometimes I wonder. Many of them seem only to show animation when they thrust out their mitts for money. Talking of which, Mr.Coot, it used to be your practice to enclose a pound every time you wrote to me. O.K. We have got over our financial problems, but a pound is still a pound and I hope you will see fit to dive south when answering this letter.
Yours sincerely,
Ronnie Scott

RONNIE'S JOKES

I certainly had a lot of laughs on the road with various bands but some of the places we had to play were pretty insalubrious.

I remember one town where the seagulls used to fly upside down. Nothing worth shitting on. And the locals are not exactly over-endowed with intelligence. When decimal currency came in they raised the school-leaving age to thirty-five. I'll give you an example of the mentality: I went into a chemist's shop up there and said to the guy behind the counter, 'Do you have cotton wool balls?' And he said, 'What do you think I am – a teddy bear?'

I understand that the only reason that Jesus wasn't born in that town was because they couldn't find three wise men. Or a virgin, for that matter. There was one woman up there who had triplets and her husband spent six months looking for the other two blokes.

PERSONAL VIEW
BY BRUCE CROWTHER

Bruce Crowther who also writes under the names 'James Grant' and 'Michael Ansara' is the author of 28 books, many of which are crime fiction. His non-fiction books include several on jazz and popular cinema. He has also written for television and for many years broadcast on jazz on local radio before he was painlessly 'rationalised'. He is a senior contributor to *The Guinness Encyclopaedia of Popular Music* and *The Guinness Who's Who of Jazz*.   J.G.

A personal view about what? ' I asked.
'Whatever you like' your editor helpfully suggested.
'Give me a clue', I persisted.
'Write about what it's like being a writer', he said, hanging up on my hysteria.
All right, on his head be it.
Can you imagine what it is like being locked in a room with nothing for company but your own, probably manic-depressive, thoughts and sheet of blank paper, knowing that if you don't transmute these three very base materials into riches beyond dreams of whatsit, your wife, kids, bank manager, agent, publisher, two dogs, two cats, and a gardenful of frogs, will make your life utterly miserable.
Well, being a writer is a bit like that. Actually, I haven't any kids. And the cats and dogs are gone to their reward, but they were always the least of my worries. After all, they didn't criticise me. They might have looked reproachfully at me out of the corners of their eyes once in a while, but they were never on my back about deadlines and was I sure I really wanted that comma in that particular place and why had I put 'kerb' instead of 'curb' and could I please let them have forty seven pages of amendments before Tuesday and would I mind replacing thirteen line drawings and a score of photographs because Helena left last week, to get married or have a baby or both, and they can't find the files with all the material they know I sent, but which they're sure I kept copies of.
I knew it, I haven't even begun and already I am turning surly. At least this tells you something you never would've believed if I hadn't just proved it to you: your editor isn't the only curmudgeon in the land.
So, what's all this to do with being a writer? (Please don't put questions after rhetorical marks. Helena.) Not a lot really, but it's only when people make suggestions like the one made by my editor that I start to wonder at the latent insanity that makes me do this for a living. (This is living?)
So what is it like? Well, I will tell you what it isn't like (trust a writer to switch a question on you like that). For a start it isn't like having a proper job. Unless you happen to have a proper job that requires you to bang in a 70-hour week, fifty plus weeks a year, with no pension, no paid holidays, no company car, no perks, no dole when the ideas run dry, and the Helenas of this world ringing you up every ten minutes asking 'You're not busy, are you?' (I think that one's rhetorical, too, Helena, but let the question mark stand).

BOOK COVERS

Part of being a writer necessitates learning how to control your blood pressure when lesser mortals would be carried off screaming to the waiting plain white van. How would you like it if one of your books (*Don't Shoot The Pianist*, written under the pseudonym of James Grant), which is about a blues-singing jazz pianist, is given a dust jacket with a picture of a gun, bullets, a glass of whiskey and a piece of sheet music. What's wrong with that you might ask. Well, try playing the music on the sheet and see how jazzy it sounds. (Yes, Helena, jazz musicians can read music, and, no, they don't make it up as they go along.) Or how about a jacket of another book (*Mace*, also by 'James Grant'), which has on it a picture of the unmistakable skyline of San Francisco. Lovely. Except for the unfortunate fact that the book is set entirely in Los Angeles. (Well, Helena, if you'd only warned me, I would have changed the plot). Then there's the jacket of *The Big Band Years* which has on its chocolate box front a silhouette drawing of a big band; a drawing which is repeated on the back of the jacket. The problem is that instead of re-drawing it someone had the bright time-saving idea of simply reversing the original. Thus, the back of the book displays in all its glory the only entirely left-handed thirteen-piece big band in history. But why all the fuss about jackets. After all, we don't judge books by their covers, do we? (Yes, I know that's a cliché, Helena, but every dog must have its day. Okay, two clichés.)
Speaking of which (judgement, I mean), how are books judged today? Certainly not on grounds of what my old school teacher referred to as literary merit. By the way, if you want to know why teachers are up in arms about plans to reintroduce spelling and grammar into the national syllabus, just ask one of them to analyse a simple sentence or define for you the difference between grammar and syntax, or whether you should use 'is' or 'are' after 'none'. They are objecting because most of them are as ignorant of such things as the pupils they are paid to teach. Never mind, twenty years from now Great Britain will be the world leader in finger-painting.
I seem to be sliding round towards the principles of literary criticism which means, I suppose, that I should watch my step, otherwise the next time your editor reviews one of my books, he will chop me off at the ankles. Well, good luck to him. At least he knows the rules by which writers live and is unlikely to level criticism at me for those things that are beyond the writer's control (Careful with that apostrophe. Helena).

CRITICS

Things like an index that is incomplete because the printer lost the last three pages of the typescript. This loss had a mildly demoralizing impact when one critic complained that the book in question was inadequate because of certain omissions. He then went on to cite artists who were, in fact, in the book, but just happened to be amongst the names accidentally omitted from the index. Actually, this goes a long way to proving a long-held suspicion that many critics whose own deadlines are pressing do not always bother to actually read the books they review. Other things beyond the author's control included transposed picture captions ('The author clearly doesn't know the difference between the band of Gene Krupa and the Coldstream Guards'— actually he does, Krupa's is the one in the funny hats) and the pictures trimmed to fit the page even if it means cutting Lester Young out of Basie band's saxophone section (only one 'a' in saxophone. Helena.)

PROPER JOB

By now, I imagine you're growing bored with all this. If he doesn't like it why doesn't he do something else, I hear you cry. For one thing, I am too old to get a proper job that requires me to bang in a 70-hour week, etcetera, etcetera (see above). For another, what other job would let me meet and socialise with real jazz people (by which I mean the musicians, not hacks like me who merely write about it?). How else would I have not only heard but also met and interviewed and once in a while made lasting friendships with so many wonderful people? So you see, it's not my fault that I do what I do, it's their fault. So don't blame me, blame Chris Barber, Sathima Benjamin, Bill Berry, Frank Capp, Tony Coe, Buster Cooper, Conte and Pete Candoli, Bob Efford, Dave Frishberg, Lionel Hampton, Carol Kidd, Anita O'Day, Nat Pierce, Dave Shepherd, Len Skeat, Marlene VerPlanck, Bob Wilber, Jimmy Witherspoon and a host of others.

Writing this last paragraph cheered me up no end and I was almost convinced that being a writer was better than working for a living, but then the telephone rang. It was my publisher. Helena has had a divorce or a baby or something and is coming back to work next month.

Oh, well, things could be worse. Your editor will probably turn out to be one of those finicky people who alters all my best bits. I'll bet he even moves some of the bloody commas. Oh, by the way, I made up the bit about Krupa and the Coldstream Guards. Everything else is true. Honest!

P.S. I thought about telling you of the time the publicity department at one of my publishers arranged a short tour during which I would plug a book on local radio stations. On the first day they had me down for four interviews, two in the morning and two in the afternoon. The locations were Leicester, Oxford, London and Bristol, in that order. 'I don't think I can manage that, Helena', I said. 'Not unless you equip me with a helicopter and one of those little jet-propelled backpack thingamajigs like that feller used at the opening of the Los Angeles Olympics. Then, I might just manage it and be back at home in Hull in time for *Coronation Street*. Otherwise it's impossible. Those towns are just too far apart'. 'Are they?' she said. 'They don't look far apart on the map in the back of my diary'. Go on, be honest. You think I made that one up, don't you?

WHISPERS, MURMURS AND ASIDES

THOSE THAT WERE THERE LOVED IT

Talking to a musician (yes, I'm an open-minded sort of chap) in the Three Greyhounds, Greek Street, run by the statuesque Ms Roxy Beaujolais, I asked him how a recent gig had gone and when he replied, 'Those that were there loved it', immediately I knew the populace had stayed away in their thousands and not to dig the artistry of him and the chaps.

Listening to the broadcast of 'Witnessing History', on BBC, a recollection of the opening night of Ronnie Scott's Club on Friday, October 30th, 1959, with Ronnie and Pete, former Scott band sideman, now pundit Benny Green, and alto-saxophonist Peter King.

Benny told the story of a one-night stand (at the Orchid Ballroom, Purley — Benny got the venue wrong) where the band's take on percentage was was £14, this munificent sum divided between nine musicians after agent's commission and travelling expenses had been deducted.

Alto-saxophonist Derek Humble exclaimed, 'I expect to work for peanuts playing jazz, but... a PEANUT!'

Every band in those halcyon touring days has known this experience. It was called 'paying your dues'.

LANCE FAIRFAX

THE JAZZMAN'S LAMENT

A stands for AGENT, who takes ten percent,
B is for BANJO — a lifetime misspent;
C is for the CRITIC who's often unkind,
D for that DRUMMER who's out of his mind;
E is for EXPERTS — the bane of my life,
F ror the FRIEND who ran off with my wife;
G for the GUV'NOR who won't pay enough,
H is for HANGOVERS when I feel rough;
I: for the INERTIA I suffer all day,
J for the JOBSWORTH who gets in the way;
K for the KEYCHANGE that bassist can't suss,
L for my LICENCE — I now go by bus;
M for the MANAGEMENT in a great flap,
N: NEW YEAR'S EVE when we're paid to play crap;
O for that OFFER I madly declined,
P for those PAYMENTS now six months behind;
Q: my QUINTET which got fired in Milan,
R for ROADIE who wrecked our new van;
S is for SEASON in Cardigan Bay,
T for the TAXMAN who won't go away;
U for the UPRIGHT that's way out of tune,
V for the VOCALIST singing *Blue Moon*;
W: WORK which gets harder to find,
X for those X-RATED thoughts in my mind;
Y for my YOUTH and the things I regret,
Zzzz for the eight hours sleep I won't get...

RON RUBIN

MICHAEL PARKINSON
talks about his long interest in jazz, the conversation occasionally turning to cricket *

Parkinson by Trog

Michael Parkinson, famed interviewer on British television and probably England's most famous Yorkshireman, is also a renowned sports journalist, a club cricketer and a keen jazz enthusiast with wide-ranging tastes and a few salty observations befitting a man from east of the Pennines. Knowing his prowess as an interviewer of the famous in his Parkinson series on BBC TV it was a somewhat unreal experience to be the interviewer of 'Parky' on his own patch, Broadcasting House, but it was an enjoyable one hour conversation that went very quickly. I wore my Ravers CC tie. One should be properly dressed for such occasions. I started the conversation imparting good wishes from Ronnie Scott and his business partner and manager of the Club, Pete King.   J.G

MP: Ah, great. Y'know, I used to employ Ronnie. I was the features editor of a magazine called *Topic* and I invited Mr Scott to write about jazz because, among his many gifts, he is a very good writer, and I used to get little slips of paper from poker sessions stating, 'Column going well, please send more money.'

JG: They seem to recall you coming into the dressing room somewhere in the Manchester area in 1953 when Ronnie was on the road with his nine-piece.

MP: No, it wasn't Manchester. It was in Moorthorpe, near Doncaster. The journalist I was indentured to — a man called Arthur Moseley — owned a dance hall called The Miners there, and I was the dogsbody. I took the money on the door, got the band on the stand, if they felt so disposed, got them their beer and washed the guv'nor's car. We had all the London bands, including the Johnny Dankworth Seven. Cleo Laine made one of her first appearances with the Seven at Moorthorpe. She didn't know how to stand, but sure could sing. It was with Ronnie's band that I first

met my old mate Benny Green. He was reading a blue cover Penguin, a classic, the first jazz musician I ever saw reading such a volume. I was about fourteen at the time. and I was very impressed.

FRANK PARR

JG: I have a very special reason for asking you the following question. Did you attend the Roses (*Lancashire CCC v Yorkshire CCC*) match that year?

MP: I can't remember.

JG: Because if you did, you would have seen someone I know very well performing against your side —

MP: Frank PARR! Wicket-keeper! Trombonist! Many years later I was playing in a charity game in Manchester and he came up to me, and I said, 'You're a trombonist, not a cricketer'.

JELLY ROLL and LOUIS ARMSTRONG

JG: Well, he didn't do badly that year. He merited an entry in the Fielding Statistics feature in *Wisden* with 38 catches and 23 stumpings. I mention this because Parr was the trombonist with Mick Mulligan's Band, George

Melly the singer. I was the agent for these hell-raisers and have the scars to prove it and Frank was the captain of the Ravers CC, originally comprised of jazz musicians, including Mick Mulligan, Wally Fawkes, and Bruce Turner, journalists and agents, me included. As you know, Frank was tipped by the cricket correspondent of *The Times* as an England prospect, but he was the only professional cricketer to become a professional jazz musician. He was an inspiring captain. Knew the game through and through. Sorry, I'm on about cricket and I'm here to ask you about your interest in jazz.

JOHNNY DODDS

MP: I don't quite recall how I first got interested in traditional jazz. I read your interview with Charlie Watts (*JARS* 101) and it was interesting that we had the same heroes. My first interests were Jelly Roll Morton and the Armstrong Hot Five. Clarinettist Johnny Dodds was one of my greatest heroes. I once wrote an essay where I compared Tom Graveney** with Johnny Dodds. I thought they were the two great

---

* With apologies to readers not interested in 'flannelled fools' capering about the green sward

** Gloucestershire and England batsman

stylists of all time. I was a purist bore. Anything recorded after 1939 I didn't want to know about. That was really my grounding.

JG: When did you first hear these records ?

MP: I can't recall. I've been trying to think since I knew I was going to talk to you. There was a friend who had a Hot Five record — 'Gut Bucket Blues' — I remember it very well and I remember thinking what an extraordinary noise they were making. I particularly loved that limpid elegance of Dodds. I've always been very attracted to stylists and Dodds had a lovely, elegant, flowing style and Armstrong, of course, the greatest jazz musician that has ever been, in my view. Then I bought Louis records on Parlophone. I got a collection of these, used to swop them around with fellow spirits and we'd bore each other shitless with our opinions.

Then I bought Bunny Berigan's record of *I Can't Get Started*, and tuned into AFN — Willis Conover — heard a different kind of jazz and started to expand my tastes. From being an ardent small group traditionalist I became interested in the big bands: Kenton, Herman, Basie, Duke and then into the modern stuff. The first ultra-modern record I ever bought was on a yellow label. Can't remember what it was called, but it was Lee Konitz playing *You Go To My Head*, and that was the start of my interest in modern jazz.

JG: Did you have any parental opposition ?

MP: Absolutely, but I used to sweeten my mother with Mantovani records and my father was a sucker for Felix Mendelssohn and his *Hawaiian Serenaders*, but that stuff was always beyond me. I was somewhere else. I was a real musical prick, I really was. We all are at that age. Such a snob. I used to read Max Jones's column in the *Melody Maker,* and because he wore a black beret, I sported one, too.

COOL PARKY

JG: Max was a founder member of the Ravers CC. A fine batsman.

MP: We didn't have a disco, but at a place called Locke Park in Barnsley, named after a local benefactor, we had a bandstand, which had long outgrown the use for which it was designed, and a friend of mine, Handley, Jiver Handley, who was a bit of a lunatic, took over the stand. He played all jazz. The opening record was always Charlie Barnet's *Skyliner,* then I heard Dizzy Gillespie for the first time — *Night In Tunisia*, *Ornithology* and all those things. I didn't lose my interest in Jelly Roll and Louis. They were my beginnings and treasured favourites and will remain so, but the effect of Dizzy and Co. was on my wardrobe. I started to wear huge crêpe-sole shoes — like landing barges — drape jackets, slim Jim ties, sported a duck's arse haircut and wore dark glasses with shades on. Oh, my God, I was cool! Dancing to modern jazz in bloody Barnsley!

JG: No doubt your mouldy fygge contemporaries condemned you for deserting what they would describe as true jazz.

MP: I had terrible rows with them. They used to wear duffle coats and open-toe sandals, smoked pipes and joined CND, but I'd moved on. They couldn't understand that one could belong to both camps.

JG: There was a lot of sartorial identification in those disputative days. It was part of the scene.

MP: Like the seediness. That's always attracted me. I remember going to Ronnie's in Gerrard Street and seeing Bill Evans.(Here MP did an imitation of Evans sprawled over the keyboard.) I also loved the atmosphere at the Flamingo with Bill Le Sage on piano, Victor Feldman on vibes, Lennie Bush on bass and Tony Crombie on drums.

JG: Who else, besides Ronnie and Johnny Dankworth, did you see in the Barnsley area ?

MP: Mick Mulligan with George Melly, Chris Barber, Ken Colyer, Freddy Randall, and Humph with Wally Fawkes.

JG: Wally was another founder member of the Ravers CC. Excellent bowler and batsman. A reluctant fielder.

MP: A fine clarinettist. Harry Gold and his Pieces of Eight I remember. That little man struggling with the enormous bass sax.

JG: Sorry to butt in again, but I saw Harry only recently, at a reunion of veteran dance band musicians. At about ten o'clock, he said, 'I must go, Jim, I'm well oiled, but I'll have a drink before I go. Make it a double, eh?' And he's ninety next February! Did you ever listen to the Yorkshire Jazz Band ?

MP: Yes, and the Saints from Manchester and on their trips north, Joe Harriott, Kenny Graham, and Kenny Baker, but the significant thing for me at the time was Stan Kenton. I couldn't get over the sound. *Intermission Riff* — a wall of sound !

OSCAR PETERSON

JG: Do you still have a collection ?

MP: Yes, I have a very wide selection, but nowadays if I buy a record I very rarely venture into unknown territory. I always go back to the classics. I'm very fond of piano players. I love piano jazz. Oscar Peterson! It's not fashionable to talk highly of Oscar, but I think he's one of the great jazz pianists of all time. There seems to be a kind of feeling that somehow he's too clever, too technical. But I think there's a muscularity in his jazz, a strength in it I find absolutely extraordinary. The way he plays with Ray Brown is perfect. A perfect marriage. Their session they recorded at the Blue Note is marvellous. I don't care what anyone says, there's some stuff in there that's unbelievable. Tatum. I never saw Tatum. I would have loved to have seen him.

JG: You would have been four years old when he came to England.

MP: Erroll Garner, another wonderful player. His *Concert By The Sea* is one of the defining pieces of jazz piano. Who else? Teddy Wilson. God almighty, I was in a bar in New York — can't recall its name — and I heard this great pianist playing somewhere in the building. I discovered where he was and there was no bugger there! I became his audience. Teddy Wilson!

What we took as a privilege, the Americans took for granted. When I was in LA I went to see the MJQ and the Eric Dolphy Quintet. There were six people and they did two sets. I doubled the audience for the second set.

JG: It makes you wonder about the economics of it all.

MP: Extraordinary. And yet the people of my generation who loved jazz were starved of it in terms of actually seeing our heroes until the exchange system started in 1956. Even then, if you were stuck up in Grimethorpe you didn't have much bloody chance of seeing them when they did come.

JG: My last interviewee was Ruby Braff. What do you think of him?

MP: I love his playing —

JG: It wasn't an easy chat, but he became fervent when we got on to piano players. It surprised me that he liked Jelly Roll Morton.

EARL HINES
and JACK TEAGARDEN

MP: It's a surprise perhaps, but understandable, because when you think of Jelly's contribution then it shouldn't be. Earl Hines, with Oscar, is my favourite. It's a funny thing, but when people talk about jazz piano nowadays they seem to overlook Earl, and I don't know why, because he had perfect musical taste.

I was a very young journalist with the *Yorkshire Evening Post*, in Doncaster. I used a little cafe and I walked in there one lunchtime and who should I see sitting at a table but Jack Teagarden and Earl Hines and the rest of the All-Stars. Teagarden and Hines in the Great North Road! I recognised Jack Teagarden immediately. It took me a minute or so to realise it was Earl Hines. I said, 'You're Jack Teagarden', and he said, 'How do you know, man?', and I said, 'I've got all your records, what on earth are you doing here?'

I wrote up that unbelievable encounter in the Doncaster edition of the *Yorkshire Evening Post*.

(THE REPORT READ: 'We saw our man eating steak and chips in a Doncaster cafe and looking very despondent. We were sure we had seen him before, but it wasn't until he got around to coffee (black) and cigarette (toasted) that we recognised him as that eminent jazzman, Jack 'Big T' Teagarden. Later we spoke to Mr T and that other aristocrat of American jazz, Earl 'Fatha' Hines. They are doing a series of one night stands with their All-Stars and Doncaster was a whistle stop en route to Bradford.

Mr Hines looked despondent, too. And so did the rest of the band, namely Cozy Cole, Max Kaminsky, Peanuts Hucko and Jack Lesberg'.

THE REASON? THE 'FLU BUG'

'Man, it really knocks you sideways', said Mr T in gravel tones familiar to jazz fans the world over. 'I reckon we've been travelling with 3,000 'flu bugs in our coach.'

We discovered that Mr T, whose first visit to England this is, liked our people ('crazy') the audiences he played to on this tour ('Man, we really flip them') and the British jazz bands he has heard ('They are the most. They gas me').

Mr Hines, in cream coloured overcoat, dark glasses and trilby hat, was very much the fugitive from a jazz band. He was as affable as a man with 'flu can be and he didn't want to do or say anything very much except 'I want to move out of this here town, 'cos I've got 'flu bugs jivin' in me.'

Mr Kaminsky, on the other hand, was more affable than a man with 'flu ought to be. 'I love this old England of yours. It's so cute and picturesque,' he said. He loves it so much he didn't spend his hour break eating, but instead he walked around Doncaster showing an avid tourist's interest in everything.

'Wonderful little town', he said. We looked to Mr T. for confirmation from the lips of the finest trombone in traditional jazz.

'Sure, real crazy. What's its name ?' he enquired as he climbed into the cream-coloured coach with five other musicians, a host of 'officials' and 3,000 'flu bugs.'

STAN GREIG

JG: I know I'm buzzing about a bit, but can you tell me about you meeting up with pianist Stan Greig during the Suez Campaign. I know Stan very well. I can boast that I am one of the few people whose name he can remember. With difficulty, but he gets there. Within five minutes or so. Not hot on names is Stan. He calls everybody 'man', but he remembers you.

MP: I certainly remember him. Like me, he was a National Serviceman. He was a mechanic. I had seen him with Humphrey Lyttelton before we were called up and I still have this blinding image of him pounding away on a broken down upright in a block of flats the Army had requisitioned in Port Said, but I can't recall how we first met.

JG: I seem to recall a programme in which you claimed to have been the youngest ever Captain in the British Army. You were nineteen.

MP: That was too bloody silly for words. It shows how daft the British Army were !

JG: Have you any abiding memories of visits to Ronnie's ?

MP: I remember Ella, Buddy Rich, Dizzy, Betty Carter. So many names. I saw Stephane Grappelli there. I love jazz violin — Stephane, Joe Venuti, Stuff Smith. I think jazz on the violin works.

I know it sounds pompous, but I think Ronnie's is very much a part of our cultural scene and for what — thirty-eight years ? I think jazz is a great art form and Ronnie's has done its best to perpetuate it. In my view a jazz musician is a great musician. We were lucky to have been around when so much was happening. From only traditional jazz the music has moved to bebop, West Coast, big bands, although, I must say I'm not sure about contemporary jazz. I like my jazz melodic, but it's strange, isn't it, that what once sounded unmelodic is now acceptable? I remember when I first heard Diz, I thought what the hell's that? — but now he sounds so tuneful. It's odd how the ear and one's perceptions change.

INTERVIEWING JAZZ GIANTS

JG: I'd like to ask you about the jazz giants you interviewed on the Parkinson programme.

MP: It was great. Duke Ellington, Count Basie, Buddy Rich, Oscar Peterson, Bud Freeman, Teddy Wilson, Stephane Grappelli, and so many more.

JG: I didn't see the show, but I hear that the Buddy Rich interview was a particular success.

MP: I liked Buddy. I think he liked me because he knew I liked jazz. He wasn't talking to a pillock. He wasn't very good at dealing with pillocks. Didn't have much time for them. I love the stories about him. I love that New York Jewish musicians' humour. When I had him on the show the first four rows of seats were occupied by drummers — sitting there gaping. I said to Harry Stoneham (*Michael's musical director*), 'It's exciting looking at his hands,' and Harry

replied, 'just look at his feet'. It was an education. On one show we had Buddy and Sammy Davis, Jnr. For some inexplicable reason, the show was filmed in Slough, where we had to take Sammy. He thought he was being kidnapped and was not best pleased when he arrived, but Buddy had a word with him and the two of them duetted. It was extraordinary. You would have thought that there was a symphony orchestra accompanying Sammy. I'm not a drum fan. I know its a necessary instrument, like the brakes of a car, but hardly a thing of beauty, but in Buddy's two hands and two feet... well, it was just magical.

BUDDY AND RONNIE

JG: Buddy appeared at the club several times and he and Ronnie sparked each other off.

MP: I can imagine !

JG: Buddy Rich would end his set and announce, 'Now Ronnie Scott is going to tell his usual old jokes,' and Ronnie would retaliate by announcing, 'And now Buddy Rich is going to play his usual old drum licks.'

MP: He was terrible martinet. Ruled the band with a rod of iron. The supreme professional and thought everyone else should be spot on. Didn't tolerate any excuses: illness, whatever. I admired him for that attitude.

We had one director who wasn't on top of the job. He rather over-rehearsed Buddy and when it came to the break, Buddy enquired what time he and the band would be needed.
'Oh, about 6.30', replied the director, and Buddy retorted, 'I don't want any of that ABOUT jazz, just give me a time', and the director replied, '6.30', and Buddy replied, 'OK, 6.30, we'll be there'. At 6.30 sharp he and the band were there. The technicians were there, I was there, but no director. I knew what was going to happen. I heard Buddy beat the band in with the director still up at the bar.

JG: That was a lesson to him.

MP: Absolutely. That's why I liked working with Buddy. The complete professional.

JG: Tell me about your interview with Duke Ellington.

MP: It was a marvellous experience. Like sitting next to God — or St. Peter at least. What a charmer!

Sadly, at this point, my allotted hour ran out. Perhaps I should have brought the subject round to cricket, which included Parky playing with British bandleader Vic Lewis's glitzy showbiz cricket X1. Hopefully, I will have another interview with Michael Parkinson to hear more about his meetings with famous American jazzmen.

Count Basie by Pennington   Buddy Rich by Pennington

INTERVIEW...
Ronnie dwells on a few occupational hazards

Sharp-eyed readers (and when it comes to noticing mistakes in these pages some of these are very sharp) will have spotted that there wasn't the usual 'Interview' with Ronnie Scott in the December/January issue of *JARS*. Ronnie had been unwell, off the scene for a bit, and instead we published Paul Pry's portrait of our scurrilous columnist Slawkenbergius and this, I may add, got a whole barrelful of worms a-seething, but that's another story... One bitterly cold snowy December evening (it was so cold the Mediterranean workshys who normally throng Frith Street had been driven into their warrens), I bearded the lion Scott in his den at the back of the club room. He was hunched over the TV set looking morose. As well he might. He was watching Bob Monkhouse, enough to make the jolliest of souls downcast.

'I hear you've been queer, Ronnie,' I enquired, solicitously.

'I beg your pardon!' the guv'nor replied sharply.

'Sorry! Usage has changed so much in recent years. One has to be so careful nowadays. One can't call a spade a spade any more, not without being accused of racism. What I meant was, I heard that you had been poorly. Which, apart from Mr. Monkhouse, explains why you are not your usual gay, sorry, jolly, self.'

'My back's been playing me up. And don't give me your horrible middle-aged leer. It's sciatica. I wish it were the other. No such luck.'

'It's all that bowing to thunderous applause after you've finished your Quintet set and told your jokes.'

MELLYITES

He sighed heavily. 'There's precious little applause now we've got George Melly. George's fans laugh at his jokes, but not mine. Getting over to them is harder than Arthur Scargill preaching socialism to a Tory Party Conference. Oscar Peterson fans titter, Buddy Rich fans giggle, Zoot Sims' audience chortles and the Jacques Loussier crowd think I'm a riot but, oh, those Mellyites.'

'You make them sound like a Hebrew tribe in the Old Testament.'

I wish they were. At least my Jewish jokes would get a hand.'

'Maybe it's because Melly's audience are a much more sophisticated lot. After all, he is known as the thinking man's entertainer. However, I hear that you went down a storm at a Christmas charity gig you did at Wormwood Scrubs. According to my informant you had them all helpless with laughter.'

Even this reminder of success failed to cheer the downcast Scott.

'How could I fail? It was a captive audience.' (Ronnie was being over-modest. His bassist, Ron Mathewson, another generally non-communicative person, and someone who has heard the Scott jokes a million times over, had been raving about the tremendous reception Ronnie got from the Scrubs' inmates.)

The phone rang and Ronnie picked it up. 'No sir, sorry. All tables are fully booked for New Year's Eve. Standing room only, I'm afraid. The charge for that, sir? Ten pounds. Five pounds one foot. That might be a better deal. It's going to be a very packed house. Melly draws a big crowd', and added, sotto voce, 'humourless lot.'

He replaced the phone and said, 'Now, what can I do for you?' That phraseology, ostensibly showing co-operativeness, means precisely the opposite with Mr. Scott. In truth it indicated that I could leave as soon as I liked, but with the triumph of hope over experience (as Samuel Johnson said of a man about to marry the second time) I had to press on, to get something to fill this page. I tried a conversational approach.

'I see... (an undeservedly famous TV 'personality') is in the Club.'

FREE-LOADERS

'SO! Has he paid to get in and how much is he spending?'

I was rather taken aback by the speed and sharpness of that riposte. Ronnie isn't a mercenary sort of fellow. In truth, he will admit to being a poor businessman — but he waxed quite heatedly on the obviously sore subject of the famous thinking their names give them access on the freeman's ticket.

'Why should they come in for free?' he enquired. 'We need every penny we can get to keep going and they can easily afford what we charge. OK if a guy's broke, or someone like Benny Goodman, whom I worship, they can be our guests, but not the likes of...' He spat out the name of a comic (who is by no means as funny as Ronnie, I may add) who presented himself at the cash desk and departed in a huff when the door staff insisted on him paying. 'That's the last we'll ever see of him.' Ronnie snorted and brightened a little at the thought.

'I get your point, but what about the publicity value. You know — noted jazz club proprietor Ronnie Scott seen enjoying a joke with Ronnie Corbett. That sort of thing.'

'I'm not your hail-fellow-well-met sort. Not with people I don't rate, anyway. And I like to think that celebrities can enjoy what's going on without being badgered or fawned upon.'

CAPTAIN'S TABLE

'Mind you, I tried the Captain's Table bit one night. The Maître d' we had at the time pestered me to give it a go. He used to fawn over the 'famous' and pestered me to give them more attention. I reluctantly agreed and told him should any notabilities come in, to invite them to dine with me.'

'You mean, Ronnie, that you actually ate at the Club? You surprise me!'

'I surprised myself. I tell you, it's one thing to be behind the mike on the bandstand and see those steaks glowing like the Milky Way on a clear night, but the close encounter at arms length is another kettle of fish, so to speak. It's enough to blind a man.'

'Anyway, no celebrities turned up, and I sat there as lonely as an oil sheikh at a barmitzvah. I told the Maître d', get somebody, anybody. I felt such a lemon sitting there by myself. He approached a man and his wife, did the fawning and beaming bit and asked them if they would dine with me. And do you know what the man said?'

'Not being present at the time, nor psychic, no, I don't.'

'No need for sarcasm. The question was rhetorical. Well, he said, 'I spent a fiver on a cab to get here, parted with fourteen notes to get in, it's going to cost me another thirty or so to sample your glowing steaks and drink that paint stripper you laughingly call the house wine, another five to get home and you're asking me to eat with the staff?! Piss off!!'

'I was quite shattered, Jim. Quite shattered. Here's me, my name in glittering neon outside, Humphrey Lyttelton nods to me at Press receptions and the like, The Queen invites me to Buckingham Palace to pin a gong on me, I'm going in 'Who's Who' and this berk turns me down.'

RAT PACK

'He sounds a rather common sort of chap, Ronnie. Shouldn't think he went to a good school. You were better off without him.'

'Oh, that wasn't all. Do you know what happened next? I know! I know! You weren't present, and you're not psychic. Well, God help me, once it got about that I was acting mein host I was joined by the Rat Pack.'

'That lot! I haven't seen them for months.'

'Eighteen, to be precise. They were copped team-handed on a mission to a mansion in Hertfordshire and got one and a half at Wormwood Scrubs. My luck they celebrated their release at the club and at my table.'

I felt genuinely sorry, albeit retrospectively, for Ronnie being lumbered with that unlovely quartet, comprising Harpie Harry, from Kingston, Jamaica; Jock Strapping, from the Gorbals, Glasgow; Giuseppe Fidlio Dodgioso, born Jubilee Dwellings, Clerkenwell, and from a long line of Sicilian hoods; and Jacko 'Bigmouth' Higso from Stepney, but usually enjoying the hospitality of Her Majesty at one of her penal institutions. In fact, he's seen the inside of most of these.

If you wished them on your worst enemy, you'd be overcome with remorse after the event for being so cruel, even to an adversary.

'Hard going, Ronnie?'

OVETT AND COE

'It was terrible but I had a bit of luck.

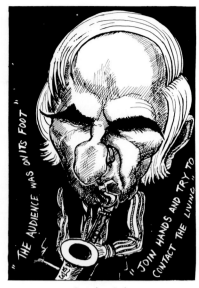

Ron by Cole

A copper member showed and they fled. I've never seen anyone move so fast. They would have put Ovett and Coe to shame. It was as though a magician had waved his wand. But my troubles weren't over. People drifted to and from the table, and in the general mêlée and me feeling disoriented after that guy's refusal and the Rat Pack, I got a bit confused. In one of those dreadful cross conversations, I got the impression that one of those present was a writer. I said, 'I believe you're a writer, Mr. Amis' and he replied, 'That's right and what do you do Mr. Scott?'

'I tell you, it wasn't my night. I decided there and then to abandon the Captain's Table bit. It's not worth the aggro.'

A grim story.   J.G.

RONNIE'S JOKES

We had a terrible audience the other night. It was the first time I'd seen dead people smoke. There was only one guy applauding and I had to tell him not to clap on his own otherwise the waiter would throw him a fish.

And when I began to do my little chat between sets he started to heckle me. 'Those jokes are terrible', he shouted. I told him: 'If I want your opinion, sir, I'll give it to you. If you really want me to be funny, I'll borrow that suit you're wearing. Somewhere in East London is a Ford Prefect with no seat covers.'

I think his problem was that he was a little stoned on a special drink we'd been serving that night – it was a mixture of one part muscatel and one part hock. We call it 'muck'. Generally speaking we get very few drunks at the Club – sometimes it seems that most of the audience has been drinking cement–and we get very few unpleasant incidents considering we're in the heart of Soho.

RONNIE AND SONNY

Sonny Rollins was first booked into Ronnie Scott's, at the 'old place', Gerrard Street in 1967 and in his book *Some of My Best Friends Are Blues* Ronnie relates how the friendship with Sonny commenced (incidentally Sonny was full of praise for the Scott Club resident pianist, Stan Tracey, saying 'You don't seem to realise over here how good a player he is'.)

When Ronnie was on one of his visits in New York he met up with Sonny. In his hotel one evening Ronnie received a call from Rollins who said, 'I am going to practise, would you like to join me?' Forever afterwards Ronnie often expressed his regret that he didn't accept the offer from this giant of the saxophone.

In October 1999 Sonny Rollins starred in a concert celebrating the Club's fortieth birthday at the Barbican and in a prior conversation to his appearance I did mention to him that Ronnie refusing the invitation is something that had haunted him ever since. Sonny recalled the conversation and politely excused himself as he was required for a photo call.

That year was indeed a year for anniversaries. It was eighty years since the first jazz band played in Britain — the Original Dixieland Jazz Band from New Orleans. It was Duke Ellington's Centennial, the 20th birthday of *JARS*, the 70th of Club director Pete King and on October 30th Ronnie Scott's Club celebrated its 40th, this milestone marked by an assembly of outstanding talent: George Benson, The Count Basie Orchestra, Carmen Bradford, Dee Dee Bridgewater, Georgie Fame and Peter King, the latter playing at Ronnie's on its opening night forty years ago.

The show started on a hilarious, yet sad, note: a tape of Ronnie cracking his famed jokes with superb timing and with that engaging little chuckle between gags. The evening was neatly compèred by Jimmy Parsons, a long time member of the Club staff.

Club director Pete King, clearly moved, praised all those who had contributed, not only to the anniversary

Pete King and Sonny thirty two years after their first meeting at Ronnie's in 1967

presentations, but the Club staff and the musicians over the years, concluding with a tribute to his wife Stella for having to share him with the Club over four decades.

EPIC SONNY ROLLINS

The Sonny Rollins concert was an equally emotive event, Sonny paying homage to the late Ronnie Scott, and to Pete King for perpetuating the name and the ethos of that institution, Ronnie Scott's Club, sentiments that were warmly applauded by an informed, capacity audience, who were captivated by his terrific performance.

He finished his second set to a standing audience clamouring for an encore, but after that final number, *Don't Stop The Carnival*, anything would have been anti-climax.

What will remain in my memory is the demonic energy of a leonine figure, his beard his mane, this king of the pride prowling the width of the stage, unleashing impassioned choruses, and with unflagging invention.

Sixty-nine years of age, he was fuelled by the regenerating force of jazz improvisation, his pre-appearance drink of a cup of coffee in the buffet room where I had a brief word with a man whose self-effacing and courteous demeanour was in a stark contrast to his dominating personality on the stage.

To describe this supreme artist as a showman would perhaps suggest clownish antics; not so; but by graphically undulating his instrument to approximate to the range of the emotions and extraordinary dynamics, he imparted another dimension to the performance. Up high there was an anguished squeal; thrust down there was a foghorn rasp that dramatically reverberated throughout the hall, but all the effects part of a logical whole.

He had an excellent band with him, the rhythm section kicked, and trombonist Clifton Anderson was an admirable foil for Sonny, but it was the leader's show. An epic performance.

Both concerts embodied the post-war history of jazz, which the Club has fully reflected in its forty years. There's barely a significant name that not appeared at its two addresses and all the musicians and singers at these concerts have long histories playing their part in the jazz pageant. They did the Club's birthday proud.   J.G.

Ronnie and Sonny in 1967 Photo: David Redfern

HERBERT COOT LETTERS

(The correspondence between Herbert Coot and Ronnie Scott, with apologies to The Henry Root Letters by William Donaldson)

10th October, 1987
Dear Mr. Scott,
Apropos the thrust in your letter of September 17 — that I 'dive south' (How graphic! I do love the colourful expressions you jazz people use) when next writing to you — I apologise most sincerely for the absence of my usual pound with my billet doux of September 10. But, alas, now a pound is a coin of the realm instead of that flimsy I used to send you, I have had to cease sending that amount with my letters.

Coinery can easily give rise to purloinery, and indeed two letters with such went amiss. One was to the Conservative Central Office, who can always do with funds, and the other to Arthur Scargill now that he is out of job.

You're not the only one to complain. Not by a long list of notabilities; indeed I now realise how much my funds were appreciated. Among those correspondees of mine who could have done with a quid to help defray their legal costs were Lester Piggott after his brush with HM Inspector of Taxes, Captain Mark Phillips after that temerararious copper booked him for doing a hundred plus on the M4 and Mr. Jeffery Archer following those dealings with a lady of easy virtue. And Mrs. Cecil Parkinson wouldn't have been averse to a pound to help pay maintenance cost to Miss Sarah Keays, either.

It's most unfortunate. It's put paid to my reputation as the country's leading philanthropist, outside of the judge dealing with Mr. Jefferey Archer's case, that is.

But, be assured, I shall continue to keep writing and the burden of this note this time is to complain — yet again — about the lighting (Ho! Ho!) at your club.

My eyes are — like a few other of my precious parts – not what they were, and only the other night I returned to what I thought was my table after visiting the gents and feeling affectionate towards my dearly beloved gave her a fond kiss and a hug. Or so I thought. It turned out to be another, younger, lady and her boyfriend, who I'd not spotted in the gloom, was very large, very muscular, very threatening and very dark.

It was a highly embarrassing, not to say alarming situation and a very displeased Mrs. Coot refused to talk to me for the rest of the night.
Yours sincerely,
Herbert Coot

15th October, 1987
Dear Mr. Coot,
Many thanks for your letter explaining the absence of your usual – and much valued pound. I get your point, and giving the matter some thought, I can see a way round the difficulty.

As we exchange correspondence some six times a year and bearing in mind the denomination of five pounds is still issued as a flimsy, why not send this at the beginning of the year and have done with it? OK, I know I could expect six pounds in normal yearly correspondence, and there's inflation, too, but I'm a reasonable man and I'll settle for a fiver. With the New Year coming up – now is the time.

Herbert Coot, mistakenly, in the stygian gloom of 47 Frith Street, embraced the lady with Frank Bruno

Regarding the lighting, I am sorry about your contretemps with Frank Bruno — that must have been a ticklish moment — but when in the past we've put up the lighting it's caused us more problems. People can see who is with who and we've had outraged wives on the phone and it's enough aggro running a club without that.
Yours sincerely,
Ronnie Scott

WHISPERS, MURMURS & ASIDES

A WOEFUL NOTE

There's not been an overwhelming response to our request that you out there, write us letters, but we did receive a rather heart-rending note from a lady who gave her real name, but requested that we use a pseudonym she provided. It read:

I was astonished to read in Private Eye *that one Sue May had been molested by a drunk at the bar in Ronnie's. I have been going to 47 Frith Street for the past ten years and have spent many, many happy hours propping up the bar when I've arrived too late for a seat and although, admittedly, I'm of a certain age (but could pass for less in what Ronnie calls lighting at the Club) I don't think I'm unattractive but never, ever, have I received as much as a touch-up.*
Where have I gone wrong? My make-up? My hairstyle? My clothes? Oh, crikey, have I got B.O? Whatever, it's troubling me no end.
Signed:
Worried Blue Eyes

CLEO LAINE Britain's First Lady of jazz

Jazz buffs, talking of American female singers, invariably use the affectionate 'familiar' first name — Bessie, Billie, Ella, Sarah, or Dinah. In England, it is the Christian name of a lady who long out-distanced all her rivals — Cleo, Cleo Laine, with the quality of her voice and the extent of her range still in its pristine strength. Her five octave range has enabled her to move in many directions outside of jazz, although this is her first and abiding love, overwhelmingly demonstrated in her latest CD, *Blue and Sentimental*, which features Gerry Mulligan, George Shearing, Joe Williams and her husband/MD, alto-saxophonist, composer and arranger, John Dankworth.

Their marriage has been one of the most enduring associations matrimonially and musically, on the British jazz scene, commencing in 1951, when the twenty-three year old Clementina Dinah Campbell auditioned for the role of girl singer with the seminal Johnny Dankworth Seven. She and John married in 1958 and have two children, bassist Alec and singer Jacqueline.

SVENGALI JOHN

Cleo readily acknowledges that husband John has been her Svengali. A consummate musician, his arrangements coaxed up the top end of her range, but in her book Cleo also generously acknowledges the help that she, the gauche novice, received from members of the Seven, pianist Bill le Sage, bassist Eric Dawson and trombonist Eddie Harvey. She recalls that she genuinely enjoyed 'paying her dues' on the hundreds of one-night stands the Seven had to play to stay in business. She also recalled the sarcasm and cynical humour, typical of the touring musician, in the band coach but she is emphatic that they were all 'gentlemen', and those who recall the Seven will know that Cleo is not putting a retrospective gloss on their characters. Well, if not exactly 'gentlemen', they were very nice guys.

In 1953 Dankworth disbanded the Seven to form his big band, with which Cleo stayed for a year, and then branched out as an actress. Again, she acknowledged the Seven. 'No matter how I assessed the years before 1958, one thing was certain: I could not have been chosen as leading lady at the Royal Court Theatre if I had not joined the Dankworth Seven. So when people say that John Dankworth is my Svengali, in this respect they are quite right. Before the Sven experience, I hardly knew how to walk on to a stage.'

ROYAL VARIETY SHOW

This was certainly not the case when playing the lead in Sandy Wilson's *Valmouth*, singing in the Brecht-Weill *Seven Deadly Sins* at the Edinburgh Festival in 1961 and in the 1971–73 London revival of Jerome Kern's *Showboat*, the Jubilee Royal Variety Show with Cliff Richard, Bob Hope, Eartha Kitt, Sophie Tucker and Rosemary Clooney, in the presence of the Queen

Cleo by Trog

and Prince Philip, and many other prestigious engagements. Also, she has performed '20th century Lieder', settings of Shakespeare and Schoenberg's *Pierrot Lunaire*. Her many, many albums include *Beyond the Blues*, *Shakespeare and All That Jazz*, *The Unbelievable Miss Cleo Laine*, *Showboat*, *Live At Carnegie Hall*, *Porgy and Bess* (with Ray Charles), *Colette* (music by John Dankworth), *The Mystery of Edwin Drood* and *Cleo Sings Sondheim*.

WAVENDON

The girl from a dull West London suburb, the illegitimate daughter of a bigamist white mother and a West Indian father, who left school at fourteen to became a hairdresser's assistant, has since rubbed shoulders with many of the great names in showbiz, as well as jazz, but, as her autobiography, *Cleo* (Simon & Schuster, 1994*)*, reveals, she hasn't forgotten her humble origins, or the people who helped her to become the success she is, and those who know Cleo will testify to her lack of affectation and her down-to-earth personality. She is rightly proud of Wavendon All-Music, at the Stables, Wavendon, which she and John founded in 1979 to present music of all kinds, and to run courses.

Of course, I had known of Cleo and her successes but it was not until the spring of 2007 when I was one of the guest speakers on their regular Sunday morning feature 'Jazz matters'. my first visit to Wavendon to see for myself the idyllic setting in which the Dankworths have established a universally famed jazz centre.

I found the Wavendon ambience quite delightful and the audience good listeners and questioners. There was some enjoyable banter with John.   J.G.

'It's an Open University summer school jazz degree field trip

Illustration: Bill Stott

HERBERT COOT LETTERS

(The correspondence between Herbert Coot and Ronnie Scott, with apologies to The Henry Root Letters by William Donaldson)

10th January, 1988
Dear Mr.Scott
I am very upset; mortified! In truth, I have never been more discombobulated in all my puff!

I searched long and hard for the right word — one so apposite – so telling – to describe that impertinent prole of a copper nicking Captain Mark Phillips for doing a ton-plus on the M4 and your editor and typesetter, or both, screwed it up into something quite rabuncolous.

The word I used — and I'll spell it out — was TEMERARIOUS, which by some gross transmogrification (see what you can do with that!) appeared as 'TEMERARARIOUS'.

I am quite shattered. Your readers will think I am illiterate or something. TEMERARARIOUS! HUH!

This was especially painful to me, because out of all the famous people with whom I regularly correspond there are two I treasure most – yourself and Mrs. Thatcher, an OBE and an OB.(Geddit?). (Mrs. Coot, who has a social conscience and votes Labour, fell about in a hysterical fit of laughter when she read this). In fact, I have had framed both your and the PM's letter of thanks for the first pound I sent you both and they hang next to each other on my study wall. They are the envy of my friends. Really, doesn't your editor check on these misprints? If I were you, I'd sack the fellow.

Yours, more in sorrow than anger,
Herbert Coot

31st January 1988
Dear Mr Coot,
I can't apologise enough for the rabuncolousness of that misprint, and that an extremely valued correspondent such as yourself should be discombobulated pains me no end.

I wouldn't wish to discombobulate anyone, not even Stan Getz, and, please be assured, I summarily carpeted the editorial staff and he absquatulated totally discombobulate.

I know exactly how you feel! Every time I pick up *JARS* I am in a state of trepidation—fearing some boner or another is going to rear up and smite me right between the eyes.

If it's any consolation to you, readers of *The Observer, Daily Telegraph, Financial Times* and *London Standard* suffer likewise. Strangely enough not so much in *The Sun, News of The World,* and *Daily Express,* but then, they don't use words of more than two syllables. My advice is that you do the same. 'Temerarious' is just asking for trouble. As for sacking the editor, the truth is we can't afford anyone better. I suppose your annoyance accounts for you not enclosing your little something as is your wont. This is particularly galling. I earnestly trust that time will soften your ire, hopefully when you next write.(See my suggestion in my letter of 10th October.)

I have seen to it personally that 'transmogrification' is not transmogrified into something rabuncolous.

Yours genuflectly,
Ronnie Scott.

4th February, 1988
Dear Mr. Scott,
I enclose a fiver (to cover me for the year, as you suggested in your letter of October 10th) if only in sheer admiration for your telling choice of words.

I will, however, take your advice and will try to limit myself to words of no more than two syllables in the future.

Yours sincerely,
Herbert Coot.

PS. Please let me know where you get your dictionaries; for use of writing to other parties, of course.

GOTHARD EXPRESS

Typical members of Ronnie Scott's Club on holiday on their way to Basle on the Gotthard Express, first class, of course.

The lady holding her purse close to her — er — private parts is obviously fearing that the cad with her might be the sort to take advantage, but one doubts if he would risk that splendid crease in his trousers.

The grim-visaged lady staring at her gentleman friend on the table opposite (as if he were something quite unappetising) is getting over — or trying to get over — a passionate affair with Ronnie Scott.

The Amazonian lady at the rear was a waitress at the Club before she struck oil — so to speak —with a rich Texan.

INTERVIEW...
of a sort, as usual

Owing to Ronnie Scott being indisposed with a recurring back complaint I was not able to conduct the 'Interview' (sic!) with him for the previous issue. In a somewhat perverse way I rather missed the agony of this exercise. For nearly three years now I've got used to gathering up my limited moral fibre and fortifying this resolve with a glass or two of Burton at the Dog and Duck before entering 47 Frith Street, for the hard graft of getting Mr Scott to talk to me, editor of his own house magazine. Long-standing readers will know what I'm on about and, indeed, some have avowed that I go on too long and too often about the cross I have to bear..

However, one evening in late April I was in the office reception collecting my fan mail from Bonita 'Bonnie' Blair, director Pete King's secretary. (Modesty would normally inhibit me from mentioning this strain on the GPO in W1, but it's an excuse to thank my readers for their unceasing stream of plaudits and may God bless you all.) I was trying to stuff this wodge of correspondence in my inadequately small briefcase when a figure, head down and in a hurry, brushed past me and disappeared into that windowless and airless cell laughingly called the office, an area which more resembles the left luggage at Waterloo station than an administration centre.

RETURN OF RONNIE

It was Ronnie, the first I'd seen of him for months. I quickly followed him in. He looked at me without any noticeable sign of enthusiasm, but this is just his way, y'know…

I thought a reminder of my name and function might be prudent with someone so notoriously forgetful.

'Name of Godbolt. Jim Godbolt. I edit your house magazine.'

'Oh, yes', he replied in a resigned fashion.

'That's a world-weary tone of voice,' I said.

'It's a world-weary guy you are looking at.'

'What's wrong Ronnie?'

'What's wrong? What's bloody right? I've been watching the news on TV. The Navy's steaming out to do battle with ships we've sold Argentina, and the Russians are backing a right wing fascist military junta. I shudder to think what the outcome will be.'

I nodded in agreement. With over a hundred years between us neither is susceptible to jingoistic elation.

The vibes were bad. Pete King quickly vacated the office. For all his tough exterior Pete's a sensitive soul and quick to conduct urgent business somewhere else in the Club when Ronnie is in a mood, but I, intrepid Scoops, had to see it through.

Ronnie sighed heavily and burped noisily. A civilised fellow is Ronnie, but he likes a good burp and that he's entitled to in his own office.

DON KINGSWELL

'Too many arbo-carbrodates, Ronnie?'

'You mean carbohydrates.'

Ronnie's hot on mispronunciation (and misspellings especially in this magazine).

'Yes, I was using one of Don Kingswell's most famous mispronunciations.'

'Don who?'

'Kingswell. He used to have an office above the Club Eleven in Windmill Street when he was managing Cy Laurie's trad band.'

'Ah, yes. Of course.' Another heavy sigh. 'That was a long time ago.'

'*Tempus Fugit* as Pete King would say.'

'Pete who?'

'Pete King. Your partner.'

'Oh yes, of course, how is he?'

'He was in the office only a minute ago'

'Really? My eyes are getting bad. Must get some new glasses. Isn't growing old awful?'

'Yes the maturing processes can have their own disadvantages. Age -related, they are called'

'Maturing processes my arse. We are decaying. Fast. Even sticking around with older people doesn't help anymore.'

I thought a little philosophical saw suitable for the occasion.

'It's sad, isn't it, that we all want to live longer but not get any older.'

'I hope you are not getting to trot out any more platitudes like that.'

He sighed an even bigger sigh, and looked glumly at the ceiling. I sighed and looked at the floor. Glumly. It was gloom, gloom, gloom.

'You are young today and old tomorrow,' I said now wallowing in the pain of it all.

'Who said that?'

'Me. I'll probably get credit for it

Illustration: Hedley Picton

when I join the great majority. There's no doubt about it, Ron, you've got to drink from the cup whilst it's overflowing or, as Kingswell would have put it 'scribble like copulating mad when there's plenty of lead in the pencil.' (Kingswell's actual words for use of youthful libido I can't possibly reproduce here).

BONNIE

'Jim, please! Our young lady Bonnie is just outside. A well brought up young lady. She wouldn't want to hear that sort of talk.'

'Young lady, Ronnie? YOUNG lady?! Heavens, I must get some new glasses as well.'

Ronnie put forefinger to lips, leaned forward and whispered, 'For Christ sake keep your voice down. I don't want her upset. She hears every word. She's got ears like a bassett hound's.'

He reached for his saxophone. Practising in that small room is the most effective way of terminating conversation with me, but ennui proved too strong and with the mother of all sighs he replaced the sax in its case.

Miss Blair bustled in, *retroussé* nose stuck high, which she depressed somewhat in my direction, sniffed as though I were something the cat had brought in, thrust some mail before Ronnie and departed without a word, though momentarily pausing to throw me a withering glance. Ronnie grimaced at me. 'You've upset her., I'll have to work like mad to get round her now. As if I haven't got enough problems.'

At that moment one of these appeared in the shape of a wild-eyed dishevelled figure. The previously crumpled Scott bristled with apprehension. The newcomer on the stage in the evening's drama was Ronnie's bassist, Ron Mathewson, a great player but not with us.

ENTRY OF RONNIE M

Now, Ronnie Scott himself distances himself as far from the grim realities of life as he can, but Ron Matthewson... why, he could be living on Mars between gigs with the Quintet. Although he's known me for twenty years or so he thinks I'm Jack Fallon. Bass player and agent/manager. Fallon is five feet seven, plump, balding, Canadian and all of eighty. I am six feet, lean, hirsute, English (Thank God!) and as for my age — put me down as twenty-nine plus.

'Where's the gig tonight, Ronnie?' enquired Matthewson.

'I've told you six times already,' snapped an irritable Scott. 'It's at the Royal Automobile Club, Pall Mall.'

'Where's that?' asked Ron M.

Eager to help, I started to give a route when Ronnie S. sharply interrupted: 'Please. Don't complicate matters with facts. It's fatal with him. He turned to the beaming Mathewson. 'Be here at nine sharp and I'll take you — lead you — down there.'

'Gee, thanks Ron. See you later. Nice to have seen you again, Jack,' and he departed as happy as a sandboy, as you might say. He had played a brief but telling part in the scenario.

Ronnie slumped back in the chair, and sadly shook his head, 'A great bass player, but...' his voice trailed away as if he couldn't summon words to describe the likeable but impossible Mathewson.

'What's on the box to cheer us up', he said, and forced himself from the chair to switch it on. Our luck! The show appearing on the screen was 'Family Fortunes' with Geoff Love and family, Bernie Winters and family and dog and, God help us, Bob Monkhouse. I am a diligent editor, I do my best to gather the thoughts of chairman Scott and nobly, I think, suffer the conditions under which I have to interview him, but this programme was more than I could reasonably stand.

I admit to having the lowest of moral fibre when it comes to watching and hearing Mr Monkhouse. I fled to the Dog and Duck up the road for a restorative pint of Burton and bumped straight into Ron Mathewson. He squinted at me as though unsure of my identity. I took the easy way out. I did my Jack Fallon imitation.   J.G.

WHISPERS, MURMURS & ASIDES

GREAT SAYINGS IN JAZZ

Some of these are probably apocryphal; others have been altered, sometimes improved on over the years; others have had the names of the principals transposed or substituted. However, they are yarns that bear re-telling and usually tell fundamental truths.

Lester Young did a gig with a mediocre trumpeter who enquired of Lester, 'Say, Prez, when was our last gig together?'

'Tonight', grunted Lester.

Jack Sheldon encountered fellow-trumpeter Chet Baker whose addictions were revealed in his lined and cadaverous features.

Sheldon: 'Say, Chet, where did you get those lines, man?'
Baker: 'They're laughter lines, man.'
Sheldon: 'Man, nothing's that funny.'

Pundit Max Harrison, reviewing editor Jim Godbolt's autobiography, *All This And Many A Dog* in the *Hampstead & Highgate Express*, enquired, 'Do we need more anecdotes about this dreary crew of boors, louts and hooligans?'

Cornettist Bobby Hackett was renowned, not only for his lyrical playing, but for not having a bad word to say about anyone. This facet of his nature intrigued a questioner who enquired of Bobby, 'What about Adolf Hitler then?'

Bobby reflected for a moment and replied, 'Well, I guess he was the best in his field.'

I am not one for high-pitched screeches on the trumpet and was pleased to read that Bobby once advertised a cornet for sale with the following words: 'Upper register entirely unused.'

CLARK 'CLARKY' TEWKSBURY

CRICKET AND JAZZ

The worlds of cricket and jazz would seem planets apart by a million light years. The first conjures up a picture of healthy, athletic chaps engaged in the contest between their bats and hard leather-cased balls, and a few pints in the pavilion when stumps are drawn. The second has the connotation of smoky dives, the participants in this subterranean world smoking substances, jokingly referred to as 'naughty- type African woodbines'.

But there are direct connections between these two worlds: both requiring unique skills from the players, involving concentration, coordination, spontaneous invention (with bat and ball) and to 'feel' the state of play. There are other similarities: a slow-scoring game that has its audience yawning in boredom or a band session that doesn't swing.

UNDERGRADUATE JAZZMEN

In the UK, the connection between cricket and jazz started as early as 1927, when band leader Fred Elizalde led a group of Cambridge University students, billed as his Cambridge Undergraduates and recorded for the Decca label.

The tenor saxophonist was Maurice Allom who was to play, as an amateur, with Sussex County Cricket Club and in 1930 made his debut in the England Test team taking a hat-trick with his fast bowling, in his first game, this against New Zealand in Auckland.

Allom recorded with Elizalde in 1929 and later in 1930, with another undergraduates band led by banjoist George Monkhouse.

In 1930 Elizalde led a band at the swank Savoy Hotel, Savoy Hill that included Americans Adrian Rollini (bass saxophone), Bobby Davis (alto and clarinet), Chelsea Quealey (trumpet) and recording extensively. Collectors items...

SPIKE HUGHES AND THE DECCA-DENTS

Another with Cambridge connections was bassist, composer Patrick 'Spike' Hughes who from 1930 to 1932 recorded a hundred titles for the Decca label, initially issued as Spike Hughes and his Decca-Dents, but a Decca executive though the 'decadent' associations unsuitable and the title was changed to 'Dance Orchestra'. At a time when there were no jazz clubs or concerts, very little jazz literature and only a few of American jazz recordings available, Hughes' band, comprised of jazz-minded dance band musicians, and how Hughes discovered their jazz ability in the climate of the time, we'll never know, as all, including Hughes, have died.

Hughes by Antony Wysard and Harry Hines, clarinettist with Hughes in 1930

Ravers CC, 1954: Left to right: Front: Frank Parr, Robin Rathborne, Wally Fawkes, Ray Smith; Rear: Pete Appleby, Bob Dawbarn, Jim Bray, Jim Godbolt, Mick Mulligan, Bruce Turner

In 1933 Hughes visited America and recorded fourteen titles with a band listed as Spike Hughes and his Negro Orchestra, but later changed, on LP issues, to Spike Hughes and his All American Orchestra. This sessions included trumpeters Shad Collins, Leonard Davis, Bill Dillard and Henry 'Red' Allen, saxophonists Benny Carter, Chu Berry and Coleman Hawkins, trombonist Dickie Wells and drummer Big Sid Catlett. Hughes played for Cambridge CCC — a minor county, but still county — cricket and the somewhat exclusive Lords Taverners. In 1954 he published an amusing book titled, *The Art of Coarse Cricket*.

In 1954 Lyn Dutton, Humphrey Lyttelton's manager, and Wally Fawkes, then Lyttelton's clarinettist, conceived, over William Younger's Scotch ale in the Blue Posts at the corner of Newman and Eastcastle Streets, off Oxford Street, a jazzman's eleven. This team included pianist George Webb, alto-saxophonist Bruce Turner, trumpeter Mick Mulligan, bassist Jim Bray, drummers Pete Appleby and Ray Smith (later founder of Ray's Jazz Shop in Shaftesbury Avenue), clarinettist Wally Fawkes, *Melody Maker* staffmen Max Jones and Bob Dawbarn and agent Jim Godbolt. The team was titled The Ravers, and lasted for fifty years, although the jazz element slowly dropped out. It was captained for twenty years by ex-Mick Mulligan trombonist Frank Parr, ex Lancashire CCC who was once tipped as an England Test wicket-keeper.

The team also included photographer Eric Jelly whose photographs frequently appeared in the *Melody Maker*. Eric was disabled and had one leg in an iron, but gamely overcame this impairment bowling off-breaks and batting with a 'runner'.

Throughout 1960s, band leader Vic Lewis, led a star-studded team comprised mainly of showbiz personalities, including Michael Parkinson. The Ravers played a fixture with Lewis and an umpire was a one-time clarinettist Harry Hines, who recorded with Spike Hughes in 1930 and later led a comedy band on the variety halls as Doctor Crock and his Crackpots. I wish I had quizzed Mr. Hines fully about

Jim Laker, Aussie tormentor, Ashes series 1956 and Tony Crombie from another world writing and recording *Laker's Day*

those days with Hughes, but he did tell me that the leader wanted him to play 'like Jimmy Dorsey'.

In the summer of 1956 England played five Tests against Australia and at Old Trafford, Manchester. Off-spinner bowler Jim Laker totalled nineteen wickets in that series, a record never achieved before or since.

LAKER'S DAY

The stunning feat helped to cinch victory over the *auld cricket* enemy — Australia. *JARS* contributor Alun Morgan, an architect by profession, but a highly respected authority on jazz old and new, watched the game on television and on that night of the achievement visited the Railway Arms, Hampstead, next to the Decca recording studio where Tony Crombie and band were recording, the line-up including Ronnie Scott and Tubby Hayes. Alun gave Tony the news of Laker's total and Crombie enquired, 'Is that good?' Alun elaborated on the feat. Tony replied, 'OK, I'll name one of the numbers as a tribute'. He called it *Laker's Day* and at the end of the number the whole band shouted 'owzat!', a corruption of the impassioned appeal 'How's that!' to the umpire by the bowler that will see the batsman trudging back to the pavilion.

JOHN BARNES'S OUTSWINGERS

For the past ten years a band led by one-time Lyttelton saxophonist, John Barnes, called the Outswingers, has

The Outswingers at Lords: from left: a represetative of Grey-Nicolls exhibiting the company's bat making equipment, Campbell Burnap, Ron Drake, John Barnes, Malcolm Harrison, Graham Read, Mike Cotton

played, during the lunch and tea intervals, on the Harris Green at Lords, the most famous cricket arena in the world. The personnel has changed over the years but a regular member is trombonist and radio presenter Campbell Burnap, ex-Acker Bilk. Campbell from 1960 was a regular Ravers member for over twenty years.

The Outswingers at one session included the American alto-saxophonist Spike Robinson, who was a regular at the seminal Club Eleven in the late forties. Spike was puzzled by the game as most Americans are. One of these I know found 'watching cricket is like watching celery grow'. The Outswingers have played at several benefits for professional cricketers and one session included bass saxophonist Harry Gold who asked John Barnes to sponsor him as member of the exclusive MCC. John told him there was an eighteen year wait to be a member and Harry replied, 'That's OK, I can wait'. He was seventy-five at the time and had he persisted with his application he, dying at the age of ninety-five, could have had two years wearing the much desired MCC tie.

John pinned the tunes they were going to play on adjacent trees, the titles given correctly but with also with cricket connections, such as *Willow Weep For Me* became 'Willow Sweep For Me', *You Go To My Head* – 'You Throw To My Head', *Red Sails in the Sunset* - 'Red Balls in the Sunset.'

Benny Green, a long time member of Ronnie Scott's bands published a massive volume entitled *The Wisden Book of Cricketers' Lives* and turned out for the Ravers CC.

HUMPHREY LYTTELTON

In the summer of 1936 a long standing fixture, Eton v. Harrow, took place at Lords (where else?), and attending the event was an Eton schoolmaster, George Lyttelton with his wife Pam and fifteen year old son Humphrey. The billing of the schools is alphabetical but no doubt, Eton would have insisted on the precedence. Half way throughout the game, Mrs Lyttelton and son left the ground and caught a taxi to Charing Cross Road to visit an instrument dealer. There the young Lyttelton was presented with a Deluxe Selmer trumpet. Payment, all of £4.50, was made by cheque, not the shop's usual practice, but the salesman, no doubt goggling at the young Lyttelton regally attired in the Eton uniform, must have realised that all was well financially. Mother and son returned to Lords, the son totally disinterested in the outcome of the game — and thinking about his new possession, made trips to the cloakroom to see if it was secure. Neither of the Lytteltons could have possibly visualised the eventual outcome of this purchase, Humph making a meteoric entry on the British jazz scene in 1947, commenced band leading in 1948 and this astonishing sixty years later, is still leading a band in addition to his broadcasting activities.

J.G.

The teenage Lyttelton in full Eton regalia

HERBERT COOT LETTERS

(The correspondence between Herbert Coot and Ronnie Scott, with apologies to The Henry Root Letters by William Donaldson)

10th March, 1988
Dear Mr Scott,

My father, Herbert Coot, and I were having one of our devotedly filial conversations over breakfast and he suggested that I write to you.

I was embarrassed to note in a letter to yourself that father quoted me as referring to your sessions as 'old folks nights', and repeating my amazement that you and your group get about without sticks, don't wear glasses, nor require assistance to mount the bandstand.

I do hope that you were not offended, but since my sentiments have been made known I would like to reiterate my admiration for you all and as you appear to be the oldest, may I enquire the secret of you being so active in your longevity. I would very much like to adopt the same regime.

Yours sincerely,
Wally Coot

17th March, 1988
Dear Wally,

I don't suppose your parents realised when they gave you your Christian name how appropriate a choice they made...

However, I'm one for helping the young in any way I can, and here is my regime. At 2 p.m. I commence my exercises: struggling to get out of bed; attempt after attempt on some afternoons and many a lesser person would give up and go back to sleep, but I like to do my share of the chores at the Club and I usually succeed in dressing at about 2.30 p.m.

My next experience in constantly pressing the clutch and accelerator and brake pedals in my car in the start-jerk-stop pattern of road travel in the journey from Chelsea to the Club. This keeps my extremities in good nick, enabling me to spring to the stand for the quintet's sets.

Once at the Club, I attend to the mountain of correspondence and answering some of the letters we get keeps me mentally agile. Like for instance,

The health-conscious Ronnie topping up his daily tar intake

a letter from a lady who said she enjoyed her visit very much, but objected to the peas she ordered as part of her meal. I had to summon the peas manager who reminded me that on the night in question he was attending a *petit pois* conference in Brussels. I had a little trouble in phrasing a reply to that lady but – a healthy mind in a healthy body – I made it eventually.

Your father once complimented me on the elegant script I used to chalk out our forthcoming attractions on the foyer notice board. Setting this out keeps my fingers — not to mention my artistic sensibilities — in trim, but naturally, I get a minion to clean off the previous lettering. It just wouldn't do for a man in my position to be seen doing the dirty work. Another factor that contributes to my glowing health is playing the saxophone. To many, this would appear as mere twiddling. Ok, but a forty minute session adds up to a lot of twiddles — and I'm standing up during this mammoth twiddle. True, I suffer trouble with my back, but that came of bending over backwards to please Stan Getz when he played at the Club ravishing us with his music and driving us mad with his tantrums. Despite these back problems I had to exercise my spine bowing to roaring applause from our audiences and bending over to sign autographs which now are probably worth a bob or two.

As for diet, I maintain a steady intake of stodge at Mama's Café, Old Compton Street, and if this surprises you (or, indeed any health faddist reading this) I'll explain.

I was on the road for yonks, travelling in a cramped, unheated bus and eating at a succession of grease-houses, one of which, on the A1, produced fare in nauseating conditions that could stand as a monument to the human body's capacity for punishment. I've been immune to almost every disease since.

Yes, I smoke forty cigarettes a day, but stubbing these out keeps my wrist muscles supple and stamping on fags in the street strengthens my toe muscles, enabling me to sprint to the bookmakers when I get a hot tip. My leg muscles are fully toned by running to the bookmakers to put money on absolute certs.

Now, for a most important bit of advice. Always, whenever and wherever, get others to peel your grapes. Some cynics I know call it the art of delegation, but it saves vital energy getting others to do the mundane chores, leaving your strength for the vitally important tasks. If you arrive at a position of authority, as I have, kick up hell to get the minions scuttling.

All this explains, I hope, how it is that at sixty-one I have the body of a man of fifty-nine, look no more than sixty, and may you grow old as gracefully and athletically as I have.

As for the rest of the chaps, they don't have to keep themselves so fit. Martin Drew, my drummer, John Critchinson, my pianist, and Ron Matthewson, my bassist, sit down for their efforts. OK, my trumpeter Dick Pearce, stands up to play, but he's the baby in the side, and he has only got a few valves to push. Nothing very tiring in that.

Ron, I must say, is the one that displays the most agility — sprinting to the bar at the end of sets and with split-second timing, manages to return the moment we resume. His right elbow is probably the most exercised in the business and his gullet muscles are in excellent shape.

Yours sincerely,

Ronnie Scott

PS. Your father used to send a little something with his letter.

Editor's footnote:

In truth, Ronnie got breathless playing chess.

Slawkenbergius

On a sunny day in April, the seductive indications of Spring treacherously enticed this hack to venture abroad without his overcoat, and to suffer a bitter wind penetrating old bones. I sought the warming of the cockles in the Three Greyhounds, 24, Greek Street, run by Ms Roxy Beaujolais, and who should I see there but our editor, James Charles Godbolt, hunched over a glass of amber-coloured fluid?

'My heart-starter, old son. Well, thanks a lot, I don't mind if I do,' as his hand automatically reached for the refill quickly supplied by Ms Beaujolais, who looked at me for the mazuma.

'You look peeved. Aggravations?', I solicitously enquired.

'Of course, old son. A day without aggro is a bonus day, and there are not too many of those about.'

I had a female on the phone this morning, asking for a Mr. Godbod. GODBOD! When they get your name wrong, old son, they're assuredly on the scrounge. This time it was a photo for free, and for a mag with a massive circulation'. We don't have a budget for music pictures, she said. I corrected her on the name bit, and was told that she didn't know me from Adam. And I don't know you from Eve, I countered, quick as a flash. What a liberty!'

'Then I had a guy on the phone whom I've repeatedly plugged, but he got the needle because I didn't run a story he sent me after we had gone to press. Then there was someone on the blower who announced himself as the 'Chairperson' of an organisation he wanted me to mention. I told him the Events column was full and he enquired, 'Then why can't you put our news on another page?' *Chutzpah*, old son. There's an awful lot of it about.'

'Anything else?', I gratuitiously enquired.

'Yes, old son, there is. There's a best-seller out at the moment called *The Daily Telegraph Book of Obituaries*, in which I have an obit on the Baroness Nica de Koenigswarter, friend of Charlie Parker and Thelonious Monk, but no credit given, no money paid and not even a complimentary copy. I tell you, it's hard being a hack.'

'How are you getting on with your new state-of-the-art computer?' I asked. A silly question.

'Don't ask, old son. It's a case of old dogs and new tricks. It's playing me up no end. It keeps admonishing me. Any day I expect it to say, 'Why's an old fart like you attempting to grapple with sophisticated equipment?'

I did an obit on dear old Spike Mackintosh, ending it with, 'He is survived by wife Diana, and sons Nick, Robert and Cameron, the latter a famous theatre impresario.' Blow me, the wretched instrument addressed me thus, and I kid you not!

'Gender-specific. A gender-neutral word like spouse may be appropriate. Would you believe it? I buy a machine to print my profundities and it gives me effing lectures in political correctness.'

But enough of human frailties and idiosyncracies of computers, It's not a perfect world. You can quote me on that profundity if you wish. Now, there's something I've been going to talk to you about for some time. It's your moniker of Slawkenbergius. People have trouble in pronouncing it. And it sounds foreign. Not that I've anything against foreigners, even though most couldn't play a straight bat to save their lives. I want something more English. What about a double-barrelled job like Montgomery-Heyworth? Aubrey Montgomery-Heyworth. That will go down well with our readers in the Shires. No? You don't fancy that? What about Valentine Cunningham. No, we can't use that. It's someone's real name. I've got it. Lance Fairfax! Lance FAIRFAX. It's got a nice English ring to it. It conjures up a clean-limbed, square-jawed, gimlet-eyed sort of chap who plays a straight bat, who doesn't funk the bouncers and walks when he gets an edge and is caught behind.' So, from now on, I'm Lance Fairfax. What's in a name, anyway?

Editor Jim Godbolt seen enjoying a joke with trombonist Jim Shepherd

BIRD, the film, reviewed by BARRY FOX

The Clint Eastwood-directed film had its British premiere in Warner West End Cinema, Leicester Square, WC2, Nov 25th 1988. Barry Fox, technical journalist, is a frequent contributor to *New Scientist* on matters audio and video, and broadcasts regularly on BBC Radio 2,3 and 4.

Jazz biopics come and jazz biopics go. Most, like that well known porno classic *Young Man With A Horn** — which has Kirk Douglas miming to Harry James pretending to be Bix Beiderbecke — are long gone and best forgotten.

Others, like the Glenn Miller and Benny Goodman stories, are fun to watch on a wet afternoon. You can laugh at the clichés, enjoy some of the music and try to spot the few historical facts among the fiction.

Clint Eastwood's new film, *Bird*, about Charlie Parker, is by no means perfect but it may well go down in history as the best biopic of them all — and create a whole new audience for Parker's music.

In the meantime Eastwood's film will surely disappoint anyone who queues in the rain expecting to see Dirty Harry or close-ups of dirty needles and ulcered arms. There's virtually no sex or violence. Even the crooked cop, who tries to sell Bird back his cabaret card for the price of a few names of suppliers, rings true.

'ALBINO' RED RODNEY

For legal reasons, there's no Miles Davis, and the young Dizzy is depicted as Mr Straight and Clean. The sequences with 'Albino' Red Rodney in the South are both funny and frank. The portrayals of Chan Parker and Nica de Koenigswarter feel right. The fact that Rodney, Dizzy, Nica, Chan all offered special thanks is an encouraging sign. If they had quarrelled with the film their names would not be on the credits.

Clint Eastwood, who both produced and directed, faced a very real technical problem. Parker died before studios started using hi-fi stereo tape recorders. So all the material available is in mid- or low-fi mono. And there never has been, and never will be, anyone who can mimic Bird's sound and fluency with sufficient accuracy to sound authentic on modern re-recording.

Bird by Pennington

LENNIE NIEHAUS

So Eastwood hired Lennie Niehaus to score a modern accompaniment for Parker's original solos — some from issued recordings, and others from off-air recordings and private tapes now owned by Chan Parker.

With modern recordings it is easy to extract solos and mix them with new accompaniment. This is because today's recordings are made on multi-track tape, with different instruments covered by different microphones and recorded on separate tracks. This is how pop stars manage to turn out a faultless recording in a studio, when they could not hope to give a similar performance live. An incompetent's vocal track can be doctored, over-dubbed, edited and rerecorded as many times as necessary to create totally artificial perfection.

But where the full sound of a band has been captured by a few microphones, connected directly to a mono (or stereo) tape recorder, it is theoretically impossible to extract one musical instrument from the mix without affecting the others. One thing you can do, as happened with the famous 1953 *Buck Clayton Jam Session on Robin's Nest*, is cut and splice different takes together to lengthen (or shorten) playing time.

TEN YEARS AGO

Ten years ago Pierre Michelot helped graft the guitar choir, Guitar Unlimited onto original recordings made by Django Reinhardt and the Hot Club Quintet between 1947 and 1953. Eastwood wanted more; Parker's solos with modern accompaniment. Lennie Niehaus hired Ray Brown, Ron Carter, Monty Alexander, Barry Harris, Johnny Guerin, Charles McPherson, John Faddis, Red Rodney and others to record new material. He also brought in engineer Robert Fernandez to try and blend the new material with Bird's original solo sound.

TECHNICAL PROBLEMS

The first step was to copy the original Parker recordings on to a modern digital studio recorder. Niehaus used a 32 track Mitsubishi recorder, because this digital format is very popular in Hollywood. He then tapped out a click track using a gadget like a hand operated metronome. This click track, which sounds like a pair of drum sticks tapped together in time with the music, was recorded on another track of the tape alongside the Parker original.

The click track was necessary because the original recordings were often live, and the tempo varied. The easiest way to stick to a strict tempo, or follow a changing tempo, is to listen to a metronome guide. Film and session musicians do it all the time, and all ten musicians hired by Niehaus work in this field — for them, following a click track is second nature.

Fernandez arranged the musicians close together, as they would play in a night club, to give a feel similar to the original recording. They listened to the click track through headphones while playing the completely fresh accompaniments which Niehaus had scored after analysing Parker's solos. He used old microphones for a period sound.

---

*The Kirk Douglas film title was changed by British distributors to *Young Man of Music*. Based on Dorothy Baker's book *Young Man with a Horn,* this title was thought unsuitable for British ears. Allegedly the story was based on the life of cornettist Bix Beiderbecke.

What ended up on a tape was the original Parker sound and completely new accompaniments recorded on separate tracks.

APPARENTLY IMPOSSIBLE TASK

This still left Fernandez with the apparently impossible task of stripping away the original Parker rhythm section before blending in the new accompaniment. He also had to suck out nightclub crowd noise and background snap, crackle, pop and hiss from the forty year-old discs and tapes.

For this he used parametric equalizers. They are like the tone controls on a hi-fi system, but they act on very narrow frequency bands.

The simplest kind of tone control, as found on cheap hi-fi systems, simply rolls off or boosts high notes while leaving low notes untouched — or vice versa. More expensive hi-fis have equalisers which attack narrower bands of sound. A professional parametric equaliser is narrower still. It can boost the level of one musical note while leaving the note next door on the scale untouched.

TRIAL AND ERROR

With a great deal of trial and error, it was possible to find the control settings which left Parker's saxophone sound — around the middle of the frequency range — more or less untouched.

This went a long way towards isolating the Parker sax sound from the backing rhythm section. But inevitably some of the sax sound overlapped with the old accompaniment, so removing the accompaniment was affecting the Parker sax sound which Eastwood was so anxious to preserve.

Fernandez thus played the very clever trick of re-shaping

the Parker solos after they had been stripped from the backing track. He did this by boosting some frequencies in the stripped sax sound to make it sound like Bird again.

Some recordings, for instance *Lester Leaps In*, varied so much in audio quality on the original, that individual bars of the music had to be doctored separately. And some original Parker recordings, made in night clubs, had so much background noise on them that it was impossible to remove. So Niehaus and Fernandez simply added extra crowd noise in stereo to mask the original.

Adding the sound of a new bright rhythm section in hi-fi stereo also helped mask any lingering traces of the rather dull mono original. And mixing in a touch of echo to the mix of old and new complemented the effect.

There are times when Parker's sax solos sound rather boxy, compared with the modern rhythm section — and in some cases the string section. And noticeable is the drummer seen playing a ride cymbal and heard on hi-hat. Doubtless saxophonists will be able to pick holes in the fingering of Forest Whitaker who plays Bird.

But on the whole it's a remarkable and respectful achievement. Anyone who feels inclined to pick nits should stop and think just how awful the film could have been if funded by someone less sympathetic to the music than Clint Eastwood.

WHISPERS, MURMURS & ASIDES

PUFF-UPS BEHIND THE PAVILION?

Now that I'm too old to act the flannelled fool, I relive golden days cavorting on the green sward by avidly reading cricket books.

One of these was The Willow Want, a volume debunking cricket myths, by Derek Birley, in which he refutes Neville Cardus's more extravagant musical analogies with our summer game, and so doing asserts, 'In fact the cricketer is more like a jazz soloist than either Mozart or his interpreter, improvising as well as performing and his art as ephemereal as that of Louis Armstrong'.

Louis Armstrong's art 'ephemeral'? Ephemeral? HERESY. The live performance — yes. But Mr. Birley, Rector of Ulster Polytechnic when he wrote this book,

is surely overlooking the vast treasury of recordings made by the immortal Louis.

It's the common belief that our great summer game is played by square-jawed, gimlet-eyed, clean-limbed chaps, doing their best for their country, or the old country (and a pound or two) and it came as a shock to see the following photograph and caption in A Spell From Laker by the late Jim Laker, formerly of Surrey and England.

What?!! Naughty-type African woodbines?!! Puff-ups behind the pavilion? I could scarcely believe my eyes! What would those disciplinarian amateur captains of yore. Lord Hawke, W.G. Grace and Douglas Jardine, have thought?

In their day, amateurs and professionals occupied separate dressing rooms and used different gates and the world a better place for it, I say.

It was something of a relief that I realised the caption referred to bruised finger-joints, an occupational hazard for custodians of the stumps. Indeed it was a relief, Jazz musicians, creatures of the night in fug-filled dens having a joint — yes — but chaps in flannels… it doesn't bear thinking about…

LANCE FAIRFAX

HUMPHREY LYTTELTON

Humphrey Lyttelton was eight-six on 23rd of May of 2007. Trumpeter, clarinettist, composer, cartoonist, author, broadcaster and genuine wit, he is also a calligraphist (his own label is called Calligraph), plays piano and alto horn and is an expert on ornithology – an extraordinarily talented man who has fully exercised his inborn gifts.

A truly exceptional character; a scion of an ancient aristocratic family, who went to Eton College (his father, George, was a master there) who became a jazz trumpeter and is now in his fifty-third year as a bandleader. Apart from considerable ability on his instruments, his aristocratic background was undoubtedly a great boost to his becoming a household name, and in his highly entertaining first volume of autobiography, aptly titled *I Play As I Please*, he acknowledges the publicity value of a background not usually associated with jazz musicians. Most bandleaders had to look for angles to publicise themselves, but his was ready-made.

His band-leading debut was at the Wood Green Jazz Club, North London in February 1948. It was a strictly traditional group, as Lyttelton had been converted to the New Orleans faith by playing with George Webb's Dixielanders, the pioneer New Orleans-style band in Britain, from April to November 1947. A personal recollection: I was the manager of the Dixielanders and in early 1947 we learned of this exceptional trumpeter playing in a North London pub.

FIRST EVER LONDON CONCERT APPEARANCE

The Dixielanders were the promoters of monthly concerts in central London under the title of the Hot Club of London, organised by myself, and we booked Lyttelton to appear as a guest with a pick-up band on one of these – all players unknown to him — on 8th March, 1947. He was a sensation. In April that year, the Dixielanders were booked for an engagement in Hawick in the Scottish Borders, a mere 400-odd miles away. The lead trumpeter, Reg Rigden, couldn't make the trip and I approached Lyttelton at the Camberwell School of Art, where he was studying, and he agreed to play the gig. The fee was a princely £7 — he didn't bat an eyelid at the prospect of an 800-mile journey there and back for seven quid. The band was booked because the promoter thought that they were — and I quote — 'darkies'. This gig led to his joining the Dixielanders, where I became acquainted with this tall trumpeter's considerable ego.

A self-portrait by Humph following his Middle East tour in 1979 recounted in his book *Why No Beethoven?*, published by Robson Books.

Humphrey was never a Hooray Henry, but had a most imperious manner. It was inevitable that he would leave the Dixielanders to form his own band. No Gentleman Ranker he. A member of that band was clarinettist Wally 'Trog' Fawkes, formerly a founder member of the Dixielanders, which commenced a twelve year association. 'Humph 'n Wally' was a familiar tag.

HUMPH'S SAXOPHONE BAND

Lyttelton gained an enormous — by jazz standards — following with his New Orleans-orientated policy, but in the mid-to late 1950s he bravely jettisoned this policy, disgusting and disturbing his mouldy fygge followers, who bitterly resented his incorporation of the hated saxophone. Such was their hostility to change that when Lyttelton appeared at a concert in Birmingham with Bruce Turner on alto saxophone, they were confronted with a banner, spread across several seats, which read: 'Go home, dirty bopper'. Such was the intensity of partisan feeling about jazz styles in those heady days. Lyttelton later engaged a variety of young bloods stylistically different from himself — Tony Coe, Joe Temperley, Kathy Stobart, Tony Mann, Dave Green, Mick Pyne, Chris Pyne, John Surman and Alan Barnes — but his style remained essentially rooted in Armstrong. Financially it was a costly exercise for Lyttelton. But, characteristically, he stuck to his guns, typical of a man who eloquently rationalised every move that he made and was not one to brook criticism.

Lyttleton at Hot Club

THE Hot Club of London is presenting the new Humphrey Lyttleton Band at its concert this Saturday, March 8 at King George's Hall, Great Russell Street, W.C.1.

Humphrey Lyttleton, outstanding jazz cornettist who also plays clarinet and piano, leads a group comprising Eddie Harvey (ex-Webb's Dixielanders) on trombone; Jerry Collins (clt.); Dick Denny (gtr.); Harry Aubrey (bass); Tim Moora (pno.); and Roy Wykes (drums).

Completing the bill are James Asman and the George Webb Dixielanders.

Cutting from *Melody Maker* advertising The Hot Club of London with Lyttelton's name misspelt — a constantly recurring experience for the Old Etonian.

Lyttelton did not like critics, but this didn't stop him from becoming one, writing pithy articles in the *Melody Maker* and *New Musical Express*, in whose pages he slagged off pundits, band agents, club and concert promoters, musicians (some of whom had played in his band) and the BBC, for which he was working. There were no targets barred for this loose cannon. Apart from his autobiography, he wrote several informative volumes under the heading of *The Best of Jazz*, where he displayed an acute perception of the jazzmen he most admired.

THE BEST OF JAZZ

His programme on Radio 2, also called *The Best of Jazz*, has been running for over thirty years and is noted for its witty commentary — delivered in that mellifluous voice — and his thorough research, but in recent years he has mellowed. The caustic asides have now been largely replaced by superlatives about people he had previously demolished, particularly in regard to the Tradders, because when he abandoned the traditional line-up, a corollary of his stylistic changes was to condemn those playing the music he had forsaken himself. Lyttelton is a man of considerable integrity, but he has made many twists and turns in his critical pronouncements over the years.

It could be said that he is not a leopard to change his spots but he's become adept at covering them up, but the old acid triumphantly emerged from occasionally. One Monday evening Humph announced, 'You will not be hearing this programme next Monday as an event of supreme, global significance takes place. It is Mick Jagger's birthday, but let me be the first to wish him many happy returns.'

He is a person I have admired more than I have liked — if you've been on the rough end of his tongue it's an experience you don't forget, but I am grateful to him for writing in Punch that he thought my autobiography, *All This and 10%*, the funniest book on jazz he had ever read, a compliment I treasure. This, furthermore, from a man about whom I had made several uncomplimentary remarks in that volume. He wrote me a very nice letter following the book's publication, which was sort of confessional, saying that his manner can be put down to acute shyness, that he would prefer to face 2000 people in a concert hall with a trumpet in his hand than to enter a room containing just half a dozen.

Humph is still touring and, if his health and lip hold out, there's no reason why he shouldn't carry on for many more years. I sincerely hope that he does, for he has made, in his music, his writing and his broadcasting, an important contribution to the British jazz scene.   J.G.

Slawkenbergius

One hot July day, I was having my modest half pint of Adnam's Best at the Three Greyhounds, 25 Greek Street, run by the statuesque Roxy Beaujolais, from Sydney, Orstrylia, and a one-time stalwart of Ronnie's door staff, when in walked our editor. Ms. Beaujolais automatically went for a certain optic, poured a measure, placed it in front of Mr. G., and looked at me for the dosh. *Plus ça change!*

'You look a bit peaky,' I said solicitously.

'So would you be if you'd had my sort of morning. Bloody technology! The Word Processor did a moody on me and I had to scrabble through the vegetable scrapings, empty plonk bottles and yoghurt cartons in the trash bin to retrieve my original longhand jottings and drafts. Give me the quill and pewter pot of ink, old son. You know where you are with these. Then the CD packed up on me. Give me your wind-up gramophone and steel needles, soft, medium and loud, and lovely old 78s. Again, you knew where you were.'

'And that's not all, old son. I popped into the Nellie Dean to enquire after Bill Colyer's health and found him, verbally speaking, in the pink. Spout uttered more words in half an hour than you'll find in *War and Peace* and the *Decline and Fall of The Roman Empire* put together. That man was vaccinated with

a gramophone needle. I staggered out into Dean Street and almost immediately met up with a Soho pest —that infernal jolly boy who stops total strangers in the street and exhorts them to smile: 'Come on', he says, 'Cheer up, *smile*, today's smile day.'

'Bloody cheek! Inflicting his ghastly bonhomie on all and sundry. If people want to walk around looking miserable, that's their business. They don't need a jollifier to tell them what to do. And what is there to smile at? The West Indians have just given us a dreadful trouncing at Edgbaston; they're still conducting atom bomb tests. I could go on.'

I nodded to Ms Beaujolais to refill the editor's tumbler and reached south for more dosh.

'That's very decent of you old son. It takes the edge off the pain,' and I continued on my rounds leaving Roxy to undgergo an occupational hazard — listening to a good old moan.

'Hear me talking to ya!' 'Spout' Colyer giving the Editor an ear-bashing. Illustration by Trog

FASCINATING RHYTHM (G. AND I. GERSHWIN)

by ALAN PLATER

Writers are obsessive about credits. Many of them are equally so about jazz. There is little to chose between filling the blank sheet of paper and playing a thirty-two bar solo. Only the time scale is different. The musician is expected to deliver instant brilliance; the writer can rub it all out and try an alternate take. However, for most writers, the delivery date was last week, so the desperation factor is about the same. The jazz obsession seems to be international. Last November I was part of a writers' Seminar in Lisbon, aimed at brainwashing young Portuguese screenwriters into good habits. Over supper, a fellow-panellist, Carlos Saboga, a Portuguese writer now living in France, initiated a game of: 'Who would we all like to be if we were born again?'

'The Duke', I replied, without hesitation.

'Eric Dolphy', said Carlos, 'except I like to sing as well, so maybe I should be a piano player'.

We all have to live out our fantasies the best way we can but the lovely thing about writing is that without leaving the desk you can be Eric Dolphy and you can sing at the same time and even if the audience doesn't know what you're on about, it's still better than going out to a proper job. Does anybody under the age of thirty remember proper jobs?

THE LAST TIME I SAW PARIS (KERN/HAMMERSTEIN)

Whatever decisions are made as a result of the Great Debate about the future of the BBC, one thing is vital: a preservation order should be placed on Derek Drescher, provider of fine jazz programmes to the Nation. Derek spent over a decade in charge of 'Desert Island Discs' so he's paid his dues. He recently asked me to introduce a concert recorded at the Glasgow Festival by Carla Bley's Very Big Band. He also suggested I interview the band-leader; unfortunately, the nearest she was going to be to London was Paris, where she was on tour with her partner, Steve Swallow,

a highly talented guitarist and a very sweet guy.

'A day trip to Paris', I said. 'Well, it sounds tough but I think we should take it on'.

The concert and the interview were broadcast on December 5th 1992. The point of the story is the entry in my diary, which reads: 'Paris with Carla'. Since all my personal papers will eventually find their way into the Hull University archive, result of a long-ago agreement in a bar with the late Phillip Larkin, that entry should give the historians something to ponder over on wet afternoons a hundred years from today.

I should also report an off-mike conversation with Carla and Steve, which ran:

'You've never played Ronnie's, have you'

'No, but we'd love to'.

'I'll put in a word when I get home'.

Another pledge honoured.

The dear departed past (Frishberg)

If the Editor has kept his word, this piece should appear in the same issue of *JARS* as my review of the new NYJO album, *These Are the Jokes*. I mention this because normally I go to great lengths to avoid being mistaken for a critic. The last time I reviewed anything with a musical content was back in the 1950s when I was failing to learn to be an architect in Newcastle. I was asked to review a student production of a Gilbert and Sullivan opera. I struck a deal that ran: 'Let me know who's in it and, providing I don't have to go, I'll give it a rave review'.

It's a very good system.

I'm now going to break the rule again and in the process, maim two birds with one stone.

From time to time people ask me whether there are going to be any more Beiderbecke series. The answer is that following in-depth discussions with James Bolam and Barbara Flynn we agreed to quit while we were still ahead. However, the third novel, *The Beiderbecke Connection*, was published by Methuen last year in conditions of great secrecy. It's a bit over-priced but otherwise it's a nice book; and that, to the best of my knowledge, is the first review that has appeared in print anywhere.

Alan Plater by Mark Herman

UNTIL THE REAL THING COMES ALONG (CAHN/CHAPLIN/FREEMAN)

My good friend, Bruce Crowther, recently occupied this column and catalogued many of the evils that beset the professional writer, but overlooked one vital element in the picture; the noble art of procrastination — constructive ways of postponing work. In the mid-60s I heard Mel Torme (acute) at a concert refer to an imaginary LP called 'Lawrence

Welk Plays Thelonious Monk', and — since all writers are thieves— I've been playing the game ever since: inventing album titles. For example: 'The Western Brothers at Newport'; 'Sing-Along-A-Mingus'; 'Billy 'Uke' Scott — The Famous Massey Hall Concert'; 'The Complete Blue Note Recordings of Harry Lester and his Hayseeds'.

It's a beautiful game because it is totally devoid of all meaning and purpose and can last for days. It's very like cricket except that anyone can join in, regardless of breeding and background, and you don't have to wear advertising logos.

DON'T BE THAT WAY (SAMPSON/GOODMAN/PARISH)

Another factor that links writers and jazz musicians is their love of ancient and bleak jokes, providing the bad taste is sincere and deeply-felt.

A story that circulated in our trade a few years ago (these days everything happened a few years ago) concerned an actor who turned up late for rehearsals at the Royal court Theatre. He said to the director:

'I'm sorry I'm late, duckie, but my father died this morning, the baby's been sick all night and my wife's left me'.

'Oh, my God', said the director, 'it's just like life, isn't it, sweetie?'

Stay cool. Love you madly.

Alan Plater has been writing for radio, television, theatre and cinema since 1961. Jazz-tinged work includes. The Beiderbecke trilogy and Misterioso — in book and television form — a jazz chamber opera. Prez, written with the late Bernie Cash and the stage musical, rent Party for the Theatre Royal, Stratford East. He is President of the Writer's Guild of Great Britain which, he claims, makes him a distant relative of Lester Young, and the front-of-house staff at Ronnie's make jokes about his anorak.

THE TALE OF TWO EDWARDS
ONE 'THE DUKE', THE OTHER A DUKE-TO-BE...

In June 1933, two Dukes (though one was yet to be titled such), both with the Christian name of Edward, met up at a party given by newspaper magnate Lord Beaverbrook at his palatial Stornoway House, set just behind St James's Street, one of the most exclusive thoroughfares in London.

Duke Ellington and his Famous Orchestra played a week at the London Palladium, booked as a 'variety act' along with singers, acrobats, jugglers and the infamous 'blue' comedian Max Miller who was banned from broadcasting on the BBC on account of his double-entendre jokes.

A somewhat bewildered band of black musicians attended an otherwise all-white gathering including many titled people, one of which was the Duke of Kent, the party being a tribute to Ellington and his men, who played a late-night session.

TOFFS ON THE DRUMS

Another guest was Edward, Prince of Wales who, like many a toff — and a very highly placed one in this case — liked to 'have a go on the drums'. Almost any drummer who has played Hooray Henry gigs will tell you of occasions when he has had to surrender his kit to an aristo, the poor owner looking on in anguish as his kit was savaged. It is one of the facts of British social history that Hoorays never wanted to 'have a go' on brass or reed instruments, although sometimes the string bass came in for a hammering from a blue blood wanting to 'have a go on that big thing'.

'Having a go' on Ellington drummer Sonny Greer's kit at the party was His Royal Highness, the Prince of Wales, due, by the grace of God, to become King, Defender of the Faith of the United Kingdom of Great Britain and Ireland, Emperor of India and of the British Dominions beyond the seas.

According to Edward Kennedy 'Duke' Ellington, HRH 'wasn't just Little Lord Fauntleroy drumming! He had a hell of a Charleston beat', but Ellington was surprised to see a royal drinking gin, this considered a low-life drink in America. Gin mills and all that.

As brandy and champagne as well as gin were consumed by Sonny and the Prince of Wales, and both, it was alleged, got 'high', HRH was addressing Sonny as 'Sonny' and Sonny was calling the prince 'The Whale'.

This must have been a piquant moment overhearing the conversation between a black drummer, a second-class citizen in his own country, and the intended future King of England. In 1936 Edward abdicated to be relegated to a mere Duke — the Duke of Windsor — and the rest is history.   J.G.

Inset: Edward the Prince of Wales, to be the Duke of Windsor after abdication. Main photo: Ellington band arrival in London, 9th June, 1933. The white man (in the centre) is impresario Jack Hylton

BRIEF ENCOUNTERS memories from the Club
by JIMMY PARSONS

In the mid-1960s, when I joined the staff, the Club had been established for a number of years already — they had moved from Gerrard Street into Frith Street. It was a challenging time for Ronnie and Pete and all who worked there, but I recall everybody sharing the same ambition and dedication as the two partners. It was a fun place to work in and when anybody got tired or stressed there was always Ronnie's humour to keep us going. It was Pete who felt the death of Ronnie most; not only was he Pete's partner but his best and closest friend. He has kept the place going since that awful day and it is a tribute to his strength, tenacity and courage that we can celebrate this forty-fifth birthday.

JUDY GARLAND

At the outbreak of the Second World War in 1939, along with several thousand kids from London, I was evacuated, and was sent with my sister to so-called foster parents in Taunton, Somerset. It was not a very happy experience, but I was taken to the cinema for the first time and saw The Wizard of Oz starring Judy Garland. It was love at first sight and I became a life-long fan.

During the late 1960s the Club would open on some Sunday evenings and it was on one of those (both Pete and Ronnie were absent) when she and her new husband appeared at the door. Although she was instantly recognisable, I was shocked by her appearance. She looked very frail and ill, but very happy. I greeted them both and escorted them to their table. We chatted for a while and she wanted to know all about the great musicians who played at the Club, and seemed to know a lot about us. She was very friendly and warm and seemed genuinely touched when I recounted how I had seen her in the cinema all those years ago and how it had affected me. I sent them a bottle of champagne on the house (sorry, Pete) and they left about two hours later. I put them in a cab and we shook hands. She promised to come back. A week later Judy Garland was dead.

LUNAR MOMENTS

While meeting Judy Garland and her husband was sheer delight, there have been nights when the encounters have not been so pleasant and, believe it or not – and it took me some time to realise this – that these coincided with the full moon! A cosmic force that always caused us bother.

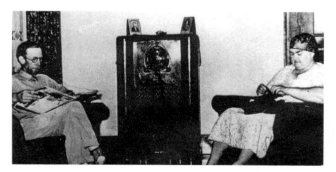

Typical Ronnie Scott's Club members having a quiet night at home

BEN WEBSTER

That great tenor saxophonist Ben Webster came to the Club to play for a month and then went on the road for a series of one-nighters. He brought with him the instruments of his newly-found hobby, photography. He had all the equipment money could buy including two expensive cameras, lenses and so on, and went about snapping everything in sight. After he had finished his engagement at the Club we went out on the road together and one of the places we visited was Coventry. I had told Ben something of the history of the city and how it had been devastated during the war and its ancient cathedral destroyed. I promised to take him to the new Cathedral so he could take some pictures. He was very excited at the prospect. We first visited the ruins and then walked around the outside of the new building with Ben snapping away happily. As we approached the main door we noticed a large sign saying 'NO PHOTOGRAPHY ALLOWED INSIDE'. Ben paused, looked at the sign and mumbled, 'We'll see about that.' Inside the church we joined the queue just starting to make the tour down the left aisle towards the high altar. As Ben pointed his camera at the altar a very small monk stepped in front of him to remind him of the 'no photography' rule. Exasperated, Ben shuffled down the aisle with the other visitors while the little monk kept bobbing up to make sure his warning had been heeded. As we reached the magnificent altar, Ben's frustration boiled over. 'Jim,' he bellowed, 'that little motherf***r's still watching me!'

Sad to say, one afternoon when Ben was rehearsing at the Club, somebody broke into his room and stole all his equipment. It was probably the monk!

AN UNEXPECTED GUEST

It was a cold and windy February night some time between midnight and 1 am. The street outside the Club was empty of passers-by and even the Italian coffee bars were deserted. Not more than fifty people remained in the Club. It was one of those nights you get mid-week early in the New Year; to put it mildly, it was quiet. The door staff had wandered back towards the warmer air of the Club, always keeping an eye on me (or so they said). I sat behind my desk and gazed towards them feeling cold, tired and bored, longing to get home to a warm bed. A sudden draught of cold night air as someone opened the front door made me swivel round fast. I looked up into the face of a well-known person. 'Jesus Christ!' I exclaimed. 'Not quite,' he said, 'but you're close.'

It was Robert Runcie, the then Archbishop of Canterbury. 'I expect you're surprised to see me here.' 'I certainly am, sir,' I said, 'please excuse my greeting. You're the last person I expected to see this evening.' He paid his admission without question and went in.

In December 2000 I had to give up the job because of my health problems but I missed Ronnie's so much that, despite now living now in Kent, I made some convoluted travel arrangements allowing me to resume my duties at the door.

PERSONAL VIEW

The following is indeed personal. It's about the colourful misspellings of my name. I trust there is some mild amusement to be had at these — though not for me, especially on cheques where my bank refuses to accept those vital slips of paper bearing the name of Godsboil (surely the ultimate in suppuration), Godsboat (the Ark?) or Judaized into Goldblatt, Goldberg, Goldstein and, most frequently, *Gold*bolt.

Spike Milligan picking up on the misspellings of my name addressed me as above.

In the June issue of *Jazz UK* there was a profile of pianist, trombonist, composer, teacher and MD Eddie Harvey, in which Eddie recalled going through a rough patch, and having to sleep on the floor of my flat.

I had forgotten that I had been Harvey-strewn, but on re-reading this tribute to my generosity I saw that his host had been one Jim *Gold*bolt. I wrote a letter of correction to *Jazz UK* which they published as their star letter with a £20 prize. My reply was: At one stage it was so common that I seriously thought about changing to the Jewish faith and I mentioned it to Ronnie Scott, né Schatt. He replied: 'I'll be happy to propose you, but at your age the operation will be most painful and possibly fatal.'

A little while later I was flattered by a profile of myself in *The Stage* regarding republication of my *A History of Jazz in Britain, 1919–50* and its accompanying 4-CD box-set, but in the subhead this Goldbolt reared his ugly head once again. Shamelessly, I repeated my *Jazz UK* letter to *The Stage*. It was printed with an amusing cartoon by John Byrne

THE COMPUTER SPEAKETH

As one barely out of the age of the quill pen and pewter pot of ink, I have come to regard the computer as a many-headed monster which, when it works, is miraculous, but is a total disaster when it doesn't. However, keeping up with the times, in the search for perfection, we run our words through the computer's spellchecker and have learned to be extremely wary about taking its advice. In this issue, for example, we have reviewed an album by one John 'Critch' Critchinson (whom we were advised should have been 'Crotch'), Old Etonian Humphrey Lyttelton narrowly avoided becoming an Old *Estonian*, and the word 'caressive' in my review of a Maxine Sullivan CD turned up as 'corrosive' — hardly

the word to describe her gentle vocalising. Recently, Radio 2 presenter Malcolm Laycock became Malcolm Laidback and my letter to Brian Attwood, editor of *The Stage*, was nearly addressed to Brian Tattooed.

LAUNCH OF PROPERBOX 88

In April, a CD launch of Properbox 88 Jazz in Britain 1919-1950 was held at Ronnie's, the distinguished guests including veterans Frank Deniz — born 1912; Coleridge Goode — born 1914; and Tommy McQuater – born 1914.

A young photographer from the West End Extra was astonished to be told their ages and enquired: 'Just what do you guys eat for breakfast?' The veterans sat together while numerous people came up to congratulate them on their contributions to the British jazz scene. All belied their ages. Ron Rubin, our resident poet, penned the following tribute:

> *From Louis, Goodman, Bean and Diz*
> *To Ronnie Scott's Boptet*
> *Here's a feast of Proper jazz*
> *In four-CD boxed set.*
> *Jim wrote his notes, compiled the discs,*
> *A launch held at the club*
> *Was chock-a-block with bonhomie,*
> *As well as booze and grub.*
> *The guests piled in, a motley bunch,*
> *With media folk galore,*
> *And jazz musicians, long in tooth –*
> *Or should one say mature?*
> *Like elder statesmen, three held court:*
> *McQuater, Goode, Deniz;*
> *Spry nonagenarians,*
> *These worthy VIPs.*
> *And younger jazzers turned up too -*
> *I spotted Campbell, B*
> *(He's sixty-five, and Pointon's just*
> *A lad of sixty-three.)*
> *But never mind the chit-chat, let's*
> *get back to all that jazz.*
> *To Fats and Duke and Humph- these discs*
> *Are bursting with pizzazz.*
> *Our music's history is there,*
> *Let's hope we needn't wait*
> *Another fifty years till Proper*
> *Brings us up to date!*

From left: Coleridge Goode, Tommy McQuater, Jim Godbolt and Frank Deniz. Tommy and Frank have since sadly passed away. Photo courtesy of *West End Extra*   J.G.

FINAL BARS

The extraordinary headline in *The Evening Standard*, 24th December, 1996, the size of which would normally be accorded to Heads of State:

It was perhaps ironic, and at the same time, touching and satisfying, that Ronnie's death received such enormous coverage in the media. Had he been able to observe this, it would certainly have afforded him wry amusement, with a comment such as, 'I could have done with that publicity on the nights at the Club when we performed for six dead Greeks'.

It was a testimony to the impact that Ronnie made in his lifetime with the public generally that the media showed so much interest. It wasn't only the quality newspapers — *The Times, The Independent, The Guardian, The Daily Telegraph, The Observer*—but also the popular press. Throughout 24th December, BBC TV and ITV covered the sad news at length with interviews with notabilities in the business, with details of his achievements and the Club that bears his name.

True, some of the reports were wildly inaccurate and speculative, but they were generally factual. Indeed, 'The Guv'nor' would have been surprised. In a way such recognition helped to soften the blow to his family, his long-standing business partner Pete King, the club staff, and a sorrowing jazz fraternity. For there is no doubt about his popularity as a musician, a wit and a person. Many stories of his kindness and generosity, especially to young musicians, have emerged.

Of course, the dark side to his character has been dwelt upon with speculation about the cause of his death.

Over the following weeks, the radio stations included tributes, these including 'Jazz Record Requests', a dedication on Jazz FM, with contributions from John Critchinson, Jim Mullen and Jim Godbolt, and Humphrey Lyttelton's 'The Best Of Jazz' on Radio 2.

THE FUNERAL

Equally extraordinary was the coverage of Ronnie's funeral on 7th January. The police cleared Frith Street of all traffic to give the cortège unhindered flow, the occasion covered by a battery of photographers and TV cameras. The leading car, bearing his coffin, was bedecked with wreaths, topped with a floral saxophone. Arriving at Golders Green Crematorium, the cortège was greeted by some eight hundred mourners, many of whom knew they may not be able to enter the chapel and about four hundred had to stand outside in arctic conditions to hear a relay of the service, conducted by Rabbi Guy Hall. It is impossible to mention all those present, but the mourners included Spike Milligan, Humphrey Lyttelton, Marion Montgomery, Cleo Laine, the *JARS* team and the Club staff.

It was a sad but not solemn occasion, punctuated by peals of laughter as various friends took to the pulpit to pay their tributes. These were Benny Green, Peter Ind, John Dankworth, Alf Summers, Rabbi Sonny Herman, a boyhood friend of Ronnie's, Mary, the mother of Ronnie's daughter Rebecca, who was also present, and Laurie, the daughter of Jo Bailey, Ronnie's companion for the last six years. The proceedings included Ronnie's long-standing friend, Joe Green, gravely intoning the *kaddish*, the Jewish mourners' prayer. The mourners filed out to the strains of Duke Ellington's *What Am I Here For?* by Stan Getz and Jimmy Rowles. This and other titles played as the congregation filed in, the tracks organised by sound engineer Peter Bould.

Before and after the service, there were touching reunions between many grey-haired veterans of the British jazz scene, who later met up at the wake held at the club that night. There was much hilarity, but this is the nature of death and wakes, and Pete King was delighted at the thanks he received from the guests. It was a situation that would have afforded Ronnie further amusement. Genuine grief was felt by the jazz fraternity at Ronnie's death and which will undoubtedly continue in their minds and hearts for the rest of their lives. They will mourn the loss of a remarkable man, the like of which will not be seen again.

Ronnie Scott's death was a shock to the jazz community, but no surprise to those close to him. Or to read that his death was probably due to an overdose. Dental problems put an end to his very being — to play music. He became extremely depressed. Pete King wanted a special issue of *JARS* to pay tribute to an exceptional person. This appeared in January 1997 with warm tributes from across the entire jazz community.

Ronnie studying form

The front page carried Trog's superb impression of Ronnie, which had appeared on the cover of Ronnie Scott's book *Some Of My Best Friends Are Blues*, and on the cover of *JARS* number 1. I decided on Trog's drawing because it so fully captured the essence of the Scott personality.

This Memorial issue carried no advertisements, the pages devoted to recollections from a wide number of people in the business, including Roy Ayers, Roxy Beaujolais, Bonny Blair, Ina Dittke and Brian Theobald of BPR, Beryl Bryden, John Chilton, Kenneth Clarke MP, Tony Coe, John Critchinson, Tony Crombie, John Dankworth, Lou Donaldson, Cindy Hacker, Wally Houser, Malcolm Laycock, Bill Lewington, Branford Marsalis, Jimmy McGriff, George Melly, Mole Jazz Shop staff, James Moody, Alun Morgan, Laurie Morgan, Dick Morrissey, Danny Moss, Alan Plater, John Prescott MP, the staff of Ray's Jazz Shop, Max Roach, Barbara Thompson, Stan Tracey, Nina Simone, Sir David Steel MP, George Webb, Mike Westbrook, and my personal tribute headed Goldblatt and Schatt with a superb depiction of same by Wally 'Trog' Fawkes. J.G.

Typical of the tributes was the following, made by John Chilton, leader of the Feetwarmers, who had accompanied George Melly for thirty years.

JOHN CHILTON recalls...

In working regularly at Ronnie Scott's Club throughout the past twenty-five years, I got to hear a lot of Ronnie Scott's tenor sax playing. I'm surprised to note that in some obituaries this side of his activities has been faintly praised. He was a wonderful, natural, jazz musician, whose skills at up-tempo playing were as remarkable as his ability to play

Invitation card to attend a memorial service, to honour Ronnie Scott, held at St. Martin-in-the-Fields, London, Charing Cross.

ballads with exquisite tenderness.

Ronnie was a likeable man, albeit a moody one, but even on his most sombre days he would suddenly say something that was delightfully funny. He was a superb compere whose masterful timing of jokes, old and new, made him a top class comedian. He loved talking about comedians and film stars of the 1930s and 1940s, but usually shunned jazz nostalgia. However, during the last week of his life I had several long conversations with him about his favourite jazz musicians, and about characters he toured with many years ago.

The Christmas season was going well, with Ronnie compèring the show, and doing some backstage practice on the tenor sax. On Monday evening, the 23rd December, just as we were getting ready to play our first set, Pete King came in and told us the sad news of Ronnie's death. In our quarter of a century together, George Melly and the Feetwarmers have never played a harder gig. Rest in peace, Ronnie.

JOHN CHILTON

ANNOUNCEMENT

Whilst the condolences are undoubtedly heartfelt, they are nothing compared with the inexpressible sorrow the undersigned feel at the passing of Ronnie Scott.

We have considered taking an advertisement to register our grief at the loss of a highly valued punter, but the severe drop in our anticipated revenue as a result of his death precludes any such expenditure and we will hav0e to content ourselves with this formal statement.

(Signed): Messrs. Coral, William Hill, Ladbrokes, Mecca and on behalf of every Honest Joe throughout Britain.

WHISPERS, MURMURS & ASIDES

FACTUALLY CHALLENGED

Back to the goof biz; on University Challenge , BBC2, four representatives of Birmingham University were asked, 'Which saxophonist opened his own club in London in the fifties?

Most of you will get that in one, but, after intense conferring, they came up with – CHARLIE PARKER!

Ronnie Scott, Caucasian, was the right answer, but when you think that the black Parker, never came to Britain, and died in 1955, four years before Ronnie opened his Club, it goes to show how jazz-ignorant the academic world is, but, what's new?

The following week four more brains were asked in whose band did John Coltrane first make his name. All of you would have given Miles Davis, but they came up with – DAVE BRUBECK! Tut! Tut!

PAUL PRY

GOLDBLATT AND SCHATT
lovable knock-about comedians

In the January/February 1997 issue of *JARS*, I wished Ronnie Scott a happy 70th birthday, together with a few anecdotes about my seventeen-year relationship with him as Editor of *JARS*. Tragically, he didn't make that birthday. I repeat that I never knew him that well. I was constantly aware of his protective wall of reserve, but have pleasant memories of conversations with him. I also had some tough moments with Ronnie. He could be a harsh task master, extremely peremptory and, depending on his mood swings, somewhat inconsistent. These conversations mostly took place in the foyer of the club, plus some fragmented exchanges in his office with him gazing at the TV screen.

Often I would try to engage his attention over some point or other and he would keep walking, I speaking in his slipstream. He had — to use horse-racing parlance — 'a good turn of foot', especially when he was hot-footing it to Ladbroke's betting shop in Bateman Street around the corner from the Club. Regarding his betting, he expressed annoyance that I referred to this in an issue of *JARS* and claimed he had given up the habit. He blandly told me that his interest in the Sport of Kings was academic — an examination of the horses' genes, the history of the trainer, the ability of the jockey, the going on the turf, and climatic conditions of the day, factors that aroused his scientific interest. OK, he might place a pound or two on now and again, just to put something back into the sport, which had so much exercised his intellectual fascination.

PO-FACED

He was the master of the comeback. When I once approached him, he said, 'Do you wish to offer your resignation?' and when I demurred, he replied, 'Oh well. Some other time then.' On another occasion he mildly enquired was it not time for me to step down and (pause) 'Make way for an *older* man. Someone (another cliff-hanging pause) with more experience?'

He'd make these queries po-faced and I was never quite certain if he meant them. It was extraordinary how immobile his features were on those occasions, the same features he often contorted into manic expressions known as 'gurning'.

He had an eagle eye for errors. Prior to printing, I invariably suffered a discomforting hour as he meticulously delineated them. I tried to get my own back one afternoon when he, on his haunches, was writing our future attractions in his quite elegant script on the blackboard in the Club's foyer. It was his waggish custom to include among the forthcoming attractions utterly improbable names; thirties film stars, like Joan Blondell, Richard Arlen, Edward Everett Horton and Eugene Pallette, and such notables as Lord Lucan, Charles Manson, the Dagenham Girl Pipers and the Luton Girls' Choir. This particular afternoon, he included Glenn Miller, but spelt 'Glenn' as 'Glen'. It was my moment of joy to point out the error. He looked up and said, 'Well, it used to be with one 'n', this little sally consistent with one of his great remarks — 'I've only been wrong once in my life and that was when I thought I was wrong!'

FLATTERED

He never ever offered me one single compliment about the magazine in all these years, but once he flattered me — albeit allusively. Engaging in repartee one afternoon, we circled each other like boxers in the ring: feinting, ducking, weaving and side-stepping — verbally speaking. It was some weeks later that secretary Bonny Blair told me that during this exchange Ronnie surreptitiously instructed her to take the telephones off the hook, not wishing the banter to be interrupted. This gesture from one of the funniest men I've ever met, I found extremely flattering, if retrospectively and allusively.

But, as I say, he never paid compliments. On the contrary. The last time I spoke to Ronnie was on Monday 9th December 1996, when he looked at the galleys for the January/February issue, which ironically, included my birthday greeting. Constantly puffing at a cigarette, he was morose and irritable. He was obviously a deeply troubled man. 'Why are there so many mistakes?' he querulously enquired.

'Human fallibility, Ronnie', I replied, and he grunted as though these considerations were not in his parlance. Indeed, he was the perfectionist in all things, although as fallible as the rest of us. But my abiding memory is of a man who made me laugh very much, whose integrity as a person and musician I admired and whose death was an awful blow.

Ronnie was Jewish, his real name Schatt, and although not in any way orthodox, he had a strong awareness of ethnic identity, which manifested itself in some very funny remarks about races generally, some of which were very politically incorrect and quite unprintable here.

At times he would pretend a strongly Jewish identity, was quick to spot anti-Semitism and also to indicate Jewish separateness. We often talked about the East End of London where he was born and I mentioned — yes, I know I've told this story before — that I had a Jewish girlfriend from the area whose mother objected to her seeing this *Goy*. He, dead-pan, said, 'Quite right too, I wish you'd leave our women alone.'

As editor of *JARS*, I have received several letters giving my surname as 'Godsboil', 'Cobalt', 'Godlio', 'Godralt', 'Godsball', and the like, but many of them Judaizing my name into 'Goldberg', 'Goldman', and my favourite, 'Goldblatt'. I said to Ronnie this was happening so frequently, I was thinking of changing to the faith, and he strongly advised against the operation...

Goldblatt and Schatt, lovable knock-about comedians available for hunt balls, barmitzvahs, car-boot sales. Charges reasonably exorbitant. Bookings must be accompanied by cash. No cheques accepted.

Ronnie was known to the general public as a stand-up comic with a familiar repertoire. This was true but I am glad to say I was one of those privileged to be constantly amused by his spontaneous wit.

Regarding our banter, I treasure Wally 'Trog' Fawkes's impression of Goldblatt and Schatt, knockabout comedians, first published in *JARS* in November/December, 1994.   J.G.

RUBINERICKS

A pianoforte player called Leake
Said 'I am completely unique
The great Hoi Polloi
Are no cause for joy'
So he formed himself into a clique

A pianoforte player called Brian
Said, 'For a large brandy I'm dyin'
With beer for a chaser
And scotch for a bracer'
(This man has a stomach of iron)

A saxophone player called Garnett
Behaved like the Devil Incarnate
When drunk and forlorn
He puked down his horn
At an interesting gig up in Barnet

A fellow called Fallabout Francis
One night rather fancied his chances
The lady was willing
But Francis, still swilling,
Collapsed into one of his trances

Well-known at the Club is Bill Colyer
When drunk there is nobody jollier
His hobby and habit
'S to jaw and to rabbit
You'd swear that the bugger could swallow yer!

Illustration: Hazeldine

The Tuba is bulky, I know,
And takes lots of effort to blow;
If your home is a bedsitter
Your wife could get bitter –
One of them might have to go...

Says Ronnie, 'I think you'll agree
Our food is completely germ-free,
The best in the land
And untouched by man's hand
For our chef's a gorilla, you see'.

RON RUBIN

193

PERSONAL VIEW

In my antiquity, I ask — where are the characters of the British jazz scene today? I refer to the likes of George Webb, Wally Fawkes, Ken Colyer, Mick Mulligan, George Melly, Sandy Brown, Humphrey Lyttelton, Diz Disley and Ian Mackintosh, on the traditional/mainstream side of the fence. Where, too, are the likes of Phil Seamen, Tubby Hayes, Tony Crombie, Flash Winston, Harry Morris, Pete King, Laurie Morgan, Kenny Graham and Lennie Bush on the 'modern' side? Not to be found, I'm afraid. You can take any of the modern crop anywhere — clean-cut characters you could introduce to your sister. You wouldn't take that chance with some of the older hands I've just mentioned. Some of them were on the wild side, but what personalities! Which brings me to one of the supreme figures of the older generation of British jazzmen — one Ronnie Scott. It has taken his death for us to fully appreciate just how much a character he was, and it is a crying shame that the indolent side of him was such that he didn't fully make use of the talents he possessed, be it actor, mimic and writer, as well as a saxophone player.

I don't exaggerate when I say that he could have been another Peter Ustinov, and Ustinov can't play tenor saxophone, nor has he led two of the most exciting jazz bands outside of America — the nine-piece and the big band.

Regarding his wit, and microphone technique, it was another crying shame that when BBC TV's Omnibus did a programme on the club's 30th anniversary, the producer, in his wisdom, didn't have Ronnie on camera for his famous spiel, even though this was firmly indicated in the synopsis provided by *JARS* editor Jim Godbolt.

One hopes that the BBC, notorious for wiping jazz material, have in their vaults the Club Eleven Reunion, made in 1985, in which there are examples of Scott's prowess at the mike. Also shown with the Club Eleven Reunion was The Street, a compilation of films, mostly of Archer Street, (in the '50s), teeming with musicians, shot on a home movie camera by trumpeter/pianist Denis Rose. Again an example of Ronnie's humour, commenting on these historic clips.

PRESS COVERAGE

Regarding the press coverage of Ronnie's death, most of this was reasonably accurate, with one or two glaring exceptions. Quite out of order was one Jane Kelly in the *Daily Mail*, referring to Ronnie's 'silly gags'. Ronnie's jokes were not silly. Like most good jokes, they bore on the absurd aspects of the human condition, their delivery was the envy of many a professional comedian and worth repetition.

Why do editors assign ignoramuses to matters about which they know nothing? Ms Kelly should stick to knitting — OK, this makes me a MCP, but it does get up my hooter to read typical misrepresentation of jazz people in the popular press.   J.G.

A BE-BOPPER'S PRAYER

Oh, give me a home
Where the flatted fifths roam
And The Smiths and the Ice Tea never play
Where Sheldon is heard, as are Monk, Miles and Bird
Where it's Newport and Montreux instead of 'The Word'
And it's a Night in Tunisia, not Beethoven's Third
And Sky's not on loudly all day

Oh, give me a land where the Glenn Miller Band
Does not creep like a rampant disease
Through the airwaves at random, with James Last in tandem
Where finally all of the stations have banned 'em
Where we'll play the changes and you'll understand them
And Diz is still playing Top C's

Oh, give me a house
Where I'll never hear Strauss
And Cliff Richard was strangled at birth
Where records by Mingus and tunes like Off Minor
Outsell Michael Jackson Oh, Carolina
Where Clayderman's albums will make way for Wynton's
We'll all drink at Birdland and dine up at Minton's
Where all the juke-boxes play Hampton Hawes
Instead of Erasure, the Fall or The Doors
There's no Little Donkeys, or Strangers On Shores.
In my Bebop Heaven on Earth
ROY DAVENPORT

I've never seen that 'ere jazz; but from what I heard that looks summat like it!
Postcard courtesy of Cambell Burnap

THE ROOM
by JIMMY PARSONS

The old room lies in total darkness now, the audience and staff have long since gone. There is no discernible noise save the buzz from the refrigerators coming up the stairs from the kitchen below; more noticeable is the lingering smell of cigarette smoke, beer and the odours given off by the human body — it will take many hours for the stale air to disperse into the walls and ceilings of the awesome room during what remains of the night. The photographs of the great and famous look out into the darkness and turn to gaze fondly in the direction of the stage where so many of them once performed and triumphed, and — could it be? — a look of sadness falls across each face.

GHOSTLY FIGURES

Slowly, almost inaudibly at first, a piano gives birth to a mournful blues. As the volume grows, bass and drums step in to establish a steady, laid-back beat. From the four corners of the room and foyer, hesitatingly at first, pale ghostly figures without any definable form step out of their photographs and begin to move towards the stage. As they take their place on the bandstand, they start to play together as a great ensemble, the best there has ever been. One by one, the soloists step forward to take centre stage and play their tribute. The great singers take up the cause to wail the blues as only they could. Suddenly the great orchestra changes the mood and plunges into a roaring up-tempo piece. The red cloths that cover the tables leap into the air to form a ghostly corps de ballet and perform their 'Dance Macabre'. Then, as if under the direction of an invisible conductor, the phantom orchestra ends its concern and, one by one, its members return slowly to their frames on the walls. Once again, the room falls silent.

Ronnie regally dressed; Illustration by Pennington

THE JAPANESE ADMIRAL

The stage is now shrouded in a swirling fog and slowly walking through it appears the one figure of a small Jewish boy dressed in the uniform of a Japanese admiral. He steps down from the stage and begins to move towards the lobby of the Club, stopping frequently to gaze up at the photographs and speaking to each one in a whisper. He pauses longer at some pictures and occasionally lifts a hand to touch a familiar face or brush away a cobweb. With each step he takes towards the entrance his body grows and changes from that of a small boy to a youth and then to a grown man. His old tenor saxophone is lying on a table in the lobby; he picks it up and plays as only he could. Ronnie Scott turns, bows to the room and walks out into the dark night. As I do now. See you later.

*In Ronnie's nightly comedy routine he used to describe the poverty of his early childhood in London's East End; his father was constantly unemployed because he was a shepherd; the family were so poor that his mother could never afford to buy him new clothes so she was forced to shop at the Army surplus stores — it was no fun for a ten year-old Jewish boy to go to school in the East end of London dressed in a Japanese admiral's uniform!

WHISPERS, MURMURS AND ASIDES

MUNCH MUSIC

It's an occupational hazard for many a jazz pianist to earn a crust tinkling the ivories while the customers chomp on salmon mousse, steak au poivre, and tiramisu, chattering and clattering the table hardware the while. 'Playing munch music,' is how the late Alan Clare described the experience, and told the tale of a lady, who, suddenly spotting Alan at the keyboard, exclaimed, 'Oh, I thought you were a tape!' Pianist (and *JARS* limerickist) Ron Rubin has played many such gigs, and one evening in a Soho restaurant was observed by cartoonist Bill Tidy making the odd grimace as his pianistic artistry was drowned by hearty guffawing and Mr. Tidy presented Ron with his impression of this musician/customer relationship, which I now reproduce, courtesy of Mr. Tidy.
PAUL PRY

BOPPING WITH SCOTT
PROPERBOX 121 - review by ALUN MORGAN

Ronnie Scott held a unique position in UK jazz. From an early age he was a central figure, an inspiration, a musician with a complete understanding of our music and the men who made it. (Nowadays it is fashionable to call such a man an icon, but my dictionary defines 'icon' as 'sacred painting, mosaic, etc, in the Orthodox Church', hardly fitting in Ronnie's case). Born Ronald Schatt at 33 South Tenter Street in London's East End on 28 January 1927 (five days before the birth of Stan Getz in Philadelphia, incidentally) he was playing gigs with local bands at the age of sixteen.

You can learn much more about Ronnie's life in Joop Visser's excellent booklet notes which accompany this 4 CD set. The first disc commences with three titles made for Decca during the year Ronnie spent in the Ted Heath band. His tone here is powerful and Hawkins-like at times although an amalgam of Charlie Ventura and Flip Phillips may be nearer the mark. I believe the 16 bars of solo tenor on *Ad Lib Frolic* is the work of Ronnie rather than fellow tenor saxist Johnny Gray.

THE INNOVATIVE ESQUIRE LABEL

No less than seventy-three of the titles making up this release came from Esquire, a label which was launched in 1948 by drummer Carlo Krahmer. (It was Carlo who helped Ronnie to get some of his earliest gigs as a teenager). Esquire played a most important part in documenting British jazz during the post-war years. Ronnie was perhaps the label's best-selling local artiste and the majority of the titles heard here originally appeared as 78s. I recall reviewing many of these for *Jazz Journal* more than half a century ago. Carlo and his partner Peter Newbrook recorded (on acetate disc) a 1948 concert at Birmingham Town Hall when boppers Denis Rose, Johnny Dankworth and Ronnie stood alongside longer established figures such as Reg Arnold and Jimmy Skidmore. When Club Eleven was formed it became a haven for adherents of the new music and the first CD in this package presents eight titles recorded at a concert put on by the club's musicians including Johnny Rogers, Tony Crombie, Tommy Pollard and, of course, Ronnie Scott. The second disc contains two quartet dates under Ronnie's leadership and a sextet session with the brilliant Jimmy Deuchar and Spike Robinson, the latter playing Parker-like alto. (Spike was stationed in England at the time with the US Navy, and became a welcome visitor to the club.)

By now Ronnie's tone had become lighter; he was acknowledging the work of the 'young Lester'. When I wrote in my *Jazz Journal* review of his version of *Too Marvellous For Words* ('a tune which Stan Getz has recorded, of course') all those years ago I received a letter of complaint from Ronnie to the effect that his version was certainly not a copy and he thought I had a duty to support British jazz! We both succeeded in living this down in later years.

JACK PARNELL's BAND

Discs Two and Three have titles made in Sweden under the leadership of pianist Arnold Ross, who was then acting as MD and accompanist to Lena Horne. Ronnie and his cohorts were in the Jack Parnell Band which was backing Lena on her European tour. The personnel of Parnell's band which recorded *The Champ* contained Ronnie and others who, for non-musical reasons, left Jack *en masse* to form Ronnie's nine-piece unit. This was one of my favourite Scott bands. It existed for nearly two and a half years and built up a wide ranging library containing excellent pieces and arrangements by band musicians (listen to Tony Crombie's delightful *Body Beautiful* for example) as well as placing on disc John Lewis's previously unrecorded *S'il Vous Plait* which had existed only on a September 1948 airshot by Miles Davis's nine-piece 'Birth of Cool' band.

After the demise of the nine-piece came the birth of Ronnie's sixteen-man big band which lasted for less than four months. Fortunately Esquire recorded the unit and the only titles which now exist are those to be found here on Disc 4. The band had some strong soloists, apart from Ronnie, including Hank Shaw and Joe Harriott, but 1955 was not the time to launch a new big band. The final two tracks in this package were made for Tempo by a quintet having the unbeatable front line of Ronnie and Jimmy Deuchar.

Following the demise of the big band, Ronnie co-led a band with Tony Crombie, then formed the Jazz Couriers with Tubby Hayes, and in October 1959 opened his club, with Pete King as manager. Ronnie died in December 1996 which means we have been without his music and his humour for more than a decade. This new Properbox release is an excellent compilation of his work from 1946 to 1956 and is also a tribute to the foresight of Carlo Krahmer and Peter Newbrook. Without their work at Esquire our knowledge of Ronnie's music would be considerably reduced. Highly recommended.

Pioneer British jazzman Harry Hayes with Alun Morgan

RONNIE SCOTT
Boppin' With Scott
(PROPERBOX 131)

As well as running the hugely successful jazz club in London, Ronnie Scott was also a world-class saxophonist and pivotal in the rise of jazz in the UK. This 81 track set focuses on Ronnie's first ten years as a professional musician when he was accompanied by the cream of British Jazz at the time. Contains 6 tracks available for the first time on CD and not available at all since the days of the 78.

TUBBY HAYES
The Little Giant
(PROPERBOX 117)

An overview of the early years of one of the most important jazz musicians the UK has ever produced. Compiled and annotated by Hayes biographer Simon Spillett. This set is the 'best available' covering this period in his career (1954-56). It also includes 5 previously unreleased tracks. 71 remastered tracks and a 44 page booklet with Tubby's story, session detail and rare photos.

JAZZ IN BRITAIN 1919-1950
(PROPERBOX 88)

This 4CD set is one of the most comprehensive surveys of the evolution of jazz music in the UK, as played by visiting luminaries from the USA as well as those who were inspired by the Americans but born and bred on home turf. It was compiled by Jim Godbolt, one of the UK's leading authorities on jazz as it has been performed in the UK, he has also written a companion book on the subject as well as the liners to this set.

Buy on line from **www.proper-records.co.uk** where full track listings and discogaphies for these and all of our other sets can be found. To purchase by telephone call **020 8676 5141.**

DAVID REDFERN
'Jazz photographer supreme' – *Buddy Rich*

David Redfern's career began in the twilight jazz clubs of 1960s London. He risked his one and only camera amongst the jiving teenage crowds. The British Trad boom was under way. His first published photos featured Kenny Ball, Chris Barber, George Melly, and the old Marquee Club.

David began photographing TV Shows like 'Ready Steady Go' and 'Thank Your Lucky Stars' which were shot during the day. Here he made many of his now classic shots of the Beatles, the Rolling Stones and Dusty Springfield.

Nights were spent at the 100 Club, Ronnie Scott's or the Marquee, where he captured on film all the jazz greats from Miles Davis to Ella Fitzgerald. These pictures were to contribute to what is now the most comprehensive jazz collection in Europe. To break into the commercial world by chasing the big American names, David became a regular visitor to the Jazz festivals in Newport, Antibes and Montreux, and the big rock festivals, photographing such greats as Hendrix and Dylan.

By the 1970s David had firmly established his name as one of the top music photographers in the business. In

1980 Pete Townsend's Eel Pie Company published David Redfern's Jazz Album. Lavishly illustrated with many of David's finest jazz photographs, it was highly acclaimed by critics and public alike. In the same year, at Frank Sinatra's request, David stepped into Terry O'Neill's shoes as official tour photographer.

In the late '80s several exhibitions featured the first 25 years: including showing his work along with Lord Lichfield and Lord Snowdon at the Kodak and Royal Photographic Society's 'Living Body' exhibition. Based on the Channel 4 TV series, it was one of the biggest exhibitions ever held by Kodak. In 1990 he was invited to put on an exhibition in Cuba to coincide with the jazz festival there.

At the beginning of 1989 David moved his music picture library REDFERNS to new premises in West London, a location now much favoured by the British music industry. The library expanded rapidly. Now covering over 26,000 different artists and styles from every musical genre, and representing some 500 photographers and collections it is the most comprehensive music picture library in the world today, with over 205,000 online at www.redferns.com.

The December '94 issue of the American publication Jazz Times featured David's work in their 'Special Collectors Edition', with select contributions from six of the world's most highly acclaimed jazz photographers. David was the only non-American to be featured. This also coincided with sale of his 1995 Jazz calendar published by the renowned calendar publishers The Ink Group.

September 1995 saw the launch of a series of ten Jazz postage stamps by the US post office. Three of David's images were used: Louis Armstrong, Thelonious Monk & Coleman Hawkins. The inclusion of the Louis Armstrong image was a result of some 38,000 signatures collected from sixty-five countries over eight years, and had a special launch in New Orleans, the birthplace of Louis Armstrong. As a point of interest the picture of Louis Armstrong was taken by David in New York in 1967, on his first visit to the USA

His book The Unclosed Eye was published by Sanctuary publishing in May 1999 with critical acclaim. The London Sunday Times Magazine published a four page feature.

The book publication coincided with exhibitions in London, New York and New Orleans, followed by one in Cork, Ireland in October 2000. The prestigious design magazine 'Creative Review' published a profile on David in their February 2001 issue. It was entitled 'Leader with Vision'. David had another exhibition in September 2001 in conjunction with the Soho Jazz & Heritage Festival in London and at the Vienne Jazz festival in June/ July 2002.

David is more active than ever in the picture business.

He has been the President of BAPLA (British Association of Picture Libraries and Agencies) for the last fifteen years, and is still traveling the world photographing music festivals and attending trade shows and conferences.

In November 2005 The Unclosed Eye expanded second edition in hardback was published by David himself. This included a 200 limited slipcase edition complete with two 10 x 8 original colour prints. David received 'The Milt Hinton Award for Excellence in Jazz Photography' in New York in

January 2007. The award recognizes lifetime achievement in jazz photography as art and history

**David's work can be seen in the books,
online at www.davidredfern.com
or at 7 Bramley Road, London W10 6SZ.
Tel: +44 (0)20 7792 2410, Mobile +44(0) 7785 367 359**

In 2005, Theatre impresario, Producer and Restaurateur, Sally Greene, became the proud new owner of Ronnie Scott's. Her purchase of the club is testament to Sally's ongoing commitment to the sympathetic restoration and rejuvenation of some of the capitals most iconic establishments,

notably, the Richmond Theatre, the Criterion — which was heralded as London's 'prettiest theatre' following Sally's painstaking restoration project, and, of course, The Old Vic. The refurbished Ronnie Scott's Club continues the long established booking of first class artist from all over the world and the revamped auditorium enabling members and guests to relax and listen in ease and comfort.

Pete King and Sally Greene. Photo: D. Sinclair

'From all the staff at Ronnie Scott's, we wish Jim, Marta and rest of the team every success with this fascinating insight into the history of the club. Nearly fifty years have already passed and we look forward to many more to come.
The Ronnie Scott's Staff '

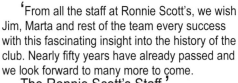

JARS BOWS OUT

The first issue of *JARS* was in August 1979 and appeared regularly, covering 159 issues up to February 2006, which welcomed Sally Greene as the new proprietor. Thereafter the Club's new management produced two issues of their magazine under a different heading, but then decided not to proceed further.

When *JARS* was folded there were no questions asked in the House of Commons, no demonstrations of regret from banner-waving *JARS* readers protesting outside 47 Frith Street. There were a few consolatory messages, but such is the transient nature of magazine journalism. A case of 'Read today and wrapping up fish and chips tomorrow', *JARS* was soon just a memory.

However, comments did appear on the net, most of them complimentary but there was one that was anything but favourable: An 'Ornate Coalman' wrote: 'Thank heavens the dire house magazine, full of old-fogey in-jokes and tired one-liners, has been overhauled. Once in while even precious objects have to be dusted, and sometimes things just go beyond their natural life span.' Another quote from him states 'I would have liked to see less of those stories repeated even more often than Ronnie's jokes. And if I had a quid for every time a 'quick as a flash' was used, the club would never have had financial problems again.'

Orn*ate Coal*man. Quick as a flash, I recognised this to be a play on the name of saxophonist Ornette Coleman, and the wit of the misspelling had me falling about in apoplectic, health-risking laughter and I had to have a lie-down immediately after. Following Mr. 'Coalman's derision, there was a slightly consoling response which read: 'I did not think that the old magazine was that bad — at least it was free, and I have seen worse.'

The most extraordinary and unexpected 'praise' came from the pen from someone who had vilified *JARS* and me for twenty years. On publication of the Club's new magazine my adversary Steve Voce commented in *Jazz Journal*: 'It's natural that, with Jim Godbolt gone, the magazine is bland. The Lurking-Pike imparted character to the pages. He was the overlord of the 'magazine' for almost four (almost three, actually, J.G.) decades. Although his humour tended to the repetitive and was sometimes only funny to its creator he was when at his best one of

Trog's caricature of myself inspired by George Melly's description of me in his Owning Up: *"Godbolt, thin and tense, his head with its pointed features crouching between his shoulders as though emerging from its burrow into a dangerous world, his eyes as cold and watchful as those of a pike in the reeds.'*

the most literate and amusing writers on jazz. Perhaps I am being unfair for I have recently been re-reading in tandem the works of S.J. Perelman ('Love is not the dying moan of a distant violin-it's a triumphant twang of a bedspring,') and Godbolt. Of course there is no contest.' (Agreed! J.G.)

Further on Voce comments on merits of my two volumes of histories of jazz in Britain (1919-50 and 1950-70) concluding: 'The volumes took many years of industry to create. In those days we chatted regularly and it seemed that he was putting all of his life into compiling and ordering bits of paper that he appeared to have amassed since his birth at the London Hippodrome on April 1, 1919.'

When my *A History of Jazz 1950-70* was published he savaged it from beginning to end. Whilst it would appear ungrateful not to acknowledge his praise of me and my books twenty years later any thanks will be heavily loaded with recollections of his hostility and wonderment as to who could lend credence to this volte-face.

As in all tastes, literary and musical, you pay your money and take your choice and never, in my twenty six years of editing *JARS*, did I ever have any illusion that its contents was unanimously acclaimed, but I like to think that its merits attracted the work of some of our finest writers on jazz music and cartoonists of the highest calibre. The general approach met with the approval for so long of two hardened veterans of the modern jazz scene, Ronnie Scott and Pete King. Yes, *JARS* is no more, but hopefully, the best of its life span over a quarter of a century is contained in these pages.

I am particularly grateful to those who advertised and with whom negotiations were always accompanied with friendly banter. My relative success in getting advertising was noticed by other magazines' editors and I received calls asking to lend my space booking talents to their pages.It inspired me to write a little poem:

Jim Godbolt, editing *JARS*, to write about jazz did aspire
And received calls from *Jazz Journal*, *Jazzwise* and *Wire*,
But, alas, for his literary graces was not the case,
They only wanted him to flog some advert space!

What an epitaph!

Sad addendum: Since Marta and I commenced work on this volume several dearly loved characters who contributed or helped with the production of *JARS* have died: Bob Glass, Jack Pennington, Brian Davis, Jimmy Brown and George Melly. I miss them all very much.

JIM GODBOLT

Jazz Floats

Chancery Cruising The Jazz Cruise Specialists

Since 1995 Chancery Cruising has been the jazz and music cruise specialist in the UK. They have sponsored and promoted Floating Jazz, Big Band and Blues extravaganzas in the Caribbean, through the Panama Canal, the Atlantic Ocean, Alaska and the Mediterranean. They have taken huge groups of music lovers onto the world's finest ships and still continue to do so. Their affiliation with Jazz At Ronnie Scott's has been a long one during which they have been pleased to announce and advertise hundreds of artists performing at the Floating Festivals.

Here are just some of them: Oscar Peterson, Joe Williams, Clark Terry, Shirley Horn, Illinois Jacquet, Tex Beneke, Dave Brubeck, Frank Foster, Milt Jackson, The Harry James Orchestra, Houston Person and Etta Jones, Gerry Mulligan, Jimmy Witherspoon, Terry Gibbs, Harry "Sweets" Edison, Stanley Turrentine, Irma Thomas, Dame Cleo Laine & Sir John Dankworth, The Artie Shaw Orchestra, Diane Schuur, Roy Hargrove, Patti Austin, Wilson Pickett, Louie Bellson, Ray Anthony, Annie Ross, Red Holloway... there are plenty more to come!

Chancery Cruising are here to stay,
so for posterity in Ronnie Scott's Jazz Farrago:
Chancery Cruising, 2-3 Cursitor Street, Chancery Lane, London, EC4A 1NE.
Telephone: (44) 020 7405 7056 • e-mail: bookings@chancerycruising.com
www.chancerycruising.com

northway publications

BOOKS ABOUT JAZZ

SOME OF MY BEST FRIENDS ARE BLUES by Ronnie Scott with Mike Hennessey
'One of the best books about jazz ever written'
Music Week
'An enthralling book about a memorable character'
Jazz at Ronnie Scott's

ALL THIS AND MANY A DOG by Jim Godbolt
'A jazz book by a man who understands that jazz is struggle, not perfection' *International Herald Tribune*

A HISTORY OF JAZZ IN BRITAIN 1919–50 by Jim Godbolt
'Enlivened throughout by the author's passion for the music itself and his narrative laced with wit' George Melly

and books about Johnny Griffin, Hank Mobley, Joe Harriott, Nat Gonella,

autobiographies by Peter King, Vic Ash, John Chilton, Coleridge Goode, Harry Gold

DOGGIN' AROUND by Alan Plater
MUSIC OUTSIDE by Ian Carr
SOLOISTS AND SIDEMEN by Peter Vacher,
A FANFARE OF MUSICAL LIMERICKS by Ron Rubin
NOTES FROM A JAZZ LIFE by Digby Fairweather
and more . . .

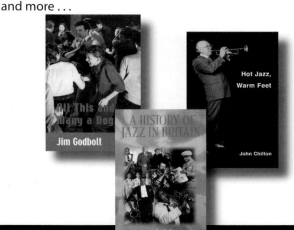

www.northwaybooks.com

201

INDEX

This index may be incomplete. Apologies for any omissions which will be included in future editions.

203